NASSAU SENIOR

AND CLASSICAL ECONOMICS

NASSAU SENIOR
AND CLASSICAL ECONOMICS

by

MARIAN BOWLEY

1967

OCTAGON BOOKS, INC.

New York

Originally published 1937, by George Allen & Unwin Ltd.

Reprinted 1967
by special arrangement with George Allen & Unwin Ltd.

OCTAGON BOOKS, INC.
175 FIFTH AVENUE
NEW YORK, N. Y. 10010

LIBRARY OF CONGRESS CATALOG CARD NUMBER: 67-18754

Printed in U.S.A. by
NOBLE OFFSET PRINTERS, INC.
NEW YORK 3, N. Y.

TO
MY PARENTS

PREFACE

IT has long been recognized that Nassau Senior merits more attention from economists than he has received. In attempting to make good this deficiency by this book I have made use of a large collection of Senior's unpublished papers which were discovered by Mr. S. Leon Levy before the War in the possession of Senior's granddaughter, Mrs. St. Loe Strachey. I should like to take this early opportunity of expressing my gratitude to Mrs. Strachey for her generosity in allowing me to use the collection and for her interest in my project.

It may be useful to say a little more about this material. Senior was Drummond Professor of Political Economy at Oxford from 1825 to 1830 and again from 1847 to 1852. A considerable number of the lectures given during the first period were either published separately or included in Senior's *Outline of Political Economy* in 1836; only five, however, of the lectures given in the second period were published. Nothing was known of the content of the unpublished lectures until Mr. Levy found them, and their recovery has added very considerably to the importance of Senior's published work in the various branches of economics. Apart from the lecture manuscripts, the most important papers in the collection are various documents relating to Senior's attitude to the Poor Laws and to the passing of the Poor Law Amendment Act of 1834; they include Senior's own account of it. (There is a copy of this account or history, originally belonging to Sir George Nicholls, in the Goldsmiths' Company's Library of Economic Literature at the University of London.)[1]

I have of course made use of Senior's published work on economic theory which is comparatively well known, and also of the considerable number of pamphlets and articles which he wrote on contemporary problems, and of the

---

[1] There is also in the same place a copy of Senior's *Outline of Political Economy* (first edition) annotated by Archbishop Whately. As is so often the case with annotated copies, it does not contain anything of interest.

journals which he kept of his travels in Ireland and on the Continent from about 1848 onwards.

In order to make use of all this data I have devoted Part I entirely to economic theory,[1] Part II to social and economic problems and added three appendices, the second of which consists of a bibliography of Senior's writings on economics, published and unpublished.

Fortunately Mrs. Strachey has relieved me of the necessity of attempting to write a biography of Senior by undertaking to do it herself, and I understand that the work is already on the way to completion. I had originally intended to give a short survey of Senior's life in order to round off the book, and its absence does, I feel, call for some explanation. In order to meet Mrs. Strachey's wishes on this matter I agreed in the end merely to include either a formal biographical statement, based principally on the article on Senior in the *Dictionary of National Biography*, or a list of the more important dates in his life. As there is not much object in reproducing what is readily accessible elsewhere, I have adopted the latter course and added to the Introduction a list of dates of the events in Senior's life which are most relevant to the main part of the text. The Introduction itself is devoted to indicating the line of approach I have adopted in estimating Senior's position in classical economics, and only includes a few references to Senior's life which appear to be necessary to make the book intelligible.

It remains to thank those people who have helped me at various stages. Professor Hayek read the bulk of Part I in its original draft, making a number of helpful suggestions

---

[1] It will be noticed in Part I, chap. 2, that I have practically ignored the mathematical economists in discussing the development of the theory of value in France, where they were more important than anywhere else. To have included them would have added to an already overgrown chapter, I believe unnecessarily. Their relation to Jevons and Walras is already well known, they appear to have been quite unknown to contemporary economists, and they were not seriously interested in the controversies between Ricardo and J. B. Say. Nor does their existence in any way weaken the argument advanced in the chapter; on the contrary it strengthens it by adding to the evidence of the development of the utility analysis by a number of scattered economists in the period between Ricardo and Jevons.

particularly with regard to references, and Mr. Redvers Opie made a number of useful criticisms at a later stage. Dr. Rosenstein-Rodan has been through the whole book, in particular he has saved me from a number of mistakes with regard to early writers on the theory of value. Mr. Beales gave me the benefit of his expert knowledge of the Poor Law. My gratitude to them is in no way diminished by the fact that I have not been able to follow their advice on all occasions.

My chief debt, however, is to Professor Robbins for his inexhaustible patience in criticizing my work during the last three years, and perhaps still more important for his generous encouragement, without which this book would probably never have been started, and would certainly never have been completed. I should add that none of these people are in any way responsible for the opinions advanced in the following pages.

My thanks are also due to the University of London for a grant from the Publication Fund towards the expenses of publishing the book, which was accepted as a thesis for the Ph.D. degree last year; also to the editors of *Economica* for allowing me to reprint an article which forms the bulk of Part I, chap. I, from *Economica*, August 1936.

I should like also to thank Miss J. Joshua for help in checking the references, Miss D. E. Ackroyd for help with the proofs and Miss I. Munroe and my father, Professor A. L. Bowley, for help with the Index.

MARIAN BOWLEY

Oxford
April 1937

CONTENTS

INTRODUCTION

As an economist Nassau William Senior has always appeared as something of a misfit. His published work, while too suggestive and original to admit of him being classed merely as follower of Ricardo, was too fragmentary to elevate him to the position of a founder of new school. In 1903, however, Professor Seligman brought to light a number of neglected British economists whose work has a strong affinity to Senior's.[1] It immediately became evident that Senior was the most distinguished of a group of economists who drew their inspiration from more varied sources than did the orthodox Ricardians. Since then it has only been a matter of time before someone undertook the fascinating task of exploring this neglected aspect of the history of economic theory in relation to Senior.

The first attempt was made by Mr. S. Leon Levy who, inspired by Professor Seligman, came to England before the War in search of Senior's unpublished lectures given at Oxford in 1826–30 and 1847–52. Mr. Levy's enterprise was rewarded almost immediately by the discovery of a mass of Senior's papers in the possession of his granddaughter Mrs. St. Loe Strachey. Mrs. Strachey generously put them at his disposal with the result that two volumes of edited extracts of Senior's writings appeared in 1929 under the title *Industrial Efficiency and Social Economy by N. W. Senior*. Mr. Levy, however, made no attempt to discuss the significance of Senior's work either in itself or in relation to the development of economic theory as a whole.[2] This particular gap has remained unclosed and it is this that I have attempted to fill in this book. It is thus neither a general history of economic theory nor precisely a monograph on Senior.

[1] *Some Neglected British Economists*, by E. Seligman. *Economic Journal*, 1903, reprinted in *Essays in Economics*, 1925.

[2] Despite the comprehensiveness of Mr. Levy's book I have found it impossible to make use of it for my purpose except for his identification in it of certain of Senior's articles. I have therefore confined myself to occasional criticisms of what seem to me to be glaring mis-selections of extracts from Senior's writings on various subjects.

It is for this reason that I have selected for my title *Nassau Senior and Classical Economics*. I do not intend by this double-barrel to introduce a line of division between Senior and the other recognized members of the classical school. In my opinion the term classical economics has become too closely associated with Ricardian economics. This is of course a matter of terminology, but there is some difficulty involved in including Senior among the classical economists if that term is taken to be approximately synonymous with Ricardo and his disciples for Senior was extremely critical of Ricardo. Three characteristics of Senior's economics emerge from a study of his work, published and unpublished: (1) his acceptance and elaboration of the utility theory of value both of goods and services under the influence of J. B. Say and Storch; (2) his critical attitude towards the Ricardian cost of production theory and assumption of perfect competition; (3) his disagreement with the Malthusian theory of population. Evidently if the term classical economists is used interchangeably with Ricardian, as it quite often is in semi-popular discussions, neither Senior, Longfield, W. F. Lloyd, nor any of the other economists to whom Professor Seligman drew attention, nor the French economists, can be included under it.

It may be protested that no one with any knowledge of the history of economic theory has ever tried to identify classical with Ricardian economics. In a sense this is true, it has been usual to consider the classical school as starting from Adam Smith and ending at Cairnes, and to treat Jevons, Walras and Menger as the founders of a new school. Nevertheless the immediate disciples of Ricardo, such as James Mill and McCulloch, have been treated as the proper representatives of British economic theory between Ricardo's death and Jevons' paper presented to the British Association in 1862. In conformity with this attitude the works of J. S. Mill and Cairnes have been regarded as the swan-songs of a dying dynasty. Consequently economists who criticized Ricardo, as for example Senior and Bailey, have been considered simply as critics who perhaps added some improvements by the way but who did not differ from him on fundamental doctrines. No attempt has been made to examine their work positively to see whether it included suggestions of a fundamental nature or was influenced by continental writers. Hence the neglect of the three or four decades after Ricardo's death and the appearance of discontinuity in the development of economic theory.

If my interpretation of the developments of the theory of value between 1823 and 1862 is correct, either it must be recognized that there were two different and more or less contemporary schools even in England, the classical or Ricardian and the utility schools, or the term classical must be disassociated from its narrow sense. The latter is the course I prefer, and I shall use the title classical school to include all those economists before Jevons who drew inspiration directly or indirectly from Adam Smith. At the risk of labouring the obvious I will elaborate my reasons for this.

In the first place it has seemed to me in studying Senior that the history of the theory of value (including distribution) can be treated most illuminatingly if viewed as the growth and later interaction of two interpretations of Adam Smith's treatment of value, viz., as a natural and market price theory and as a labour theory which derived the value of commodities from the labour involved in producing them. On the whole it is true to say that the former was dominant in France, where it was developed particularly by J. B. Say, and the latter in England during the first quarter of the nineteenth century. But after Ricardo's death important work was done in England, Ireland, France and Germany, by economists who tried to combine whatever was useful in the developments of these two interpretations by relating the utility to the cost of production analysis. In making this attempt a number of them either stated or hinted at the marginal analysis of value. By the 'seventies at the latest the confusions and difficulties produced by the divergent developments of Adam Smith's treatment of value had been pretty well resolved. The clear statements of the marginal utility theory given by Jevons, Walras and

Menger, mark the close of this preliminary period and the opening of one in which the marginal utility analysis became the accepted basis for further progress.[1]

In the second place this use of the term conforms to popular usage in discussions of the attitudes of economists to *laissez-faire*. A distinction is frequently made between classical economists and others, the former being generally associated with the free-trade opposition to most kinds of Government intervention thought to have been inspired by Adam Smith and the Radical Philosophers. Both Senior and the French economists as well as the strict Ricardians are usually included together for the purposes of such discussions. As I deal with this topic at some length in Part II with particular reference to Senior's attitude the use of the term classical in the same sense is suitable.

I have treated Senior throughout therefore as belonging to the classical school of what may be called the second generation. In order to show his place in the history of economics I have been obliged to discuss at considerable length other members of the school both of the first and second generations. Thus in the first chapter on scope and method I have started from the Ricardo–Malthus controversy and surveyed the views of McCulloch, Torrens and J. B. Say, before reaching Senior. In the second chapter on the theory of value I have attempted to show the divergent lines of thought starting from the *Wealth of Nations* and followed them up as briefly as possible. This appeared to me to be necessary in order to show up the background of Senior's work; even this is not the end of discussions of other economists as continual reference to contemporary writers on the utility theory of value proved necessary. It was possible, however, to confine the succeeding four chapters on rent, capital, wages, money and international trade, respectively, more closely to Senior as the back-

---

[1] From the point of view of the history of scope and method it is not necessary, of course, to make any distinction between the classical economists in my sense and more modern ones. This is so obvious, however, that it is not misleading to retain the distinction in dealing with this subject, and in Part I, chap. I, I have done so for the sake of uniformity.

ground to them had been included to some extent in the second chapter.

The second part of the book is devoted to the development of Senior's opinions on Government intervention and his work as a social reformer. I have isolated the discussion of the Poor Laws and devoted the whole of the second chapter to it, for it was on the question of Poor Law reform that Senior did his most important work. In the first chapter I have tried to cover the rest of Senior's numerous writings and activities in the field of economic and social policy, and for this fortunately I have been able to make use of the very important group of unpublished lectures which Senior delivered at Oxford between 1847 and 1852.[1] I have made no attempt in these chapters to give a complete account of contemporary opinion on these questions, but have merely indicated the attitudes of other economists where it seemed necessary.

A few words as to Senior's general political position are necessary to explain these chapters. Although Senior knew a considerable number of philosophical radicals including the Mills, he was never, as far as I am aware, one himself. From the time he finished his first period as Drummond Professor of Political Economy at Oxford in 1830 he was effectually a member of the Whig party and a valued adviser on economic matters. In that year, for example, he was asked by Lord Melbourne to investigate the position under the laws relating to combinations, and Lord Howick suggested to him that it would be useful to investigate the problems of poor relief in Ireland. The results of the former inquiry were never published, but those of the latter were published as *A Letter to Lord Howick, on a legal provision for the Irish Poor, etc.*[2] Without doubt this pamphlet was one of the reasons for his appointment to the Poor Law Commission of 1832–4 which afforded him his long wished for opportunity to try to rehabilitate the agricultural labourers.[3] It is important also to draw attention to his well-known

[1] By the kind permission of Mrs. St. Loe Strachey.
[2] Cf. Part II, chap. I, pp. 277 et seq. and 242–52 below.
[3] *Cornhill Magazine*, Vol. x, 1864, p. 254. Obituary notice of Senior.

friendship with Archbishop Whately which stimulated his permanent interest in Irish affairs, for the economic and social problems of Ireland had some influence on his outlook on Government intervention in general. It was no doubt partly as a consequence of his reputation with the Whigs that he was able to find a channel for the expression of his opinions on economic matters in the 'forties in the *Edinburgh Review*. He was indeed regarded as a most valued contributor to it.[1]

There is one other general point that is perhaps worth mentioning here: Senior was, as his *Journals* show,[2] a keen and observant traveller both in Ireland and on the Continent, and was familiar at least during the last decade or so of his life with economic conditions outside Great Britain. I have come across no indication that he met any of the German economists, but he knew most of the writers on economics in France and Italy, even before going abroad.

I am extremely conscious that the absence of any outline of Senior's life must give this book a sort of decapitated appearance, but as I explained in the Preface it did not in the end seem feasible to include one. I can only hope that the few explanations given in the preceding pages together with the list of dates given below and the bibliography given in Appendix II contain sufficient information to make the text intelligible. There is of course a good deal of information as to Senior's life easily accessible in a number of books: for example in his own published *Journals*, in the book by his daughter, Mrs. M. C. M. Simpson, *Many Memories of Many People*, in various biographies and collections of letters, e.g. that of Archbishop Whately, Mrs. Grote's life of her husband, *George Ticknor's Life and Letters* (Vol. II), the *Selected Correspondence of Macvey Napier*, J. L. Mallet's Diaries in *The Proceedings of the Political Economy Club* (Vol. VI), and of course in the *Dictionary of National Biography*. For an authoritative biography, however, we shall have to wait for the publication of Mrs. St. Loe Strachey's book based on hitherto unpublished material.

[1] *Selected Correspondence of Macvey Napier*, 1879, pp. 352, 379, 387, etc.
[2] For a list of Senior's published *Journals* see Appendix II below.

LIST OF DATES IMPORTANT IN THE LIFE OF NASSAU SENIOR (1790–1864)[1, 2]

1790   Nassau William Senior the economist was born at Compton Beauchamp in Berkshire, eldest son of John Raven Senior, Vicar of Durnford.

1803–7   educated at Eton.

1807   Demy of Magdalen College, Oxford.

1811   obtained a first class in degree examination.

1812   B.A. Oxford and Probationary Fellow of Magdalen.

1813   Vinerian Scholar, Oxford; entered Sugden's chambers in Lincoln's Inn to read for the Bar.

1817   certified as a conveyancer.

1819   called to the Bar.

1821   married Mary Charlotte Mair. (He had two children by his marriage.)

published an article on the Corn Laws in the *Quarterly Review*.

1823   elected a member of the Political Economy Club. (He remained a member for the rest of his life except for the years 1848–53 during which he resigned.)[3]

1825–30   First Drummond Professor of Political Economy at Oxford.

published:

1826   Appendix to Whately's *Logic* on Definitions in Political Economy.

1827   Introductory Lecture on Political Economy.

1828   Three Lectures on the Transmission of the Precious Metals, etc.

1829   Two Lectures on Population, together with a Correspondence between the author and the Rev. T. R. Malthus.

1830   Three Lectures on the Cost of Obtaining Money, etc.

Three Lectures on Wages, with a Preface on the Causes and Remedies of the Present Distress.

[1] Most of the dates included in this list are to be found in the *Dictionary of National Biography*.

For a complete list of Senior's published works on economics see Appendix II below.

[2] I have not attempted to make a record of Senior's activities as a lawyer.

[3] *Proceedings of the Political Economy Club*, Vol. VI. List of members.

1830[1] invited by Lord Melbourne to report on the state of the Laws relating to Combinations. (Report finished in 1831, unpublished.)

started inquiry into the Irish Poor Laws at the suggestion of Lord Howick. (Inquiry published in 1831 as *A Letter to Lord Howick, on a legal provision for the Irish Poor, etc.*)

1831 appointed Professor of Political Economy at King's College, London. He was forced to resign soon after his appointment owing to his advocacy of the confiscation of some of the revenues of the Established Church in Ireland for the benefit of the Roman Catholics.[2] This opinion was advanced in the *Letter to Lord Howick* referred to above and in *A Letter to Lord Howick on Commutation of Tithes and a Provision for the Roman Catholic Clergy in Ireland.*[3]

1832-4 member of the Commission for inquiring into the Administration and Operation of the Poor Laws.

1835 published a pamphlet *On National Property and on the prospects of the present Administration and of their Successors.*

1836 appointed Master in Chancery.

consulted by Lord John Russell on Irish Poor Law Reform.[4]

published first edition of the *Outline of Political Economy* as part of the *Encyclopedia Metropitana.*

1837 visited cotton factories in Lancashire and published the *Letters on the Factory Act.*

1841 finished drawing up the Report of the Commission on the Condition of the Unemployed Hand-loom Weavers.[5]

1841-49 contributed a number of articles to the *Edinburgh Review* on economic subjects.

1847-52 appointed Drummond Professor of Political Economy at Oxford for the second time.

published:

1849 Lecture on the Production of Wealth.

1852 Four Introductory Lectures on Political Economy.

[1] See Part II, chap. I, pp. 277 et seq. and 242-52 below.

[2] *Proceedings of the Political Economy Club*, Vol. VI, pp. 236 and 261.

[3] The only evidence I have for the existence of this second pamphlet is that it was reviewed under this title in the *Quarterly Review*, Vol. 46, January 1832, Art. V. This may have been merely a second review of the *Letter to Lord Howick on a legal provision for the Irish Poor, etc.*, which was reviewed in Article IV of the same issue. In consequence I have not listed it separately in the Bibliographical Appendix.

[4] See Appendix I, p. 336 below.   [5] See Part II, chap. I, pp. 258 et seq. below.

1857 appointed member of the Royal Commission on Popular Education.
1860 President of Section F of the British Association for the Advancement of Science.
1862 gave evidence before the Select Committee on Poor Relief.
1863 President of the Education Department of the National Association for the Promotion of Social Science.

PART I
ECONOMIC THEORY

CHAPTER 1

SCOPE AND METHOD

THE adherence of the majority of economists in England to the deductive method in economics is very often regarded as merely one more sign of their blind loyalty to the classical tradition.[1] But it is only in comparison with the intensity and persistence of methodological controversies on the Continent that there seems to have been little discussion in England during the nineteenth century. It is natural perhaps that the members of the historical and empirical schools should only have noticed such English discussions of method as were stimulated by their own attacks, but in this respect they have shown a lamentable disregard of their own avowed principles of research and failed to appreciate the history of the methodology they have criticized. By attempting to explain away the existence of the classical school of method in terms of contemporary philosophy and institutions, they have overlooked the actual development of the methods they were criticizing. In fact, whatever may have been their mistakes, the adherents to the classical method have possessed a far greater understanding of its problems than their critics have either given them credit for or displayed themselves.

The classical economists themselves displayed a very real interest in putting their own house in order, a fact which perhaps accounts for their apparent indifference to the

---

[1] The criticisms of the various branches of the Historical School do not directly concern us here, but it is of some interest to notice that it attracted its most distinguished English adherents, J. K. Ingram and Cliffe Leslie, at a time when it was most under the influence of Roscher and Knies, both of whom admitted the importance of the results of the classical analysis. For the most extreme criticisms of the deductive method see Schmoller, *Grundfragen der Socialpolitik und der Volkswirtschaftslehre*, and for a reply see Menger, *Untersuchungen über die Methode der Socialwissenschaften und der Politischen Oekonomie insbesondere*. Cf. also Robbins, *The Nature and Significance of Economic Science*, second edition, for a more recent defence. For a very tolerant account of the issues in the nineteenth century controversies see H. Sidgwick, *The Principles of Political Economy*, Introduction.

developments of divergent schools of method, of which they
were not by any means unaware.[1] For this reason it seems
to be more useful to examine the way they dealt with their
own problems than to follow the historians over the well-
worn field of the relation of classical economics to Benthamism.[2] Everything possible, right and wrong, must have been
said by now in interpretation of the philosophical background of English nineteenth-century economics;—the
result of it all is merely to leave a profound scepticism as
to the value of such explanations if, instead of reading
commentaries on the Classics, one reads the Classics
themselves. Another and perhaps a more fundamental
reason for taking this course is the failure of the attempts to
explain away the significance of the classical methodology
to account either for the continuity in treatment between
Ricardo and Marshall, or for the growth of deductive
schools in Austria and Lausanne. I shall therefore ignore the
explanations plausible and otherwise that have been given
of the general loyalty of English economists to the deductive
method in economics, and limit myself to following out the
attempts that were made to define that method.

Actually the controversies within the deductive school
have no logical connection with what may roughly be called
the historical approach.[3] All the protagonists have started

[1] Marshall (*Principles of Economics*) appears to have underrated English
development of method by an over-generous attempt to give credit to the work
of the German historical school. In Appendix C, par. 4, with a remarkable disregard of Senior's and Cairnes' attempts to distinguish between the science and
the art of economics, he says, "It is only recently, and to a great extent through
the wholesome influence of the criticisms of the historical school, that prominence
has been given to that distinction in economics which corresponds to the distinction between strategy and tactics in warfare." Actually Senior used
a similar analogy.

[2] Cf. Schumpeter, *Dogmen- und Methodengeschichte*, III, "Das klassische
System," par. 5, and Bonar, *Philosophy and Political Economy*, Bk. III, chap. 2.

[3] Dr. Kaufmann has recently suggested that the only difference between the
deductive and empirical methods is as to the desirability of formulating general
or particular laws in particular cases, pointing out that each method makes
use of an assumption as to the nature of cause and effect and is therefore, to
that extent, hypothetical (*Review of Economic Studies*, February 1934, "The
Concept of Law in Economic Science"). Welcome though any attempt to
bring about a rapprochement between the exponents of the various methods
may be, Dr. Kaufmann appears in this respect to have gone too far and merged

from the basis that there are permanent uniformities in economic behaviour; the disputes have been concerned with the question of how far it is possible to simplify the data of economic analysis in order to examine certain aspects more closely, without omitting anything organically connected with the fundamental problems;—or put more technically, how few, and how simple, are the terms of the economic functions which are sufficient to determine the relations between all the relevant variables? Essentially it is this question which has occupied the centre of interest from the beginning of last century to the present day. With the exception of John Stuart Mill, who attempted to introduce the economic man as a hypothetical basis of economic analysis,[1] and a few of his followers, English economists have always started from the idea that the initial premises must include the whole range of data relevant to the pricing process; the principal problem has been to decide what the data are. Thus the methodological significance of the formulation of the marginal theory of value in terms of choices between scarce satisfactions is recognized as its contribution to the solution of this problem by completing both the premises of the Ricardian theory and that theory itself.[2] Similarly, Pareto's criticism of Marshall's use of the "one at a time" method on the assumption that the data

three questions at least into one. The first and most fundamental is as to the existence of independent uniformities of economic phenomena; until agreement is reached upon this point it is useless to try to consider the dispute between the sociological historians and the deductive economists as a question of degree. The second is as to the best method of finding economic laws, the empirical versus the deductive; this in fact is a question of degree turning on opinion as to practicability, etc., and it is this question that Kaufmann really resolves, but it had been done long ago. Cf. below, pp. 52–9. The third is as to the best method of dealing with particular problems, whether by applying general laws which do not take into account the particular premises, or by treating all premises as particular and ignoring the general implications. This is perhaps a dispute which is really one of degree, but, if it is treated as one, there is a danger of obscuring the divergence in outlook involved between the difference of emphasis on general and particular propositions respectively. Cf. discussion of the Senior–Mill–Cairnes controversy below, pp. 59–64.

[1] J. S. Mill, *Essays on Unsettled Questions*, "On the Definition of Political Economy; and on the Method of Investigation Proper to it."

[2] See Wicksteed, Vol. II, *Collected Works*, "The Scope and Method of Political Economy in the Light of the 'Marginal' Theory of Value and Distribution."

excluded had either no organic influence on the results, or was of the second order of smalls, turned on the same point.[1] Finally we can point to the interest that has been excited by recent discussions of "the path" towards equilibrium which have cast doubts upon the validity of both Marshall's and Pareto's analyses on the same grounds.[2]

I

Although the first methodological discussion of importance in England was that between Malthus, Ricardo and Say, its significance can only be appreciated from a review of their relation to Adam Smith. In investigating the influences affecting the wealth of nations, Adam Smith started from a realistic study of the productivity of labour. It was a natural procedure to try to explain the most striking economic phenomena of all, the organization of productive capacity to supply wants through the price system. The explanation of the existence of price at all he found in the inherent disposition to "truck and barter";[3] as a corollary it emerged that no one would accept a lower reward for his productive effort than he need, or, turned round the reverse

[1] See *Principles of Economics*, Appendices B, C, D, for the fullest exposition of Marshall's method. His justification of the use of the hypothetical method is to be found in Appendix C, par. 2, in its most concise form. "It is true that the forces with which economics deals have one advantage for deductive treatment in the fact that their method of combination is, as Mill observed, that of mechanics rather than of chemistry. That is to say, when we know the action of two economic forces separately . . . we can predict fairly well their conjoint action, without waiting for specific experience of it." Pareto's particular objection to the literary economists was just this assumption. *Manuel d'Économie Politique*, chap. 3, par. 219.

[2] See Wicksteed's criticism of Marshall's theory of consumer's surplus. *Collected Works*, Vol. II, pp. 467–73. The problem has, however, cropped up in practically all discussions of the concept of a perfect market, see for example Wicksell's criticism of Jevons in *Über Wert, Kapital, und Rente*, chap. 1, par. 5. Recently the problem has been stated in general terms by Dr. Rosenstein-Rodan, "Das Zeitmoment in der mathematischen Theorie des wirtschaftlichen Gleichgewichtes," *Zeitschrift für Nationalökonomie*, May 1929, pp. 129–42, and "The Rôle of Time in Economic Theory," *Economica*, February 1934.

[3] *Wealth of Nations*, Bk. I, chap. 2, Vol. I, p. 15, Cannan's edition (all page references are to Cannan's edition). For a general account of Adam Smith's method see Marshall's *Principles of Economics*, Appendix B, par. 4 to the end.

way, pay more to obtain those goods which he wanted than he was obliged to. The whole fabric of Adam Smith's analysis developed from this essentially realistic basis. From it he drew the general conclusion that the maximum output of the goods desired would result from freedom of action in economic transactions, within a legal framework of security of property. There is little in the *Wealth of Nations* to suggest that this would produce the most ethically desirable distribution of wealth, but in examining contemporary institutions Adam Smith judged them by what might be called the productivity criterion. As far as the pure theory of economics was concerned this was perfectly straightforward, the basic premises neither included, nor excluded, any motivation except the desire to satisfy needs in the easiest available manner. Nor did Adam Smith attempt to define the quantity or type of goods individuals might desire, except by whatever can be read into his general remark on the nature of human desires, that although the capacity of the human stomach is limited, the desire for variety and the ambition of man have no assignable limits.[1] Adam Smith simply set out to explain the mechanism by which these desires were satisfied, and drew certain conclusions as to the efficiency of competition.[2] The organon of economic analysis contained in the *Wealth of Nations* was thus essentially realistic. If the premises were correct and complete and the reasoning logical the laws deduced described tendencies present in the actual world. It was this systematic attempt at explanation of economic phenomena that Ricardo and Malthus started out to complete and, if necessary, correct.[3]

Approached from this angle the dispute on method between Malthus and Ricardo—hailed so often as the first indication of admission of the weakness of the deductive

---

[1] *Wealth of Nations*, Bk. I, chap. II, Vol. I, p. 165.

[2] Adam Smith was well aware of the importance of education in relation to perfect mobility and therefore perfect competition, and advocated State education (Ibid., Bk. V, chap. I, Conclusion, Vol. II, pp. 300–1).

[3] Ricardo, *Principles of Political Economy and Taxation*. Preface to the first edition. Malthus' *Principles of Political Economy*, first edition, 1820, p. 3. (All references are to this edition.)

method—turns out to be merely a question of the applicability of the latter's analysis to particular problems depending on the completeness of the premises on which that analysis was based. A study of the Introduction to Malthus' *Principles* shows clearly enough that the difference between them was due to a difference in objective. Malthus wanted an explanation of certain short-period problems; Ricardo's analysis being devoted to the long period did not supply it. And Malthus, not altogether appreciating this, jumped to the conclusion that there was something wrong with the analysis, and attempted to point out why. Thus he remarked on the impossibility that

"any propositions the practical application of which depend upon the agency of so variable a being as man, and the qualities of so variable a compound as the soil, can ever admit of the same kinds of proof, or lead to the same certain conclusions as those which relate to figure and number."[1]

Taken by itself, this passage is perhaps open to interpretation as a denial of the possibility of the existence of general laws. But if it is considered in connection with his intention of correcting certain mistakes of Adam Smith's and with subsequent passages of the Introduction, it seems intended to apply to the interpretation of particular cases. Malthus went on in a few pages to point out the cause of the mistaken attempts at interpretation due to

"a precipitate attempt to simplify and generalize; and while their more practical opponents draw too hasty inferences from a frequent appeal to partial facts, these writers run into a contrary extreme, and do not sufficiently try their theories by a reference to that enlarged and comprehensive experience which, on so complicated a subject, can alone establish their truth and utility."

and a page farther on he added:

"The same tendency to simplify and generalize, produces a still greater disinclination to allow of modifications, limitations, and exceptions to any rule or proposition, than to admit the operation of more causes than one."[2]

[1] Malthus, *Principles of Political Economy*, p. 1.   [2] Ibid., pp. 6 and 7.

It is open, I think, to question whether Malthus thought that this criticism[1] was against the incompleteness of the premises of general laws or against the incompleteness of supplementary premises in particular cases. In view of the relation between his theory of value and his own theory of gluts the former interpretation seems correct, but if these passages are compared with a later one, the latter:

"One of the specific objects of the present work is to prepare the general rules of political economy for practical application by a frequent reference to experience, and by taking as comprehensive a view as I can of all the causes that concur in the production of particular phenomena."[2]

At most those who attempt to find in Malthus the father of the empirical method in economics may read in this an admission that our knowledge of general principles and of their application to particular problems would be improved by a more careful investigation of the premises—a suggestion that few deductive economists would venture to deny. It is fairly evident, however, that Ricardo regarded the criticism not in this light so much as a failure on Malthus' part to understand either his objects or his attempts to achieve them. Thus he wrote to Hutches Trower about Malthus' *Principles of Political Economy* that

"This is a question of fact and degree, not of principle, and it is one of my complaints against him that he does not answer your principle but wishes to show that you have taken your case so wide, that it could under no circumstances exist; but however limited might be your case, the same principle is involved, and it is that which should be answered."[3]

In trying to explain to Malthus the source of their disagreement he wrote:

"Our differences may in some respects, I think, be ascribed to your considering my book as more practical than I intended

[1] Malthus, *Principles of Political Economy*, pp. 8–9. This criticism was directed against the orthodox attitude to the theory of gluts, among other things.
[2] Ibid., p. 21.
[3] Letter from Ricardo to Hutches Trower, September 15, 1820, referring to Malthus' *Principles of Political Economy*, chap. 3, pp. 145–6, on rent. *Letters from Ricardo to Hutches Trower*, edited Bonar and Hollander, 1899, p. 121.

it to be. My object was to elucidate principles, and to do this I imagined strong cases, that I might show the operation of those principles."[1]

In introducing strong cases, however, Ricardo had taken an important new step in the development of economic analysis. Although there is no question that fundamentally Ricardo's general premises were as much based on reality as Adam Smith's since they were the same, Ricardo deliberately abstracted from certain conditions of the real world and conducted mental experiments as to the mutual interaction of basic tendencies if freed from disturbances. The realization of the equilibrium depicted in his experiment is not, he knew, possible in the real world owing to continual changes in technique, habits, etc.; nevertheless, he believed that the general direction of the tendencies towards equilibrium exhibited under his experimental conditions, exist in the real world. Clearly his belief in the validity of such hypothetical experiments was only justifiable if the premises left out were not integral parts of the premises considered, and could therefore be allowed for afterwards, as Marshall explained, if the nature of economic reactions are mechanical and not chemical.[2] Now it is possible to argue that the mechanism of short-period adjustment is an essential part of long period adjustments, and therefore

[1] Letter from Ricardo to Malthus. May 4, 1820. *Letters from Ricardo to Malthus*, edited Bonar, 1887, pp. 166–7.

[2] Malthus continually objected that Ricardo reached the conclusion that the landlords' interests were usually opposed to those of the community, because he neglected to consider the effect of improvements. Ricardo replied in great detail in the "Notes" (edited Hollander and Gregory, 1928) on chap. 3 of Malthus' *Principles*, pointing out that Malthus' analysis was wrong, and that the difference was not in this respect at any rate due to inadequate premises.

The instance most frequently referred to, however, is Ricardo's statement that a tax on wages would always be passed on. His critics maintain that this conclusion was based on his assumption that wages were always at the minimum consistent with maintaining the population. This is, however, incorrect, as Ricardo explained, both in the *Principles* (chap. 16, pp. 203–5, Gonner's edition) and in a letter to McCulloch on March 29, 1820, that under all circumstances the amount deducted from wages would be returned in an increased demand for labour by the Government. *Letters of David Ricardo to John Ramsay McCulloch, 1816–1823*, edited Hollander, 1895, pp. 54–6.

In fact, from the methodological point of view Ricardo's record is much better than his critics admit.

that the latter must be explained in the same terms as the former. If this is the case, then Ricardo's failure to analyse short-period pricing problems led to an incorrect interpretation of the permanent tendencies of the pricing process, and his results were in fact not directly applicable to the actual world. Malthus' criticism of Ricardo's value analysis in this respect came to just this,[1] but not being stated clearly in methodological terms did not present the issue in an obvious way. This service was performed by J. B. Say in correspondence with Ricardo and Malthus, and in the Discours Préliminaire of his *Traité*.

Casting round for a scientific method to apply to economics Say adopted the most usual method of the natural sciences, for since both dealt with concrete facts it appeared at first sight that the method which had been so successful in the one case would be suitable in the other. The only possible way he considered of finding the correct premises of economics—and it is to be observed that in common with everyone else he assumed the necessity of realistic premises — is by the intensive and extensive observation of facts:

"En économie politique, comme en physique, comme en tout, on a fait des systèmes avant d'établir des vérités; c'est-à-dire qu'on a donné pour la vérité des conceptions gratuités, de pures assertions. Plus tard, on a appliqué à cette science les méthodes qui ont tant contribué, depuis Bacon, aux progrès de toutes les autres; c'est-à-dire la méthode expérimentale, qui consiste essentiellement à n'admettre comme vrais que les faits dont l'observation et l'expérience ont démontré la réalité, et comme des vérités constantes que les conclusions qu'on en peut tirer naturellement."[2]

He distinguished, however, between sciences that are solely concerned with collecting and classifying facts, and those that have reached a stage of deduction from facts.

"De là naissent deux genres de sciences: les sciences qu'on peut nommer *descriptives*, qui consistent à nommer et à classer les choses, comme la botanique ou l'histoire naturelle; et les

[1] Malthus, *Principles of Political Economy*, chap. 2, sects. ii and iii.
[2] *Traité d'Économie Politique*, Discours Préliminaire, p. 3, sixth edition. (All page references are to this edition unless otherwise stated.)

sciences *expérimentales*, qui nous font connaître les actions réciproques que les choses exercent les unes sur les autres, ou en d'autres termes la liaison des effets avec leurs causes; telles sont la physique et la chimie."[1]

Economics of course belongs to the latter class and statistics to the former. So far so good, but Say naturally, like others who have followed the same path in method, promptly got into difficulties in explaining how economists, who cannot make experiments, are to isolate essential and constant facts from the unessential which they observe. By suddenly begging the question he attempted to get over the difficulty by saying that the general observation of common phenomena is the necessary preliminary to formulating economic premises (a method which in fact differs not at all from ordinary methods of the English economists).

"L'économie politique . . . est établie sur des fondemens inébranlables, du moment que les principes qui lui servent de base sont les déductions rigoureuses de faits généraux incontestables. Les faits généraux sont, à la vérité, fondés sur l'observation des faits particuliers, mais on a pu choisir les faits particuliers les mieux observés, les mieux constatés, ceux dont on a été soi-même le témoin; . . . Enfin, combien peu de faits particuliers sont complètement avérés! Combien peu d'entre eux sont observés avec toutes leurs circonstances! Et, en les supposant bien avérés, bien observés et bien décrits, combien n'y en a-t-il pas qui ne prouvent rien, ou qui prouvent le contraire de ce qu'on veut établir."[2]

A few pages further on he laid still further insistence on the necessity of selecting only general facts and ignoring the collection of details.

"Il faut donc, pour parvenir à la vérité, connaître, non beaucoup de faits, mais les faits essentiels et véritablement influens, les envisager sous toutes leurs faces, et surtout en tirer des conséquences justes, être assuré que l'effet qu'on leur attribue vient réellement d'eux, et non d'ailleurs. Tout autre connaissance de faits est un amas d'où il ne résulte rien, une érudition d'almanach."[3]

[1] *Traité d'Économie Politique*, Discours Préliminaire, p. 4.
[2] Ibid., p. 6.   [3] Ibid., p. 10.

In attempting to explain how the premises of economics are discovered, Say had really demonstrated the impossibility of treating economics as an experimental science and had merely emphasized the necessity of starting from complete premises. He criticized the Ricardian analysis for this reason as being built on premises imperfectly founded on facts, and therefore, according to Say, pure assumptions with no necessary relevance to the actual world.

". . . des économistes anglais de l'école de David Ricardo . . . sans employer les formules algébriques trop évidemment inapplicables à l'économie politique, ont voulu y introduire un genre d'argumentation auquel je crois, en thèse générale, qu'elle se refuse de même que toutes les sciences qui ne reconnaissent pour fondement que l'expérience : je veux dire l'argumentation qui repose sur des abstractions."[1]

The particular object singled out for attack was of course the Ricardian theory of rent. Say described it as based in the first place on data not true of the world, and then built up by successive stages of argument into a colossal edifice with the result that the conclusions were contradicted by experience. The ensuing controversies were therefore, he declared, endless and futile, and distracted attention from serious problems by their "scholastic" dialectics.[2]

Like Malthus', Say's attack was on what he believed to be the application of laws deduced from imperfect premises to the explanation of economic phenomena, and his sympathy with Malthus in this respect was natural and genuine, though he disagreed with Malthus' application of this criticism to Ricardo's treatment of his theory of gluts.[3] Ricardo's reply was inevitably the same, that Say did not understand him.[4]

Another critic of Ricardo within the classical school deserves mention for the clarity with which he saw the issue between Ricardo and Malthus in terms of the com-

---

[1] *Traité d'Économie Politique*, Discours Préliminaire, p. 15.
[2] Ibid., p. 16.
[3] *Mélanges de J. B. Say*. Letter from Say to Malthus, February 24, 1827.
[4] Letter from Ricardo to Hutches Trower, December 14, 1822. *Letters, etc.*, edited Bonar and Hollander, 1899, pp. 196–7.

pleteness of premises. In the Preface to the *Essay on Wealth*, Torrens remarked that Ricardo by generalizing too hastily

"fails to establish his principles on a sufficiently extensive induction. In the inventive faculty, and in the power of pure and continuous ratiocination, he has seldom been surpassed; but in the capacity for accurate observation his pre-eminence is less apparent."[1]

Malthus on the other hand is described as exhibiting

"throughout his writings, an intellectual character, altogether opposite to that which has been here described. He possesses in a very eminent degree the faculty for observing particular phenomena, but is somewhat deficient in that power of analysis which distinguishes between coincidence and necessary connexion, and enables us to trace the sequence of causes and effects. If Mr. Ricardo generalizes too much, Mr. Malthus generalizes too little."[2]

He concluded the preface by remarking that:

"Had the analytical method of induction from particular cases been more frequently resorted to by Mr. Ricardo, that most original and profound economist would not by his recent deviations from his original doctrines, have retarded the progress of the science for which he has achieved so much; and had this method been adopted by Mr. Malthus, he would not have appeared as the ingenious opponent of the new theory of profit, which may be traced by a process of reasoning, self-evident in all its steps, from those discoveries respecting the nature and origin of rent which he himself has made."[3]

McCulloch, in adopting wholesale Ricardo's analysis, stated explicitly the real nature of economic science and the applicability of its laws to the real world. It apparently never occurred to him to doubt that Ricardo was treating Adam Smith's premises in the same way as the latter himself had. He explained that the conclusions of political economy are founded on principles which form "a part of the original constitution of man," and that their operation "may, like that of the mechanical principles, be

---

[1] *Essay on the Production of Wealth*, Introduction, p. iv.
[2] Ibid., p. iv.   [3] Ibid., pp. x–xiii.

traced by the aid of observation and analysis." Not content, however, with this bald statement, he remarked on the existence of degree and even exception of application in special cases.

"The principles which determine the production and accumulation of wealth are inherent in our nature, and exert a powerful, but not always the same degree of influence over the conduct of every individual; and the theorist must, therefore, satisfy himself with framing rules which explain their operation in the majority of instances, leaving it to the sagacity of the observer to modify them so as to suit individual cases."[1]

McCulloch followed up this general statement by explaining that the basic economic premises must be founded on extensive induction and a study of history, a precept which he himself failed to carry out as far as the inherent principles of human nature were concerned. This admission of the necessity of induction did not, however, save him from Say singling him out as one of the worst offenders in respect of the Ricardian habits of reasoning from assumed premises.[2]

It is difficult in face of this sort of discussion of the unsatisfactory character of Ricardo's premises to maintain that the classical economists, even of Ricardo's generation, were either unaware of, or indifferent to, the problems involved in the use of their own methods. But it is important to notice that not one of them seriously questioned the existence of general laws of economics, although McCulloch was the only one to make the slightest attempt to state the premises relating to human behaviour on which they were based; they all tacitly accepted Adam Smith's description.

[1] *Principles of Political Economy*, Introduction, pp. 14–15, third edition.

[2] McCulloch, *Principles*, Introduction, pp. 15 et seq., third edition, J. B. Say, op. cit., Discours Préliminaire, p. 16 n. Say's criticism, which was based on McCulloch's evidence before the Committee on the Export of Machinery 1824–5, was in this instance due to his own failure to understand McCulloch's use of the term "high" and "low" wages in the Ricardian sense of proportions. Senior also criticized McCulloch's evidence but merely as an example of the confusion arising from Ricardo's terminology. Senior, *Political Economy*, pp. 143–8.

Richard Jones, however, standing outside the ring of the classical school, protested vigorously against the general attitude. He objected that the narrow view of economics, adopted by the bulk of the classical economists, ignored one of the most important and interesting aspects of economics, the relation between economic influences and social institutions. He urged that economists should be historically-minded and view the past course of the development of human society in order that they might understand and advise statesmen on the institutions most conducive to the future happiness and prosperity of the human race. In brief, he looked upon sociology as a branch of economics, thus reversing Comte's treatment of economics as a branch of sociology. But still more important, perhaps, Jones also criticized the classics for ignoring the relativity of economic laws. Like List some years later, he argued that the general economic laws were neither interesting nor useful in dealing with societies in which the institutions and customs were such that the economic forces analysed by Ricardo, for instance, were practically nullified. In short, Richard Jones was an isolated representative of the historical method in England in the 'thirties. But he immersed himself to such an extent in detailed historical studies that his more philosophical disquisitions were overshadowed by his accumulations of facts, and he was regarded by his contemporaries as a statistician rather than as an innovator in methodology.[1]

The criticism which has so often been levelled against the early classics, that they applied their economic conclusions to questions of policy without considering non-economic aspects, is, as far as the art of economics is concerned, quite ridiculous by definition. Nevertheless, it is reasonable to criticize a number of them for dogmatizing too readily on the precepts of the art of economics (or as it is now more generally called applied economics) before they had made sufficient progress with the science. McCulloch is frequently

---

[1] *Introductory Lecture at King's College*, London, February 27, 1833. Jones never fulfilled his ambition of completing a study of distribution on socio-economic lines, but his *Essay on Rent*, 1831, and the remains of his lectures (reprinted in his *Literary Remains*, 1859) probably give a fair indication of what he was aiming at.

held up as one of the worst offenders in this respect. He was
was certainly convinced that

"The object of Political Economy is to point out the means
by which the industry of man may be rendered most productive
of those necessaries, comforts, and enjoyments, which constitute
wealth; to ascertain the circumstances most favourable for its
accumulation; the proportions in which it is divided among
the different classes of the community; and the mode in which
it may be most advantageously consumed."[1]

Furthermore, he evidently had little doubt that it was
possible to begin to realize this object, for he was pretty
well satisfied as to the soundness and universality of his
premises and the theory built on them. A very considerable
part of his *Principles* was in consequence devoted to expounding the art.

Say held similar views with respect to his own version
of economic theory, and although he conscientiously kept
the *Traité* free from excursions outside the field of pure
science, he devoted the energy of his old age to expounding
various applications of economic theory in the *Cours*.

Malthus, too, was anxious to develop the art of economics,
and explained that one of the chief objects of his *Principles*
was to prepare the "general rules of political economy for
practical application." Moreover, by emphasizing the
exceptions and limitations to the general laws, he intended
to point out the exceptions which must be made to *laissez-
faire* as a general policy.[2] It would be rash to conclude
from this, in view of Malthus' general inexactitude of
thought, that he meant that economic theory justified a
general policy of *laissez-faire* and that the sole exceptions
to that policy were to be found on economic grounds. But
his controversy with Senior on population certainly lends
colour to the interpretation, and it is obvious that, as a
result of his preoccupation with population problems, he
was deeply impressed by the futility and danger of Government interference in social and economic questions, except

[1] McCulloch, *Principles*, Introduction, p. 7, third edition.
[2] Malthus, *Principles of Political Economy*, Introduction, pp. 21 and 13–14.

in the sphere of education.[1] Ricardo's attitude is naturally
more difficult to discover but on one point at least he
followed Malthus' lead, by applying the conclusions of
population theory to a condemnation of the Poor Laws.[2]

The critics of the classical economists are on less firm
ground when they inveigh against the latter's discourses
on Government policy in general as distinct from the
economic aspects of policy. It is true, of course, that on the
score of methodological clarity such discourses are out of
place in treatises on economics. But there is no reason for
assuming merely because they were included, that they
were written without taking the non-economic aspects of
policy into consideration. It must be remembered too that
some of the worst offenders in the eyes of these critics, such
as James Mill and McCulloch, were philosophical Radicals,
and were active in politics.[3] It is scarcely reasonable to
criticize them because the conclusions of their political
philosophy ran parallel in many respects to those of their
economic investigations.

II

It is evident that by the time Senior went to lecture at
Oxford in 1826 the principal problems of the deductive
method in economics had been raised in one form or another.
But with the exception of Say's Discours Préliminaire, no
attempt had been made to consider systematically how far
the open, or tacit, claims as to reality and completeness of
the premises were justified. This gap Senior attempted to
fill in his Introductory lecture and the succeeding lectures
on the fundamental propositions, and at intervals during
his whole active life as an economist.

[1] Malthus' correspondence with Senior, published with Senior's *Two
Lectures on Population*, 1829. Cf. also *Principles of Political Economy*, Introduction,
pp. 13–15.

[2] Letters from Ricardo to Hutches Trower, December 10, 1817, and January
26, 1818. *Letters, etc.*, edited Bonar and Hollander, 1899, pp. 42–3, 47–8.

[3] For a discussion of the opinions of the classical economists on social policy
see Part II, chap. I, pp. 272–7 below.

For Senior's views on the relation between economic theory and policy,
etc., see below.

The Introductory lecture delivered at Oxford in 1826, though not in itself an important contribution to the solution of problems of scope, showed the main lines of approach which he subsequently developed. As his chief interest in economics was the light it might be expected to throw on the social questions connected with the prevalent poverty of the working classes, it is not surprising that he started with a wide definition of Political Economy as

"the science which teaches in what wealth consists—by what agents it is produced—and according to what laws it is distributed—and what are the institutions and customs by which production may be facilitated and distribution regulated, so as to give the largest possible amount of wealth to each individual."[1]

He went on immediately to justify this definition by explaining the nature of the premises on which it was founded:

"The first, or theoretic branch, that which explains the nature, production, and distribution of wealth, will be found to rest on a very few general propositions, which are the result of observation, or consciousness, and which almost every man, as soon as he hears them, admits, as familiar to his thoughts, or at least, as included in his previous knowledge.

Its conclusions are also nearly as general as its premises—those which relate to the nature and production of wealth, are universally true; and, though those which relate to the distribution of wealth, are liable to be affected by peculiar institutions of particular countries—in the cases, for instance, of slavery, corn laws, or poor-laws—the natural state of things can be laid down as the general rule, and the anomalies produced by particular disturbing causes can be afterwards accounted for."[2]

This general idea of the nature of a science of economics based on general premises covering the major phenomena affecting economic propositions, he retained unchanged to the end of his life, expanding it in the *Political Economy* in 1836, and in the Lectures of 1847.

As to the second branch, the practical, however, Senior's

---

[1] *Introductory Lecture*, 1826, published 1827, p. 7.   [2] Ibid., pp. 7–8.

opinion underwent two major modifications in 1836 and in 1847, but in 1826 he allowed this branch the same general position as McCulloch.

"The practical branch of the science, that of which the office is to ascertain what institutions are most favourable to wealth, is a far more arduous study. Many of its premises, indeed, rest on the same evidence as those of the first branch; for they are the conclusions of that branch:—but it has many which depend on induction from phenomena, numerous, difficult of enumeration, and of which the real sequence often differs widely from the apparent one. The machinery of civilized society is worked by so many antagonistic springs; the dislike of labour, the desire for immediate enjoyment, the love of accumulation are so perpetually counteracting one another, and they produce such opposite conduct, not only in different individuals, but in whole masses of people, that we are liable to the greatest mistakes when we endeavour to assign motives to past conduct, or to predict the conduct which a new motive will produce."[1]

Even in 1826 Senior laid little claim to a degree of authority for the practical branch comparable with that claimed for the theoretical, and maintained that it was inattention to the necessary distinction between them that had brought economics into disrepute in many quarters. Nevertheless, at this stage he suggested that many of the most important practical conclusions rest so immediately on those of the theoretical branch as to have the same certainty. He did not explain which practical conclusions these were.

"Inattention to the distinction between the practical and the theoretic branches of Political Economy, appears to me to have occasioned much of the difference of opinion which prevails as to the certainty of its conclusions. Those who assert that it approaches to the accuracy of logic or mechanics, must either have confined their attention to the theoretic branch, or have forgotten that the practical branch must sometimes draw its premises from particular facts, respecting particular climates, soils, and seasons; and must sometimes take into account the

[1] *Introductory Lecture*, 1826, published 1827, pp. 8-9.

influence of every human passion and appetite, under every modification of government and knowledge.

"On the other hand, the uncertainty which affects many of the investigations of Political Economists, has been rashly attributed to them all. Because from probable premises they have deduced only probable conclusions, it has been sometimes supposed that probability, and that of a low degree, is all they can attain."[1]

But he almost immediately introduced the important modification mentioned above:

"I hope, also, to show that many conclusions, and those of the highest importance, in the practical branch, rest so immediately on the conclusions of the theoretic branch as to possess equal certainty and universality."[2]

Despite this rather nebulous attempt to differentiate between the certainty of theoretical analysis, and the uncertainty attaching to its application to particular cases, there was already a significant difference between Senior's statement and McCulloch's. Senior stressed the unpredictability of human actions, the complex of human passions, the variations in civilized development, without attempting to relegate them to the category of not very important exceptions like McCulloch, who only admitted that occasionally discretion has to be used in dealing with particular problems.[3]

Probably, however, Senior's discussion of the fundamental premises in economics was the most significant difference between his treatment of method and that of most of his predecessors. Not merely were they selected so as to cover all at once the main phenomena which could affect economic data, but he went into their validity and universality with the greatest care. He laid down four fundamental propositions and a fundamental definition which can be summarized briefly as follows:

The definition was that of wealth: this Senior defined to cover all goods and services which possess utility and are

---

[1] *Introductory Lecture*, 1826, published 1827, p. 10.
[2] Ibid., p. 11.   [3] See pp. 38–9 above.

scarce, in other words everything which enters into the circle of exchange.[1] The importance of this definition became evident immediately he stated the first fundamental proposition:

"That every person is desirous to obtain, with as little sacrifice as possible, as much as possible of the articles of wealth."[2]

Now this proposition is the common one at the basis of all classical economics, and it is only by defining wealth to cover all services as well as material goods that it is possible to claim that it covers the complex of actions which may influence the pricing process. As long as wealth is confined to material goods, the applicability of economic laws is limited to only a portion of the objects of exchange, and depends on the assumption that the objects excluded have no significant influence on the pricing process of the commodities included. Any such assumption according to the marginal theory of price necessarily prevents economics having any claim to be based on positive premises.[3] It is arguable, however, that, as far as a physical cost of production theory is valid, this is not true, as the characteristic of the theory is the determination of price by comparisons of physical cost; in consequence it is possible to limit the circle of exchange as much as desired. Instead of being unrealistic the application of the analysis is merely artificially limited. It seems to me possible that the realization of this independence accounts for the cheerful way in which Ricardo omitted to consider the pricing process of services; and that he forgot that this could not justify the exclusion of services from the circle of exchange in the short run, where he admitted that demand has considerable influence. It is less understandable that Malthus, who started by maintain-

---

[1] *Introductory Lecture*, 1826, published 1827, p. 30.

[2] Ibid., p. 30.

[3] It is not clear from Say's *Traité* whether he thought that Malthus' and Ricardo's omission of immaterial goods from wealth destroyed the validity of their theories of value as applied to the actual world.

ing that demand is as important an influence as cost of production, should deliberately exclude services from consideration.

Senior, however, was not content with this vital alteration. His explanation of the way in which the desire for wealth affects both the demand for individual commodities and services, and the willingness to take action in order to obtain that wealth, is clearly an essential part of the proof of the universal sufficiency of this motive to account for human action in connection with wealth. The detailed discussion of these points is of course the substance of the theories of value, wages, profits, rent, etc. (and will be taken up in the appropriate chapters), but the basic lines of the influence and the scope of the motive Senior explained in general terms in discussing the first proposition:

"In stating that every man desires to obtain additional wealth with as little sacrifice as possible, we must not be supposed to mean that everybody, or indeed anybody, wishes for an indefinite quantity of everything; still less as stating that wealth, though the universal, either is, or ought to be, the principal object of human desire. What we mean to state is, that no person feels his whole wants to be adequately supplied; that every person has some unsatisfied desires which he believes that additional wealth would gratify. The nature and urgency of each individual's wants are as various as the differences in individual character. Some may wish for power, others for distinction, others for leisure; some require bodily, and others mental amusement; some are anxious to produce important advantage to the public; and there are few—perhaps there are none—who, if it could be done by a wish, would not benefit their acquaintances and friends. Money seems to be the only object for which the desire is universal; and it is so because money is abstract wealth. . . .

"An equal diversity exists in the amount and the kind of the sacrifice which different individuals, or even the same individual, will encounter in the pursuit of wealth. And not only is the same sacrifice more severe to one than to another, as some will not give up ease or leisure for study, others good air and a country life, and others recreation and society, but the absolute desire for wealth on the one hand, and the absolute will to encounter toils and privations in its pursuit on the other, are stronger in some men than in others."[1]

It is difficult to find any better statement of the essential premises of the economics of choice, or of the reality and sufficiency of those premises, as a basis for a theory of value applicable to the real world, even in modern literature.

The other three fundamental propositions are premises which Senior thought would cover the main observed phenomena necessary to the theory of distribution and production.

(2) "That the Population of the World, or, in other words, the number of persons inhabiting it, is limited only by moral or physical evil, or by fear of a deficiency of those articles of wealth which the habits of the individuals of each class of its inhabitants lead them to require."

(3) "That the power of Labour, and of the other instruments of production which produce wealth, may be indefinitely increased by using their Products as the means of further Production."

(4) "That agricultural skill remaining the same, additional Labour employed on the land within a given district produces in general a less proportionate return, or, in other words, that though, with every increase of the labour bestowed, the aggregate return is increased, the increase of the return is not in proportion to the increase of the Labour."[2]

The inclusion of the doctrine of population among the fundamental propositions may seem surprising in view of Senior's general views on the probability of subsistence increasing at least as fast as, if not faster than, population. But it must be remembered that Senior only thought this to be true where there were adequate opportunities for the counteracting motive of ambition to have effect.

The third and fourth propositions are of course merely

[1] *Political Economy*, p. 27. The bulk of the discussions of the Fundamental Propositions in the *Political Economy* was taken unaltered from the first course of Lectures. Lectures, 1826–7, Course i, lecture 2. (All page references to the *Political Economy* are to the sixth edition, see Appendix ii.)

[2] *Political Economy*, p. 26. Except for minor verbal differences this statement is the same as in the *Introductory Lecture* referred to above (Lectures, 1826–30, Course i, lecture 1).

statements of the productivity of capital and of the law of diminishing returns in agriculture, both derived from observation.

The first two propositions are thus based primarily on principles of human nature, and the last two on general empirical observation. Senior's general attitude to method, an attitude which he elaborated but never changed, was that theoretical economics is a deductive science based on a group of premises which cover the main data relevant to the specific objects of the science, and which are drawn from the real world by consciousness and observation. Economics is thus, he argued, as much a real science as any of the natural sciences, but owing to the type of data used is not an empirical science in the ordinary sense of the term.[1]

The publication of the *Political Economy* in 1836 marked an important change in Senior's attitude towards the scope of economics as a whole and its relation to policy, though the treatment of the nature and premises of economic theory was simply incorporated from the Lectures. He now limited economics strictly to the field of pure theory:

". . . the science which treats of the Nature, the Production, and the Distribution of Wealth."[2]

The explanation of the change that he himself gave was that it is beyond the bounds of human capacity to study all the other branches of knowledge necessary to apply economic conclusions to particular cases, or to give advice on policy at the same time as mastering economic theory.

"We believe that such inquiries far exceed the bounds of any treatise, and indeed the powers of any single mind. We believe that by confining our own and the readers' attention to the Nature, Production, and Distribution of Wealth, we shall produce a more clear, and complete, and instructive work, than if we allowed ourselves to wander into the more interesting and more important, but far less definite fields by which the comparatively narrow path of Political Economy is surrounded.

[1] This idea was developed at length in the later Lectures, 1847–52. See below.
[2] *Political Economy*, p. 1.

The question is, To what extent and under what circumstances the possession of Wealth is, on the whole, beneficial or injurious to its possessor, or to the society of which he is a member?— What distribution of Wealth is most desirable in each different state of society?—and, What are the means by which any given country can facilitate such a distribution?—all these are questions of great interest and difficulty, but no more form part of the science of Political Economy, in the sense in which we use that term, then Navigation forms part of the science of Astronomy. The principles supplied by Political Economy are indeed necessary elements in their solution, but they are not the only, or even the most important elements. The writer who pursues such investigations is in fact engaged on the great science of legislation; a science which requires a knowledge of the general principles supplied by Political Economy, but differs from it essentially in its subject, its premises, and its conclusions. The subject of legislation is not Wealth, but human Welfare."[1]

By this demarcation of economics the economist is not even allowed to tender advice; his function is no longer to analyse the effect of institutions and customs with the object of giving advice on how to increase wealth, but merely to state general economic principles which the legislator may be justified in ignoring.

"But his conclusions, whatever be their generality and their truth, do not authorize him in adding a single syllable of advice. That privilege belongs to the writer or the statesman who has considered all the causes which may promote or impede the general welfare of those whom he addresses, not to the theorist who has considered only one, though among the most important, of those causes. The business of a Political Economist is neither to recommend nor to dissuade, but to state general principles, which it is fatal to neglect, but neither advisable, nor perhaps practicable, to use as the sole, or even the principal, guides in the actual conduct of affairs. . . . To decide in each case how far those conclusions are to be acted upon belongs to the art of government, an art to which Political Economy is only one of many subservient sciences; which involves the consideration of motives, of which the desire for Wealth is only one among many, and aims at objects to which the possession of Wealth is only a subordinate means."[2]

[1] *Political Economy*, p. 2.   [2] Ibid., p. 3.

This severe limitation of the field of economists, not because their conclusions are inapplicable to real life, nor because they are hypothetical, but because there may be a divergence between economic criteria and the criteria of government was indeed an important admission; it should have gone some way to dispel the popular belief that the classical economists automatically identified social and economic criteria. This sudden change of mind must be attributed, I think, to Senior's practical experience derived from his investigations into the state of Ireland and from his position on the Poor Law Commission, which brought home to him the variety of non-economic considerations involved in any far-reaching policy.[1]

Senior himself maintained that the confusion of the science of Political Economy with the arts to which it is subsidiary, accounted for the lack of progress in the science for two reasons. First, that it had "excited in the public unfavourable prejudices," because people thought that economists ought to deal with welfare as well as wealth on the one hand, and confused wealth with welfare on the other. Secondly, that it misled economists "both with respect to the object of their science and the means of obtaining it"; the former by seducing them into vague fields of conjecture from which no practical results might be expected; the latter by encouraging the belief that economics consisted in the collection of vast quantities of facts. The collection of facts he allowed to be necessary in any problem of applied economics, but did little to improve the laws of economics which were based on a few general facts:

". . . the facts on which the general principles of the science rest may be stated in a very few sentences, and indeed in a very few words. But that the reasoning from these facts, the drawing from them of correct conclusions, is a matter of great difficulty, may be inferred from the imperfect state in which the science is now found after it has been so long and so intensely studied."[2]

---

[1] The similarity of this opinion with Say's (*Traité*, Discours Préliminaire, pp. 1 and 2) is another indication of the generality of the discussions of economic method.   [2] *Political Economy*, p. 4.

In 1836 in short Senior limited the science of economics to an exact science based on the positive premises contained in four fundamental propositions and the definition of wealth. The existence of an art of economics he denied categorically. Everything that is normally included in the art of economics Senior classed indiscriminately as the art of government; any proposition that had for its object welfare rather than wealth is part of the science of legislation, and the only work that economists are capable of doing, *qua* economists, is to formulate general principles of economics and apply them to particular problems.

In effect, Senior's Introduction to the *Political Economy* was inspired by the belief that economists had bitten off more than they could chew. The entirely arbitrary line which he drew between the work of examining particular applications of economic principles and that of drawing conclusions from them as to the most economic way of increasing wealth, which is after all the sole subject of the art, can only be explained on this basis. He was not in fact laying down a real methodological distinction, but merely giving expression to his own opinion on the parlous state of economics in general.[1]

III

Senior's return to Oxford in 1847 gave him an opportunity of dealing with questions of scope and method at greater length than before. The need of such a procedure was greater he believed, probably rightly, than earlier, for, despite the triumph of the teaching of economists in matters of fiscal policy, the validity of the general body of economic theory was being attacked under the impression that it was the foundation of a policy of *laissez-faire* in social questions. Public attention was focussed on the social problems of the industrial towns, stimulated by the innumerable reports

---

[1] McCulloch protested strongly against this excision of the art from economics (*Principles of Political Economy*, Preface to third edition, pp. vii–xi), for he naturally thought that the main work of formulating principles had been completed by Ricardo, and the only fresh fields for economists were those of the art.

on their conditions and the increasingly powerful working-class agitation. By associating the opposition of economists, such as McCulloch and Senior himself, to the ten-hour movement with a general policy of *laissez-faire*, it was easy enough for the man in the street to overlook the reforming movements which the same economists supported. At the same time business interests were not above claiming the support of economic theory whenever it might be useful in opposing social legislation, and the romantic younger section of the Tory Party inspired by Carlyle had made economists the special target for their criticisms of industrialism.[1] Some attempt to present the different issues mixed up in this opposition by explaining the foundations and scope of economics was obviously necessary, if only as a protest against the prevalent misconceptions.

With this object in view Senior set out to overhaul the foundations of economic method. In marked contrast to J. S. Mill, he maintained that economics was seriously inadequate and showing little sign of improvement. This lack of progress he traced back to three factors: first, that everyone was personally interested in the results of economic analysis, a fact which militated against impartiality; secondly, that the general interest in the subject had led to the invasion of the field by people with no general background of economics, and interested only in one aspect which they took out of its setting; thirdly, the inability of economists to realize the limitations of their own knowledge. It was this third difficulty, one which he had attempted to deal with in the *Political Economy*, that affected his general discussion of method:

"But many who have avowedly devoted themselves to its pursuit, seem to have misdirected their efforts, for want of a clear conception of the object of their investigations, of the manner in which they ought to be conducted, or the nature of the difficulties to be surmounted. If the teacher of political economy have not decided whether he is engaged on a science

[1] Cf. Schumpeter, *Dogmen- und Methodengeschichte*, Part iii, "Das klassische System," par. 6, and Leslie Stephens, *English Utilitarians*, Vol. iii, chap. 3, sec. ii.

or on an art, whether it is his duty to explain phenomena or to deliver precepts, whether his principal business is to observe facts or to deduce inferences, whether his premises are all physical truths or depend partly on assumption—his work, though it may contain partial views of the highest value, cannot possibly form a clear or a consistent whole."[1]

Senior's attempt to clear up these obscurities involved him in yet another attempt to decide whether there is an art of economics as well as a science, and in an inquiry into the nature of the evidence on which economic theory is founded.

The problem of the existence of an art of economics was one upon which Senior found it difficult to make up his mind. In 1826 he had already admitted the existence of the art in fairly generous terms; in 1836, bothered no doubt by the importance of the non-economic considerations involved in the solution of any problem, he had gone to the other extreme and limited economics solely to the science in the hope of saving the reputation of economic theory from confusion with that of any particular policy. By 1847, however, he had changed his mind again, returned to a middle position, and admitted that an art of economics might exist—in fact that there were two possible arts as well as the science. He now defined the science as stating "the laws regulating the production and distribution of wealth, so far as they depend on the action of the human mind," introducing the last clause to avoid any confusion of economics with technology. The art might be defined, he suggested, as either "the art which points out the institutions and habits most conducive to the production and accumulation of wealth," or as "the art which points out the institutions and habits most conducive to that production, accumulation, and distribution of wealth, which is most favourable to the happiness of mankind."[2]

Both these definitions of the art of economics were, he thought, attractive and plausible, but he denied that it was yet possible for either art actually to exist.

[1] Lectures, 1847–52, Course I, lecture I, published 1852, pp. 15–16.
[2] Ibid., lecture 3, published 1852, p. 36.

"I have already remarked that all the practical arts draw their principles from sciences. If, however, the teacher of an art were to attempt to teach also the different sciences on which it is founded, his treatise would want unity of subject, and would be inconveniently long. He generally, therefore, assumes his scientific principles as established, and refers to them as well known. . . . Many of the sciences and of the arts which are subservient to Political Economy may be thus treated. . . .

"There is one science, however, to which this treatment cannot as yet be applied, and it is the science most intimately connected with the art of Political Economy, that is to say, the science which states the laws regulating the production, accumulation, and distribution of wealth, or in other words the science (as distinguished from the art) of Political Economy itself. The time [,I trust,] will come, [perhaps within the lives of some of us], when the outline of the science will be clearly made out and generally recognized, . . . I scarcely need repeat how far this is from being the case at present."[1]

Thus, although Senior admitted the possibility of economics being treated as an art of direct assistance in problems of policy, he refused to admit that it was justifiable to discuss these problems *qua* economists. His own discussions of social problems, he said, were undertaken not as an economist, but as a moralist or statesman, and he did not expect from his readers "the full conviction which follows scientific reasoning, but the qualified assent which is given to the precepts of an art."[2]

But Senior realized that the authority of economics did not only depend on its connection or lack of connection with particular policies, but also on the foundation of its claim to explain actual phenomena. It was in attempting to resolve this second problem that he made his most important contribution to the methodology of economics.

Sciences, he argued, can be divided into the physical, which study the properties of matter, and the mental, which study "the sensations, faculties, and habits of the human mind, and regard in matter only the qualities which produce

[1] Lectures, 1847–52, Course I, lecture 3, pp. 51–2. The words enclosed in square brackets are crossed out in Senior's own copy of this lecture.
[2] Ibid., lecture 3, pp. 55–6.

them." The only sources from which premises for either group can be drawn are observation, consciousness and hypothesis, the physical sciences depending on observation and hypothesis, the mental mainly on consciousness.

"The physical sciences, being only secondarily conversant with mind, draw their premises almost exclusively from observation or hypothesis. Those which treat only of magnitude and number, or, as they are usually called, the pure sciences, draw them altogether from hypothesis. . . . Those which abstain from hypothesis depend on observation. . . . They disregard almost entirely the phenomenon of consciousness. The physical *arts* are almost exclusively based on observation. As their object is to produce positive effects, they trust as little as possible to hypothesis; and the mental phenomena which they have to consider are generally few and simple. . . .

"On the other hand, the mental sciences and the mental arts draw their premises principally from consciousness. The subjects with which they are chiefly conversant are the workings of the human mind. And the only mind whose workings a man really knows is his own."[1]

To complete Senior's classification before considering its validity, it is necessary to notice his description of the major difficulty of mental sciences related to the inability to make experiments, and his actual classification of economics as a mental science. The difficulty is the vital one of justifying the interpretation of the workings of other people's minds in terms of one's own.

"When a man endeavours to discover what is passing in the mind of another, by reflecting on what has passed, or is passing in his own, the certainty of the result depends of course on the degree in which the two minds coincide. The educated man, therefore, estimates ill the feelings and the faculties of the uneducated, the adult those of the child, the sane those of the insane, the civilized man those of the savage. And this accounts for the constant mismanagement of the lower orders, and of children, madmen, and savages, by their intellectual and moral superiors. . . . The mental peculiarities of other men are likely

[1] Lectures, 1847–52, Course 1, lecture 2, published 1852, pp. 26–7.

to mislead him in particular instances. His own mental peculiarities are likely to mislead him on all occasions."[1]

This difficulty of interpretation, which makes the inability of the mental sciences to conduct experiments so serious, is only partly eliminated by the possibility of conducting experiments on our own minds.

"When we direct our attention to the workings of our own minds, that is to say, when we search for premises by means of consciousness instead of by means of observation, our powers of trying experiments are much greater."[2]

After this discussion in general terms we might have expected a detailed discussion of how far the premises of economics are derived from observation or consciousness, but Senior left this out and classed economics as a mental science purely on account of the nature of its subject-matter.

"Unquestionably the political economist has much to do with matter. The phenomena attending the production of material wealth occupy a great part of his attention; and these depend mainly on the laws of matter. The efficacy of machinery, the diminishing productiveness, under certain circumstances, of successive applications of capital to land, and the fecundity and longevity of the human species, are all important premises in Political Economy, and are all laws of matter. But the political economist dwells on them only with reference to the mental phenomena which they serve to explain; he considers them as among the motives to the accumulation of capital, as among the sources of rent, as among the regulators of profit, and as among the causes which promote or retard the pressure of population on subsistence."

He ended his explanation by pointing out that:

"All the technical terms, therefore, of Political Economy, represent either purely mental ideas, such as *demand, utility, value,* and *abstinence,* or objects which, though some of them may be material, are considered by the Political Economist so far

---

[1] Lectures, 1847–52, Course I, lecture 2, pp. 27–8.
[2] Ibid., p. 31.

only as they are the results or the causes of certain affectations of the human mind, such as *wealth, capital, rent, wages,* and *profits.*"[1]

Senior's classification of economics as a mental study was objected to by Cairnes,[2] who declared that it no more investigated the laws of mind than of matter, and must be classed as a hybrid. The question was, however, largely one of terminology, since Cairnes did not dispute that the characteristic of the mental sciences, inability to experiment, was common to economics.

By pointing out this particular condition of economic science, and using it to explain the futility of trying to find its premises by detailed induction, Senior demonstrated the inapplicability of the Baconian method to economics, lip-service to which had led to inconsistencies in economic methodology. Say, for example, starting with a full-dress statement of the necessity of using the Baconian method had finally concealed the difficulty of applying it in question-begging terms; Torrens had more elaborately, but equally vaguely, talked of the synthesis of the results of induction; while McCulloch, after stating that induction was as necessary in economics as in physical sciences, had simply ignored the problem. Nor has any other exponent of the empirical approach managed to get over the difficulty, except by deciding beforehand from general observation, and/or consciousness, the uniformities to be isolated and then confining their observations to them—scarcely a scientific procedure. In fact, the use made of detailed induction by both schools in formulating premises has been confined to testing their generality. Thus although the issue between the two schools can, if Dr. Kaufmann likes,[3] be called one of degree not of principle, it is really simply one of the relative practicability of the two methods and can only

[1] Lectures, 1847–52, Course I, lecture 2, pp. 33 and 34–5. This point of view is similar to that advanced in J. S. Mill's essay, "On the Definition of Political Economy, etc.," in *Essays on Unsettled Questions,* etc. A summary of Senior's views on method is contained in his review of J. S. Mill's *Principles of Political Economy* in the *Edinburgh Review,* 1848.

[2] Cairnes, *Logical Method of Political Economy,* Lecture II, par. I.

[3] See note 3 on p. 28.

be decided on that basis. The deductive economists can no more claim greater truth for their laws than the natural scientists, for in both cases they depend on the same factors—the validity of the premises and the logic of the argument. In short, as both Mill and Senior appreciated, the dispute is not one of the absolute merits of either method but of its relative suitability to economics.

The resolution of the confusion of this question of induction, however, was merely a preliminary to the more important question of the nature of the premises of economic science. The distinction between empirical and deductive sciences has, Senior pointed out, a corollary in the characteristic ability of the mental sciences to substitute general observations based on consciousness for specific observations. It follows that the premises of economics may be founded on general observation aided by consciousness. The most important of the fundamental uniformities derived by Senior in this way was of course the general desire for wealth.

So far Senior, Mill and Cairnes were in complete agreement, but the next step in the analysis, one of great interest, involved a breach between Mill and Senior, which left Cairnes more or less facing all ways in his attempt to bridge it.[1] Senior's concept of hypothetical sciences was that they are based, either from necessity or choice, on assumed premises, by which he meant that some data are selected, in the case of economics by observation and consciousness, while other data almost equally relevant are excluded. Consequently the relation of the laws of hypothetical sciences to the real world is ambiguous, they may or may not be present as tendencies. To treat economics as a hypothetical science in this way he believed to be both unnecessary and dangerous, and it was on these grounds that he criticized Mill's concept of the economic man. Mill had maintained that since the desire for wealth is the human motive most relevant to economics, man may be regarded by economists as motivated solely by it. The

[1] *Logical Method of Political Economy*, Lecture ii, par. 3.

abstraction from reality involved simplifies the analysis, but as he admitted makes economics essentially a hypothetical science.[1]

"What is now commonly understood by the term 'Political Economy' is not the science of speculative politics, but a branch of that science. It does not treat of the whole of man's nature as modified by the social state, nor of the whole conduct of man in society. It is concerned with him solely as a being who desires to possess wealth, and who is capable of judging the comparative efficacy of means for obtaining that end. It predicts only such of the phenomena of the social state as take place in consequence of the pursuit of wealth. It makes entire abstraction of every other human passion or motive; except those which may be regarded as perpetually antagonizing principles to the desire for wealth, namely, aversion to labour, and desire of present enjoyment of costly indulgences. These it takes, to a certain extent, into its calculations, because these do not merely, like other desires, occasionally conflict with the pursuit of wealth, but accompany it always as a drag, or impediment, and are therefore inseparably mixed up in the consideration of it. Political Economy considers mankind as occupied solely in acquiring and consuming wealth; and aims at showing what is the course of action into which mankind, living in a state of society, would be impelled, if that motive, except in the degree in which it is checked by the two perpetual counter-motives above adverted to, were absolute ruler of all their actions. . . . The science then proceeds to investigate the laws which govern these several operations, under the supposition that man is a being who is determined, by the necessity of his nature, to prefer a greater portion of wealth to a smaller in all cases, without any other exception than that constituted by the two counter-motives already specified. Not that any political economist was ever so absurd as to suppose that mankind are really thus constituted, but because this is the mode in which science must necessarily proceed. When an effect depends upon a concurrence of causes, those causes must be studied one at a time, and their laws separately investigated, if we wish, through

[1] Mill considered that the *a priori* method, as he termed the hypothetical method, was the only one suitable to abstract or mental sciences: "On the Definition of Political Economy, etc.," in *Essays on Unsettled Questions*, third edition, pp. 143–5.

the causes, to obtain the power of either predicting or controlling the effect; . . . The manner in which it necessarily proceeds is that of treating the main and acknowledged end as if it were the sole end; which, of all hypotheses equally simple, is the nearest to the truth."[1]

Mill's argument was thus simply that the method applicable to the mental sciences is, by reason of their complicated nature and the impossibility of making experiments, that of deduction from hypothetical premises based on selected data of particular importance and modification in applying the resulting conclusions to actual phenomena. When it is remembered that Mill confined wealth to material goods the inadequacy of this hypothesis for investigating the pricing process becomes obvious. His two counteracting forces to the desire for wealth, the desires for leisure and immediate enjoyment, cover only a small section of the influences affecting the intensity of the desire for wealth, in particular omitting the concept of net advantages and the interdependence of values.

Senior's opposition was vigorous:

"But neither the reasoning of Mr. Mill, nor the example of Mr. Ricardo, induce me to treat Political Economy as a hypothetical science. I do not think it necessary, and, if unnecessary, I do not think it desirable.

"It appears to me, that if we substitute for Mr. Mill's hypothesis, that wealth and costly enjoyment are the *only* objects of human desire, the statement that they are universal and constant objects of desire, that they are desired by all men and at all times, we shall have laid an equally firm foundation for our subsequent reasonings, and have put a truth in the place of an arbitrary assumption. We shall not, it is true, from the fact

[1] *Essays on Unsettled Questions*, third edition, pp. 137–9. This passage also occurs in Mill's *System of Logic* (Bk. VI, chap. 9, par. 3) which was published in the preceding year, 1843; the substance of the argument is the same in both places. The more extensive discussion of the nature of the "social science" in the *System of Logic* shows, however, that Mill regarded each of its branch sciences as based on hypotheses in so far as they do not include among their premises a statement of the laws of evolution of social institutions or customs. This reason is not the same as, though it is related to, the particular reason, discussed in the text above, by which Mill justified his opinion that economics is founded on hypothetical premises.

that by acting in a particular manner a labourer may obtain higher wages, a capitalist higher profits, or a landlord higher rent, be able to infer that they will certainly act in that manner, but we shall be able to infer that they will do so in the absence of disturbing causes. And if we are able, as will frequently be the case, to state the cases in which these causes may be expected to exist, and the force with which they are likely to operate, we shall have removed all objection to the positive as opposed to the hypothetical treatment of the science."[1, 2]

Senior's particular objections to the hypothetical treatment were the perpetual danger of forgetting the hypothetical nature of the premises, its abstractness which he thought unattractive, and the absence of any check on the results by experience.

Cairnes attempted to resolve the difference between the two into a question of terminology by demonstrating that, to a considerable extent, the question as to whether a science should be considered hypothetical or positive, depends merely on whether we are considering the nature of the premises, or the immediate applicability of results.[3] But this approach conceals the more important question which was really in dispute between Senior, Mill and Ricardo, and which Cairnes himself suggests: the question of the completeness of the premises. It is obvious that the actual result of a general law in any particular case will depend on the supplementary premises involved. The result is not determinate *a priori* from the general law, although that is based on positive premises. The general law expresses, as it were, the constant relations in the system of equations, the particular supplementary premises give the values of the variables. Neither Senior nor anyone else denied that.

[1] Lectures, 1847–8, Course I, lecture 4, published 1852, pp. 62–3.

[2] Senior's substitution of net advantages for earnings is equivalent to defining in general terms the relation between all the variables which influence the distribution of resources between occupations, instead of leaving that relation to be considered afresh in each particular case.

[3] Cairnes, *Logical Method of Political Economy*, Lecture II, par. 3. Cf. J. N. Keynes, *Scope and Method of Political Economy*, chap. 7, for a somewhat similar account of this controversy and for a description of Bagehot's position. Cf. also Edgeworth's review of Marshall's *Principles* in *Papers relating to Political Economy*, Vol. III, p. 65.

But if the premises of the general law are not complete, a knowledge of the supplementary premises will only give the result if the missing link is included in the supplementary premises.[1] Thus in the question of the definition of the desire for wealth: if it is stated in Mill's form that everyone always prefers wealth to anything else, with the added warning that it is only a hypothesis, the constant relation between the desire for wealth and all other conflicting motives is not defined completely by the general law. It remains necessary to introduce a further premise in each individual case stating the general relation of other motives to that of the desire for wealth, as well as evaluating the actual variables. Now Senior's explanation of the desire for wealth includes information as to the interconnections between the variables. In justice to Mill it must be remembered that he safeguarded himself by regarding this statement as a hypothesis, but Cairnes took Mill's statement as a positive premise qualifying it by saying that it was incomplete, but not indicating the possible importance of that incompleteness.[2]

It is evident, of course, that it was much easier for Senior than for Mill to bring the premises of the desire for wealth out of the realm of hypothesis, since he included immaterial goods in wealth, while Mill excluded them. In this connection the sense in which Senior used the term hypothetical is of interest in the development of the theory of value. Frequent criticisms have been directed against the marginal theory because it is asserted that its general formulation does not cover all the variables, but leaves them to be fitted in. The reply has been to prove, by explaining the completeness of the premises, that the *ceteris paribus* clauses are unnecessary, and that therefore the theory corresponds with reality since it includes all the relevant variables.

As long as wealth was confined to material goods the necessity of the hypothesis of the economic man, though

---

[1] Cairnes, *Logical Method of Political Economy*, Lecture II, par. 3. See also Lecture III, pars. 3 and 4.

[2] This distinction was evidently considered so important by Senior as to constitute it one of principle.

unperceived by anyone before J. S. Mill, was a fact, since it is impossible to deny the influence of desires other than the fundamental desire for wealth (so defined) on values in the real world. Although in the "long run" the Ricardian cost of production theory of value approximately eliminates this difficulty, it does not in the "short run." It is possible that the adoption of the Smithian limitation of wealth to material goods is the real explanation of the persistence of the interest in the cost of production theory which, being applicable only in the "long run," so conveniently evaded these complexities.

In conclusion, it is of interest to draw attention to a recent illustration of the continuity of the discussion of the problems of the deductive method which has been furnished by Professor Mises in his book *Grundprobleme der Nationalökonomie*. Professor Mises argues that economic analysis must proceed from positive premises which are "complete" in the sense used throughout this chapter, and that the essential premise is the recognized characteristic of man to truck and barter: "Menschliches Handeln ist bewusstes Verhalten des Menschen."[1] From this one fundamental characteristic all the general concepts of economics which are relevant to the formulation of general laws are derived.[2] Clearly this is the same approach as Senior's, and resembles Mill's as far as the derivation of economic concepts from the initial premise is concerned, but it differs in regard to the nature of that premise itself. Allowing for Professor Mises' particular use of the term *a priori*, his interpretation of the significance of the Senior-Mill-Cairnes controversy as an attempt to complete and elucidate the nature of the basic premises of economics is the same as that adopted here.[3]

The only fundamental difference between Mises' general attitude and Senior's lies in Mises' apparent denial of the possibility of using any general empirical data, i.e. facts of general observation, as initial premises. This difference,

[1] Ludwig von Mises, *Grundprobleme der Nationalökonomie*, 1933, p. 22.
[2] Ibid., pp. 22–34. "Umfang und Bedeutung des Systems der apriorischen Sätze."   [3] Ibid., pp. 18–20.

however, turns upon Mises' basic ideas of the nature of thought, and though of general philosophical importance, has little special relevance to economic method as such.

If the preceding account of the methodological discussions of the first part of the nineteenth century is correct it must be admitted that Senior, not Cairnes, was the most important writer on scope and method among the classical economists. Not only was Senior's contribution more original than that of Cairnes, but it has far more importance in relation to modern discussions of method. His attempt to formulate the premises of the theory of value in such a way as to make economics a positive science, foreshadowed the later discussions of the methodological significance of the marginal theory of value. With regard to the scope of economics Senior was not particularly original, but the difficulty he experienced in making up his mind is of considerable historical interest in that it was caused by realization of the importance of dissociating economics from the policy of *laissez-faire* at least as early as 1836. In short, Senior's attitude to the problems of the scope and method of economics had much in common with that of modern economists, and his contributions to their solution anticipated many of those of the last fifty or sixty years.

CHAPTER 2

THE THEORY OF VALUE

It has always been recognized that Senior's work on the theory of value was of some originality, that in many ways he saw further and more clearly than most of his contemporaries. Nevertheless no serious attempt has been made to assign to it any definite place in the development of value theory. This is natural enough since Senior neither founded a school nor exercised any very definite influence on other economists. Judged by these criteria therefore Senior can be dismissed as of comparatively little importance. Even Jevons paid tribute to Senior only as one among many of the prophets of the marginal utility theory. But if Senior's work is examined from the standpoint of, as it were, its topographical position, it immediately assumes significance as a signpost on the route from Ricardo's theory to Jevons'. By considering it from this aspect an interesting light is thrown on the evolution of the marginal theory, and the contributions of the various anticipators fall into place in a line of continuous development from Ricardo to Jevons.

So much has been learnt in the last three or four decades of these neglected contributions, that it is really necessary to revise the traditional view that a revolution occurred in economics with John Stuart Mill's recantation of the wage fund theory in 1869. There may perhaps be little doubt that Mill thought he had started a revolution by admitting the justice of many of Thornton's criticisms of the wage-fund theory, but in fact Mill was a long way behind the times in his economic theory. He and his immediate followers apparently believed that nothing much of fundamental interest to economists had been written since Ricardo's death, and, still more important, they somehow managed to give that impression to many of their contemporaries and successors. This was a complete delusion, for both in England and on the Continent very considerable progress had been made in the development of Ricardo's theories and their reconciliation with J. B. Say's between 1823 and 1869. With this process Jevons, Menger and Walras made no distinct break, for they refined and completed theories that had been in the air for several decades. In short, the idea needs revision that the period between Ricardo's first edition of his *Principles* in 1817 and Jevons' communication to the British Association in 1862 witnessed the rise, decline and fall of the empire of the classical economists.

This chapter is a tentative attempt at revision, based on an examination of the relation between Senior's contribution to the theory of value and those of other economists of the first half of the nineteenth century. To put the development of the theory of value during this period into perspective it is necessary to go back to the *Wealth of Nations* and find the origins of the four groups into which the economists of the first part of the nineteenth century can be divided: viz., the French School, particularly Say and his immediate followers; the Ricardians; the group which we may call the English Dissenters, which includes economists as far apart in time as Lauderdale and Macleod;[1] and the German theorists from Hüfeland to von Mangoldt. This classification is adopted simply for purposes of exposition, and no merit is claimed for it except that it isolates that group of English economists who were intermediate between Ricardo and Say in outlook and were remarkably akin to the Germans.

I

Adam Smith's adoption of the consumers' concept of wealth—"the necessaries and conveniences of life"—together with the theory of the "hidden hand," finally turned economic speculation towards the discovery of the mechanism connecting production with consumers' demand.[2]

---

[1] This group may reasonably be said to have descended from Dugald Stewart.

[2] *Wealth of Nations*, edited Cannan (1904, second edition 1924), Vol. 1, p. 1. (All volume and page references are to the Cannan editions unless otherwise stated.) This concept of wealth was not, of course, new. It was already incorporated in economic speculation, e.g. in the works of Petty, Boisguilbert,

These were the major themes on which subsequent theories were the variation. Adam Smith's own theory of value and distribution was merely a complex of suggestions directed partly to explaining the central ideas, and partly to evolving a method of measuring the progress of wealth by some sort of index number. It is the lack of co-ordination of this complex which appears to me to be the explanation of the segregation of economists into two schools of thought, the Ricardian and the Continental under the leadership of Say, during the first quarter of the nineteenth century.

In the three chapters on value in the *Wealth of Nations*[1] there are three logically distinct ideas, two of which were of particular importance to subsequent developments of value theory: the working out of the theory of natural prices from its origin in the Glasgow Lectures of 1755,[2] the semi-independent labour theory of value, and the attempt to find an invariable measure of value. It is worth while trying to trace their evolution from the *Lectures* to the *Wealth of Nations*.

In the *Lectures* it appears that the section on price and wages was introduced simply to indicate that a mechanism existed by which the free play of self-interest would bring about maximum "opulence." Labour was the only factor of production taken into consideration, and the natural price of labour was simply explained to be an amount "sufficient to maintain him [the labourer] during the time of labour, to defray the expense of education, and to compensate the risk of not living long enough, and of not succeeding in his business."[3] The natural price of any commodity must therefore, Adam Smith declared, be sufficient to cover the natural price of the labour used in its production. In this

---

Cantillon, North, etc., as well as those of Galiani, Turgot and Condillac. Similarly the idea of the equilibrating "hidden hand" was not peculiar to the *Wealth of Nations*, but merely expounded in it so as to attract great attention. Condillac (*Du Commerce et du Gouvernement*, 1776) started from this approach also.

[1] *Wealth of Nations*, Bk. I, chap. 5, "Of the real and nominal Price of Commodities"; chap. 6, "Of the component Parts of the Price of Commodities"; chap. 7, "Of the natural and market Price of Commodities."

[2] *Lectures of Adam Smith*, edited Cannan, pp. 173–82.   [3] Ibid., p. 176.

way relative labour costs, based on the cost of production of labour, were introduced as the determinants of equilibrium values. The influence of demand and scarcity on market price is important in causing the distribution of labour between the production of different commodities, so as to achieve this equality.

It was a very short step, but nevertheless in a completely new direction, from this position to the Labour Theory put forward in the *Wealth of Nations*, where the philosophical derivation of all value from labour—"labour the original purchase price"—is said to be due not to the cost of production of the labourer, but to the actual disutility of labour.[1]

"Equal quantities of labour, at all times and places, may be said to be of equal value to the labourer. In his ordinary state of health, strength, and spirits; in the ordinary degree of his skill and dexterity, he must always lay down the same portion of his ease, his liberty, and his happiness. The price which he pays must always be the same, whatever may be the quantity of goods which he receives in return for it."[2]

If the Lecture notes give a correct account of his original theory we must surely conclude that Adam Smith intended to develop a real physical theory of value by introducing this new concept of physical disutility into the *Wealth of Nations*. In Chapter 5 it is made clear that the commodity price of labour is only called its real price in conformity with the usual sense of real as distinct from money, and has nothing to do with the determination of value.[3]

The difficulties introduced into the sweet simplicity of the labour theory by different grades of labour, and by land and capital, led, however, to its abandonment in favour of a development of the germs of the natural price theory

---

[1] *Wealth of Nations*, Bk. 1, chaps. 5 and 6.
[2] Ibid., Bk. 1, chap. 5, Vol. 1, p. 35.
[3] Cf. C. M. Walsh, *The Fundamental Problem in Monetary Science* (1903), Part 11, chap. 2, for a very subtle exposition of the various threads in Adam Smith's attempt to find both a measure of value and a standard of value. Dr. Walsh does not, I think, sufficiently emphasize Adam Smith's hope of finding a standard by which to measure changes in total national wealth.

contained in the Lectures.[1] Allowing for the complications introduced by considering the natural prices of more than one factor, which led obviously to some sort of theory of distribution, the final development of the natural-price-cum-cost-of-production theory was obviously much more related to the original theory of the Lectures than to the labour theory.

The use of labour as a measure of value lingered on throughout the *Wealth of Nations*, however, to the great confusion of later generations, though as soon as land and capital were introduced the "quantity of labour used" was dropped in favour of the "quantity of labour commanded."[2] This was logical enough, as in the primitive society to which the labour theory applied, the determinant, the measure and the source of value all coincided, and "the quantity of labour commonly employed in acquiring or producing any commodity" was rightly said to be "the only circumstance which can regulate the quantity of labour which it [the commodity] ought commonly to purchase, command, or exchange for."[3] The retention of the "labour commanded" as a measure of value was consistent with Adam Smith's insistence on the invariableness of the sacrifice caused by labouring, and he explained that this was its purpose since—

"The real value of all the different component parts of price, it must be observed, is measured by the quantity of labour which they can, each of them, purchase or command. Labour measures the value not only of that part of price which resolves itself into labour, but of that which resolves itself into rent, and of that which resolves itself into profit."[4]

[1] Samuel Bailey was one of the earliest economists to point to the seriousness of the problem of different grades of labour which both Adam Smith and Ricardo were inclined to consider of minor importance. Its real importance has been abundantly shown in the history of the extension of the rent analysis, and the specific use of the theory of non-competing groups to deal with it; the former implying a marginal productivity, and the latter a productivity, theory in the explanation of wages. *Dissertation on the Nature, Measures, and Causes of Value* (1825), chap. 11, pp. 207-15 of the reprint in the London School of Economics series of Scarce Tracts in Economics and Political Science. (All references are to this reprint.)

[2] *Wealth of Nations*, Bk. 1, chap. 6, Vol. 1, pp. 49-52.

[3] Ibid., Bk. 1, chap. 6, Vol. 1, pp. 49-50.

[4] Ibid., Bk. 1, chap. 6, Vol. 1, p. 52.

This conclusion is really independent of the theory of value, and not as Ricardo thought simply the result of confusion ;[1] like the later introduction of corn as a measure of value, it is merely an attempt to measure wealth by an invariable standard.

The labour theory thus disappeared as an explanation of the wider problems of equilibrium in an advanced society, but the expansion of the natural price theory did not proceed easily.[2] The natural price of a commodity, Adam Smith laid down, is that which just covers the natural rates of rent, wages and profits, of the land, labour and capital that are used in producing it and bringing it to market.[3] To relate this natural price to market price was of course simple enough, and also to deduce that the whole income of the community resolved into rent, wages and profits.[4] But the problem of the causal relationship between the respective natural prices of commodities and factors, the former being dependent on the latter, produced apparently insurmountable difficulties. The natural price of labour in the *Wealth of Nations* depends only in the limit on the cost of production of labour, and the connection between its natural price when it is not subsistence level and the price of commodities is never squarely faced. Thus at the end of the chapter "Of the natural and market Price of Commodities" the purpose of the next two chapters is declared to be the explanation of "the circumstances which naturally determine the rate of wages, and in what manner those circumstances are affected by the riches or poverty, by the advancing, stationary, or declining state of the society," and similarly with respect to profits.[5]

It is surprising to find in these chapters no indications that the natural rates of wages and profits are seriously connected with the cost of production of labour and capital,[6]

[1] Ricardo, *Principles of Political Economy and Taxation*, chap. 1, pp. 7–14. (All references are to E. C. K. Gonner's edition in Bohn's Libraries, unless otherwise stated.)   [2] *Wealth of Nations*, Bk. 1, chaps. 6 and 7.
[3] Ibid., Bk. 1, chap. 7, Vol. 1, p. 57.
[4] Ibid., Bk. 1, chap. 7, Vol. 1, pp. 58–9, and chap. 6, Vol. 1, p. 52.
[5] Ibid., Bk. 1, chap. 7, Vol. 1, p. 65.
[6] Ibid., chaps. 8 and 9. Adam Smith does not appear to have regarded the stationary state when wages and profits would have reached their minima, as the state of natural equilibrium. In the first four paragraphs of Bk. 1, chap. 7,

for according to the Lectures the natural price of labour is fixed by its cost of production. Even in the Lectures, however, Adam Smith did not discuss how this cost is determined in relation to the increasing, stationary or declining state of society.

According to the *Wealth of Nations* the minimum level of subsistence forms the lower limit of wages, but above this limit the natural rate was treated simply as the current general rate dependent on the ratio of the supply of labour to the capitalists' funds.[1] Similarly with profits, although there is a minimum rate necessary to compensate capitalists for occasional losses,[2] the natural rate itself is simply whatever the current general rate happens to be. This depends on the supply of capital which depends on the wealth of the country, and the opportunities for employing it which

he explains that the ordinary or average rates both of wages and profits are the natural rates: "These ordinary or average rates may be called the natural rates of wages, profit, and rent, at the time and place in which they commonly prevail" (Vol. 1, p. 57). At the end of the same chapter we are told that he is going to explain the variations in these natural rates which are the component parts of the price of commodities, and which vary according to the advancing, stationary or declining condition of society (Vol. 1, p. 65). The identification of "natural" rates with customary minima in classical economics is due to Ricardo's restriction of equilibrium analysis to stationary equilibrium, not to anything in the *Wealth of Nations*. Rightly or wrongly Adam Smith appeared to regard equilibrium as achieved whenever discrepancies in earnings in different occupations are so adjusted that there is no incentive for factors to change their positions (cf. Bk. 1, chap. 10, Vol. 1, p. 101). See Gide and Rist, *History of Economic Doctrines*, pp. 68–93, for a general discussion of the idea of "natural" in the *Wealth of Nations* as a philosophical rather than a technical concept.

[1] Thus we are told to start with that "the produce of labour constitutes the natural recompense or wages of labour." It is only because of the scarcity of land and capital that the labourer does not receive the whole produce; it follows that what he does "naturally" receive depends on how much the other factors leave him and this depends on the advancing, stationary or declining state of society, which determines the size of the funds destined for the payment of wages. It is evident that things can be natural in Smith's sense in an advancing society, for he says with regard to the surplus over and above the funds necessary for the maintenance of the landlord, etc., "Increase this surplus, and he will naturally increase the number of those servants." Similarly, increase the surplus of the capitalist and he will "naturally increase the number of his journeymen," and finally, "The demand for those who live by wages, therefore, naturally increases with the increase of national wealth, and cannot possibly increase without it" (*Wealth of Nations*, Bk. 1, chap. 8, Vol. 1, pp. 66–8, 71).

[2] *Wealth of Nations*, Bk. 1, chap. 9. Cf. Part 1, chap. 4, pp. 138–9 below.

increase with the opening of new channels of trade or methods of production.[1]

In fact, Adam Smith nowhere produced a theory of natural wages and profits parallel to the natural prices of commodities and labour of the Lectures, and he left unsolved the vital question of what constituted the demands for factors of production. In addition, he made incompleteness a source of confusion by raising the question of why he devoted so much time to explaining that all value was derived from labour, and to introducing a labour theory of value only to abandon it later on.

The suggestion that he evolved the labour theory simply as an alternative way of stating the natural price theory in a special case seems inadequate, for he was aware that there was a weakness in the labour theory when different grades of labour were involved—a weakness not so apparent in the natural price theory. Considering the obscurity of the reason for Adam Smith's changeover, it is not surprising that Ricardo thought that he had intended to work out the labour theory but got confused,[2] nor on the other hand that Say disregarded it as an irrelevant digression.

Finally, Adam Smith introduced a quite different source of confusion into the theory of value by distinguishing between productive and unproductive labour. It must not be thought, however, that he himself got into difficulties

---

[1] Adam Smith's treatment of profits is closely parallel to that of wages; in the *Wealth of Nations*, Bk. 1, chap. 9, Vol. 1, p. 89, he explained that "The rise and fall in the profits of stock depend upon the same causes with the rise and fall in the wages of labour, the increasing or declining state of the wealth of the society." His preoccupation with the average or current rate of wages and profits is illustrated on the same page: "It is not easy, it has already been observed, to ascertain what are the average wages of labour, even in a particular place, and at a particular time. We can, even in this case, seldom determine more than what are the most usual wages. But even this can seldom be done with regard to the profits of stock." The same identification of natural with average or usual is equally clear in the treatment of rent: "Rent, considered as the price paid for the use of land, is naturally the highest which the tenant can afford to pay in the actual circumstances of the land," and after explaining that this may be miscalculated through ignorance, he adds, "This portion, however, may still be considered as the natural rent of land, or the rent for which it is naturally meant that land should for the most part be let" (Ibid., Bk. 1, chap. 11, Vol. 1, p. 145).

[2] *Principles of Political Economy and Taxation*, chap. 1, pp. 7–14.

over this, as it was introduced long after the chapters on value proper, but it is inconceivable that if he had had clear ideas on the source of demand for factors of production that he would have introduced it in that particular way. At any rate, it formed a great stumbling-block to economists after him, in the way of formulating a productivity theory of wages.[1]

II

The development and propagation of the ideas of Adam Smith in France were conditioned by a number of circumstances peculiar to that country. Most important of these were the influence of the Physiocrats and of the tradition of utility analysis, the comparative backwardness of industry, and the French Revolution and the ensuing wars.

The prestige of the Physiocrats, though an asset from the point of view of breaking down Mercantilism, necessarily meant that the acceptance of the whole teaching of the *Wealth of Nations* was hindered by the existence of a comparatively new group of economic ideas which had not lost their initial hold. The backwardness of French industry compared with English at the same time tended to increase

---

[1] *Principles of Political Economy and Taxation*, Bk. II, chap. 3, "Of the Accumulation of Capital, or of productive and unproductive Labour." It is fairly obvious that the distinction was introduced purely in connection with the definition of wealth from the capital instead of the income aspect of Bk. I. Cf. Cannan, *Theories of Production and Distribution*, pp. 14–31.

Succeeding economists very rarely kept this distinction in mind and simply defined wealth without differentiating between capital and income, thus limiting the scope of value theory to material goods and ignoring unproductive labour. The sort of confusion this led to is illustrated *par excellence* by Malthus' analysis of gluts. Samuel Read is an interesting exception to the usual confusion, and accepted Adam Smith's distinction and deliberately made capital co-existent with wealth. *Right to Vendible Property*, 1829, Bk. I, chap. 7, p. 65, and more generally in chaps. 1 and 4. On the Continent Say distinguished clearly between the two aspects including immaterial goods in wealth, but only some of them in capital. *Traité*, Bk. I, chap. 13, and Epitome, p. 596. Some years later Courcelle-Seneuil and Cherbuliez made use of a curious compromise, defining wealth mainly from the capital aspect and therefore excluding immaterial goods, but including them in their treatment of value. *Traité théorique et pratique*, second edition, 1867, Bk. I, chap. 1, sect. 4, and Bk. II, chaps. 2 and 5. *Précis de la Science Economique*, Bk. I, chap. 3, and Bk. II, chap 2, respectively.

the prestige of an agricultural system of economics, and to prevent the growth of an industrial interest to which an attack on the restrictions of industry would be welcome.[1] The influence of the revolution itself is, of course, impossible to summarize, but a few aspects of it must be noticed. The mere existence of revolution inevitably created profound disturbances in the economic system, and created a general atmosphere of unrest in the intellectual life of France; in addition, the revolution itself was a signal triumph for the ideas of freedom, to which a sudden extinguisher was applied by the wars and the despotism of Napoleon. To some extent as a result of this, French Liberals were engaged to a much greater degree in expounding the principles of political and economic freedom in opposition to the Government on the one side, and the Utopian Socialists on the other, than in working them out in detail. Sociological and philosophical treatments of economic problems and attempts to find a justification of economic freedom were thus important in France at a time when strictly scientific treatises were being written in England. Even Destutt de Tracey's *Traité* was written as part of a system of philosophy, while Dunoyer's *Liberté de Travail* was devoted to finding a philosophical justification for an economic and social policy of extreme *laissez-faire*. Naturally, too, the very backwardness of industrial development in France encouraged many people to believe that increased productivity would solve many social problems; at the same time the comparative absence of a food and population problem made abstract discussions of distribution, such as the Malthusian-Ricardian rent analysis, appear irrelevant and barren.[2]

[1] For an account of these influences on French economic thought see *Revue d'Histoire des Doctrines Économiques*, 1912, pp. 317–42, "L'œuvre économique de Germain Garnier," by E. Allix.

[2] It is no doubt true that Say did not fully understand the Ricardian rent analysis (*Mélanges de J. B. Say*, Letter from Ricardo to Say, January 11, 1820, and Say's reply, March 2, 1820), but it is also clear that he thought it unimportant and did not bother. (See p. 79 below.) In general it was not misunderstood in France, for Destutt de Tracey and Rossi as well as later writers incorporated it in their systems, and Bastiat understood it well enough to appreciate its implications as to landlords.

Against this general background the peculiar merits and defects of J. B. Say's approach to economics, as well as his divergencies from contemporary English economists, stand out with great clarity. Say's purpose in writing the *Traité* in 1803, a purpose which became intensified as time went on, was to explain and clarify the main doctrines of the *Wealth of Nations* for the benefit of France, and to expose the fallacies of the Physiocrats.[1]

With this object in mind and influenced by Condillac,[2] Say started the *Traité* by an exhaustive discussion of the consumers' concept of production in order to abolish the peculiar prestige of land. The characteristic of goods having value is, he said, that they should have utility and be limited in supply, therefore "Production is never a creation of matter, but a creation of utility. It is not measured according to the length, the volume, or the weight, of the product, but according to the utility it has been given."[3] Naturally after this declaration as to the nature of production Say could find no use for Adam Smith's distinction between productive and unproductive labour. He argued that he drew a false distinction between the utility of goods and the utility of services by ignoring that the common characteristic of all factors and commodities possessing value is their ability to provide the consumer with a scarce utility.[4]

Say's whole theory of value and distribution was built on the foundation of this connection between utility and productivity. The whole tenor of his mind and purpose was against going back to the obscurities of the labour theory of value, either for itself, or to find out why land had become property, or capital come into existence. Adam Smith's own account was far from clear and in any case

---

[1] *Traité*, Discours Préliminaire, pp. 37–9, sixth edition, 1841. (All references to this edition, unless otherwise stated.)

[2] Say was very mean in his acknowledgments to Condillac (Discours Préliminaire, p. 26), but the existence of the tradition of a utility approach to value in France influenced his own interpretation of the *Wealth of Nations* profoundly. Cf. Teilhac, *Œuvre Économique de J. B. Say*, 1927, Part II, chaps. 1 and 2.

[3] *Traité*, Bk. I, chap. I, p. 58.   [4] Ibid., Bk. I, chap. 13, pp. 123–4.

purely hypothetical. Thus it was natural for Say to try to dovetail the equilibrium content of the theory of market and natural prices into his own theory of utility and scarcity as determinants of value. In the chapter entitled "Des fondemens de la valeur des choses," he explained that "Évaluer une chose, c'est déclarer qu'elle doit être estimée autant qu'une certaine quantité d'une autre chose qu'on désigne."[1] Cost of production where it exists is the lower limit to price since it limits the extent of the supply, and general productivity is the upper limit as it is the factor regulating the total amount that can be given in exchange for a particular commodity. In between these boundaries value depends on scarcity and utility. Thus the values of commodities that can be reproduced are limited in equilibrium by their costs of production, but the values of those of which the supply is fixed have no lower limits.[2] Superficially regarded Say's theory seems to come to the same thing as Adam Smith's theory of natural prices, but Say's emphasis on the point that value is derived from utility, and that cost is important only as it limits "the extent of the supply," constitutes a fundamental difference from Adam Smith's emphasis on the derivation of value from costs.

Say's path-breaking divergence from the *Wealth of Nations*, however, lay less in this analysis of value than in his deduction from it, that the values of factors are derived from the value of their products, and his development of the doctrine of productive services from the latter. From the correspondence with Malthus and Ricardo, he himself appears to have regarded this as one of his most important contributions. It can be summarized as follows: the values of the productive services of the factors of production are derived from their ability to create utility, hence from the value of their products. The entrepreneur demands the services of factors because he can use them to create valuable products, and the amount he is willing to pay them depends on what he considers to be their powers to perform this function—

"The current value of productive exertion is founded upon the value of an infinity of products compared one with another;

[1] *Traité*, Bk. II, chap. I, p. 313.   [2] Ibid., Bk. II, chap. I, pp. 315–21.

that the value of products is not founded upon that of productive agency as some authors have erroneously affirmed; and that, since the desire of an object, and consequently its value, originates in its utility, it is the ability to create the utility wherein originates that desire, that gives value to productive agency; which value is proportionate to the importance of its co-operation in the business of production, and forms, in respect to each product individually, what is called the cost of its production."[1]

This is certainly far from being complete but it is a considerable advance, and contains the germ of the concept of value-opportunity costs as distinct from the physical-opportunity costs implied in the labour and cost of production theories of value. Unfortunately Say never explained the way in which the productivity, or productive importance, of each factor is determined. It appears from subsequent chapters that, other things being equal, the relative scarcity of a factor affects its relative productive importance, and he simply assumed that this decreases as the supply of the factor increases and vice versa.

To complete this outline of a price system, Say adopted a causal connection between wages and profit and the total supplies of labour and capital. He considered, however, the income from fixed capital to be akin to the rent from land, since neither effect the respective supplies and therefore they have no minimum.[2] This distinction between land and other factors was not of nearly as much significance to Say as might be expected. Rent, he considered, enters into the cost of production like the reward of other factors, for it is only in the hypothetical long run that the functional connection between income and total supplies of factors can have any

---

[1] This passage is taken from the fourth edition of Say's *Traité* (translated by Prinsep, 1821), Bk. II, chap. I, p. 8. It does not appear in the sixth edition, but it expresses so clearly the actual doctrine of productive services which Say never really altered that it seems legitimate to quote it here. There is also an interesting footnote attached: "It must not be inferred that I mean to say, that the productive agency exerted in raising a product, whose charges of production have amounted to 4 fr. although it is saleable for 3 fr. only, is therefore worth but 3 fr. My position merely implies, that the amount of productive service has, in such a case, raised a value of 3 fr. only, though it might have raised a value of 4 fr."

[2] *Traité*, Bk. II, chaps. 5, 7, 8, 9, and Bk. I, chap. 13, p. 130.

influence on value, and in the meantime there are so many other disturbing influences that such speculation about the connection is uninteresting. Thus Say wrote to Ricardo in 1821 in answer to the latter's criticism of his scant treatment of rent,

"permittez-moi, de vous dire, mon cher monsieur, que ces questions, me paraissent moins importantes qu' à vous, et que j'évite, par-dessous tout, des abstractions qui n'ont, je vous en demande bien pardon, rien d'applicable dans la vie réelle."[1]

Say's attitude on this question must undoubtedly be ascribed partly to the absence in France of a population problem and the accompanying spectre of rising costs of production of food, partly to the backwardness of French industry and agriculture compared to English, which made the boundaries to increasing wealth seem further off, and perhaps also to the tradition, *par excellence*, of the Physiocrats of the supreme productivity of land.

The theory of value as expounded by Say formed the backbone of French economics for the first half of the century and there were few developments of interest in pure theory except by the mathematicians. Destutt de Tracey reproduced Say's analysis and threw some light on the measurement of value.[2] He attached considerable importance to the Ricardian-Malthusian rent analysis but threw no further light on the theory of value. After him, until the as-it-were official theories of the optimists were advanced by Bastiat, the critics of economic theory, such as Sismondi and Comte, were more active than its supporters. Dunoyer, it is true, was an exception to this inactivity, but, instead of developing economics further, he devoted himself to writing philosophical treatises in defence of liberty, depending on Say's analysis to show its economic aspect.[3] There was, however, an uncomfortable fact which could not be long overlooked by any optimistic group: that Say had merely sidetracked the Malthusian doctrines, not disproved them. Until Bastiat no serious attempt was made to deal

[1] *Mélanges de J. B. Say*, Letter to Ricardo, July 19, 1821.
[2] *Elemens d'Idéologie*, Vol. IV, pp. 156–65, second edition, 1818.
[3] Dunoyer, *Nouveau Traité d'Économie Sociale*, 1830. *De la Liberté du Travail*, 1845.

with this problem. Bastiat aimed not merely at justifying incomes from land by an extension of his theory of services —an attempt which amounted to nothing more than Say's utility concept attached very shakily to the past sacrifice of bringing land into cultivation—but also at disproving the Ricardian thesis that, *ceteris paribus*, the landlords gain at the expense of the community if population increases. This attempt,[1] though not of much ultimate theoretical significance, as it was based on moral rather than economic reasoning, is interesting as an attempt to make the real cost theory into a moral basis for *laissez-faire*. The praise which Jevons bestowed on Bastiat for keeping the "torch of demand theory burning"[2] is to say the least of it exaggerated, and it is difficult, in face of the latter's religious convictions of ultimate harmony, to credit the uncompleted sections of his argument with much scientific value.

The remarkable developments of mathematical economics in France must, I think, be associated with the tradition of analysis from the end of demand. In particular, Cournot's analysis of competition by way of monopoly[3] has an interesting similarity to Senior's angle of approach, though it is impossible to know whether he was acquainted with the latter's *Political Economy* in 1838.

Pellegrino Rossi should be mentioned as the French disciple of Senior, for, though an Italian by birth, he succeeded J. B. Say at the Collège de France in 1833. It is interesting to notice that while adopting Say's value concept, he insisted that the Ricardian theory of value was necessary to give it precision, while at the same time he criticized Ricardo [for not paying sufficient attention to the prevalence of monopoly conditions.[4]

[1] Bastiat, *Economic Harmonies*, chap. 9.

[2] Jevons, *The Principles of Economics*, 1905, chap. 3, p. 8.

[3] *Mathematical Principles of the Theory of Wealth*, 1838. For an explanation of the neglect of the French mathematical economists in this chapter see Preface, p. 10, note 1 above.

[4] Rossi is sometimes regarded as Ricardo's continental popularizer, but he follows Senior much more closely than Ricardo. His *Cours d'Économie Politique* was first published in four volumes in 1840, 1841, 1851, and 1854 respectively; it contained a considerable number of his lectures given at the Collège de France.

The later French economists, Chevalier, Courcelle-Seneuil, Cherbuliez, Joseph Garnier, were so eclectic as to be uninteresting theoretically. They adopted Say's analysis of value, Senior's theory of abstinence, and J. S. Mill's and Rae's treatment of saving, and Ricardo's stationary state. Courcelle-Seneuil, for instance, in his survey of the development of economic theory, referred to Senior as clearing up the problems of cost of production, and to Mill as throwing light on the accumulation of capital. In short, they took Say's *Traité* as their basis, and added precision to his analysis from the works of the English and some of the German economists.[1]

III

Ricardo, in contrast to Say, was quite unable to pass lightly over the problem of the introduction of the labour theory of value into the *Wealth of Nations*. In any case by 1817 the theories of rent and population had been newly worked out by West and Malthus, and any attempt in England to re-examine the nature and determinants of value had to take them into account. As Ricardo explained in his preface they had thrown fresh light on the natural course of wages, rent and profit, and his object was to rework the theories of his predecessors with the help of the new tools.[2] It was obvious that the new theories had little connection with the short run, and thus from the beginning Ricardo set to work with his eyes on the distant state of ultimate equilibrium, where the tendencies of rent and population could be fully worked out.[3]

Adam Smith's labour theory of value had been broken down by the introduction of land and capital to claim shares in the total product. This had created the paradox that the amount of labour embodied in a commodity exchanged

[1] Courcelle-Seneuil, *Traité théoretique et practique d'Économie Politique*, second edition, 1867, Vol. 1, p. 490. Cf. Schumpeter, *Dogmen- und Methodengeschichte*, III, "Das klassiche System."

[2] Ricardo, *Principles of Political Economy and Taxation*, Preface, pp. 1–2.

[3] Ricardo's *Letters to Malthus*, edited Bonar, 1887, p. 127. Ricardo's letter to Malthus, January 24, 1817.

for a smaller amount of labour embodied in wages. As long as the value of labour itself was assumed to be constant, this was obviously inconsistent with the derivation of all value from labour and its determination by the relative quantities used; evidently, since the premise of the whole theory was that equal quantities of labour of the same kind are of equal value, in equilibrium they must exchange for each other. There were two ways out of this impasse other than the crude exploitation theory: to admit either that capital and land are productive, or that the value of labour is variable. Both of these Adam Smith denied in theory, though he accepted the first in fact; Ricardo, on the other hand, boldly chose the second. There were three problems to be dealt with: to show that labour was the ultimate source of value, that the relative quantities used were the determinants of value, and to find a more complete explanation of the shares of capital and land in the produce than crude exploitation.

Ricardo's solutions to all these depended on the theories of rent and population. Land could be eliminated from the sources of value since it could be shown that rent was a residual payment, a true surplus over costs of production which did not affect the availability of productive resources. Capital was merely accumulated, or indirect, labour and therefore introduced no new source of productivity. Labour was, therefore, isolated as the sole source of value. The question of the determinants of value could be solved on the same lines. Land was eliminated again by the theory of rent and commodities were considered to be exchanged on the basis of relative quantities of direct and indirect labour.[1] The difficulty of profits still remained—why should labour embodied in a commodity exchange for less labour in the form of wages for both direct and indirect labour. The principle of population, however, came to the rescue at this point by showing that the cost of production of labour, i.e. the amount of labour, direct and indirect, necessary to procure any given level of subsistence varies, and that therefore by the labour theory itself the value of

[1] *Principles*, chap. 1, "On Value," sects. 1–3; chap. 2, "On Rent."

labour varies.[1] This means, of course, that labour has no claim to any share other than the equilibrium rate of wages, and therefore. the receipt by labour of less than the whole product does not invalidate the labour theory of value.

This solution, however, did not explain the existence of profits, although it prevented them disturbing the theory of the determination of value as long as the assumption was made that the capital structure of production was the same for different commodities, except in a minority of cases. Unfortunately for Ricardo's reconstruction of the labour theory, his analysis of stationary equilibrium involved a functional connection between profits and the supply of capital.[2] Thus the existence of profits had to be tacitly admitted to have some connection with real costs of production. Ricardo attempted to avoid these uncomfortable implications by divorcing distribution from value—writing to McCulloch in 1820, he concluded:—

"I sometimes think that if I were to write the chapter on value again which is in my book, I should acknowledge that the relative value of commodities was regulated by two causes instead of by one, namely, by the relative quantity of labour necessary to produce the commodities in question, and by the rate of profit for the time that the capital remained dormant, and until the commodities were brought to market. Perhaps I should find the difficulties nearly as great in this view of the subject as in that which I have adopted.

"After all, the great questions of Rent, Wages, and Profits must be explained by the proportions in which the whole produce is divided between landlords, capitalists, and labourers, and which are not essentially connected with the doctrine of value."[3]

It is evident that the difficulty of fitting capital into the labour theory of value had become more and more obvious to Ricardo as time went on. In the second edition of the *Principles* (1819) he divided Chapter 1, On Value, into sections with headings which started by stating (section 2)

---

[1] *Principles*, chap. 1, pp. 10–11; chap. 5, "On Wages," pp. 70–5, 78.

[2] Ibid., chap. 6, "On Profits," pp. 98–103.

[3] Ricardo's letter to McCulloch, June 13, 1820. *Letters of David Ricardo to J. R. McCulloch*, edited T. H. Hollander, 1895, p. 72.

that capital accumulation made no difference to the labour theory, and went on (sections 3 and 4) to state that this was modified by the use of machinery and by the unequal durability of fixed capital, and by differences in the rapidity of circulation of capital through the process of production. The modification of the labour theory had it seems already become of sufficient importance in 1819 to be dignified by special headings. By 1821 these qualifications had assumed even greater importance, and in the third edition of that date the heading of section 3 was altered to draw attention to the necessity of adding indirect to direct labour in comparing the quantities of labour used in making commodities. But the most important innovation in the third edition is the addition of a footnote to section 6.

"Mr. Malthus appears to think that it is a part of my doctrine that the cost and value of a thing should be the same;—it is, if he means by cost, 'cost of production including profits.' "[1]

Ricardo's preoccupation with the complexities of value theory are further illustrated by his correspondence with McCulloch, to whom he wrote in 1819 that he was not satisfied with his account of value, adding that the fault lay in his exposition, not in the doctrine. In 1822 he complained that McCulloch was too rigid in his treatment, since he did not admit that even where the same quantities of labour were used in making two commodities their relative values might vary solely on account of changes in the value of labour, adding, "and yet the fact appears to me undeniable." Again in 1823 Ricardo wrote that he found it difficult to show why he had selected labour as a measure of value when confronted with cases such as the wine in the cellar, or the oak tree, but that he remained convinced that it was the best possible measure.[2]

[1] See Cannan, *Review of Economic Theory*, pp. 176-7. Marshall, in the *Principles of Economics*, Appendix 1, attributed far too clear ideas to Ricardo on this matter, probably because he did not compare the three editions of Ricardo's chapter, On Value, Ricardo, *Principles*, p. 39 n. This footnote is based on Ricardo's reply to Malthus' criticism of him in his *Principles* (chap. 2, sect. 2). *Notes on Malthus*, 1820, edited Gregory and Hollander, 1928, pp. 14-15.

[2] *Letters of David Ricardo to J. R. McCulloch*, edited Hollander, 1895, pp. 47-8, December 18, 1819; pp. 131-2, March 19, 1822; and pp. 153-4, August 8,

Although it seems that to the end of his life Ricardo hankered after the labour theory of value, he replaced it to all intents and purposes by a cost of production theory applicable to a certain field of analysis. Thus to some extent he justified the emphasis on costs in Adam Smith's explanation of natural prices. The completeness of the new version was not always recognized by his contemporaries, and its association with the labour theory prevented any serious attempt being made before Senior to reconcile it with Say's demand theory. According to Ricardo's analysis the values of commodities are determined, under conditions of constant cost, by the relative costs of production; even the payment of rents for land does not really upset this, it merely involves the introduction of the concept of a no-rent margin, intensive or extensive. The position of the margin is not itself directly dependent on demand, but can be found from the functions of the fertility of land, of the supply of capital, and of the supply of labour, since the functions of capital and labour together show the total returns which must be yielded at the margin of cultivation in equilibrium.

Compared with Ricardo's very real achievement in abstract analysis, Say's work necessarily appeared superficial and to have been directed solely to the elucidation of what Ricardians considered the simple problems of market value.[1] In point of fact, neither Say nor Ricardo appeared to have realized clearly that the main source of their differences lay in their interests in different periods of time. Between them they had introduced three different lengths, the shortest of all which covered the problems of market price, a quasi-long period in which the prices of products had time to be equated to their money costs of production, and the true long period of stationary equilibrium in which the distinction between value and physical costs of factors of production became relevant. They both

1823. Finally Ricardo said definitely that he had come to the conclusion that capital was something more than accumulated labour. Ibid., pp. 174–8, August 21, 1823.

[1] *Letters of David Ricardo to J. R. McCulloch*, edited Hollander, 1895, p. 105, April 25, 1821. Agreeing with a criticism (probably McCulloch's) of Say in the *Scotsman*.

dealt with all three, but Say attached more importance to the first two and regarded the third as irrelevant, while Ricardo deliberately took the first for granted and pretty well ignored the second. The divergence in their interests is illustrated in a letter from Say to Ricardo in 1815 in connection with the latter's controversy with Malthus on rent, ". . . .je regarde comme comparativement peu important le profit propre, le profit inhérent à ces deux instrumens"; and again in 1820, "Il me semble que vous ne pouvez déterminer la quantité et qualité de travail que par le prix que l'on paie pour l'obtenir."[1]

Despite their unfailing belief in Ricardo neither James Mill nor McCulloch appreciated the conditions under which Ricardo worked out his analysis, and quite failed to understand his difficulties with capital. To the end of their days they asserted that profits were the payment for indirect labour, thus hopelessly confusing capital replacement with the net return on capital.[2] Their version of the Ricardian theory may, through its simplification, have contributed to its authority among the non-professional economists, but it made it appear even more vulnerable to attack to the initiated by obscuring the importance of Ricardo's suggestions on capital.

Of all the adherents, good, bad and indifferent, of Ricardo, De Quincey was the only one to appreciate the equilibrium significance of his analysis. He was refreshingly clear as to the relation between market price and equilibrium price, and realized that Ricardo introduced the chapter On Market Price simply to provide against the criticism that his results did not conform to the observed phenomena on the market.[3] Most of Malthus' criticisms were due, De Quincey believed, to a failure to appreciate this. On the actual theory of value he was not so clear, attributing much greater validity to the labour theory than Ricardo himself

[1] *Mélanges de J. B. Say*. Letters to Ricardo, December 2, 1815, and March 2, 1820.

[2] James Mill, *Elements of Political Economy*, chap. 3, third edition, pp. 98–101. McCulloch, *Principles of Political Economy*, Part II, chap. 1, and Part II, chap. 4, pp. 371–3, fourth edition, 1849.

[3] De Quincey, *Logic of Political Economy*, 1844, chap. 2, "Market Value."

did. On the other hand, he understood the enormous importance attached to rent, which he called one of the "well-heads of his [Ricardo's] economy."[1]

The position of Malthus among the Ricardians is more than a little difficult to define. On the whole, for reasons which will emerge, it seems to me better to discuss him here than to put him among the demand theorists proper. Diametrically opposed to De Quincey, he kept up a guerilla war on Ricardo in a "spirit of high promise and trivial performance."[2] It must be admitted at once that he had some excellent ideas on the subject of demand, and that De Quincey and Ricardo were not altogether fair to him. His habitual confusion on everything except population in contrast to their own clarity must have made his persistent attacks peculiarly irritating both to Ricardo and to his devotee.

Malthus' contributions to the theory of demand seem to have been due not so much to an adequate analysis of demand as to his interest in short-run problems, for in the end his theory of long-run price was essentially the same as the cost of production theory.[3] If he had approached the subject more on the lines of Say he might have been able to carry out the suggestions of his first chapter; as it was by the adoption of the limitation of the theory of value to material goods by his definition of wealth[4] he made it logically impossible to explain wages on anything but a cost of production basis. In this way he ended up with the usual cost of production theory of long-period price.

He opened his introduction with an attack on Ricardian methods, declaring it to be impossible for economic laws, which depend on such variable factors as human beings and land, to be proved in the same way, or to lead to conclusions as certain as those of mathematics.[5] A little further on he maintains that "a precipitate attempt to simplify and

[1] De Quincey, *Logic of Political Economy*, 1844, chap. 4, "On Rent," p. 174.
[2] Ibid., chap. 5, "Profits," p. 254.
[3] Malthus, *Principles of Political Economy*, first edition, 1820. (All page references to this edition.)
[4] Ibid., chap. 1, sect. 1, p. 28, and sect. 2.
[5] Ibid., Introduction, p. 1.

to generalize" on the one hand and "hasty inferences from a frequent appeal to partial facts" on the other have hindered the progress of knowledge.[1] Clearly a failure to produce a thorough and consistent system of equilibrium was not likely to worry Malthus, nor the existence of apparent anomalies to make him overhaul his principles.

In the first chapter he made a number of admirable remarks on the connection between demand and value, pointing out that the cost of production only influences long-run price by affecting the supply.[2] But when he tried to explain the determination of the prices of factors, he did not really succeed in getting away from Ricardo's theories, though he started in a promising way by stating that they must be determined in the same way as those of commodities.[3] Consistently with the stress on demand Malthus abandoned the labour theory of value, but at the same time betrayed the fact that his interest in market value was so great that he did not realize what Ricardo meant by the cost of production:

"We have the power indeed arbitrarily to call the labour which has been employed upon a commodity its real value; but in so doing we use words in a different sense from that in which they are customarily used; we confound at once the very important distinction between cost and value; and render it almost impossible to explain, with clearness, the main stimulus to the production of wealth, which, in fact, depends upon this distinction.[4]

But if we cannot count this rejection of the labour theory as a proof that Malthus knew what he meant by demand, how are we to account for the earlier correct remarks upon the influence of demand on the value of commodities? I suggest in the first place that the explanation lies in his interest in short-run value problems, in particular over-production which superficially at any rate is primarily a question of demand. Secondly, that failing to understand the analysis of long-run equilibrium, he came to the natural

[1] Malthus, *Principles of Political Economy*, Introduction, p. 6. Cf. Part 1, chap. 1, pp. 9–13.   [2] Ibid., chap. 2, pp. 72–8.
[3] Ibid., chap. 2, pp. 78–83.   [4] Ibid., chap. 1, p. 61.

conclusion that as it did not help to solve the problems he was interested in it must necessarily be wrong. Obviously as long as he insisted that unproductive labour was necessary in order to maintain demand, he could not admit that demand did not influence the position of ultimate equilibrium, although he had no general theory of value that could seriously compete with Ricardo's. We can only conclude that Malthus' so-called demand theory of value was the result of his own particular interests and a misunderstanding of Ricardo.[1] This contention derives further support from his emphasis on the distinction between productive and unproductive labour, which eliminated the question of the value of services from his analysis of demand from the beginning. His contemporaries were surely right in believing that his whole theory of value was originated to explain gluts, and stood or fell with the explanation. McCulloch's remark that Malthus had been highly overrated as an economist was justified in this respect at least.[2]

I have examined Malthus' position in this detail because he is so often taken as one of the forerunners of modern value theory. I have attempted to show this is misleading and does not do justice to the demand theorists. On the other hand, his failure to understand Ricardo was so great that it is impossible to really call him a Ricardian. The simplest solution is probably to abandon the attempt to classify him at all.

John Stuart Mill and Cairnes must be mentioned among the Ricardians both for completeness and as an indication of how little the developments that had been going on were publicly appreciated. Although Mill declared initially that there was nothing to be added to Ricardo's theory of value, he himself adopted a very cautious attitude to the labour theory.[3] The only contribution of Senior's that he took any

[1] Ricardo's letter to Malthus, January 24, 1817, op. cit., edited Bonar, 1887, p. 128.

[2] *McCulloch's Letters to Ricardo*, edited Hollander, 1931, p. 12, letter December 5, 1819.

[3] J. S. Mill, *Principles of Political Economy*, Bk. ii, chap. i, par. i.

notice of was the introduction of the term "abstinence" to indicate the real cost of capital when he found it necessary to use Ricardo's real cost theory rather than his labour theory. Though the discussion of "peculiar cases of value" was an interesting innovation it has little significance for the general development of the theory, for he simply put it in as one of the group of exceptions with which Ricardian economics had always been garnished. Much the same is true of his use of a demand curve in the theory of international values.[1]

Although Cairnes was an obstructionist of the first order in many respects, he managed to do some useful work in drawing attention to what he called the cases of "reciprocal demand" in the determination of the value of labour. But as he was of the opinion that one set of general principles could not be expected to deal with all the complexities of economic phenomena, he naturally did not think it necessary to ask whether the existence of such an important class of exceptions shed any new light on the general theory of imputation. It is perhaps worth noticing that the idea of non-competing groups was already contained in the generalization of the theory of rent and Bailey's criticisms of Ricardo, as well as in J. S. Mill's theory of reciprocal demand in international trade.[2]

Torrens must for all practical purposes be accounted a Ricardian in his adaptation of the cost of production theory. He himself apparently believed that, because he had given up the labour theory, he had made a new departure.[3] His statements at the Political Economy Club in the 'thirties that the bulk of Ricardo's theory of value and rent had been

---

[1] J. S. Mill, *Principles of Political Economy*, Bk. III, chaps. 16 and 18.

[2] Cairnes, *Leading Principles of Political Economy*, Part I, chap. 3.

[3] Torrens, *Essay on the Production of Wealth*, first edition, 1821, pp. vi and vii, 34–8 and 51–5. Torrens was not alone in thinking that he had made innovations. His contemporaries, including Ricardo, had a very high opinion of him. Senior referred to his treatment of value as illuminating (*Political Economy*, sixth edition, p. 98). Samuel Read expressed the highest respect for him and agreed with much of what he wrote on value and profits. For a discussion of modern neglect of Torrens see E. Seligman, *Essays in Economics*, 1925, "Some Neglected British Economists."

disproved by Bailey, are explicable,[1] since Bailey, though criticizing Ricardo, was prepared to concede the validity of the cost of production theory in a limited field. Torrens himself did not in his *Essay on the Production of Wealth* go as far as Bailey in admitting the influence of demand.

IV

The other group of economists in England, whom I have called the "dissenters," were spread thinly through the half-century of our period. They neither wrote so much as the Ricardians nor made so spectacular an impression on the public, nor were they members of any particular party. It must be admitted that their work, except Longfield's and Senior's, does not give the impression of the same intellectual stature as that of Ricardo's and the Mills'. But they are of importance as people interested in economic problems to whom the labour theory of value approach did not seem obviously correct, and who started from a different angle, like Lauderdale, or else attacked it on its own grounds of theory.

In 1804 Lauderdale[2] adopted approximately the same interpretation of the theory of value in the *Wealth of Nations* as J. B. Say. In the first chapter of his *Public Wealth*, considering the nature of value, he decided that it depends on utility and scarcity, that is demand and supply, and that it is affected by a change on either side, and therefore that it is determined by no intrinsic quality. Naturally it

---

[1] In 1828 Torrens asked the question whether the definition of wealth as material commodities possessing utility and limited in supply was adequate; and in 1831 whether any of the principles enunciated by Ricardo were still admitted to be correct. According to J. L. Mallet's account of the discussion Torrens answered the latter question in the negative, saying that Bailey had proved that Ricardo's theories were wrong. J. L. Mallet's Diaries, *Proceedings of the Political Economy Club*, Vol. VI (1921), pp. 30, 223–43.

[2] *An Inquiry into the Nature and Origin of Public Wealth, and into the Means and Causes of its Increase*, first edition, 1804. Lauderdale evidently interpreted the *Wealth of Nations* with the aid of Condillac's *Du Commerce et du Gouvernement*.

is impossible to find a constant standard of value if it is considered in this relative way, and Lauderdale did not bother to pursue the matter further. The connection between value and cost of production under perfect competition is through the latter's influence on supply which is, he thought, on exactly the same footing as demand.[1] On the crucial question of the prices of factors of production he held practically the same view as Say, that they are equally derived from their productivity on which the demand for them depends, and from their supply which has some functional connection with their prices.[2] Consistently with this approach Lauderdale attacked the distinction between productive and unproductive labour as being inconsistent with the concept of value, and in any case impossible to base on the difference between durable and non-durable goods.[3]

Although the theory of public and private wealth and the attack on the sinking fund advanced in Lauderdale's book are absurd, it cannot, I think, be said that they invalidate his claim to be considered the forerunner of the demand school in England. The close resemblance between his approach and Say's and the clarity of his views on the subject, prevent the very absurdity of his other theories from damaging his reputation. After all, the whole mistake of the theory of public wealth was based on a fallacy as to the elasticity of demand for certain groups of commodities in particular instances.[4] Even Lord Brougham in the *Edinburgh Review*, in a scathing and sarcastic article, was forced to admit that on the pure theory of value his ideas were clear, and to consider them separately from the rest.[5] Additionally, and this perhaps is conclusive, he had considerable influence on certain early German writers, notably

[1] *An Inquiry into the Nature and Origin of Public Wealth, and into the Means and Causes of its Increase*, chap. 1, pp. 11–20, first edition. (All references are to this edition.)

[2] Ibid., chap. 3, especially pp. 167–8.

[3] Ibid., chap. 3, pp. 132–53.

[4] Ibid., chaps. 4 and 5.

[5] *Edinburgh Review*, July 1804. For identification of Brougham as the reviewer see W. A. Copinger on the "Authors of the first hundred numbers of *Edinburgh Review* Articles (1802–30)."

Hüfeland, who produced a pure psychological theory of value.[1]

The first important criticism of Ricardo in England appeared in Bailey's *Critical Dissertation on the Nature, Measures and Causes of Value*. This essay was remarkable for its appreciation of the dependence of Ricardo's system on a physical or real conception of cost and value. Bailey pointed out that since value was admitted to be a relation between two things and to be dependent on a "state of mind,"[2] it was a contradiction in terms to say that any commodity had intrinsic value on any grounds whatever. It followed that the attempt to derive value from physical cost of production was absurd. This criticism did not prevent him from accepting cost of production or even, with appropriate qualifications, relative amounts of labour used, as the determinant of value under conditions of constant costs. But he remarked very pertinently that it is absurd to call this a theory of value when the exceptions admitted are so important. Naturally he thought the exceptions to be more important than Ricardo admitted, and insisted that the case of goods not reproducible except at increasing costs, such as all which are produced with the aid of land, should have been treated separately as a case of monopoly. He also suggested that the existence of different grades of labour raises the same problems as different capital structures.[3] Finally, he extended the rent analysis to wages for special skill, talent, etc.[4] Throughout his criticisms the influence of Say is very marked, and Bailey was in fact criticizing certain sections of Ricardo's system in the light of Say's general results.

Senior's theory of value is a landmark in the development

---

[1] Hüfeland, *Neue Grundlegung der Staatswirtschaftskunst*, 2 vols., 1807–13.

[2] *Critical Dissertation on the Nature, Measures and Causes of Value*, 1825, reprinted in the London School of Economics series of reprints of scarce tracts in Economics and Political Science, chap. I, pp. 1–11, and Note A, pp. 233–41. (All page references are to the reprint.)

[3] Ibid., chap. 11, pp. 207–15.

[4] Ibid., chap. 11, pp. 196–7.

of the post-Ricardian period.[1] He inherited the legacy of
the Ricardian discussions of the first quarter of the century,
and he knew personally the economists of his time without
being bound to mental stagnation by intimate friendships
like Mill and McCulloch, since his friends belonged to the
Whig political circles or to the law. Not merely this, but he
brought to the subject an intelligence trained to a nicety
of definition by his legal education, while his outside
interests brought him into direct contact with most of the
pressing social problems of the time.

Without doubt the two economists who had most influence
on the development of his economics were Say and Ricardo.
It is tempting to consider Bailey as also of some importance
although Senior never referred to the Dissertation in connection with the theory of value, for it is difficult to believe that
he had not come across it by the time he started lecturing at
Oxford in 1826. Nevertheless in some respects he seems to
have been nearly as impervious to fresh suggestions on the
subject of value as were most of his contemporaries. The
theory of value developed in his first group of lectures at
Oxford appeared unchanged throughout the numerous
editions of the *Political Economy*, despite additional reading
of foreign economists and the contributions of his English
and Irish contemporaries. Longfield is only mentioned once
in the whole of his writings on theory published and unpublished; Banfield did not fare very much better, and both
Isaac Butt and W. F. Lloyd were ignored, though they
sent him copies of their lectures. Hermann was the only
economist who seems to have had any influence on his later
work, and even he only affected Senior's value theory
indirectly.

It was natural that Senior, with his kink for definition,

---

[1] Professor Seligman has discovered two other economists earlier than
Senior who belong to this group: John Craig, who extended the rent analysis
to the income of fixed capital, and hinted at the connection between marginal
utility and value (*Remarks on some fundamental doctrines in Political Economy*, 1821),
and John Rooke, who stated that value was determined by demand and the
marginal cost of production as a general principle (*An Inquiry into the Principles
of National Wealth*, 1824, p. 26). "On some Neglected British Economists," in
Essays in Economics, E. Seligman.

should approach the theory of value via discussion of the definitions of wealth. Defining wealth as "all those things, and those things only, . . . which have value"[1] he adopted Say's discussion of the derivation of value from utility and scarcity, and stated that it depends on the possession of three characteristics—utility, limitation in supply, and transferableness.[2]

He carried Say's analysis further, however, to show the essential relativity of utility.

"Utility, however," he said, "denotes no intrinsic quality in the things which we call useful; it merely expresses their relations to the pains and pleasures of mankind. And, as the susceptibility of pain and pleasure from particular objects is created and modified by causes innumerable, and constantly varying, we find an endless diversity in the relative utility of different objects to different persons, a diversity which is the motive of all exchanges."

The limitation of supply Senior considered the most important element in value. This, however, did not imply a return to the cost of production theory, but rather a further discussion of the relation of limitation of supply to utility and vice versa. For, surprisingly enough, it is under this heading that the famous discussion of wants which was admired by Jevons,[4] and which led to the formulation of the marginal utility concept, is included. This principle of limitation acts through the human desire for variety and distinction, for, Senior explained, if it were not for these desires the wants of man would cease with the provision of the simple necessaries and comforts of life. It was in his attempt to explain the influence of the desire for variety that Senior formulated the law of diminishing marginal utility :—

"It is obvious, however, that our desires do not aim so much at quantity as at diversity. Not only are there limits to the pleasure which the commodities of any given class can afford, but the pleasure diminishes in a rapidly increasing ratio long before those limits are reached. Two articles of the same kind

---

[1] *Political Economy*, sixth edition, p. 6. (All references are to this edition.)
[2] Ibid., p. 6.   [3] Ibid., p. 7.
[4] Jevons, *Principles of Economics*, 1905, chap. 3, pp. 1–4; and the *Theory of Political Economy*, chap. 3, p. 40, third edition.

will seldom afford twice the pleasure of one, and still less will ten give five times the pleasure of two. In proportion, therefore, as any article is abundant, the number of those who are provided with it, and do not wish, or wish but little to increase their provision, is likely to be great; and, so far as they are concerned, the additional supply loses all, or nearly all, its utility."[1]

The third attribute of a commodity possessing value is transferability. Under this heading Senior discussed the inclusion of immaterial goods under wealth. The ability to transfer material goods is obvious, he argued, but although immaterial goods are imperfectly transferable, as long as some utility which can be transferred is derived from these immaterial goods, they must be included in wealth. If some of the advantages of skill can be sold to, or hired by, other people that skill can have value, e.g. the physical strength of a navvy or the skill of a lawyer, etc.[2] This argument disposed of the distinction between material and immaterial goods in a way similar to Say's and Lauderdale's, and makes it clear that the determination of the values of these different services belongs to the major problems of economics.

In the actual discussion of value Senior defined his attitude to the cost of production by insisting that, except for very short periods, variations in supply should be used to mean variations in the force of the obstacles by which the supply is limited, whatever their nature.[3] One of the most obvious obstacles is the cost of the production of the commodity in question. Except for this casual reference we

---

[1] Senior, *Political Economy*, pp. 11–13. Quotation from p. 12.

[2] Ibid., pp. 8–11. Ferrara (*Esame Storico-critico di Economisti*, Vol. i, p. 482) criticized the inclusion of transferability among the constituents of value. Senior himself, however, suggested in his later lectures (Lectures, 1847–52, Course IV, lecture 6) that transferability would be more properly called a condition than a constituent of value. His discussion, nevertheless, was of more relevance than Ferrara admitted since both Courcelle-Seneuil (op. cit., p. 27, second edition) and Samuel Read (op. cit., pp. 1–9) included lack of transferability among the objections to including immaterial goods in wealth.

[3] Ibid., p. 16. Senior's use of this concept of variations in supply is illustrated in his lecture on *The Value of Money*, delivered in 1829, published 1840, reprinted in London School of Economics series of reprints of scarce tracts in Economics and Political Science, p. 55 of the reprint.

get through the general discussion on the nature of wealth and value without any analysis of the cost of production.

In criticizing the derivation of wealth from labour or the cost of production, Senior maintained that Ricardo was wrong; first because he introduced a partial cause, labour cost, instead of the general cause, scarcity, which gives value to labour itself, and secondly because the applicability of the cost of production theory is limited.[1]

So far Senior's theory was entirely in the French tradition except for the greater precision of statement, a precision due one might suppose to the necessity of explaining his position *vis-à-vis* the Ricardians. The further developments of the relation of cost of production to value, however, were original both in purpose and result. They formed the first serious attempt to explain the connection between the utility and the cost of production approaches. It is particularly noticeable that Senior considered the latter to be essentially misleading although not entirely wrong. It must not be assumed because he completed the elements of the real cost analysis by introducing "abstinence" as the sacrifice behind capital, that his principal object was to clarify Ricardo's analysis.[2] He recognized the necessity of explaining the basis of the scarcity of goods by explaining the scarcity of the factors of production, neither more nor less.

He showed that Ricardo's cost of production theory is sufficient only in the special case of constant costs which implies perfect accessibility of all factors to all producers. It follows that, wherever either increasing or diminishing returns exist, the cost of production theory is inadequate, in particular where land is a scarce factor—

"where the only natural agents employed are those which are universally accessible, and therefore are practically unlimited in supply, the utility of the produce, or in other words, its power,

[1] *Political Economy*, pp. 24–5.

[2] Ibid., pp. 97–8. Senior's innovations in the theory of value have often been regarded by his contemporaries, e.g. J. S. Mill, Courcelle-Seneuil, as well as by historians such as Cannan and Böhm-Bawerk, as merely completing the cost of production theory See note 1, on p. 151 below. Senior himself was quite aware that Ricardo had changed from a labour theory to a cost of production theory in his third edition. Ibid., p. 98.

directly or indirectly, of producing gratification, or preventing pain, must be in proportion to the sacrifices made to produce it, unless the producer has misapplied his exertions; since no man would willingly employ a given amount of labour or abstinence in producing one commodity, if he could obtain more gratification by devoting them to the production of another."[1]

Since Senior regarded the cost of production as composed of wages, capital replacement and profits, it is clear that no difficulty was involved in comparing the costs of goods made with different capital structures. Given the rates of wages and profits, as determined according to his theory of wages and capital, real physical costs can be reduced in all cases to money terms. That this was his opinion is shown by his remark that the equilibrium prices of commodities produced under conditions of constant costs, must be sufficient to afford the ordinary rates of remuneration to labour and abstinence.[2] Even in this case, however, Senior did not admit that cost of production is the final cause of price, it is merely the "regulator."[3] This is the only point at which his theory coincided with Ricardo's, and, since he excluded commodities made with scarce natural agents, he denied the applicability of Ricardo's analysis to any case in which rent arises.

The majority of the problems which the theory of value has to explain come in consequence into the sphere of monopoly analysis defined by imperfect accessibility of all factors to all producers. The importance of demand relatively to cost of production in determining equilibrium values depends, Senior argued, on the degree of monopoly present in the production of each commodity. He distinguished five cases, which he summarized as follows:

"Effects of the cost of production on price:—We have seen that production may take place under five different circumstances.

1. Absence of all monopoly—all persons being capable of producing with equal advantage.

---

[1] *Political Economy*, p. 97. This passage is printed in italics in the original.
[2] Ibid., p. 101.　　　　　　　　　　　　　[3] Ibid., p. 102.

2. A monopoly under which the monopolist has not the exclusive power of producing, but exclusive facilities as a producer, which may be employed indefinitely with equal or increasing advantage.

3. A monopoly under which the monopolist is the only producer, and cannot increase the amount of his produce.

4. A monopoly under which the monopolist is the only producer, and can increase indefinitely, with equal or increasing advantage, the amount of his produce.

5. A monopoly under which the monopolist is not the only producer, but has peculiar facilities which diminish and ultimately disappear as he increases the amount of his produce."[1]

The first case, Senior explained, is that of constant costs already dealt with, where price must equal wages, capital replacement and profits. In the next three cases value is related to the cost of production by no general rules. In case 2, for which he gave patent rights as an example, price is prevented by competition from rising above the cost of production without the use of monopolized productive agent. But in this case, owing to the economies of large-scale production, price will tend towards the monopolist's own cost of production, and the exact position will depend on the actual conditions of production and demand. Case 3 is, of course, that of absolute scarcity in which there is no upper limit to price, but only a lower limit formed by the cost of production, if any. Case 4 is the same as case 2, except, as it is absolute monopoly, there will be no upper limit to price. Case 5 is the most important, as it includes production under conditions of differential advantages and diminishing returns, and therefore rents arise. (It includes agriculture.) Price in this case has "a constant tendency to coincide with the cost of that portion which is continued to be produced at the greatest expense," this portion depending on the demand.[2] This case practically covers the majority of value problems, for even where all producers are equally well situated they will all have to

[1] *Political Economy*, p. 111.

[2] Ibid., p. 115. This, of course, is Ricardian, *except* that where Ricardo used the given conditions of the supply of labour and capital to determine the margin, Senior relied on the demand for the produce.

use some scarce natural agent whose price varies with the amount demanded.[1]

Actually this last case is even more general than appears from this account, as Senior defined rent as "the revenue offered spontaneously by nature or by accident," including under the former all outstanding human ability, and under the latter the returns on fixed capital goods that are now called quasi-rent.[2]

It must be admitted, I think, that up to this point Senior was successful in his attempt to reconcile Ricardo's analysis with Say's, by the method of classifying the major cases of value according to the relative importance of demand and cost of production as actual determinants. In dealing with the contiguous problems of the values of factors of production, however, he failed to carry the analysis to its logical conclusion with sufficient certainty to reach satisfactory results. His attempt is nevertheless interesting both in comparison to parallel work in Germany,[3] and in itself. It is on this part of Senior's work that the later lectures throw a certain amount of fresh light, without which it is difficult to decide how far he really considered the generalization of the theory of rent important, and how far he derived the income of factors from their product.[4]

The problem confronting Senior was to determine the importance of the real cost of production of factors and the value of the products of factors, respectively, in the distribution of the total product. He had explained the real cost of production at an early stage as abstinence and labour, following and completing Ricardo's analysis.[5]

[1] *Political Economy*, pp. 103–18. Prof. R. T. Ely drew attention to Senior's analysis of monopoly in 1899. *Report of Proceedings of the American Economic Association*, 1899, pp. 89–102.

[2] *Political Economy*, pp. 128 et seq. Senior never explained how far these quasi-rents entered into long run costs of production. Cf. Part I, chap. 3, pp. 129 et seq. below.

[3] See Section v below.

[4] In the Lectures, 1847–52, Senior devoted very little attention to value as such, but in the lectures on the "Classification of Instruments of Production and on Capital," he laid great emphasis on the importance of rent and adopted a new definition of capital. (Course II, lectures 2, 3, and 4.) See note on p. 116 for an account of the differences between his treatment of value in the *Political Economy* and the later lectures.   [5] Senior, *Political Economy*, p. 101.

But he denied the relevance of the Malthusian theory of the cost of production of the labourer to the actual problem of distribution. Instead he returned to Adam Smith's concept of the real cost of labour as consisting in the actual disutility of labour, just as he himself defined the real cost of capital as the disutility of the abstinence involved in saving. Capital and labour were therefore exactly parallel in this respect.[1]

Senior's next step was to redefine the distributive shares. He generalized the theory of rent to explain the incomes of all factors of production the supply of which have no real cost basis either in the long or short run, i.e. land, fixed capital, special skill and talents, or some special opportunity such as the monopolists of cases 2, 3, and 4 above.[2] This was simply a restatement of the doctrine of productive services in terms of Ricardian rent. It was worked out in the *Political Economy* but was stated in such a way as to leave it uncertain how far he really thought it important. From the 1847–52 Lectures, however, it becomes clear that it was a fundamental part of his theory of distribution.[3] Here not only did he repeat the original analysis of rent more clearly, but he redefined capital to include land on the grounds that it is impossible to distinguish between capital and land in practice, as capital (in the limited sense as the result of abstinence) has a constant tendency to approximate to land by losing its mobility by investment in durable goods.[4] Senior admitted this change in his definition to be due to Hermann's influence, but he also explained in addition that the characteristic of land lies in its immobility rather than any absolute limitation of supply.[5]

[1] *Political Economy*, pp. 89, 128, 140. Not only did Senior discuss population at the beginning of the *Political Economy* quite separately from wages, but he disagreed with Malthus fundamentally in that he believed that the instinct of man to better his position was stronger than the instinct of propagation in civilized and free countries. This was considered at great length in the 1847–52 lectures. See Chap. 3 below.

[2] Ibid., pp. 89–95, 102, 128–30. See Part I, chap. 3 below, Section II.

[3] Lectures, 1847–52, Course II, lecture 2.   [4] Ibid.

[5] Ibid., Course III, lecture I. This was pointed out still earlier in England by Samuel Read (op. cit., Bk. II, chap. 7, pp. 300–2). For the effect of this change in definition on Senior's theory of capital, see Part I, chap. 4 below, pp. 159 et seq.

This extension of the rent analysis left Senior with the problems of the wages of ordinary labour and of the interest on circulating capital to solve. In the *Political Economy* he was singularly unsuccessful in making his general position clear, and it is usually considered that the Abstinence theory of capital was advanced as an integral part of the cost of production theory of value and distribution, and is very little more.[1] While this is justified perhaps from a study of the *Political Economy* alone, the lectures on money and the developments of the later lectures put the matter in a different light.

Senior's idea that the return to resources employed in the export trades is entirely dependent on the value of the produce is the main basis of his whole explanation of international price levels, and there can be little doubt that he himself regarded this as an obvious conclusion from his general theory of value and imputation. For example, in the lecture *On the Cost of Obtaining Money* he explained that differences in the wages between countries are due to the differences in capacity to produce valuable goods and service, just as differences in earnings between individuals in the same country are.[2] This passage is perhaps sufficient evidence that Senior approached distribution from a productivity aspect, but since his introduction of abstinence as a real cost has led to the opposite opinion, it is important to clear up the confusion more specifically. To begin with, there is nothing actually inconsistent with the derivation of the income of capital from the value of its product in the section on capital in the *Political Economy*, though it is open to other interpretations.[3] The discussions of the abstinence involved in saving and the productivity of capital[4] can be legitimately taken as an analysis of the

---

[1] Cannan, *Review of Economic Theory*, p. 187. Böhm-Bawerk, *Capital and Interest*, p. 285. Smart's translation. Cf. p. 97, n. 2 above.

[2] *Three Lectures on the Cost of Obtaining Money and on Some Effects of Private and Government Paper Money*, p. 14. London School of Economics series of reprints of scarce tracts in Economics and Political Science. The lecture was delivered in 1829 and published in 1830. See Part I, chap. 6, pp. 222–3 below.

[3] *Political Economy*, pp. 58–81.

[4] It is noticeable that another early English abstinence theorist, Poulett Scrope, laid great emphasis on the productivity of capital as the determinant of the rate of interest from the side of demand. See chap. 4, pp. 143–4 below.

conditions of supply of capital, and as an incomplete explanation of the reasons for the demand for capital respectively. In addition there are *a priori* grounds for considering that Senior derived profits from the productivity of capital—his general approach to value and his extension of the rent concept, especially in its later form. If this is a correct interpretation, his theory amounts to saying that the equilibrium rate of profits, or interest, is determined by the equalization of demand, depending on the productivity of capital, and supply at a level just sufficient to pay for the sacrifice involved in saving. This is in fact very similar to Marshall's theory.

In support of this interpretation there are two interesting passages in the 1847 lectures:

"The comparative utility of commodities depends partly on the intensity of the pleasure they afford, and partly on their durability. . . .

"Nearly the same causes determine the comparative utility of instruments. It depends partly on their efficiency and partly on their durability. . . .

"The comparative utility of materials depends partly on the utility of the commodities or instruments of which they are the materials, partly on the facility or difficulty with which they can be converted into those commodities or instruments, and partly on the time which that conversion takes."

A little further on, in discussing the supply of capital, he explained that the extent of each individual's providence is determined by the "degree of future advantage" which will induce him to sacrifice a given amount of present enjoyment for a given time.[1]

It must be admitted that Senior's theory of wages was far less clear than his theory of capital, but its independence of the cost of production theory of value is obvious. Essentially a productivity theory, its statement in terms of the wage fund[2]

[1] Lectures, 1847–52. Course II, lecture 9. See Part I, chap. 4, p. 162 below. Like most English economists of the time, Senior generally used the terms profits and interest interchangeably.

[2] Ferrara is one of the few historians of economic theory who have really emphasized the importance of Senior's position in the development of the theory of value. His main criticisms of Senior's exposition are: (1) That he distinguishes scarcity from utility as a cause of value. Strictly, no doubt,

merely shows that, in common with most English economists, Senior thought that the payment of wages out of circulating capital (the amount of which was quite often assumed fixed at the beginning of each production period) involved a special and difficult problem. It is not surprising that he failed to resolve the problem, and that in attempting to do so he lost the opportunity of working out a theory of wages parallel to that either of rent or of profits. In short, Senior's theory of wages was an unsuccessful attempt to elucidate the relation between the dependence of wages on the productivity of labour and the connection between wages and capital, and not a relapse into the Ricardian separation of the values of factors from the values of their products.[1]

It was principally because Senior failed in this way to connect his modifications of the Ricardian theory of value with any definite conclusions on the incomes of the factors of production, that his work attracted so little notice. What was the point of all this elaborate discussion of utility and of the various cases of monopoly, critics asked, if it threw no light on distribution? The extension of the rent concept was disliked, and seemed put to little practical use in the *Political Economy*; its relation to costs in different time periods was not worked out, and seemed merely a source of confusion. To Malthusians his heterodoxy on population left

Ferrara is correct in stating that scarcity is an influence affecting the utility of a commodity rather than an independent cause of value. But it was natural under the circumstances of the period 1826–30, when Senior evolved his theory, that he should have separated scarcity from utility and it has, in fact, been accepted as a convenient method of approach. (2) That Senior generally spoke of cost of production instead of "reproduction," and did not differentiate sufficiently clearly between the economic concept of the production of equivalent satisfaction and the technical concept of the production of similar commodities. (3) That Senior was wrong in limiting the applicability of the theory of value to exchange in a society. Despite these very pertinent criticisms Ferrara admits that Senior had grasped the essence of the modern theory of value. Ferrara, *Esame Storico-Critico di Economisti*, Vol. 1, pp. 472–93.

[1] *Political Economy*, pp. 140–99. Senior's theory of the wage fund was repeated in a very abbreviated form in his review of J. S. Mill's *Principles* and *Essays* in the *Edinburgh Review*, 1848. For some unknown reason Mr. Levy has taken all his extracts on the wage fund (Senior's *Industrial Efficiency*, Vol. 11, Part IX, chap. 4) from this review instead of from the lectures published in 1830, which were incorporated in the *Political Economy* in 1836. See Part 1, chap. 5, Sect. IV.

a nasty flavour behind, and at the same time deprived his analysis of that completeness from the equilibrium aspect that had given so much force to Ricardo's work. It is easy to see how sterile his results appeared to the orthodox. With all his labour he had apparently only redescribed some of their own analysis, though the introduction of the new word "abstinence" was admitted to be useful.

Senior's achievements were, however, remarkable. With the aid of Say he had demolished the labour and the real cost of production theories of value, and with the aid of Ricardo's rent theory he had made a useful reclassification of the factors of production, and shown at what points the real cost theory and the relative utility theory of value fitted into each other. Starting with the extreme case of perfect accessibility of all factors of production, he had worked a classification through to the case of perfect monopoly, or perfect inaccessibility of factors, showing how cost of production had *pari passu* a smaller and smaller influence on price. Thus in effect he fused the two developments of value theory whose origins are to be found in the *Wealth of Nations*, and whose discrepancies split the world of economists into two sections, each of which believed that they were right but could not prove the other wrong. Even his apparent failures in the field of distribution are important. His Ricardianesque strain forced him to look for some more precise explanation than Say provided which would be consistent with the analysis of equilibrium of the very long period in which the distinction between rent and other forms of income is significant. That he failed to find the solution is less important than the fact that, even at this stage, he realized that the rent analysis was important, even although the theory of value with which it had been originally connected turned out to be only a special case.

Senior's theory of value was received coldly by the more important English economists, being either ignored or criticized. In the *Edinburgh Review* his extension of the rent concept was objected to on the grounds of being useless, and in any case wrong. It was said to be useless because Senior admitted the inconvenience of the new terminology it involved, and wrong because according to the reviewer if pushed to its logical extreme the term rent must be applied to all monopoly incomes and unusual profits, and also to explain the difference in earnings between an Englishman and a Hindoo.[1] The obvious implication of the generalization of the rent analysis that marginal productivity analysis is relevant to the pricing of all factors simply did not occur to the reviewer, but, considering Senior's own obscurity on this point, that is not after all to be wondered at.

McCulloch, as was to be expected, would have none of Senior's theory of value. He devoted some space in his *Principles* to asserting that even in the case of the golden aeroliths the labour theory of value holds good, for, he argued, labour is needed to pick up aeroliths and to produce such gold as is not rained down from heaven. He seems also to have included Senior in his comment on continental economists' treatment of value, as that of persons "who stumble at the very threshold of the science," and of whom it is "but too clear" that they "have yet to make themselves acquainted with its merest elements."[2] The truth indeed was only with McCulloch and his labour theory of value.

Despite this unfavourable reception by the big guns of economics, Senior was not isolated in his approach to value, even in England in the 'thirties. Archbishop Whately held the same views on value and distribution,[3] and had the most admirable ideas on rent as the consequence of immobilities of certain factors or groups of factors—ideas similar to those behind Senior's generalization of the rent analysis.[4] It is possible, of course, that Senior derived his

[1] Review of Senior's *Political Economy*, 1836, in the *Edinburgh Review*, October 1837, pp. 73–102.   [2] McCulloch's *Principles*, third edition, pp. 69 et seq.
[3] Whately, *Introductory Lectures on Political Economy*, 1831, first edition, 1831. Lecture I, pp. 8–9, second edition 1832, and IX, pp. 252–3; also *Easy Lessons on Money Matters for the use of Young People*, sixth edition, 1842, Lesson 5, "On Value," and Lesson 6, "On Wages." For Whately's discussion with Senior on the treatment of rent in this book see chap. 3 below, p. 131, n. 2.
[4] The Appendix on "Ambiguous Terms," of which the section on economic terms was written by Senior, in Whately's *Elements of Logic* (1826) contain Senior's first published suggestions on the generalization of rent (pp. 389–96, fifth edition, 1834, particularly pp. 392–3). The suggestion was taken up by C. F. Cotterill, *The Doctrines of Value as set forth by Adam Smith, etc.*, 1831.

ideas on this subject from Whately, but it appears to be improbable since there is no sign that the latter took any active interest in theoretical economics before he held the Drummond Chair in succession to Senior. Indeed, judging from the references to Senior in Whately's published lectures, he was in Senior's debt in matters of economics. This is further borne out by their voluminous but fragmentary correspondence, in which Senior looks to Whately for help with questions of logic, and vice versa in regard to economic theory proper.

More important than Whately, C. Poulett Scrope, M.P., published a theory of value and distribution which had much in common with Senior's in *The Principles of Political Economy*, 1833. Value he declared to be entirely relative, and to be determined by cost of production only in those rare cases where there was perfect competition.[1] Thus far he made no advance on Bailey, but he took a step forward in an admirable explanation of the substitutability of commodities. On distribution his debt to Samuel Read and Senior is obvious. In explaining net profits as the reward for abstinence, he accepted the theory hinted at in 1829 by Read, whose book he reviewed in the *Quarterly Review* in 1831; on wages he adopted explicitly Senior's theory as published in the lectures *On the Cost of Obtaining Money*, 1830. In the same article he said, in reference to these lectures:

"The subject of wages has been lately treated by Mr. Senior with some novelty, and his views, with certain corrections, appear to us to be sound. . . . Mr. Senior has omitted to remark that all this is true only of the price of labour in a natural state of things, uninfluenced by taxation, monopolies, restrictions, or legal interference."[2]

Scrope had a very high opinion of Senior as an economist,

Cotterill is one of the economists discovered by Professor Seligman. See "On Some Neglected British Economists," op. cit., and Part 1, chap. 3 below, p. 131, notes.

[1] Article in the *Quarterly Review* on McCulloch and Read, January 1831, Vol. XLIV, Art. 1, pp. 1–52, and expanded in his *Principles*, 1833, chaps. 8 and 9.

[2] *Quarterly Review*, January 1831, Art. 1, pp. 31–2. Also included in the *Principles*, pp. 87–9, first edition.

and apparently derived moral support from finding a considerable measure of agreement with him on points on which he differed from the strict Ricardians. For instance, he says, "we were gratified to find this able writer agreeing with us on several of the points in which we have ventured to differ most widely from the prevailing opinions," and he remarked with obvious regret that "even Senior" agreed with Ricardo, McCulloch, etc., on rent.[1]

It is tempting to think that Senior started a utility tradition at Oxford during his first tenure of the Drummond Chair, for after Whately gave it up to become Archbishop of Dublin in 1831, it was occupied by William Forster Lloyd, an utility theorist of importance.[2] Lloyd expounded the theory of marginal utility, in his solitary remaining lecture on value, with the greatest clarity and with more precision than Senior. In it he explained that—

"An increase of quantity will at length exhaust, or satisfy to the utmost, the demand for any specific object of desire."

and further on,

"In its ultimate sense, [value] undoubtedly signifies a feeling of the mind, which shows itself always at the margin of separation between satisfied and unsatisfied wants."[3]

Lloyd's lecture was published in 1834, two years before Senior's appeared in the *Political Economy*. Unless, therefore, Lloyd had had access to them before publication in some way or another it is difficult to see how he could have been influenced by Senior. But passages in Lloyd's lecture on value are so like parallel passages on the variability of wants as a basis of the desire for wealth, and on the decreasing

[1] *Quarterly Review*, November 1831, Art. IV, p. 81, note *. The points in question were the harmful effects of the export of food from a poor country to pay rents to absentee landlords, the distinction between wealth and welfare and the paramount importance of the sufficiency of food.

[2] Cf. "On Some Neglected British Economists," *Economic Journal*, XIII, 1903, pp. 335 et seq., and 511 et seq., reprinted in *Essays in Economics*, 1925, chap. 3. Lloyd is probably the most important of the discoveries made by Professor Seligman in his search for the origin of the utility theory.

[3] *Lecture on the Notion of Value*, 1833, published 1834, pp. 9 and 16.

significance of a commodity as its supply increases, in Senior's manuscript lectures,[1] that it is almost impossible to believe that Lloyd did not know Senior's work. The matter cannot be settled, but it is not unreasonable to conjecture that Lloyd, who was lecturing on mathematics at Christ Church, Oxford, in 1824, knew Senior, and either saw the original lectures or heard what was in them in the same way as Whately appears to have done.[2]

Whether Lloyd evolved his ideas on value independently or not, there is no doubt that Montifort Longfield's explanation of both the marginal utility and marginal productivity analyses was worked out independently.[3] Longfield's application of the marginal analysis was far more complete than either Senior's or Lloyd's, but for all that Senior never referred to him on the subject of value in the later editions of the *Political Economy*, or in his lectures 1847–52. In Ireland, however, Longfield bid fair to set up a distinctive school of economists, for his immediate successor in the Whately Chair, Isaac Butt, deliberately accepted his analysis. Butt, however, was no mere plagiarist. He attempted to work the marginal productivity theory out in detail to explain the imputation of the value of a product to the various factors of production jointly used to make it.[4] It is significant to notice that Butt considered that Say, Longfield and

---

[1] For Senior on value see above, pp. 93 et seq. Lloyd's *Lecture on the Notion of Value*, pp. 7–10.

[2] *Dictionary of National Biography*.

[3] Longfield, *Lectures on Political Economy*, 1833, published 1834, reprinted in the London School of Economics Series of Scarce Tracts in Economics and Political Science, Lectures VI, IX, and X. It is obvious that Senior and Longfield must have met some time while Whately was Archbishop of Dublin, but there are no remaining signs of any correspondence. That Senior knew of the Lectures is proved by their mention in a letter from Whately to him (January 11, 1834), in which the latter says that he did not hear them delivered but that they are about to be published. Senior's only reference to Longfield is to his *Lectures on Commerce and Absenteeism* in the discussion of the effects of absenteeism on wages. *Political Economy*, p. 161.

[4] *Lectures on Rent, Profits and Labour*, 1837, published 1838, pp. 21–32. Butt remarks truly enough that the marginal productivity theory of wages and profits "seems obvious and simple enough, but until the appearance of Dr. Longfield's Lectures it was not thought of" (p. 23). For an account of Butt see Seligman, op. cit. Butt is among Professor Seligman's discoveries.

Senior were the most important writers on economics to study, and that he did not mention Ricardo in this connection.[1]

For published appreciation of his own contribution to value theory in England, Senior had to wait for Banfield's 1844 lectures at Cambridge, published in 1845.[2] These lectures were given in order to inform Cambridge economists of recent developments of economic theory on the Continent. For some reason or other Banfield was particularly well acquainted with the work of foreign economists; he seems to have been the first English economist to mention Von Thünen, and the only one besides Senior to have read Hermann. As was to be expected in lectures of this type, economic theory was approached from the side of demand. Banfield referred in the Preface to the enormous change made in economics by the subjective theory of value "which demands of producers at least as much attention to the physical and mental improvement of their consuming fellow-citizens as to the mechanical operations" of production. He also suggested that wages will depend on "the utility of the instrument of which a man understands the use." In the actual lectures the main stress was laid on the essential relativity and intensity of wants as the whole basis of economics as a science, and he discussed the nature, gradation and relativity of wants, thus of the utility of goods and services which satisfy them. For the details of the discussion of this aspect of economics he referred to Say, Storch, Senior, Rossi and Hermann. He took particular pains to point out the close affinity between Senior's position and that of the continental economists, quoting appreciatively Senior's classification of wants, and awarding to him the credit for disposing finally of the cost of production theory of value and clearing up the confusion on the nature of utility. He himself went a little further by denying that

[1] *Introductory Lecture*, 1837, published 1837, note viii, p. 66.
[2] Published under the title of *The Organization of Industry*, 1845. Senior only referred to Banfield twice in his later lectures and then not to his remarks on value, i.e. 1847–52, Course II, lecture 3, reference to Banfield's definition of capital; Course III, lecture 2, reference to Banfield's description of rents outside Brussels in his *Letters to Sir Robert Peel*.

there is any distinction between the concepts of value in use and value in exchange.[1]

Although Banfield was by no means an original economist, or a first-class interpreter of other people's ideas, he did succeed in grasping the connection between a demand or utility theory of value and the pricing of factors of production. He realized that much of the obscurities of Ricardo were due to lack of treatment of this aspect.

Between Banfield and Jevons there was a long and dreary gap in the development of the theory of value in England, and no one took any notice of Senior's theory. Although Longe and Thornton must be included among the Dissenters, their contributions were confined to the analysis of the demand for labour, and they added little to the general theory *per se*.[2] But it is perhaps of some significance that questions of wages were frequently introduced at the Political Economy Club, and that Ricardo's statement that wages and profits varied inversely was attacked by Bailey, Read, Scrope, Longfield and Banfield.[3] The question of wages was in fact recognized by all the Dissenters as one of the crucial problems to be resolved by a satisfactory theory of value.

V

Although the British writers on theory who attempted to resolve the obscurities generated by Ricardo and Say's opposing conclusions were few in number and small in volume of output, they gain enormously in significance from their parallelism with continental writers of the same period. Senior's attempt to reconcile Ricardo and Say in particular, important though it is in the interpretation

[1] Banfield, *The Organization of Industry*, Preface, pp. 1–2, 6. Lecture 1 and particularly the end of Lecture 3.

[2] Francis D. Longe, *Refutation of the Wage Fund Theory*, 1866. W. T. Thornton, *On Labour, its Wrongful Claims and Rightful Dues*, 1869. H. D. Macleod must be mentioned as an upholder of the utility analysis or as a vigorous critic of Ricardo and J. S. Mill (*Elements of Political Economy*, 1858, chap. 2). He did not, however, make any new contribution of importance in this field.

[3] Bailey, op. cit., chap. 4. Read, op. cit., Bk. II, chap. 6, sect. 2. Scrope, *Quarterly Review*, January 1831, Art. 1, and *Principles*, 1833, chap. 7. Longfield, op. cit., Lecture IX, pp. 182–6 of L.S.E. reprint. Banfield, op. cit., p. 31.

of the work of his English contemporaries, becomes still more so by a comparison with German developments of theory.[1] No effort to estimate his place in the general evolution of the theory of value would be complete without a brief reference to this aspect, for not merely had he much in common with them, but was considerably interested in and influenced by their work.[2]

In Germany in the second and third quarters of the nineteenth century, three theorists, Hermann, von Thünen and von Mangoldt, stand out as exponents of the German tradition of analysis before it became submerged by the Historical School. This tradition was based primarily on Say's interpretation of the *Wealth of Nations*, but a considerable amount of clarification and development of the utility theory had already been carried out by their predecessors. By 1813, for instance, Hüfeland,[3] drawing mainly on the work of Say and Lauderdale, had evolved a pure subjective and psychological theory of value, and had introduced the idea of rent of talents. In many ways his treatment of the relation between the subjective valuations of utility and the cost of production was superior to Say's. As a result Hermann, in reviewing Senior's *Political Economy* in 1836, was able to claim that many of Senior's conclusions in the discussion of value were already accepted as a matter of course in Germany.[4] Hermann himself had reached much the same position as Senior on the general theory of value, and stated

[1] For an account of the interconnection between British and French economics in the post-Ricardian period see above, Sect. II and Sect. IV particularly.

[2] The only German economist mentioned by Senior in his Appendix to Whately's *Logic* (1826) is Storch. It was probably from Storch's *Cours d'Économie Politique* that Senior got the idea of generalizing rent. See chap. 3 below. Between 1826 and 1847–52 Senior became acquainted with the work of Hermann (*Staatswirtschaftliche Untersuchungen*) and of Rau (*Grundsätze der Volkswirthschaftslehre*). In both of these he must have read of von Thünen's *Isolirte Staat* and he explained that he derived a general knowledge of German economists from Rau. Lectures, 1847–52, Course II, lecture 2.

[3] *Neue Grundlegung der Staatswirthschaftskunst*, 1807–13 Other early German economists worked on lines similar to Hüfeland, such as Fulda, Von Soden, Sartorius, Lotz. See Schumpeter, *Dogmen- und Methodengeschichte*, Part III, "Das klassische System."

[4] *Gelehrte Anzeigen*, Munich, 1836.

his results with much more decision and clarity.[1] He welcomed Senior's work as the first attempt in England to develop Ricardo's theory of value, and bring it into line with continental thought. Actually, despite the remarkable similarity between their respective syntheses of the theories of Ricardo and Say, there were important differences in the theory of imputation which show the greater influence of Ricardo on Senior. Hermann in fact made no attempt to deal with the theory of ultimate stationary equilibrium. Where Senior emphasized the abstinence aspect of capital and the real sacrifice of labour, Hermann propounded the "Use" theory of interest and a productivity theory of wages.[2] But Senior's attempt to explain the relation of wages to capital met with some appreciation from Hermann in the review of the *Political Economy*, though the latter did not really tackle the problem himself. The greatest difference between them was in their treatments of rent: Hermann considered rent as essentially the income of factors which happened to be immobile, though he approved of Senior's generalization of it to rents of opportunity and talent.[3] He insisted rather obscurely that rent is closely similar to interest and enters into cost, without explaining the time period to which he was referring, and criticized Senior for his retention of the real cost distinction between the two categories.[4] A more detailed discussion of their treatments of special problems will be taken up in subsequent chapters, all that is necessary to point out here is the very considerable degree of similarity between their attempts to deal with Ricardo and Say's teaching in the narrower field of value theory, at approximately the same date.

The publication in 1850 of the second part of von Thünen's *Der Isolirte Staat* containing a general statement of the theory of marginal productivity is another interesting

[1] *Staatswirtschaftliche Untersuchungen*, first edition, 1832, chap. 4.

[2] Ibid., chap. 3, "Vom Kapital," chap. 5, "Vom Gewinn" and chap. 6, "Vom Kapital."

[3] *Gelehrte Anzeigen*, op. cit.

[4] *Staatswirtschaftliche Untersuchungen*, chap. 5, sects. 1 and 2, and *Gelehrte Anzeigen*. It was largely as a result of these criticisms in the review that Senior changed his definitions of capital. Lectures, 1847–52, Course II, lecture 2.

sign of the general movement. Von Thünen's struggles
with the theory of wages show that, in common with English
writers, he found great difficulty in elucidating the relation
of labour to capital.[1] He also accepted the extension of the
rent analysis to capital, but emphasized the temporary
durability of many forms of fixed capital.[2]

Another and most important ramification of the same
tendency is found in von Mangoldt's essay on Profits, in
which a complete and detailed theory of profits is based on
the rent analysis.[3] It is in his *Grundriss*, however, that the
most striking confirmation of what I have called the evolu-
tionary interpretation of the history of economic theory is
to be found. The *Grundriss* was written as a short introduction
to the standard German text-books, such as Roscher's and
Rau's, and was not therefore meant to be the vehicle of new
ideas.[4] It contains, nevertheless, not merely a perfectly
clear treatment of utility and the cost of production in
relation to value, but also a brief and explicit statement of
the derivation of the values of factors from their marginal
productivities.[5] Still further, von Mangoldt was perfectly
clear as to the relation between the real cost analysis of
Ricardo in the long period and the shorter period analysis
of Hermann and Say.[6]

Against this background it is surely not far-fetched to
suggest that Gossen's[7] statement of the law of diminishing
marginal utility in 1854 was a brilliant, but not surprising,
interpretation of the ideas generally current at that time.[8]

---

[1] *Der Isolirte Staat*, Part II, 1850, pp. 10 and 11 and 162–93. The whole of
Part II centres on the problems of wages.

[2] Ibid., Part I, pp. 14–20, second edition, 1842. This part was first published
in 1826 and may have influenced Hermann's belief as to the common characteristics of land and fixed capital. Cf. chap. 4, pp. 152–6 below.

[3] *Lehre vom Unternehmergewinn*, 1855.

[4] *Grundriss der Volkswirthschaftslehre (Ein Leitfaden für Vorlesungen an Hoch-
schulen und für das Privatstudium)*, first edition, 1863, Preface.

[5] Ibid., Bk. III, chap. 3, sect. i; Bk. IV, chap. 3, pp. 117 and 131.

[6] Ibid., Bk. IV, chap. 1, pp. 93–5; chap. 3, pp. 101–2; Bk. III, chap. 3, sect. i.

[7] Gossen, *Entwickelung der Gesetze des Menschlichen Verkehrs*, 1854.

[8] Among the German economists who had clear ideas on utility, though
they added nothing new, were Hildebrand and Knies. See Carl Diehl,
Entwicklung der Wert- und Preistheorie im 19 Jahrhundert in *Entwicklung der Deutschen
Volkswirtschaftslehre*, edited by Schmoller, Part I, 1908.

VI

If the preceding brief outline of the work of economists between Ricardo and Jevons is correct, the picturesque view of the rise, ascendancy and fall of the dictatorship of the classics must be abandoned or modified. From the point of view of the popular interpreters of economics this of course is not so, but that is irrelevant to the argument put forward in this chapter. No one will deny that the orthodox school in England, and the optimists in France, were supremely successful in keeping in the public eye, but that is not the criterion by which the importance of developments in theory can be judged. The question of how far the work of Jevons, Menger and Walras really constituted a breach with that of their predecessors is the relevant one, whether we are to attach more importance to their acknowledged forerunners than to accidental shots in the dark. It seems to me that the opinion here put forward is at least plausible: that the five decades after Ricardo's death witnessed an attempt on the part of numerous economists to solve the paradox arising from the French and Ricardian schools each believing themselves to be right, but unable to prove the other wrong. The widespread character of this search for a way out of the jungle of conflicting theories of value seems to me to make it more impressive than if it had been limited to a compact body of economists led by one pioneer. Much the same difficulties were reached and partially solved in very similar ways by writers who, though they frequently knew each other's work, were by no means each other's pupils.

In this work Senior was the outstanding figure in England, and it is only by regarding him from this aspect that it is possible to appreciate both the successes and failures of his theories. The rigid classical bigot of history books, the "also ran" in the history of theory, the tiresome, rather dilettante critic that he appeared to some people, is seen in a new light as an important figure in the evolution of modern economic theory.

This attitude towards the economists of the intermediate

period, 1825–72, in no way detracts from the brilliance of the achievements of the trio Jevons, Menger and Walras. They, after all, finally recognized and gave unity to the solutions which the scattered bands of their predecessors had indicated.

BIBLIOGRAPHICAL NOTE ON SENIOR'S THEORY OF VALUE

In the Lectures, 1826–30, Senior developed the theory of value which he held, as far as is known, for the rest of his life. Course 1, lectures 2 and 3, on the "Nature of Wealth" and the "Nature of Value," respectively, are exactly the same as in the *Political Economy*, pp. 6–22, except for the omission of some examples. Course 111, lectures 1, 2 and 3, "On the Cost of Production," "On Price where Competition is Unequal," "General Laws of Price continued," respectively, are exactly the same as the *Political Economy*, pp. 95–118, except for the omission of one example. In 1847–52 Senior's statement of the theory of value was definitely inferior to this earlier statement. The lecture on the Universal Desire for Wealth, Course 1, lecture 5, is a rambling recapitulation of pp. 27–9 of the *Political Economy*, while the whole of the rest of the theory of value was squashed into two lectures (Course IV, lectures 6 and 7) and lost both in clarity of statement and arrangement. In particular: the explanation of diminishing marginal utility was omitted from the discussion of limitation of supply; monopolies were classified in a bewildering number of sub-divisions which add nothing new, and for no apparent reason he included one new division covering cases in which "the producer who strains his powers finds them gradually diminish," a case which, if a case of monopoly at all, belongs to the class of diminishing returns. These lectures also omit any discussion of the rarity of cases of perfect competition. The only interesting theoretical discussion in either of these lectures is that of the tendencies of economies of large-scale production to increase the size of the firm (see below, Part 1, chap. 3, p. 123, note 1). It is one of the most amazing things in S. Leon Levy's editing of Senior's papers that he took the whole of his chapters (op. cit., Vol. 11, Part VI, chap. 1, and chap. 3, sect. 3) on Senior's theory of value from these two very inferior lectures, which can only be explained away by suggesting that Senior wrote them when he was either bored or in a great hurry.

CHAPTER 3

POPULATION AND RENT

THE connection between the theories of population and rent in Ricardo's analysis of stationary equilibrium were at once the basis of its completeness and the origin of its most insidious weakness. The theory of wages based on the law of population was essentially applicable only to the very long run and, therefore, converted his equilibrium analysis into an analysis of secular tendencies towards a stationary state—an analysis really involving complicated assumptions about the speeds of reaction of economic phenomena. Interest in Ricardo's stationary analysis thus depended on a belief in the theory of population and naturally disappeared as soon as that theory was abandoned; the importance of the analysis of stationary equilibrium was recognized again only when the concept was redefined in the last three decades of the century.

The comparative indifference to population problems on the Continent thus naturally, but illogically, involved indifference to the Ricardian treatment of rent. As soon, however, as certain German economists such as Hüfeland, Storch, Hermann and von Mangoldt realized that the concept of rent could be generalized to explain other income than that from land, it became one of their most important analytical tools.[1] Just the opposite tendency was apparent in England. The attraction of the rent analysis waned with the influence of Malthus at the very time that the possibilities of extending the category of land were being realized by Bailey, Senior and Whately.

The arrangement of the discussion of population, variable returns and rent in Senior's *Political Economy* is typical of his

---

[1] Storch, *Cours d'Économie Politique*, 1815; Hüfeland, *Neue Grundlegung der Staatswirtschaftskunst*, 1807–13, first edition; Hermann, *Staatswirtschaftliche Untersuchungen*, 1832; von Mangoldt, *Lehre vom Unternehmergewinn*, 1855.

In France still less interest was exhibited in rent analysis of any sort, and with the exception of Bastiat's attempt to disprove the Ricardian theory nothing of importance was written on it.

"betwixt and between" position between Ricardo and the continental economists. Population is dealt with and dismissed by the development of the second fundamental proposition, variable returns further on in the development of the fourth, and rent quite separately in the second part of the book devoted to distribution.[1] Population problems, in Senior's opinion, were separate from the rest of economic theory, just because, like Say, he never really thought the Ricardian connection of the law of population with stationary equilibrium of much interest, for the excellent reason that he had not much faith in that law.

I

The publication of the two lectures on population and the correspondence with Malthus[2] first attracted attention to the heterodoxy of Senior's attitude to the population question. The main thesis of the lectures, which reappeared in the *Political Economy*, was that the desire of man to better his position in the world was at least as important as the sexual desires. In stating his thesis Senior realized that he was flying in the face of orthodoxy:

"But I must admit that this is not the received opinion. The popular doctrine certainly is that population has a tendency to increase beyond the means of subsistence, or, in other words, that, whatever be the existing means of subsistence, population

---

[1] *Political Economy*—"Population," pp. 29–50; "Variable Returns," pp. 81–6; "Rent," pp. 88–140; "Rent of Land," pp. 105–11 and 115–19. The differences between the *Political Economy* and the lectures of 1826–30 are as follows: Population—the treatment in the *Political Economy* included an account of the correspondence with Malthus. Rent—the discussion on pp. 88–95 was not in the lectures, pp. 95–118 are word for word the same as Course III, lectures 1–3, pp. 118–40 are not among the remaining lectures, but, according to Levy, Course IV included two lectures on "Rent, Profit and Wages," which might tally with these pages. *Senior's Industrial Efficiency, etc.*, Vol. II, p. 377. In any case, the most important discussion in these pages is that of the problems of classification of different types of income, and that was already published in brief in Senior's Appendix to Whately's *Logic*, 1826, pp. 389–96 and especially p. 393, fifth edition. See note 1, p. 128, below and Bibliographical Appendix.

[2] *Two Lectures on Population, to which is added a correspondence between the author and the Rev. T. R. Malthus*, published 1829.

has a tendency fully to come up with them, and even to struggle to pass beyond them, and is kept back principally by the vice and misery which that struggle occasions. I admit that population has the power (considered abstractedly) so to increase, and I admit that, under the influence of unwise institutions, that power may be exercised, and the amount of subsistence bear a smaller proportion than before to the number of people; and that vice and misery, more or less intense and diffused, according to the circumstances of each case, must be the result. What I deny is, that, under wise institutions, there is any tendency to this state of things. I believe the tendency to be just the reverse."[1]

In the *Political Economy* this paragraph was omitted and he contented himself with remarking that:

"If it be conceded that there exists in the human race a natural tendency to advance from barbarism to civilization, and that the means of subsistence are proportionably more abundant in a civilized than in a savage state, and neither of these propositions can be denied, it must follow that there is a natural tendency in subsistence to increase in a greater ratio than population."[2]

But Senior was far from thinking that an unlimited increase in population was a good thing, even if subsistence kept up:

"But although we believe that, as civilization advances, the pressure of population on subsistence is a decreasing evil, we are far from denying the prevalence of this pressure in all long-settled countries; . . . We believe that there are few portions of Europe the inhabitants of which would not now be richer if their numbers were fewer, and would not be richer hereafter if they were now to retard the rate at which their population is increasing."[3]

Malthus' exposition of the Law of Population was, Senior argued, incomplete, since he stated that there was a constant tendency for population to increase faster than subsistence in the absence of either the positive or negative checks, as though this in fact happened. Whereas, according

[1] *Two Lectures on Population, etc.*, pp. 35–6.
[2] *Political Economy*, p. 48.
[3] Ibid., p. 42.

to Senior, he should have said that this tendency was opposed by the opposite tendency of man to try and better his position:

"You would still say, that in the absence of disturbing causes, population has a tendency to increase faster than food, because the comparative increase of the former is a mere compliance with our natural wishes, the comparative increase of the latter is all effort and self-denial. I should still say, that, in the absence of disturbing causes, food has a tendency to increase faster than population, because, in fact, it has generally done so, and because I consider the desire of bettering our condition as natural a wish as the desire for marriage."[1]

Senior went as far as to declare that it was almost as true that subsistence tended to increase as fast as or faster than population, as the reverse. Although Whately tried to pour oil on the troubled waters by suggesting that the difference of opinion was due to difference in the meaning attached to the word tendency, the source of the dispute was really more fundamental.[2] Despite Senior's statement in the correspondence (after Malthus had admitted agreement with his explanation) that he and Malthus were in complete agreement, it is pretty obvious on examination of it that they were not.[3] After further reflection, Senior remarked in the *Political Economy* that certain passages in the last edition of the *Essay on Population* were inconsistent with Malthus' letters to him:

"Mr. Malthus's opinions appear to have been considerably modified in the course of his long and brilliant philosophical career. In the first edition of his great work, the principle of

[1] *Two Lectures on Population, etc.*, p. 58: Letter from Senior to Malthus, March 15, 1829.

[2] Whately, *Lectures on Political Economy*, Lecture IX, pp. 248–50, 2nd edition, referred to by Senior, *Political Economy*, p. 47.

[3] *Two Lectures on Population, etc.*, pp. 82–90: Letters from Malthus to Senior, March 31, 1829, and Senior to Malthus, April 9, 1829. It is obvious from these letters that Malthus was not really convinced; in his letter to Senior he asserts that if the Corn Laws were repealed and the price of food fell, population might be expected to increase suddenly and rapidly up to the margin of subsistence, unless some important institutional change took place. This is the purest milk of the extreme doctrine.

population was represented as an insurmountable obstacle to the permanent welfare of the mass of mankind. And even in the last edition, the following passages are open to the same construction; . . .

"But when the opposite doctrine, namely, that, in the absence of disturbing causes, subsistence is likely to increase more rapidly than population, was brought before him by Mr. Senior, he appears to have disavowed, we will not say his former expressions, but the inferences to which they lead."[1]

Though he was willing to credit Malthus with the latter opinion, and also James Mill and McCulloch, he considered that the extreme way in which they expressed their opinions was misleading to the general public and dangerous to the cause of reform.[2]

Dr. Bonar is scarcely fair to Senior when, referring to this dispute, he triumphantly announces that Senior withdrew from his original position admitting that he had misunderstood Malthus.[3] In the light of the passage quoted above from the *Political Economy*, and still more of a passage in the 1847–52 lectures, it is clear that this admission was due partly to a belief that Malthus did agree with him, and partly to a desire to do justice to his distinguished and generally maligned adversary. In the later lectures he roundly asserted that Malthus adhered to his fatalist pessimism throughout his life:

"In fact Mr. Malthus's views were to the end somewhat exaggerated and somewhat distorted by the train of thought which originally suggested them."

And he added further on:

"So exclusively indeed was Malthus's attention fixed on Vice and Misery as the checks to population that it was not until his

[1] *Political Economy*, pp. 45 and 46.

[2] Ibid., pp. 49–50. In the letters Senior expressed himself more forcibly on this point, saying that extreme statements of the Malthusian theory by reputable economists had been made into "the stalking-horse of negligence and injustice, the favourite objection to every project for rendering the resources of the country more productive." Letter from Senior to Malthus, April 9, 1829, *Two Lectures on Population, etc.*, p. 89.

[3] *Malthus and his Work*, second edition, 1924, pp. 3–4.

work had passed through more than one edition that he introduced among those checks, moral restraint."[1]

There was in fact a real difference in outlook which no
amount of beating about the bush could conceal. Senior
was really of the opinion that the progress of the human
race was due to an inherent strain of ambition which,
given reasonably favourable circumstances, was sufficient
to maintain subsistence at least on a level with population.
Drawing on his knowledge of Irish conditions, he contrasted
the results of the lack of this ambition with its presence by
comparing Irish and English standards of living. Nor was
he prepared to agree that the difference was due to a difference in prudence or foresight between the two races, but
insisted that it was the effect of centuries of misrule and a
vicious system of land-tenure which had killed all ambition
among the Irish.[2] In short, he thought that a satisfactory
solution to the population problem is only possible when
racial characteristics and social institutions give full play
to the natural ambition of man.

Senior's cheerfulness as to the future of the human race
was considerably reinforced by his interpretation of the laws
of variable returns in industry and agriculture.

The fourth Proposition on which economics is founded is,
according to Senior, that "additional labour when applied
in manufactures is *more*, when applied in agriculture is *less*,
efficient in proportion."[3] His usual search for precision led
him to expose the false parallelism between the two parts
of the statement. He pointed out that economists, in discussing increasing returns in manufactures, tacitly assume
that the raw materials are increased in proportion to the
finished product. The increased returns to labour, etc.,
however, are due, he pointed out, not to producing more
from the same physical source, for that is not possible
except within narrow limits, but to the economies of large-
scale production by which an increase of labour in the

---

[1] Lectures, 1847–52, Course III, lecture 4.

[2] *Letter to Lord Howick on a legal provision for the Irish Poor*, 1831, pp. 43–4.
See Appendix 1 below.

[3] *Political Economy*, pp. 81–6. Quotation from p. 81.

same proportion as the raw materials is rendered unnecessary. If the amount of raw material is kept constant the application of increased labour and capital must result in rapidly vanishing returns. In agriculture, on the other hand, increased quantities of labour and capital are applied to the same quantity of the raw material, land. It is obvious that the increased product which results, though after a point in decreasing proportion, is caused not by the economies of large-scale production, which are very limited in agriculture, but by the superiority of land in this respect compared to any other raw material. He summarized the correct version of the proposition as follows:

"The advantage possessed by land in repaying increased labour, though employed on the same materials, with a constantly increasing produce, is overbalanced by the diminishing proportion which the increase of the produce generally bears to the increase of the labour. And the disadvantage of manufactures in requiring for every increase of produce an equal increase of materials, is overbalanced by the constantly increasing facility with which the increased quantity of materials is worked up."[1]

Senior admitted two exceptions to decreasing returns in agriculture, improvements in methods of land tenure and in skill in production:—

"But the proposition that we have been endeavouring to

[1] *Political Economy*, p. 83. Senior expanded this line of thought a little in the 1847–52 lectures, Course IV, lecture 7, where he gave an excellent account of the tendency for the economies of large-scale production to lead to cutthroat competition and the concentration of output on a comparatively small number of large firms. He concluded by saying: "I believe that there is no great manufacture in which more sales do not take place below the cost of production (including in the cost of production average remuneration for the abstinence of the capitalists, or, in other words, average profits) than above it." For this reason he said the price of manufactured goods is generally regulated by the cost of production of the manufacturer who enjoys the greatest productive advantages. (It must be assumed that Senior was still including overhead costs in costs of production.) The statement was not, of course, meant to apply to equilibrium conditions, but as a description of the actual situation in a highly competitive industry it gives as good an idea as any other generalization.

illustrate, though general, is not universal; it is subject to material exceptions. In the first place, the negligence or ignorance of the occupier or proprietor, or obstacles of ownership, often prevent for a long time particular portions of land from being subjected to the average degree of labour bestowed on land of equal capability. Increased labour, when at length bestowed on land so circumstanced, may fairly be expected to be as productive, indeed more productive, than the average of agricultural labour. . . .

"But the most important exception to the general rule takes place when increase of labour is accompanied by increase of skill. More efficient implements, a better rotation of crops, a greater division of labour, in short, improvements in the art of agriculture generally accompany the increase of agricultural labour. They always accompany that increase when it is accompanied by an increase of capital as well as of the population of a country; and they always counteract, and often outweigh the inferiority of diminished proportional powers of the soil to which they are applied."[1]

This belief that skill tended to increase in some sort of relation to population and capital, which is in such sharp contrast to the orthodox Malthusian doctrine, was not peculiar to Senior. It was stated in a more extreme way by Read and Scrope, who maintained that under good government this fortunate conjuncture always occurred.[2] Senior, however, qualified his statement by pointing out that it was beyond the bounds of belief that the powers of the soil would "increase geometrically for ever, whatever be the amount of labour employed on it." The apparent note of pessimism introduced by this admission was immediately counteracted in the next paragraph—

"On the other hand, every increase in the number of manufacturing labourers is accompanied, not merely by a corresponding, but by an increased productive power. . . . The only check by which we can predict that the progress of our manufactures will in time be retarded, is the increasing difficulty of importing materials and food. If the importation of raw produce could

---

[1] *Political Economy*, pp. 85–6.
[2] Read, *Natural Grounds of a Right to Vendible Property*, 1829, Bk. 1, chap. 10, sect. iv. Scrope, *Principles of Political Economy*, 1833, chap. 11.

keep pace with the power of working it up, there would be no limit to the increase of wealth and population."[1]

This sort of optimism with regard to manufacturing progress is the explanation of the general change of attitude on population problems which began to be noticeable in the 'thirties. However much the population increased the powers of manufacturing seemed to increase more rapidly, and with the latter, once free trade could be established, so would the power of importing food and materials. But this cheerful attitude was not the basic reason for Senior's opposition to Malthus, and he expressly said (referring to Scrope) that he did not belong to the group who believed

"that an increase of numbers is necessarily accompanied, not merely by a positive, but by a relative increase of productive power; that density of population is the cause and the test of prosperity; and that, 'were every nation under the sun to be released from all the natural and artificial checks on their increase, and to start off breeding at the fastest possible rate, many, very many generations must elapse before any necessary pressure could be felt.' "[2]

At the same time he admitted that wealth per head in most countries would probably be greater if population were smaller, and that it would increase more rapidly if population increased less rapidly in the future. This, however, is a very different thing from maintaining that the inherent characteristics of man were such as to prevent all progress.[3] To Senior it was much more the question of the optimum rate of progress rather than no progress at all that was involved in the population problem in civilized countries. On the whole he expected rent would be increased more by the general increase in wealth than by the resort to inferior land. The tendency of population in what he calls a highly civilized country is, he argued, to increase productivity in general, including that of labour applied to

[1] *Political Economy*, p. 86.　　　　　　[2] Ibid., p. 43.
[3] See p. 118 above and *Proceedings of the Political Economy Club*, J. L. Mallet's *Diaries* (p. 265), where Mallet, describing a debate, says that Senior and Tooke declared that subsistence was more likely to increase faster than population than vice versa.

agriculture, and to increase the absolute amount of rent rather than the relative share of the landlords. Nevertheless he maintained that this relative share would be less if population were smaller.[1] Evidently Senior very nearly discovered the optimum theory of population.[2]

II

Senior's generalization of the theory of rent is at once a justification of his own legal attention to problems of definition and classification and of the English real cost approach to value problems. He explained in introducing the section on distribution that it covered the question of how all that is produced is divided among the ultimate consumers, i.e. it deals with the laws which govern all exchanges as well as with those which apply specifically to those "exchanges in which the owners of the different productive instruments exchange specifically with one another the produce of those instruments."[3]

Although in treating the rent of land Senior accepted the ordinary account of its differential aspect,[4] he did not in fact derive rent solely from this characteristic. He maintained in opposition to Ricardo that rent might contain no differential element at all, since if land were all of the same quality and could only be cultivated at all by a fixed amount of labour and capital per acre, rent would still arise if all the land were occupied:

[1] *Political Economy*, pp. 138–9.

[2] During the second tenure of the Drummond Chair, 1847–52, Senior added nothing to his original theory of population. Although he devoted three lectures to the "Efficiency of Capital applied to Agriculture," and eight to population problems (Course iii, lectures 1–9, and Course iv, lectures 1 and 2), the only changes that he made were terminological, "destructive" instead of "positive" checks, and "prudence" instead of "moral restraint" (Course iii, lecture 4). He expanded the whole question with illustrations and laid great emphasis on the possibilities of colonization; he also drew attention to the elementary consideration which Malthus overlooked, that the destructive checks, war and disease, etc., checked production as well as population (Course iii, lecture 8).

[3] *Political Economy*, p. 88.

[4] Ibid., pp. 105–11 and 115–18.

"Again, he (Ricardo) has often spoken of the existence of rent as dependent on the cultivation of land of different degrees of fertility, or on the fact that the same land repays, with a proportionably smaller return, the application of additional capital. And yet it is clear that if we suppose the existence of a populous and opulent district of great but uniform fertility, giving a large return to a given expenditure of capital, but incapable of giving any return whatever on a less expenditure, or any greater return on a larger expenditure, such a district would afford a high rent, though every rood of land and every portion of capital applied to it would be equally productive."[1]

It is evident that Senior had either ignored transport costs, or made implicit assumptions as to the distribution of the population, but these objections do not invalidate his criticism of Ricardo who also usually ignored these considerations. Consistently with this illustration of scarcity rent, Senior defined rent as "all that nature or fortune bestows either without any exertion on the part of the recipient, or in addition to the average remuneration for the exercise of industry or the employment of capital."[2] Apart from this difference, or rather addition, which indicated his approach to the generalization of rents, Senior accepted the Ricardian theory, and defended it against Say's criticism.[3] He made, however, two protests in the interests of precision against Ricardo's method of exposition: that in insisting correctly that rent was the result of the niggardliness of nature, Ricardo had omitted to point out that rent could not exist at all if some land did not yield a surplus over the costs of cultivation; and that he gave the impression that the extension of cultivation caused a rise in rent instead of being the means of counteracting that rise.[4]

[1] *Political Economy*, p. 118. A similar proof of the possibility of pure scarcity rents was given by W. F. Lloyd. *Lecture on Rent*, published 1837, and another proof by Longfield, *Lectures on Political Economy*, Lecture 7, pp. 133-4 of the reprint in the London School of Economics series of reprints of scarce tracts in Economics and Political Science.

[2] *Political Economy*, p. 92. See note pp. 131-2 below.

[3] Ibid., pp. 116-17.

[4] Ibid., pp. 137-9, and p. 118. He added to the latter protest that "The inaccuracy is so obvious that we can scarcely suppose it to have misled any reader of tolerable care and acuteness."

Senior's love of classification led him to take up the suggestions made by other writers that the rent analysis had not been fully developed in the theory of distribution. The necessary preliminary step to any analysis of distribution was, he realized, to define the parties to that distribution exactly. The characteristic of the labourer, he said, was to labour and receive wages as reward for his labour, of the capitalist to abstain from present enjoyments and receive profits. On the other hand, the characteristic of the recipient of rent is to enjoy an income by virtue not of any sacrifice but of his ownership of property which is not the result of his sacrifice—most obviously the ownership of natural agents. Any income that is due to ownership of any sort not based on sacrifice falls under this head, which thus includes all income from institutionally or legally created property such as patent rights. By a simple process of elimination, therefore, Senior concluded that any income that does not correspond to a real sacrifice cannot be included in wages or profits but comes under rent. Since rent has a pure scarcity as distinct from a differential aspect, it covers all incomes derived from the possession of a useful quality, either uniform or differentiated, wh'ch is not generally accessible.[1] Senior explained the position reached by this process of definition as follows:

"The payment made by a manufacturer to a patentee, for the use of the privilege of using the patent process, is usually termed, in commercial language, a Rent; and under the same head must be ranked all the peculiar advantages of situation

---

[1] *Political Economy*, pp. 88–95. It is fairly obvious that the discussion on these pages was added for the sake of clarity to the earlier treatment in the lectures which was apparently contained in the first two lectures of Course IV (see note 1 on p. 118 above). The best account of these questions of classification is in Senior's Appendix to Whately's *Logic* (published 1826), pp. 389–96, quotation from p. 393, fifth edition, 1834. "In the classification of revenues, either Rent ought to have been omitted as a genus, or considered only as an anomalous interruption of the general uniformity of wages and profits, or all the accidental sources of revenue ought to have been included in one genus, of which the Rent of land would have formed the principal species." It seems probable that Senior's attention was attracted to this problem by Storch's treatment of rent in the *Cours d'Économie Politique*, Bk. III, which he mentioned in the Appendix.

or connection, and all extraordinary qualities of body and mind. The surplus revenue which they occasion beyond average wages and profits, is a revenue for which no additional sacrifice has been made. The proprietor of these advantages differs from a landlord only in the circumstance that he cannot in general let them out to be used by another, and must consequently either allow them to be useless or turn them to account himself. He is forced, therefore, always to employ on them his own industry, and generally his own capital, and receives not only rent, but wages and profit. If, therefore, the established division is adhered to, and all that is produced is to be divided into rent, profit, and wages . . . and if wages and profit are to be considered as the rewards of peculiar sacrifices, the former the remuneration for labour, and the latter for abstinence from immediate enjoyment, it is clear that under the term 'rent' must be included all that is obtained without any sacrifice.''[1]

Once this position had been reached the application of the rent analysis to certain types of income should have been plain sailing, but just here in the *Political Economy* Senior became extraordinarily timid in applying it. The elaborate classification of monopolies was of course based entirely on this method of definition, but it is noticeable that the actual exposition of the theory of rent was limited to the case of land. In the section headed "Relative Proportions of Rent, Profit, and Wages," his difficulties are more obvious. Rent once defined as "the revenue spontaneously offered by nature or accident" turned out to be extremely difficult to identify. He lost sight of the general theoretical aspect of the real cost concept by suggesting that all income from any form of property ought to be called rent, once it has passed by inheritance or gift out of the hands of the person who originally acquired it as the result of the sacrifice of labour or abstinence. The fact that this is not of any importance in relation to the total supplies of factors escaped his notice, as also the difficult problem of how far the maintenance of the source of income by its new owner by maintaining the capital intact should be regarded as a sacrifice. On the other hand he was quite

---

[1] *Political Economy*, pp. 91–2.

clear as to the nature of rent when he said that fortuitous
profits arising from short-period advantages, such as the
possession of war stores on the outbreak of war, are really
rents.[1] From a comparison of this passage together with
an earlier one on the effects of short-period fluctuations in
prices on the income from fixed capital and a later one on
the immobility of capital in general, it is evident that
Senior was attempting to find the distinction between
interest, quasi-rent and rent.[2] Unfortunately, however,
since he omitted to compare the effects of short-period
with long-period limitations of supply he never got the
matter cleared up, although he seems to have realized that
the time element is the key to the difficulty. Exactly analogous
problems arise in wage theory in connection with wages in
different occupations, but in dealing with them he never
so much as mentioned rent and relapsed into the Smithian
distinctions plus a paragraph on the immobility of labour
as a cause of differences in rates of wages.

It is noticeable among Senior's many omissions in the
discussion that he did not attempt to apply the marginal
side of the rent analysis to any case except that of land, nor
did he suggest that rent can ever enter into cost of production.
He had in fact got into magnificent confusion—he had
explained that rent is the income which accrues without
any sacrifice and is a result not a cause of price, but it
appears as an element indistinguishable in practice from
wages and profits. How then is it possible that it should not
in any way affect price? Senior never faced this question at
all; if he had he might have succeeded in elucidating the
connection between value-opportunity costs and physical-
opportunity costs. All we have to go upon in the *Political
Economy*, or for that matter anywhere in his writings, is
that where rent arises price "has a constant tendency to
coincide with the cost of production of that portion which
is continued to be produced at the greatest expense. . . .
The difference between the price and the cost of production is Rent."[3] And we know from the initial discussion

---

[1] *Political Economy*, pp. 128–30.
[2] Ibid., pp. 102, 219–20.   [3] Ibid., p. 115.

that cost includes no payment for rare abilities or natural agents, or even for such things as patents. Nor is it easy to reconcile Senior's analysis with his elaborate example of a watchmaker calculating the cost of production of a watch, and including in it interest on the capital invested in buying the land for his factory. Here we explicitly are told that rent enters into the price:

"There are few things of which the price seems to consist more exclusively of wages and profits than a watch; but if we trace it from the mine to the pocket of the purchaser, we shall be struck by the payment of rent (the invariable sign of the agency of some instrument not universally accessible) at every stage of its progress . . . [here follows a list of the number of stages at which rent was paid.] . . . The whole amount of all these different payments forms probably a very small portion of the value of the watch; . . . What remains consists of the wages of the workmen, and the profits of the capitalist who paid those wages in advance."[1]

It is not surprising that in the review of the *Political Economy* in the *Edinburgh Review* the innovations in the theory of rent were singled out for attack.[2] Senior was criticized

[1] *Political Economy*, p. 112.

[2] *Edinburgh Review*, October 1837, pp. 73–102. Even in England the extension of the rent concept was not altogether strange or unwelcome. Bailey had already extended it to wages in 1825 and still earlier Craig had extended it to the income from fixed capital, while C. F. Cotterill had taken up Senior's suggestion from the Appendix to Whately's *Logic* in 1831. (See Part 1, chap. 2, p. 106, note 3, and note 1 on p. 128 above.) Sir Travers Twiss, another of the holders of the Drummond Chair of Political Economy, mentioned the rent of machines as due to their immobility. *View of the Progress of Political Economy since the Sixteenth Century*, published 1847, p. 181. But the most thorough adopter of the rent analysis was Whately, who seized upon Senior's suggestion in the Appendix that rent was interruption of the tendencies to equalities of wages and profits. In a letter to Senior in reply to the latter's criticism of his treatment (in *Easy Lessons on Money Matters*, etc., first edition, 1835, chap. 10) of rent, hire and interest as belonging to the same class, he expounded the nature of rent as follows: ". . . about Rent being a certain bonus super-added by the bounty of nature, giving the land the power of *producing more than the support* of the cultivators, etc.—If land practically unlimited no rent; if limited rent paid, though but for a beach to dry nets on, etc. The question may be regarded as merely one of *convenience for teaching*. . . . You can judge whether the treatise—or a longer or fuller one—would have

on the ground that he introduced a new classification which he was unable to distinguish in real life from the old. This was not any more a criticism of the classification itself, as the reviewer seemed to think, than was Richard Jones' attack on the whole of the Ricardian theory of rent merely because economic rent is not always separable in fact from actual rent. Senior himself was quite clear about the analytical distinction between rent, wages and profits, though he admitted that it is inconvenient as they are generally mixed up. But the reviewer went further than this in criticizing the generalization of rent as such. Most of the objections raised are, however, due simply to the natural misunderstanding of Senior's use of the term "average" when he really meant modal rate of wages or profits. He also suggested that the whole difference between a Hindoo's wages and an English workman's ought to be called rent. This is a much more important criticism of the whole rent approach to distribution but has nothing to do with the sphere of application of the rent analysis as visualized by Senior.

By the time of his second tenure of the Drummond Chair (1847–52) Senior's views on rent had undergone a considerable modification as a result of Hermann's criticisms.

gained, or would not have lost, in clearness and simplicity, by taking in Rent as one of three heads. There it is noticed incidentally, as an occasional element in cost, yet enough is said, and I think clearly said, about it in proportion to the sale of the work. . . . The most natural course of proceeding therefore seems to be, to regard Labour and Abstinence as the moving *powers*, and all kinds and degrees of *monopoly*—natural and artificial—as a sort of *friction*, producing various degrees of disturbance; as when a body is moved through a resisting medium of various densities, and over a smooth or rough surface." (Senior MSS., no date.) Whately apparently agreed with Say that rent enters into the cost of production, for in some notes on the first edition of Senior's *Political Economy*, pp. 98–100, he wrote: "It seems to me that the natural price or cost of production of a commodity must remunerate every one who was necessary to its production; and if so both the landlord and the capitalist must be remunerated as well as the labourer." He also brought the matter up at the Political Economy Club by asking whether in writing a book on Political Economy it was "more convenient to treat rent as a separate source of revenue or as the effect of disturbing causes." June 1, 1843. *Proceedings of the Political Economy Club*, p. 55.
    Rather later John Stuart Mill accepted the generalization of rent to extra income due to favourable opportunities of production, talents, etc. He did not, however, seem to think that it threw any light on the theory of value. *Principles*, Bk. III, chap. 5, par. 4.

In his review of the *Political Economy* Hermann had approved of the generalization of the rent concept, but objected: that Senior did not emphasize the importance of the productivity or utility of the source of rent; that owing to his false distinction between land and capital he failed to explain changes in the value of capital; finally, that he was wrong in saying that rent did not enter into costs.[1] Hermann's own position on these points was not always clear. It is true that his general approach to distribution excluded any treatment of real costs as it was based entirely on value, as distinct from physical, productivity.[2] But he was not justified in saying that Senior had ignored this in his treatment of rent and monopoly. Senior, however, I think as a result of these criticisms, did emphasize the whole influence of productivity more in 1847 than earlier.[3]

Hermann's view of rent was essentially as a quasi-rent, the current return on fixed capital. Like Say he entirely ignored the difference between factors of production which are fixed in supply in the long run and those which are variable. In so far as he considered rent separately in the long run it was simply as the necessary payment for a productive service, and it seems likely that it was only in the long run that he considered it as entering into costs. He was not, however, explicit about this, and did not discuss it in criticizing Senior's definition of cost of production.

In 1847 Senior had accepted Hermann's point of view that land and capital were really the same genus, justifying this change for two reasons. He pointed out that they are not distinguishable in practice.[4] This difficulty in itself seemed an inadequate reason for the change as he had always been aware of it, and it is really his acceptance of the argument that the sole distinguishing feature of land is not its scarcity but its immobility through space that gives the clue to the change in attitude:

[1] *Gelehrte Anzeigen*, Munich, 1836.
[2] *Staatswirtschaftliche Untersuchungen*, chaps. 3–6.
[3] Lectures, 1847–52, Course II, lectures 4, 7–9.
[4] Ibid., Course II, lecture 2 ; see chap. 4, pp. 156 et seq. below.

"One of the most important peculiarities of Land is its immobility. . . .

"If, like all the other productive instruments and materials land could be transported to the places where it is wanted we should not, at least in the present state of the population of the world, have to complain of its limitation in quantity. . . . Its immobility limits the quantity accessible to the inhabitants of every district."[1]

Despite this Senior retained the distinction between rent and interest on the basis of the definition of costs, though he laid much greater emphasis on the generalization of the rent analysis than before, and expanded this aspect with numerous examples.[2] It becomes evident in these lectures that he thought it important in explaining phenomena of distribution and exchange arising from imperfect accessibility of factors of production.

Ultimately, therefore, the difference between Senior and Hermann was reduced to the former maintaining that in the last analysis the payment of rent was not a cost of production, while the latter maintained that it was. Senior gained from the real cost approach the appreciation of the fundamental distinction between the fixed and flexible supplies of factors in relation to costs in equilibrium, while Hermann was nearer to the appreciation of opportunity costs in terms of value.

The use of the rent analysis in Germany is of some interest. Hüfeland, one of the earliest exponents of the extension of rent to natural abilities, accepted the whole Ricardian analysis and agreed that rent had no connection with costs. He suggested that all rents were a peculiar type of profit, a surplus above whatever the necessary minimum price might be for any factor.[3] A more far-

---

[1] Lectures, 1847–52, Course III, lecture 1. This passage was originally in Course II, lecture 1, but in rearranging the lectures in an attempt to make a treatise out of them Senior altered its position. Cf. Part I, chap. 2, pp. 101–2 above.

[2] Ibid., Course II, lecture 2; Course II, lectures 8 and 9. For a discussion of the relation of the rent analysis to Senior's theory of capital, see chap. 4 below.

[3] *Neue Grundlegung der Staatswirthschaftskunst* (1807–13), Part IIIB, sect. 2. In und nach dem Tausche.

reaching generalization of the rent concept was made by Storch about the same time. Storch's treatment is not altogether satisfactory. He started by explaining that the entire payments for unusual abilities or talents are in the nature of rents, because they are not the rewards for any sacrifice or real cost. He went on, however, to treat all the income from capital as rent, only distinguishing at a later stage between the rent of fixed and of circulating capital respectively. The latter, he said, is really interest and must be sufficient to compensate the sacrifice involved in saving; it is this rent, or rather interest, which is the basis for comparing all other incomes from capital, since fixed capital gradually wears out and will only be replaced if the rent is at least equivalent to interest. In effect Storch sketched out a theory of quasi-rents and despite the confusion in exposition was much clearer on the whole question than any of the economists who borrowed the idea from him before von Mangoldt.[1] Hermann, as we have seen, appears to have considered rent as a cost under most circumstances, possibly deriving this from Say, or else from von Thünen's emphasis on immobility of land rather than its fixity in supply. Neither Say nor Hermann seems to have realized completely the significance of the differential element of rent in relation to costs. Von Mangoldt, as might have been expected, had refreshingly clear ideas on the subject of rent. Rent, he said, is always a surplus over costs, whether it is the rent of land, of natural abilities or of fixed capital, or entrepreneurial rent. It is only as fixed capital becomes circulating, or rather free, capital that the return on it has any relationship to the supply of capital to any particular employment, but at that stage the return on capital becomes interest, not rent. The only obscurity he left was in the connection between the rent of abilities and opportunity costs in the short run, and this may perhaps be generalized from his discussion of entrepreneurial rents.[2]

The generalization of the theory of rent depended in fact on two concepts which had only partially emerged in

---

[1] *Cours d'Économie Politique*, Bk. III, chaps. 5 and 8–13. See note 2 on p. 112 above. [2] *Grundriss der Volkswirthschaftslehre*, Bk. IV, chap. 3, sect. 4.

the period with which we are dealing: quasi-rents in relation to rent proper and value-opportunity costs compared to real or physical-opportunity costs. From the point of view of this chapter the fact that the attempts were made to fill the gap left in value theory by the absence of these concepts is of importance; it illustrates once more the existence of a continuous thread of development in economics after 1825, and the position of Senior in that process.[1]

[1] Marshall's indebtedness to these earlier efforts is obvious in his treatment of quasi-rent. He himself refers to Senior, John Stuart Mill, Hermann and von Mangoldt, laying particular stress on Senior's contribution: "Senior seemed on the point of perceiving that the key of the difficulty was held by the element of time: but here as elsewhere he contented himself with suggestions; he did not work them out." *Principles*, Bk. v, chap. 10, par. 3, note, p. 432, fifth edition.

CHAPTER 4

CAPITAL AND INTEREST

THE original abstinence theory of interest for which Senior is famous has long been recognized as the most complete of the classical theories, and under various names has become incorporated in the general corpus of economic theory. Nevertheless as soon as this same theory is considered in relation to the classical analysis it is regarded merely as the necessary missing link in the cost of production theory of value, and hence only significant as far as that theory is significant. The paradox of this situation has been overlooked for the simple reason that Senior's work has not been regarded as an attempt to build a system embodying the achievements of Say as well as Ricardo. But it would be really rather odd if the capital theory of one of the outstanding exponents of the utility approach served merely to complete a theory of value with which he disagreed, and, if this were the case, it would be impossible to explain why most later theories of capital have depended in some way on the idea of abstinence in Senior's *Political Economy*. It is evident that there must be some peculiar fascination in the abstinence theory which needs to be unearthed.[1] A little consideration of Senior's exposition shows that this attraction is connected with his development of the analysis of the role of time in economics which originated in Adam Smith's attempt to substantiate the labour theory of value.

Senior's later lectures, 1847–52, are of considerable interest in this connection since they show both his preoccupation with this rather than the ordinary cost aspect,[2]

---

[1] For the connection between Senior's interest in the wage-fund theory and his treatment of the time element in capital see next chapter, sect. iv.

[2] The original course of lectures (Lectures, 1826–30, Course II) which, according to S. Leon Levy (*Senior's Industrial Efficiency*, Vol. II, p. 377), dealt with capital and abstinence, is now missing, and the earliest statement of the theory left is that in the *Political Economy*, pp. 58–81, 1836. In the later Lectures, 1847–52, Course II, lectures 2–9, delivered in 1848–9, contains the

and Hermann's influence on him which led him to change his definition of capital. There can be little doubt that if Senior had realized his hope of publishing a complete treatise on economics the confusion over the real significance of his theory of capital would not have arisen.

I

By introducing capital into economics "under the wing," as Cannan puts it, of the division of labour, Adam Smith caused that preoccupation with the fact of the superior physical productivity of time-using processes of production which characterized Ricardo's treatment of capital. The realization of the benefits of the division of labour, Adam Smith observed, takes time; during that time the labourer must live. It is therefore necessary that someone should accumulate subsistence as a condition of production. These accumulations are the simplest form of capital[1]; machinery, tools, stocks of all sorts and human skill and knowledge are simply mere complicated forms.

According to Adam Smith's first treatment of capital in close connection with the labour theory of value, the accumulation made necessary by the time-using processes is realized in the indirect application of labour. Capital as such has therefore no claim to a special share of the product once the indirect labour is paid for, and derives its income simply from exploitation. The idea that saving involved a sacrifice of the same nature as labour was not considered at this stage. In the later and more extended treatment of capital, particularly in the sections on natural prices, both the simplicity and analytical clarity of the original discussion was lost. The time aspect of capital became more and more

whole of his later version, but the most complete summary of the distinction between productive and unproductive consumption in relation to capital is contained in Course I, lecture 8. *The Production of Wealth*, 1847, published 1849.

[1] *Wealth of Nations*, edited Cannan, Bk. I, chap. 6, Vol. I, pp. 49–50. The clearest statement of the function of capital as a fund of subsistence is contained, however, in the Introduction to Bk. II "Of the Nature, Accumulation, and Employment of Stock," Vol. I, pp. 258–60. (All page references are to Cannan's edition.)

buried under the enumeration of the different forms of capital, and appeared to be flatly contradicted by the exclusion of subsistence in the hands of the labourer from capital.[1] There were, however, certain suggestions scattered about the discussion that profits are the compensation for the real cost of accumulation, as well as a payment necessary to induce the capitalist to invest in certain lines of production. It was constantly explained that parsimony and frugality are necessary to the accumulation of capital, and Adam Smith seemed just on the point of explaining that this sacrifice must be compensated by profits, but never actually did so. It is true that he maintained that there is a minimum rate of return below which interest cannot fall without diminishing savings, but this he stated to be necessary to cover the risk of loss and the trouble involved in investment.[2] This analysis of capital, though clearly containing so much of fundamental importance, implicitly denied that capital was an independent source of productivity.

By taking up the labour theory of value Ricardo brought himself face to face with the questions of if, and how far, capital was to be admitted as a distinct factor of production. He could not get away with a mere description of the various forms of capital drawn from the commercial world, such as filled up so many discussions of the theory of capital.[3] He had to consider the problem of whether Adam Smith's original analysis of the nature of capital was correct, and, if so, how far that justified the denial of independent productivity to capital. In short, whether capital is simply accumulated labour or not. If this were answered in the negative, how was he to account for the apparent connection between the rate of interest and the total supply of capital? This connection was absolutely essential to the stationary state analysis, and could scarcely be explained on any other than a real cost basis. If there was a real cost basis to the

---

[1] *Wealth of Nations*, Bk. II, chap. I, Vol. I, pp. 261–8.

[2] Ibid., Bk. I, chap. 9. Cf. Part I, chap. 2, pp. 71–3 above, particularly p. 73, note I.

[3] Cf., for example, Say, Rossi, J. S. Mill, McCulloch, etc.

accumulation of capital, how could the denial of productivity with its concomitant of exploitation be persisted in?[1]

This fundamental tenet of the English School as to the flexibility of the supply of capital led to the most curious paradoxes in capital theory. The concept of stationary equilibrium necessitated the use of a functional connection between the return on capital and its total supply, that is, to a recognition of a real cost behind the accumulation of capital. At the same time the admission in the *Wealth of Nations* that the natural price of capital forms part of the costs of production was an incentive to treat it as reflecting a real cost to economists who were convinced, *a priori*, of the overwhelming importance of real costs as a whole. In consequence McCulloch and James Mill, after giving 'the devil his due' in reproducing the pure labour theory of value and the explanation of capital as simply accumulated labour, slid peacefully over to describing the physical productivity of capital, the stationary state analysis, the cost of production, and the importance of the accumulation of capital. Nevertheless, this did not prevent either of them from maintaining that the gross receipts of capital, i.e. profits and replacement, are merely the payment of past labour. McCulloch's blindness in this matter was so complete that he was ready to defend the thesis that the enhanced value of matured wine is entirely due to accumulated labour, against all critics.[2]

Considering all this it is not surprising to find that, though the theories of value from which Say and McCulloch approached capital were poles apart, they were in tolerable agreement both on the question of what was to be included in capital, and in explaining interest by the actual productivity of capital and its scarcity.

Torrens and Malthus were at least considerably more clear-headed in frankly admitting a cost of production as

[1] Cf. Part I, chap. 2, pp. 81 et seq. above.

[2] James Mill, *Elements of Political Economy*, chap. 3. McCulloch, *Principles of Political Economy*, pp. 371–3, fourth edition. This inconsistency was pointed out with great vigour by Samuel Read, *Right to Vendible Property*, 1829, Bk. II, chap. 5, note on pp. 247–9, and by Scrope, *Quarterly Review*, January 1831, Art. I; and *Principles of Political Economy*, chap. 7.

distinct from a labour theory of value, but, as far as improving the idea of capital was concerned, they were no better than the others. They had, however, this advantage over continental writers, that they retained with emphasis the subsistence fund function of capital.[1]

By deliberately taking over the labour theory of value Ricardo was, however, in a different position to his disciples. They might, and would, copy his theories without very fundamental criticism, but he had to satisfy himself as to their validity. The difficulties arising from the existence of different capital structures of production obviously had to be dealt with. In the first edition they were admitted, but consideration of them deferred, but in the interval between the successive editions he seriously tried to resolve the problem of whether they involved the breakdown of the concept of capital simply as accumulated labour. The examination of the test case of wine in a cellar brought him to the conclusion that there is some other element besides accumulated labour[2] involved in capital. This extra element to be recognized is, he thought, waiting or time, and explains why goods made with the same amount of labour, direct and indirect, but having different capital structures, have different values. Profits are therefore in some sort paid for the productive service involved by the time factor. It became obvious to Ricardo that the solution to the problem of capital is connected with the length of waiting on the supply side and the productivity of waiting on the demand side.[3]

Senior's theory of capital was effectively the same as Ricardo's, only much more carefully elaborated; perhaps it

[1] Malthus, *Principles of Political Economy*, 1820, chap. 2, sect. 3. Torrens, *Essay on the Production of Wealth*, first edition, 1821, chap. 1, pp. 26–47.

[2] Letter to McCulloch, August 8, 1823. *Ricardo's Letters to McCulloch*, edited Hollander, 1895, p. 153. See also Part 1, chap. 2, p. 84 above.

[3] For a very charitable interpretation of Ricardo's capital theory see V. Edelberg, "The Ricardian Theory of Profits," *Economica*, February 1933. Jevons also believed that Ricardo had grasped the whole essence of the theory of capital. *Theory of Political Economy*, p. 221, third edition. Böhm-Bawerk characteristically could see so little virtue in Ricardo's treatment of capital that he classed it among the Colourless theories. *Capital and Interest*, pp. 87–96, Smart's translation.

would be more correct to say that he started just where Ricardo left off, and worked out the ideas contained in Ricardo's later admissions. The third fundamental proposition stated the observed premise, "That the powers of Labour, and of the other instruments which produce wealth, may be indefinitely increased by using their Products as the means of further Production." But the utilization of intermediate products involves a consideration of the means by which it can take place and leads naturally to an analysis of the factors of production. These Senior divided into two classes, primary and secondary; the former covers labour and natural agents, and the latter abstinence.[1]

In order to avoid any suggestion that the term labour can be extended to include capital, Senior defined it as "the voluntary exertion of bodily or mental faculties for the purpose of production," explaining that:

"Peculiar notions respecting the causes of value have, however, led some Economists to employ the term labour in senses so different from its common acceptation, that for some time to come it will be dangerous to use the word without explanation. We have already observed that many recent writers have considered value as solely dependent on labour. When pressed to explain how wine in a cellar, or an oak in its progress from a sapling to a tree, could, on this principle, increase in value, they replied that they considered the improvement of the wine and the growth of the tree as so much additional labour bestowed on each. We do not quite understand the meaning of this reply; but we have given a definition of labour, lest we should be supposed to include in it the unassisted operations of nature."

The second group of primary factors, natural agents, include "every productive agent, so far as it does not derive its powers from the act of man."[2]

These two agents alone do not, he declared, make possible the use of intermediate products to make further products. In order to take advantage of the roundabout method of production, the secondary instrument, abstinence, must be combined with the primary agents, since roundabout production takes time. Abstinence is defined

[1] *Political Economy*, pp. 26, 57–60.   [2] Ibid., p. 57.

to indicate the real cost of saving and the peculiar productive function of waiting, as follows, "a term by which we express the conduct of a person who either abstains from the unproductive use of what he can command, or designedly prefers the production of remote to that of immediate results."

Capital is the result of the combination of the primary and secondary factors, or in other words, of the application of current resources to future production. It is thus essentially a derived factor of production. Its ordinary definition, Senior pointed out, as "*an article of wealth, the result of human exertion, employed in the production or distribution of wealth,*" implies this complex nature.

"It is evident that Capital thus defined is not a simple productive instrument: it is in most cases the result of all the three productive instruments combined. Some natural agent must have afforded the material, some delay of enjoyment must in general have reserved it from unproductive use, and some labour must in general have been employed to prepare and preserve it. *By the word Abstinence, we wish to express that agent, distinct from labour and the agency of nature, the concurrence of which is necessary to the existence of capital, and which stands in the same relation to profit as labour does to wages.*"[1]

It is evident that Senior had at last succeeded in making explicit the underlying ideas of the Ricardian analysis of time. Capital is, according to this passage, neither labour nor land, nor any particular combination of them, but is the intermediate product which results from the application of their current uses to provision for the future by postponing present consumption. The productivity of capital is explained at the same time as originating in the release of current resources for making intermediate products by the same postponement of enjoyment; in short, the application of resources to remote ends makes roundabout methods of production possible.

Senior's claim to be considered the originator of the abstinence theory has been challenged by two authorities,

[1] *Political Economy*, pp. 58, 59. Senior's italics.

Allix and Opie, who have pressed the claims of Germain Garnier and Scrope respectively.[1] There is no doubt that each of these economists has some claim in this respect, but actual priority can only be proved in the case of Garnier, for Senior's lectures on abstinence were given, it appears from S. Leon Levy's account, in 1827–28, that is several years before Scrope's article in the *Quarterly Review* or his book (1833) was published.[2] In any case neither of them did much more than show that there was a real cost behind the accumulation of capital; they did not work out at all completely the mutual relation between the aspects of abstinence as a productive element in spreading productive resources through time, and as an influence limiting the supply of capital. If anyone has a more serious claim to be considered the originator of the abstinence theory than Senior, that person is Storch, who does not seem to have been considered in this connection.[3] Storch not only introduced abstinence as a factor influencing the supply of capital, but explained with great lucidity the connection between the total supply of capital and the respective supplies of fixed and circulating capital. He did not, however, explain the productive aspect of abstinence except by rather vague implication.

It is disappointing that with this excellent basis to start from Senior failed to give a really adequate account of the things of which capital consists—machinery, tools, buildings used for trade, etc., improvements of land, unsold stocks of any sort, materials, money, acquired skill and knowledge,

[1] For statements of the claims of these economists to be considered as the originators of the abstinence theory see W. Hasbach in Schmoller's *Jahrbuch für Gesetzgebung*, Vol. 29 (3), 1905, pp. 323–4, and E. Allix in the *Revue d'Histoire des Doctrines Économiques*, 1912, and R. Opie, "A Neglected British Economist," in the *Quarterly Journal of Economics*, 1930, pp. 101–37.

[2] Scrope, *Quarterly Review*, Art. 1, January 1831, p. 18, and *Principles of Political Economy*, 1833, chap. 7, pp. 148–54.

[3] For an account of Storch's treatment of capital see p. 154 below. It is possible to put forward a claim for Samuel Bailey as an anticipator of the theory, for he asserted that there is a natural preference for present to future goods of a like kind, adding: "Thus time is really a consideration which may influence both buyers and sellers." Bailey denied that capital could be merely accumulated labour. *Dissertation on the Nature, Measures and Causes of Value*, pp. 217–23, London School of Economics reprint.

durable consumption goods let out by their owners, and the necessaries of life in the possession of labourers and capitalists. Except for the last two items, the enumeration is taken directly from Adam Smith[1] without any detailed explanation of why Senior considered it correct, beyond the remark that—

"This enumeration contains, perhaps, some useless distinctions, and, we think, two improper exclusions; but, generally speaking, it gives an excellent view of the different species of capital."[2]

Adam Smith's "improper exclusions" were, of course, subsistence in the hands of the labourers and capitalists, and durable consumption goods let out by the owner. Senior's attitude to these vexed questions was determined by his use of the distinction between productive and unproductive consumption.

"Productive consumption," he said, "is that use of a commodity which occasions an ulterior product. Unproductive consumption is of course that use which occasions no ulterior product. The characteristic of unproductive consumption is, that it adds to the enjoyment of no one but the consumer himself. Its only effect upon the rest of the community is to diminish *pro tanto* the mass of commodities applicable to their use."[3]

Subsistence in the hands of the labourers is included in capital because it will be productively consumed by the labourers who will thus be made capable of producing an ulterior product—

"And in what does the consumption of food by a labourer differ from that of coals by the steam engine? Simply in this, that the labourer derives pleasure from what he consumes, and the steam engine does not."[4]

But the whole of this distinction appears to be merely

---

[1] *Wealth of Nations*, Bk. II, chap. I, Vol. I, pp. 264–5.
[2] *Political Economy*, p. 64.   [3] Ibid., p. 54.
[4] Ibid., p. 64. Senior explained the distinction in just the same way in 1847–52, Course I, lecture 8, "On Production."

letting in a fallacious concept of productivity based on ulterior products, instead of on ulterior utility.[1] If the value of a commodity is derived from its utility, then the criterion of productivity turns on whether the good or service in question yields an utility or not. If goods in the hands of consumers are not consumed because their future consumption will yield a greater utility than their present (and all consumption goods held at all come into this category), then, by Senior's own definition of capital, all such consumption goods are capital. A further distinction between consumption which is necessary and that which is not, does not appear to me to be one which has relevance to a general classification of capital goods, quite apart from the inconsistency in not making such a distinction in the case of the wage fund in the hands of capitalists, which consists of subsistence wages plus "luxury" wages.

Senior's other distinction between durable goods used and hired out, respectively, by their owners involves the same misconception. The owner derives revenue just as much in the one case as in the other; in the former it is in the form of money, and in the latter in the form of the utility of the services received. In neither case is it correct to speak of unproductive rather than productive consumption.[2] Nevertheless, despite these inconsistencies and omissions, Senior's exposition of the nature of capital remains

---

[1] The distinction between productive and unproductive labour and/or consumption was primarily connected with capital and appeared in some form or other throughout English classical economics (for Adam Smith's use of the distinction see Part 1, chap. 2, pp. 73–4 above). The most complete treatment of the matter is to be found in J. S. Mill's *Essays on Unsettled Questions*, "On the Words Productive and Unproductive." In this essay, after defining wealth as "permanent sources of enjoyment, whether material or immaterial" (p. 82, third edition), Mill maintained that though labour devoted to services was only productive if it does, and is intended to, contribute to the maintenance or increase of these sources, all labour realized in material commodities is productive. It followed, he thought, that only consumption necessary to maintenance of these sources, including labour, is productive (ibid., pp. 82–8). Senior's use of the distinction in the sphere of consumption was thus directly in the English tradition, though fundamentally inconsistent with his own income concept of wealth and his definition of abstinence.

[2] *Political Economy*, pp. 64–6.

as the most complete exposition of the English tradition of capital theory before Jevons.[1]

The omissions and inconsistencies of Senior's enumeration of types of capital led inevitably to a limitation of his statement of the advantages to be derived from the use of capital to the use of implements and the division of labour. He pointed out that, except for a small number of unimportant exceptions, the use of any implement implied the exercise of abstinence.

"It will be observed that we consider the use of all implements as implying an exercise of abstinence, using that word in our extended sense as comprehending all preference of remote to immediate results."[2]

In the same section Senior explained at some length the way in which capital makes the division of labour and the use of tools possible.[3] Commenting on the passage referring to this point in the Introduction to Book II of the *Wealth of Nations*, he suggested that, if taken literally, it gives the impression that Adam Smith thought that all the stock necessary to support the labourer must be accumulated beforehand. This idea, he explained, is incorrect, since all that is necessary is that resources should be so employed as to ensure a flow of the necessary subsistence and materials as they are needed:

"Nor is it absolutely necessary in any case, though, if Adam Smith's words were taken literally, such a necessity might be inferred, that, before a man dedicates himself to a peculiar branch of production, a stock of goods should be stored up to supply him with subsistence, materials, and tools, till his own product has been completed and sold. That he must be kept supplied with these articles is true; but they need not have been stored up before he first sets to work, they may have been pro-

---

[1] Senior's objection to Ricardo's distinction between fixed and circulating capital as one merely of degree, at first sight seems a denial of the importance of the time element. On the whole, however, the criticism is more likely to be due to his excessive desire to make clear lines of classification between different phenomena. Senior, *Political Economy*, pp. 62-3, and Ricardo's *Principles*, chap. 1, sect. 4.

[2] *Political Economy*, p. 68.   [3] Ibid., pp. 67-81.

duced while his work was in progress. . . . It is probable, however, that Adam Smith's real meaning was, not that the identical supplies which will be wanted in a course of progressive industry must be already collected when the process which they are to assist or remunerate is about to be begun, but that a fund or source must then exist from which they may be drawn as they are required. That fund must comprise in specie some of the things wanted. The painter must have his canvas, the weaver his loom and materials, not enough, perhaps, to complete his web, but to commence it. As to those commodities, however, which the workman subsequently requires, it is enough if the fund on which he relies is a productive fund, keeping pace with his wants, and virtually set apart to answer them."[1]

This is the clearest statement of the process of production in English economic literature of the first half of the nine-teenth century. If it had been digested by Senior and his contemporaries the evolution of the wage fund theory might have had a different history, instead of being stultified by being stated as a mere mathematical identity.

Senior had satisfactorily accounted for the demand for capital, and therefore abstinence, by the superior physical productivity of the roundabout method of production which can only be utilized if future is preferred to present enjoyment.[2] The really serious omission in this explanation was that of the function of capital in making possible adjustments between the marginal utility of income at different points of time. After his treatment of productive and unproductive consumption this was of course inevitable, though he defined abstinence quite generally enough to include it. His exposition of the conditions affecting the supply of abstinence did, however, contain suggestions of a time disagio.

[1] *Political Economy*, pp. 78–9.

[2] It seems to me that Böhm-Bawerk, even allowing for his unwillingness to admit anticipators, quite genuinely failed to realize how much of his own theory was in Senior. *Capital and Interest*, Bk. IV, chap. 2, Smart's translation. Jevons, on the other hand, specifically mentioned Senior's theory as the necessary and natural complement to Ricardo's; a fact which those who have regarded Senior's explanation of abstinence merely as part of a cost theory would have done well to consider. *Theory of Political Economy*, pp. 232–4, third edition.

The creation of capital, he explained, involves a definite present and painful sacrifice—abstinence from present consumption—which people will only undertake with some prospect of reward:

"Profits and Wages differ in almost all respects from Rent. They are each subject to a minimum and a maximum. They are subject to a minimum, because each of them is the result of a sacrifice. It may be difficult to say what is the minimum with respect to profit, but it is clear that every capitalist, as a motive to abstain from the immediate and unproductive enjoyment of his capital, must require some remuneration exceeding the lowest that is conceivable. . . . On the other hand, as the rate of wages depends in a great measure on the number of labourers, and the rate of profit on the amount of capital, both high wages and high profits have a tendency to produce their own diminution."[1]

The question of why people should prefer present to future goods was left by Senior in obscurity except in so far as he related an inability to realize the future, that is a lack of providence, to an unwillingness to abstain:

"To abstain from the enjoyment which is in our power, or to seek distant rather than immediate results, are among the most painful exertions of the human will. It is true that such exertions are made, and indeed are frequent in every state of society, except perhaps in the very lowest, and have been made in the very lowest, for society could not otherwise have improved; but of all the means by which man can be raised in the scale of being, abstinence, as it is perhaps the most effective, is the slowest in its increase, and the latest generally diffused. Among nations, those that are the least civilized, and among the different classes of the same nation, those which are the worst educated, are almost the most improvident, and consequently the least abstinent."[2]

---

[1] *Political Economy*, p. 140.

[2] Ibid., pp. 59–60. Senior's explanation of the motives influencing people's preferences between present and future was lamentably incomplete, and inferior to Rae's. (*Statement of some New Principles on the Subject of Political Economy*, 1834, chaps. 6 and 7 of Mixter's reprint, 1905.) Probably, however, the best account was given by J. S. Mill, who was indebted to both Senior and Rae. (*Principles of Political Economy*, Bk. II, chap. 15, par. 1, and Bk. I, chap. 11, par. 2.) Mill also explained in detail the circumstances which affect individual desires to change the time-shape of their income streams (Ibid., Bk. IV, chap. 4, par. 3.)

Senior's theory of capital and interest was thus based on an explanation of the demand for capital due to the peculiar productivity of capital, and of the supply of capital in terms of the real cost of saving. As we have already pointed out, the connection between time and productivity was introduced in the *Wealth of Nations*, but only admitted as making capital an independent source of productivity by Ricardo after considerable intellectual struggle. It was from this basis that Senior started to analyse in more detail the relation between capital and other factors, and the nature of the real cost which appeared to limit the supply of capital. In identifying this cost and calling it 'abstinence,' Senior was thus only making explicit the connection between the supply of capital and its price, which had been assumed without explanation by Ricardo—

"The term 'cost of production' must be familiar to those who are acquainted with the writings of modern Economists; but, like most terms in political economy, though currently used, it has never been accurately defined; and it appears to us impossible that it should have been defined without the assistance of the term 'abstinence,' or some equivalent expression. . . .

"In a note to the third edition, p. 46, Mr. Ricardo admits that profit also forms part of the cost of production. Mr. Mill, by a stretch of language, in the convenience of which we cannot concur, includes profit under the term labour. The definitions of Mr. Ricardo and Mr. Mill appear, therefore, to coincide; and that adopted by Mr. Malthus only differs from them in referring, not to the labour that *has* been employed, but to that which must be employed if the production must be continued. In this respect the language of Mr. Malthus is undoubtedly the most correct. The sacrifices that *have* been made to produce a given commodity have no effect on its value. All that the purchaser considers is the amount of sacrifice that its production would require at the time of the exchange. . . . And when Mr. Ricardo and Mr. Mill speak of the labour which *has* been employed on a commodity as affecting its value, they must be understood as implying that the circumstances of production remain unchanged."[1]

[1] *Political Economy*, pp. 97–8.

This explanation, however, did not mark a regression to a cost of production theory of value either of capital or of commodities; it placed profits and wages on equal footings. The mere mention of real costs of production does not imply that value is determined solely by cost of production. For this reason Cannan's and Böhm-Bawerk's criticism of Senior's abstinence theory, on the grounds that it was tied up with a cost of production theory of value, are entirely beside the point.[1] Except where production takes place under conditions of constant costs, as Senior devoted the greatest care to point out, costs are only one of the elements determining value. Even in the former case he denied that value is derived from labour or abstinence, or from any other cost; it is merely regulated by costs. As regards the relation of the cost of abstinence to the actual value of abstinence, Senior never made the suggestion that this cost is the sole determinant of price. In fact, he spent far more time in explaining why abstinence is productive than why it is scarce. In the absence of direct evidence to the contrary, it is more reasonable to assume that Senior derived the income of all factors from the value of their products, rather than from their respective costs of production. There are, however, a number of passages that quite definitely support this interpretation in relation to the rent analysis—

"We will begin by recurring to a subject to which we have already alluded, the frequent difficulty of deciding whether a given revenue ought or ought not to be called Rent. When an estate has been for some time leased to a careful tenant, it generally receives permanent ameliorations, which enable the owner, at the expiration of the lease, to obtain a higher rent. . . . Is the increase of revenue rent or profit? It arises from an additional fertility, now inseparably attached to the land. It is received by the owner without sacrifice on his part. It is, in fact, undistinguishable from the previous rent. On the other hand, its existence is owing to the abstinence of the farmer, who devoted

---

[1] Böhm-Bawerk, *Capital and Interest*, Bk. IV, chap. 2, pp. 285–6, Smart's translation; Cannan, *Review of Economic Theory*, p. 187; *Theories of Production and Distribution*, pp. 213–14.

to a distant object—the amelioration of the land—labour which he might have employed in producing immediate enjoyment for himself. If the owner of the estate had farmed it himself, and had directed labour to be employed on its permanent improvement, the additional produce occasioned by those improvements would clearly have been termed profit. It appears, therefore, most convenient to term it profit when occasioned by the improvements made by a tenant."[1]

It is abundantly evident in this passage that Senior derived profits, the reward for abstinence, directly from the value of that extra produce made possible by that abstinence. Since rent has always been admitted to be derived directly from the value of the produce of land, it is evident that if profits merge into rent in certain circumstances they must be derived from the value of the produce of abstinence. The position is made even clearer in a passage a few lines further on in the same discussion:

". . . for all useful purposes the distinction of profit from rent ceases as soon as the capital, from which a given revenue arises, has become, whether by gift or by inheritance, the property of a person to whose abstinence and exertions it did not owe its creation? The revenue arising from a dock, or a wharf, or a canal, is profit in the hands of the *original constructor*. It is the reward of *his* abstinence, in having employed capital for the purposes of production instead of for those of enjoyment. But in the hands of his heir it has all the attributes of rent. It is to him the gift of fortune, not the result of a sacrifice."[2]

II

Senior's attention was first seriously attracted to non-Ricardian theories of capital by Hermann's review of the *Political Economy* in 1836.[3] From this time Senior came under the influence of continental capital theory. Hermann was the only continental economist who could be said to have anything like a coherent theory of capital, and it is neces-

---

[1] *Political Economy*, pp. 128–9. Cf. Part I, chap. 5, sect. III below.
[2] Ibid., p. 129.   [3] *Gelehrte Anzeigen*, Munich, 1836.

sary to give some account of it in order to appreciate its effect on Senior.

Hermann's theory of capital and interest was really an elaboration of Storch's generalization of rent to capital and Say's theory of productive services. It followed from Say's analysis of value that the value of resources which yield scarce useful services is derived from, and in some way determined by, the value of those services. In consequence, Say treated capital on exactly the same footing as labour and land. Durable goods, machines and instruments, like land yield a series of productive services, and their value is thus determined like that of land by the same sort of summation of the values of the series.[1] It is important to notice that as far as this fixed capital was concerned Say took little notice of the time element. Circulating capital, however, he treated as in some way advances to labour necessary because production took time. He regarded it as self-evident that the return on circulating capital must, *ceteris paribus*, be the same in all occupations; and that this return is determined by the value of the services of more or less current resources in these different occupations.[2] His explanation of why these advances of wages and materials to labour should be capable of yielding a net return in the form of interest was not at all clear.[3] It was evident to Say, however, that, once the rate of interest on circulating capital is determined, all the services of land and fixed capital are discounted by this rate. Therefore as capital goods wear out, whether they are replaced or not depends on the expected yield being equal to the rate of interest. What was not at all obvious from Say's explanation was how the all-important rate of interest is really determined, for, though it is clear that he thought it dependent on the supply and demand for free capital, he did not really explain either the source of that demand or why the supply was limited. The most significant feature of Say's

---

[1] *Traité d'Économie Politique*, Bk. i, chap. 13, p. 130; Bk. ii, chap. 9, sect. i. Cf. Part i, chap. 2, pp. 77–9 above.

[2] Ibid., Bk. ii, chap. 8.

[3] Cf. Böhm-Bawerk, op. cit., Bk. iii, chaps. 3–8.

treatment was, however, the implied inclusion of the rent of land and the profits on capital in the same genus.[1]

The implications of Say's analysis were more fully elaborated by Storch. Storch started his discussion of capital by considering the return on capital as a rent,[2] he then proceeded to distinguish between the rent of fixed capital and the rent of circulating or free capital which he said was really interest. Interest, he explained, is necessary to recompense the sacrifice of saving, i.e. is payment for abstinence. The value of fixed capital is necessarily determined by discounting its series of services by the rate of interest; as fixed capital wears out it will only be replaced if capital yields at least as much in that use as in any other.[3] Like Say he did not explain the source of the demand for capital, but he was much clearer about its supply and the long-run distinction between fixed capital and land— that the former might dissolve into free capital and then disappear as capital altogether while the latter cannot. Thus Storch, apart from explaining clearly the temporary nature of capital as contrasted with the permanency of land by stressing the possibility of fixed capital disappearing altogether, explained why the total supply of capital was limited.

Hermann simply took some of the ideas of Say and some of those of Storch and elaborated them, making what was really a very impressive theory of capital from them by his superior analytical ability.

Say had suggested that land and fixed capital are really very similar and yield series of productive services in the same way, and Storch had in the first instance designated the yield of all capital rent. Hermann went further and declared that land is really a form of capital because both

---

[1] Say said quite definitely in a letter to Ricardo that he was not interested in the Malthus-Ricardo controversy on rent, because he regarded rent as a form of profits, the profits derived from the employment of land being similar to those derived from the employment of capital. *Mélanges de J. B. Say.* Letter to Ricardo, December 2, 1815.

[2] *Cours d'Économie Politique,* 1815, Bk. iii, chap. 8.

[3] Ibid., 1815, Bk. iii, chaps. 9 and 10.

yield productive services whose values are determined in exactly the same way—

"Am wenigsten Rücksicht verdient die Unterscheidung, dass Grund und Boden von Natur bestehe, Kapital Folge früherer Ersparniss an erzeugten Güter sey; da die Beobachtung, dass ein Vorrath früherer Erzeugnisse die Production fördert und ergiebiger macht, während er sich seinem Tauschwerth nach erhält, wohl zuerst auf der Begriff des Kapitals führte, Ersparniss zu seyn aber keineswegs jetzt mehr nothwendiges Merkmal des Kapitals ist."

Naturally Hermann advanced as another reason for not distinguishing between land and capital the actual difficulty of distinguishing between them in practice.[1]

The actual services, or uses as he called them, of capital, including land, are scarce, and therefore the payment for them by way of rent was, he argued like Say, a cost of production.[2] So far everything seems simple, but when Hermann came to the actual theory of interest as such, the danger of his definition became clear. He apparently thought that it absolved him from considering why capital, including free capital, was scarce, and he simply ignored the question of the total supply of capital. If this assumption, which is really equivalent to one of a fixed supply of capital, is allowed, his further explanation of how the rate of interest is determined must be admitted to be among the best in early capital theory.[3]

The return to fixed capital, he pointed out, is the difference between total receipts and primary costs and replacements, and may be either above or below the current rate of interest. This return he classed as a rent. As soon as a piece of fixed capital changes hands it will be valued in the market by discounting this rent by the current rate of interest, allowance being made for the risks, etc., peculiar to that line of investment. Thus the return on this fixed

---

[1] *Staatswirtschaftliche Untersuchungen*, chap. 3, "Begriff des Kapitals," par. 4. Quotation from p. 49. (All page references are to the 1924 reprint of the first edition.)

[2] Ibid., chap. 5, "Vom Gewinn," pp. 151–99.   [3] Ibid., pp. 200–65.

capital after changing hands will be brought into line with the returns to be derived from any other employment of capital. This must necessarily, he argued, be so, as the buyer of fixed capital is an owner of free capital for which the market is perfectly competitive. This made clear that it is the conditions ruling in the market for free capital that are important in determining the rate of interest. The supply of free capital is limited and it can be invested in a number of alternative ways which are expected to yield returns over and above the original amount invested; previously invested fixed capital must be valued in such a way as to yield the same return as the competing opportunities for the investment of free capital, if it is to change hands. This may result in a loss or gain of capital to the original owner. Circulating capital, in Hermann's view, will naturally tend to yield more nearly the current rate of interest on new investments than fixed, any deficit being thrown on the latter.[1]

The fundamental defect of Say's theory of capital in failing to account specifically for the productivity of capital was only partially remedied by Hermann's theory that there are opportunities for the employment of capital which will yield a surplus over primary costs and replacements.[2] Any suggestion of the time-elements in production having anything to do with it was completely lacking, since for Hermann, as for Say, the simplicity of the idea of productive services had over-simplified the whole problem of capital and labour.

Hermann's inclusion of land in capital had a great attraction for Senior, for it appeared to get over the difficulty of deciding what is rent and what is profits, and in the Lectures in 1847–52 he adopted Hermann's definition of capital. After explaining that the traditional three-fold classification of the instruments of production, based on the consideration that the revenue from land is due solely to the bounty of nature, not to any form of human exertion, and has neither a maximum nor a minimum, has a good deal

[1] *Staatswirtschaftliche Untersuchungen*, pp. 267–89.
[2] Ibid., pp. 145–51, 267–74.

to be said for it, he went on to explain why he was giving it up:

". . . but neither Adam Smith nor the Physiocrats seem to have been fully aware that the greater part of what we call rent is merely profit on the capital employed in fitting the land for use. Still less did they perceive that the remainder is the gift not of nature but of monopoly, not of abundance, but of scarcity, and exists wherever an instrument of production not universally accessible is employed, and shows itself in profits and in wages, whenever the one or other rises above the general average. To give all such extra profit and extra wages the name of rent would I think be an inconvenient departure from ordinary language. . . . In the great majority of cases in which wages or profits rise beyond the average, the causes are imperceptible, even to those persons who gain by them. They are the compound operation of many obscure peculiarities. Tact in obtaining good customers or employers and avoiding bad ones, favourable opportunities caught or neglected or never presented, the conduct of friends and of enemies, and of rivals and of supporters —these and many other causes to which, because we know them only by their effects, we give the name of chance, apportion the whole aggregate of wages and profits among the millions of producers in a great country. It is often difficult to distinguish profit from wages. The adding a third sort of revenue to which a portion of what is usually called profit or wages is to be attributed appears to me an unnecessary complication."[1]

This is far enough away from a cost of production theory of distribution, though the theoretical distinction between profits and rent apparently remains. Senior's attitude towards the whole question was not based entirely on the same reasoning as Hermann's, for Hermann maintained that there is not even a theoretical distinction between rent and profit, or land and capital. They both, however, agreed that an important reason for classing them together was the physical difficulty of distinguishing between capital invested in agricultural improvements, etc., and the original powers of the soil—

"But the great objection to the treating land as a separate instrument of production, is the difficulty which will be more

[1] Lectures, 1847–52, Course II, lecture 2.

clearly shown as we go on, of framing any definition of capital from which land can be excluded."[1]

Senior's emphasis on the monopoly element in many incomes and prices which was among the reasons for his inclusion of land in capital was almost entirely lacking in Hermann's analysis. He pointed out also that the monopoly element in the rent of land is not peculiar to land, but is common to practically all forms of revenue. But Senior gave still another reason for treating land as capital; he realized that the characteristic of land is its immobility in space not its absolute scarcity, and that therefore if the demand for it increases sufficiently to cover transport costs, etc., more will come into use.[2] Hence it appeared that the classical reason for distinguishing between land and capital on the basis of the connection of supply with returns was not so valid as had generally been thought.

According to these lines of reasoning, it is not at all obvious why any distinction should be made between capital and man. Senior, however, considered that not only would this be confusing, but that since man was after all the conscious agent in production he should be distinguished from the passive agent.

"I have already shown that land cannot be conveniently excluded from the term capital: If man is also to be included in it there is but one instrument of production, namely capital, and rent and wages are mere species of profit. It appears to me that this classification and nomenclature would be inconvenient.

"It seems to me that man as the intelligent instrument of production is an instrument differing in kind from brute and inanimate agents: that his existence and his increase are the results of causes differing from those by which they are produced and augmented: that most of the services which he performs are such as they cannot effect; and that the reward which he receives is governed by principles differing from those which regulate the remuneration paid for their use. On these grounds

---

[1] Lectures, 1847–52, Course II, lecture 2. Cf. Hermann, Staatswirts-chaftsliche Untersuchungen, chap. 3, par. 4, pp. 48–50.

[2] Lectures, 1847–52, Course III, lecture 1. See Part I, chap. 3, pp. 133–4 above.

I consider knowledge and skill not as capital, and productive of profit, but as qualities of man, and therefore productive of wages."[1]

The instruments of production are therefore, Senior decided, capital, or "material wealth used productively," and man.

Senior devoted nearly a whole course of lectures to elaborating his theory of capital to meet this new classification. He started by criticizing most of the existing definitions of capital on the ground that they failed to crystallize the essence of capital because they did not distinguish completely between resources devoted to present and future enjoyment respectively. In actual fact this meant that in his opinion practically all the definitions were defective, either because they excluded finished goods in the hands of retailers and subsistence funds in the hands of labourers, or because they included too much and made capital synonymous with wealth.[2] This criticism is of fundamental importance to Senior's theory. For, though the actual form it took in a distinction between productive and unproductive consumption is incorrect, the underlying idea that the distribution of resources through time is essential to the existence of capital, is made sufficiently clear in his discussion:

"Each of these two classes of definitions appear to have been influenced by the opinion expressly maintained by Mr. McCulloch that the question whether a given commodity ought or not to be classed under the head capital, depends on the intrinsic qualities of that commodity, not on the use which is made of it."

And a few pages further on:

"But when we come to apply the definition we find that it

[1] Lectures, 1847–52, Course II, lecture 3.
[2] Ibid., Course II, lectures 2 and 3. The English definitions quoted were those of Banfield, Lauderdale, Malthus, Mrs. Marcet, McCulloch, James Mill, J. S. Mill, Ricardo, Adam Smith and Torrens. American: Carey, Cooper, Hamilton, Ramsey, Tucker, Vethake, and Wayland. French: Droz, Dutens, Ganilh, J. B. Say and Leon Say, and Rossi and Florez-Estrada whom Senior included with the French. German: Hermann, Rau and Storch. On the whole, the Americans went wrong, according to Senior, by making capital synonymous with wealth while the English and Germans generally excluded some item or other which they should have included.

includes commodities which do not produce the effects attributed by Mr. McCulloch to capital. . . .

"How do the 1,500 horses that we see every summer evening in Hyde Park, assist in the division of labour, or in the execution of work, or in economizing labour, or rendering it more efficient? It is quite true that neither the identity nor the capacity of the horse is affected by the use that is made of him, but whether he be, or be not an instrument of production depends on that use, and on that use only."[1]

It has already been pointed out that Senior, in attempting to explain that the essence of capitalistic production is the distribution of resources through time, became confused with regard to the distribution of income through time by means of investment in durable consumption goods, and also got muddled about productive and unproductive consumption of income. It is this latter confusion which led him to retain in 1848 the distinction between necessary and unnecessary subsistence funds in the hands of the final consumer, explaining that he defined capital ". . . not with reference to the revenue which it procures but to the assistance which it affords."

Within this limited meaning of production he defined capital as "material wealth employed productively."

After describing, as in the *Political Economy*, the importance of capital in facilitating the division of labour and the use of instruments, he went on to the importance of abstinence in the formation of capital—[3]

"To a certain extent it is the gift of nature. Nature gave to man all the globe and all its contents: . . . Scarcely any gift of nature, however, except the sea, is of much service to man until he has fashioned it to his use. And that fashion in general contributes to its utility much more than the mere bounty of nature. The ore out of which an anchor has been made had

[1] Lectures, 1847–52, Course II, lecture 3.
[2] Ibid., Course II, lecture 4. Cf. pp. 144 et seq. above.
[3] This order of explanation differed from that in the *Political Economy*, where abstinence was explained before the actual productivity of capital was described. Apart from this inversion the description of the productivity of capitalistic production due to the use of machinery and the division of labour was much the same in 1847–52 as in 1836.

little value while it was buried in the mine. A second cause therefore of the existence of capital is human industry.

"All the products of human industry are not capital, or the word capital would be synonymous with the word wealth. Capital . . . is wealth destined to be employed productively. Something therefore besides nature and industry must concur to produce it, and to that third something, to the cause which occasions a given article of wealth to be used productively I give the name of abstinence. By that term I express the conduct of a person who either abstains from the unproductive use of what he can command or designedly prefers the production of remote to that of immediate results. The union of industry and abstinence I express by the term accumulation."[1]

It is evident that, as in 1836, Senior thought the existence of capital to be dependent on the willingness of people to devote present resources to future production, and its function that of making possible the realization of more productive roundabout methods of production. In order to make still clearer the relation of capital to time, Senior introduced a distinction between "frugality" and "providence," which he regarded as species of the same genus abstinence. Frugality he defined as "the mere refraining from the use of a commodity," and "providence" as the "employment of labour to produce remote results."[2]

Possibly as a result of Rae's elaboration of the motives influencing saving,[3] Senior devoted more attention in 1847–52 than in 1836 to the relation of the return on capital to the supply of capital, and to the opportunities for investment—

"In fact it is in general the average price paid for the purchase or for the hire of durable instruments, and, in particular, the average number of years' purchase of land, and the average interest of money, which decides, in every particular society, the extent to which a member of that society will carry his providence,

---

[1] Lectures, 1847–52, Course II, lecture 8.
[2] Ibid., Course II, lecture 9.
[3] Rae, *Statement of some New Principles of Political Economy*. Senior knew Rae's book by 1848, at any rate, since he mentioned his account of the improvidence of Indians (ibid., chap. 7 of Mixter's edition, pp. 66 et seq.) in Course II, lecture 9.

or, in other words, what degree of future advantage will induce him to sacrifice for a given time a given amount of the means of present enjoyment."[1]

Those people, he explained, whose providence was either below or above the average providence of their contemporaries will naturally consume or accumulate their capitals respectively:

"Those whose providence is less than the average providence of the society in which they live, if they are born poor, remain poor. The average remuneration of abstinence appears to them inadequate. . . . Those on the other hand who are born rich, if deficient in ordinary providence do not remain rich. They can part with the instruments from which their incomes are derived for sums which according to their estimate of the present compared to the future are above their value. . . .

"Those whose providence exceeds that of the society in which they live become rich. They become purchasers of the productive instruments which the improvident sell. They work up materials affording a return rather more distant or a profit rather smaller than those generally used, and of those instruments they can choose the most certain. With every fall of the ordinary rate of interest the sphere of providence is extended. As long as the interest of money is 5 per cent undertakings likely to produce only $4\frac{1}{2}$ per cent, however convenient or useful to the public, are not engaged in by individuals of only average providence. Let interest sink to 4 per cent, they are eagerly sought for, and those which have been preoccupied by men of more than ordinary providence now afford a more than ordinary profit."[2]

In many ways Senior's treatment of capital in 1847–52 was a great improvement on his earlier effort, but the theory was not altogether coherent. He never really explained the relation of the rate of interest to the maintenance of fixed capital. This gave his exposition a sort of disjointedness which he could have avoided by including part of Storch's discussion of the matter. It must be admitted,

[1] Lectures, 1847–52, Course II, lecture 9.
[2] Ibid. For a closely similar treatment, see J. S. Mill, *Principles of Political Economy*, Bk. IV, chap. 4, par. 3. Mill refers to the "rate which an average person will deem to be an equivalent for abstinence." Senior certainly knew Mill's discussion and was very likely influenced by it.

too, that his actual explanation of the relation of the sacrifice of saving to the motives for saving was not nearly as adequate as those of Rae and J. S. Mill. Indeed, if Senior's claim to have made an important original contribution to theory of capital rested on this aspect of the abstinence analysis it would not be very strong, but as we have endeavoured to show this is not the most interesting part of Senior's treatment.

III

Apart from the actual merits of his analysis, it must be admitted that Senior's introduction of the idea of abstinence had more definite influence on the future course of theory than any of his more general contributions. (This, of course, only refers to the exposition in the *Political Economy*. The later developments were contained only in unpublished lectures.) From 1836 onwards the inadequacy of the cost of production theory of value in explaining the cost of production of capital was remedied by the simple but magical word "abstinence"; it was from this aspect that J. S. Mill hailed it with such relief and incorporated it more or less permanently in English capital theory.[1] Where the cost of production theory of value was never accepted, as for instance in France and Germany, the usefulness of the term was recognized in this connection in the same way as Senior himself recognized it, as a concept necessary to complete the analysis of costs rather than that of value.[2]

It was not until Jevons' generation that the aspect of the abstinence theory parallel to Ricardo's theory of capital was recognized. It is this part of the theory that is now dominant in England, no doubt owing to Marshall's recognition of it, and alteration of the actual word "abstinence" to "waiting."[3] In consequence, Senior's direct influence on

[1] J. S. Mill, *Principles of Political Economy*, Bk. 1, chap. 2, pars. 2 and 4. Cf. note 2 on p. 97 and note 1 on p. 151 above.

[2] E.g. by Rossi, Courcelle-Seneuil, von Mangoldt, etc.

[3] Jevons, *Theory of Political Economy*, pp. 232–4, third edition (see note 2 on p. 148 above), and Marshall, *Principles of Economics*, Bk. iv, chap. 7, pars. 8–9, fifth edition.

the development of English capital theory has probably been greater than that of any other classical economist. Outside England, however, his theory has been severely criticized, particularly by Böhm-Bawerk and Irving Fisher.

Their main criticism is that saving itself does not involve any particular cost additional to that always involved in choosing between scarce satisfactions; abstinence therefore cannot, they argue, be separated from any other form of sacrifice.[1] Superficially this criticism seems justified, but even if it is admitted, the problem still remains of accounting for the scarcity of the supply of capital as such. Böhm-Bawerk recognized this, and attempted to overcome it by his analysis of the three grounds of the higher value of present compared with future goods—the technical superiority of present over future resources, the better provision for the future than the present, and the psychological under-valuation of the future.[2] It is unnecessary to discuss his failure to establish the first of these grounds as an independent explanation, for it has been shown *ad nauseam*, and does not directly concern us here. The last ground, however, is of importance, for it is evident that the existence of a time disagio is as good an explanation of the limitation of the supply of capital as the sacrifice of saving, or abstinence. The question is whether it is really a different explanation, or the same turned round and expanded. It seems evident to me that if there was no under-valuation of the future there would be no peculiar sacrifice attached to saving beyond that attached to any choice between scarce satis-factions, for there would then be no difference between distributing the income streams between various present expenditures, and between present and future expenditures. The eonomizing of resources would always be naturally three-dimensional. If, on the other hand, there was in general a time disagio, it would mean that people in fact experienced a peculiar difficulty and dissatisfaction in

---

[1] Böhm-Bawerk, *Capital and Interest*, Bk. IV, chap. 2. Fisher, *The Rate of Interest*, chap. 3, pars. 8–13, pp. 42–52.

[2] *Positive Theory of Capital*, Vol. I, Bk. IV, chap. I.

having to take the future into account when considering their expenditure; in short, that the existence of a time discount was due to the sacrifice or disutility of saving, or in Senior's terminology, the pain of exercising abstinence.

Irving Fisher's criticism taken in connection with his income concept of capital makes this clearer, and at the same time affords an explanation of why he criticized the abstinence theory. Fisher, in regarding the whole problem of capital and interest as one of the equilization of the marginal utility of income flows through time, deliberately includes in capital all sources of future income, such as stocks of consumption goods and durable consumption goods whoever they are owned by. Capital, he explains, is total wealth considered as a stock at a point of time, income is the total services derived from all stock in this sense, regarded as a flow through time.[1] Now Senior attempted to avoid this wide concept of capital by using the distinction between productive and unproductive consumption; the attempt was quite unnecessary with regard to the aspect of abstinence he was endeavouring to stress, namely, the distribution of scarce resources through time. Under these circumstances, and in the absence of the later lectures, Fisher rather naturally has regarded the abstinence theory as the negation of the wide approach which he favours, and as an offshoot only of the cost of production treatment. It is probable, too, that Fisher's interest in the detailed analysis of the various factors influencing the emergence of individual time disagios has prevented him from appreciating fully the connection between the existence of a general disagio and the sacrifice behind the exercise of providence. But this is precisely the fundamental disutility of providence which prevents individuals from distributing their incomes through time so as to maximize utility over their lives as a whole.

If this interpretation of Böhm-Bawerk's and Fisher's criticism is correct, it is reasonable to believe that Senior's influence was really important outside as well as inside

[1] "What is Capital?" *Economic Journal*, 1896, Vol. vi, pp. 509–34; *The Rate of Interest*, chaps. 8 and 9.

England. All the comparatively modern attempts in Europe and America to extend the marginal utility analysis to the distribution of resources through time by means of the concept of time agios are, directly or indirectly, descendants of Senior's theory of abstinence.

CHAPTER 5

THE THEORY OF WAGES

It is customary when describing the development of the theory of wages, to dismiss a great part of the classical doctrines as either an application of the Malthusian theory of population, or as merely the wage fund, and to welcome F. A. Walker's "produce-less-deductions" theory as the first serious sign of better things. This appears to me to be not merely misleading, but actually incorrect. It is undoubtedly true that the majority of English writers laid greater emphasis in their formal analysis of wages on elements other than the productivity of labour. But the whole of the Ricardian long-period analysis was built on the foundations of the *Wealth of Nations*, and implied some sort of "produce-less-deductions" theory.

In the treatment of the wage-fund theory itself, the general obscurity about the importance of time in production lay at the root of much of the apparent absurdities of the doctrine. Later critics, such as Longe and Walker, did very little to clear up this fundamental difficulty, and limited themselves quite often to the mere reiteration that labour is paid out of its product.

The disappointing failure of the theory of wages to develop during the first part of the nineteenth century may be attributed to three difficulties: the preoccupation with distribution to each factor as a whole, or lump-sum as contrasted with unit distribution, the complexity of the time element, and in England the line taken by Ricardo in value theory. The main elements in wage theory which corresponded to these difficulties were productivity, the wage fund, or more generally the relation of capital to labour, and population.

On all these topics Senior had a good deal to say, much of it disjointedly, and a certain amount without throwing any light on the question. Nevertheless his attempts are of some significance as illustrating the general progress of economic theory, and the complexity of the problem of fitting Ricardian and continental theories together. Senior himself was as obviously dissatisfied with his results as Ricardo had been with his own theory of value.[1] The arrangement of any discussion of wage theory is a matter of considerable difficulty owing to the complexity of the three elements involved, and the numerous sidelights thrown on the main issues by the discussions of subsidiary points. It seems to me simplest to start by analysing the treatment of the main strands of wage theory in the *Wealth of Nations*, and to trace the development of each separately. The chapter will thus fall into six parts: 1. Adam Smith's theory of wages. 2. The population element. 3. Productivity. 4. The wage fund. 5. Wages in different occupations, and finally an attempt to draw together the threads of Senior's discussions and show their significance.

I.

The treatment of wages in the *Wealth of Nations* indicated the main ideas which were destined to enter into the discussions of wages for the following three-quarters of a century. But it is important to notice that the emphasis laid by Adam Smith on the different elements of wage theory differed considerably from that of his followers, both on the Continent and in England.

According to his account of the labour theory of value the total amount produced forms the reward of labour, the wage or return for labour is thus directly dependent on the physical productivity of labour.[2] Differences between earnings in different occupations were dismissed at this stage by explaining that the higgling of the market will cause allowance to be made for the different degrees of skill and hardship.[3] This is, of course, physical distribution, for the idea of value distribution is automatically excluded by the

---

[1] *Political Economy*, pp. 194–200, where Senior was attempting to decide what determines "the average period of advance of capital," one of the most important influences on wages he admitted that there is no means of finding out!

[2] *Wealth of Nations*, Vol. 1, Bk. 1, chap. 8, "Wages," p. 66.

[3] Ibid., Vol. 1, Bk. 1, chap. 5, p. 33; chap. 6, p. 49.

definition of value in terms of labour—a definition which clearly made it logically impossible to ask what the value of a unit of labour might be. This resulted in a basic ambiguity as to productivity which persisted in English economics for a long time, since the productivity of labour as a whole was considered only in physical terms, while its productivity in different occupations was measured in value terms by the mechanism of supply and demand.[1] It was in this double use of the term that the cleavage in Ricardian Economics between the long-period and short-period theories of distribution originated. The long-run value of labour was based simply on the physical productivity of labourers in producing subsistence for labourers, while in the short run resources were considered to be distributed between different occupations by variations in the value productivity of labour, capital and land, determined by the demand and supply for a particular product.[2] To return, however, to Adam Smith's own theory. The change from a simple to a complex society led to the introduction of a "produce-less-deductions" theory of wages, but in itself this did not affect the basic dependence of wages on the productivity of labour.[3]

When Adam Smith tried to deal with the theory of natural prices, however, the influence of productivity became obscured. Quite logically he introduced the idea that wages are limited by the funds destined for the employment of labour, since it is just the necessity of advancing wages that characterizes an advanced society.[4] These funds turn out to be composed both of revenue and circulating capital; this is not important except to show that Adam Smith had no very clear ideas as to the determination of the size of

---

[1] *Wealth of Nations*, Vol. 1, Bk. 1, chap. 10, "On Wages and Profits in the different Employments of Labour and Stock," Introduction and sect. 1, pp. 101 et seq.

[2] Ricardo, *Principles of Political Economy*, chap. 5, "On Wages," pars. 35, 36 and 37, pp. 70–5; chap. 4, "On natural and market Price." Gonner's edition. (All page references to this edition.)

[3] *Wealth of Nations*, Vol. 1, Bk. 1, chap. 6, pp. 49–56; chap. 8, pp. 66–7.

[4] Ibid., Vol. 1, Bk. 1, chap. 8, pp. 66–8, 70–1; Bk. 11, Introduction, pp. 258–9.

the funds.[1] The idea of the wage fund is in no way inconsistent with the "produce-less-deductions" theory on the assumption that equilibrium is reached; obviously in equilibrium the total produce of labour will exactly equal the wages already advanced plus the natural return to capital and land. The fact that the natural price of capital was inadequately explained in the *Wealth of Nations* does not alter this, but it does explain the gradual omission of any serious connection of the wage fund with productivity by later economists.

The later omission of the productivity of labour arose, it appears, from a certain ambiguity in the use of the term natural price. It is fairly obvious that Adam Smith regarded the natural prices of labour and capital not as stationary equilibrium prices, but as current average prices.[2] The natural price of labour depends, according to the *Wealth of Nations*, on the extent of the employers' funds divided by the number of labourers. These funds may increase, decrease, or remain stationary according to the progress of society, which depends on general conditions explained in various places. There is no indication that any one of these states, progressive, declining, or stationary, is any more natural than any other. Owing, however, to the propagation habits of the human race it appears that wages will tend to be above, below, or at subsistence level in these respective circumstances.[3] On the other hand, according to Adam Smith's theory of value, the natural prices of commodities are based on their costs of production, that is on the natural prices of the factors; the latter have, however, no direct connection with the costs of production of the factors themselves. Thus the prices of commodities may be in

---

[1] See note 1 on p. 145 above and Taussig, *Wages and Capital*, Part II, chap. 7, pp. 141–6 of the reprint in the London School of Economics series of reprints of scarce tracts in Economics and Political Science.

[2] See Part I, chap. 2, "On Value"; note 6 on p. 71 and note 1 on p. 72 above.

[3] *Wealth of Nations*, Vol. I, Bk. I, chap. 8, p. 73. "Though the wealth of a country should be very great, yet if it has long been stationary, we must not expect to find the wages of labour very high in it. . . . The hands, on the contrary, would, in this case, naturally multiply beyond their employment."

equilibrium when the state of society is not stationary; for the natural price of labour is determined in the past by the decision which determined the size of the funds for the employment of labour, while the natural price of capital is determined in the present residually, since it is merely the current average rate of profits.[1] Thus commodities may exchange for their natural prices, i.e. the ratios of the sums of the natural prices of factors used, even though these latter are changing. This is possible because the natural price of capital being residually determined can absorb any increased productivity of labour. It is only in the next production period after the increase of the available funds that the increased product of labour will show in wages. In other words, Adam Smith appears to have regarded the natural price of labour as given from the past, and that of capital as a residual in the present. In the case of a perfectly stationary society this, of course, is simple enough, but under any other conditions it obscures the connection between the productivity of labour and the wages of labour. Naturally by the time Ricardo had limited the idea of a wage fund to the short period and the use of the term natural prices to long-period stationary equilibrium, the confusion as to the connection between wages as determined by the wage fund and by the productivity of labour was complete. Enemies of trade unions were able to assert without fear of contradiction that an increase in the wage of one group of labourers could only take place at the expense of others.

Finally, it is necessary to refer to Adam Smith's distinction between productive and unproductive labour.[2] This distinction which turned into such a stumbling-block later, was introduced in the *Wealth of Nations* only as part of the

---

[1] *Wealth of Nations*, Vol. 1, Bk. 1, chap. 9. Adam Smith did not define profits anywhere, and the natural rate of profits appeared in the *Wealth of Nations* to be simply the ordinary current rate, judging from the trouble he took to find out what that current rate was. Cf. Part 1, chap. 2, note 1 on p. 73 above. We are told, however, that the employer must receive something above the expenses of wages and materials and remuneration for his trouble in order to induce him to bother to invest capital. (Ibid., Vol. 1, Bk. 1, chap. 6, p. 50.) Cf. Cannan, *Theories of Production and Distribution*, pp. 200–3.

[2] *Wealth of Nations*, Vol. 1, Bk. 11, chap. 3. See Part 1, chap. 2, pp. 73–4 above.

explanation of the causes affecting the growth of wealth. It played no part in the actual discussion of the influences determining wages, except in so far as it explained causes indirectly affecting the size of the fund.

We can sum up the various sources of difficulty introduced by Adam Smith into the discussion of wages as follows: The productivity of labour is essentially important to his theory, but his introduction of the idea of a fund for the payment of wages confused the connection between wages and productivity. He seemed to treat the natural price of labour as independent of the cost of production of labour except in a stationary state, which he does not appear to have thought of as the natural state *par excellence*. Finally, the whole idea of the labour theory of value introduced the approach to wages, not by asking the simple question of how the value of unit of labour is determined, but by asking how the total share of labour in the final product is determined.

II.

In Adam Smith's treatment of wages the element of population had only an incidental influence on wages.[1] With the development of the rent analysis and the Malthusian theory of population it became, however, one of the most important considerations to be taken into account. Not merely did the theory of population introduce an important law of the supply of labour, but in Ricardo's hands it became an essential element in the determination of equilibrium. On the basis of these two functions of the theory of population subsequent wage theories can be classified parallel to the classification of the theories of value. The predominantly continental school which considered the relation between population and wages only from the first aspect if at all; and the Ricardian, which incorporated it into the theory of equilibrium value.

(1) *The Supply of Labour.*—Lauderdale, rather surprisingly, took no notice of the theory of population from either aspect

[1] See p. 72 above.

even in the second edition of his *Public Wealth*.[1] Some of the French economists, however, took Malthus' contribution seriously from the point of view that it threw light on the possibility of wages being lowered to subsistence level by the automatic expansion of population. Thus Say devoted a chapter at the end of the book on the "Distribution of Wealth" to the tendency of population to be limited by subsistence. He also incorporated in his theory of wages the idea that the supply of unskilled labour tends to increase or diminish with the fluctuations of wages about the customary standard of living.[2] Compared with Say, Destutt de Tracey devoted more attention to the Ricardian attitude to population and the probabilities of a stationary state. Nevertheless, he was too faithful a follower of Say to suggest that this had any relevance to wages, except by affecting the productivity of labour on which he explicitly said that wages depend.[3] The majority of continental economists, when they took any notice of population theory at all, copied Say in considering the possibility of changes in the size of population merely from the supply aspect. Hüfeland, Dunoyer, and von Mangoldt, for instance, considered population from this point of view, while Courcelle-Seneuil ignored it altogether.[4] Bastiat was of course an exception, since he thought the Ricardian analysis of the relation between population and rent of sufficient importance to be worth trying to disprove.[5]

Senior had more affinity to the continental group than to the Ricardian, but his position is somewhat peculiar. He considered Malthus' theory of great importance, and the

[1] *An Inquiry into the Nature and Origin of Public Wealth*, second edition, 1819, chap. 3, "Of the Sources of Wealth."
[2] *Traité d'Économie Politique*, Bk. II, chap. 11, "De la Population dans ses rapportes avec l'économie politique," and chap. 7, "Des Revenues Industriels," pp. 372–4, sixth edition.
[3] Destutt de Tracey, *Traité d'Économie Politique*, chap. 9, "La Population," and chap. 3, "De la mésure de l'utilité, ou des Valeurs," pp. 93–4.
[4] Hüfeland, *Neue Grundlegung der Staatswirthschaftskunst*, Part B, sect. 2, "In und nach dem Tausche." Dunoyer, *De la Liberté du Travail*, 1845, Bk. IV, chap. 10, pp. 408–71. Von Mangoldt, *Grundriss*, 1863, Bk. IV, chap. 3, pp. 133–6. Courcelle-Seneuil, *Traité theorique et practique*, 1858, Vol. I, Bk. 2, chap. 5, par. 4.
[5] Bastiat, *Economic Harmonies*, chaps. 14 and 16.

connection between rent, population and distribution as elucidated by Ricardo to be formally correct, but while admitting all this he neither made it a fundamental part of the theory of value nor of wages. As was explained in the chapter on Rent,[1] Senior denied the reality of any tendency for the pressure of population to bring about a stationary state. His denial, however, depended on his belief that the increase of population tends to produce improvements and increase productivity per head, and on his reliance on the ambition, prudence and forethought of the human race. Only if these influences failed to materialize would he admit the immanence of stationary equilibrium in the Ricardian sense.

It was obvious, therefore, that the theory of wages based on the Malthus-Ricardo analysis was bound to be of little interest to Senior. Since he admitted the derivation of values of factors from the value of their product and had done his best to dispose of the cost of production theory of value, any cost of production theory of wages would have been thoroughly inconsistent with his analysis of value. But in so far as the theory of population threw light on the supply of labour it might perhaps have been expected to be of some use to him, for he admitted the importance of supplies of factors in the determination of relative shares in the total product.[2]

Even from limited aspect, however, Senior's treatment of population in relation to wages is very scanty. The discussion of population proper is completely separated from that of the theory of wages in the *Political Economy*, and no mention of wages is made in it.[3] It is confined to a discussion of whether Malthus was right or wrong in his general outlook on the population problem as a whole. When we turn to the sections on distribution, it is really only by courtesy that we can say that Senior discussed the theory of population in relation to wages at all. The first heading that is in any way relevant is: "Causes on which the Proportionate

---

[1] See Part I, chap. 2, pp. 103–5 and chap. 3, pp. 118 et seq. above.

[2] *Political Economy*, p. 140.

[3] Ibid., "Population," pp. 29–50; "Wages," pp. 140–93.

Amount of Rent depends." Under this the question, which has little obvious connection with population theory, of whether rent depends on the fertility of the soil or the lack of fertility is the principal topic of discussion. Ricardo's excessive concentration on the comparative unfertility of land as the cause of rent is criticized. Pursuing this point, Senior reached the only consideration of population in this section, and even this has nothing specifically to do with wages:[1]

"Mr. Ricardo's attention seems to have been confined to the evil. But rent might be enormously increased without the increase of that evil, or even though that evil should be diminished. If the proprietor of a single estate could by a wish triple its produce, he would augment in a much greater ratio its rent. Would this increase be owing to the parsimony of nature? It may be said that it would be owing to the comparative unproductiveness of the rest of the country. It must be admitted that, if we could suddenly triple the productive powers of all the land in this country, the population remaining the same, the whole amount of rent would fall, and the condition of all classes, except of that comparatively small class which subsists on the rent of land, would be much improved. But if our population were also tripled, rents would be prodigiously increased, the situation of the landlords would be improved, and that of no other class deteriorated. In fact, the condition of all other classes would be improved, as the increased division of labour and ease of communication occasioned by a greater density of population would cheapen and improve our manufactures. If the population, instead of being tripled, were only doubled the situation of the country would be still better."[2]

This passage is not and was not intended to be a fundamental criticism of Ricardo, but as an indication of the small importance Senior attached to the stationary state analysis in distribution it has some interest.

The next section is headed "Proportionate Amounts of Profit and Wages"; in this the only passages of any relevance are the following:

[1] *Political Economy*, pp. 135–40. See also Part I, chap. 3, sect. I, above.
[2] *Political Economy*, pp. 138–9.

"The minimum at which wages can be permanently fixed is of course the sum necessary to enable the existing labouring population to subsist. On the other hand, as the rate of wages depends in a great measure on the number of labourers, and the rate of profit on the amount of capital, both high wages and high profits have a tendency to produce their own diminution. High wages, by stimulating an increase of population, and therefore an increase of the number of labourers, and high profits, by occasioning an increase in capital."

Senior went on to remark that although there is no obvious maximum to either profits or wages, "in no country have profits continued for any considerable period at the average rate of 50 per cent per annum, or wages at such a rate as to afford the labourer ten times the amount necessary for the subsistence of a family."[1] Beyond these nebulous passages there is nothing in Senior's formulation of the theory of wages to indicate that the theory of population had ever existed!

(2) *The Ricardian Use of Population Theory in the determination of Wages.*—The essential irrelevance of the theory of population to Senior's theory of wages is made even more obvious in contrast to its use by Ricardo. Ricardo started by confining the term natural price to the cost of production both for commodities and factors. This, of course, was only made possible by the adaptation of the Malthusian law of population into a theory of wages. With the help of the rent analysis the natural rate of wages became the rate which just suffices to maintain the supply of labour stationary at the customary standard of living. Since Ricardo was primarily only interested in the long-run analysis of the stationary state, this population theory of wages was his only well-thought-out explanation of wages. For the short run he was content initially with a loose formulation of the idea of the wage fund.[2] But in the third edition of his *Principles* he realized that the population theory was so much in the long run that it offered no explanation of the

[1] *Political Economy*, p. 140.
[2] *Principles*, chap. 5, "On Wages," pp. 71–5; chap. 16, "Taxes on Wages," pp. 203–4, 209. Gonner's edition.

effect of machinery on wages and of various other everyday important problems, and he devoted considerable attention to the wage fund.[1] It seems probable that this increased interest was also partly due to his changed opinion as to the difficulties of the capital theory with which the wage-fund theory was closely connected.

This tendency, started by Ricardo, gradually grew after his death, and interest in population theories of wages sank more into the background, even with McCulloch.[2] J. S. Mill, for example, devoted comparatively little attention to purely population theories of wages, and Cairnes in attempting, as he thought, to rehabilitate Ricardo concentrated almost exclusively on the wage fund. From this point of view Senior was in harmony with contemporary English development in his lack of interest in the connection between population and wages.

III.

In discussing Adam Smith's treatment of the influence of productivity on wages, it was pointed out that the idea of valuing labour was eliminated by the labour theory of value itself: that as labour was the standard and the source of value, there was no question of investigating how and why labour was valuable. Instead the problem of wages was envisaged as, given the total product, what does labour manage to retain after the deduction of profits and rent? It followed that economics was concerned with the product of labour as a whole, not with the value of a unit of labour. Essentially this attitude lasted in England for the first half of the nineteenth century. Wages were regarded with a few exceptions not as derived from the value of the product of a unit of labour, but as some physical amount which

[1] *Principles*, chap. 31, "On Machinery." Cf. Taussig, *Wages and Capital*, Part II, chap. 9.

[2] McCulloch explained definitely enough that the value of labour was determined by the cost of producing labour in his *Principles* (third edition, Part III, chap. 2, pp. 385 et seq.), even in the later editions, but in his pamphlet, *On the Circumstances which determine the Rate of Wages*, first edition, 1826, he concentrated exclusively on the wage fund.

derived its value from the value of the labour involved in producing it.

Obviously since Ricardo founded his whole analysis on the labour theory of value this was necessarily his approach. Its natural development would have been on an obvious produce-less-deductions line, but the introduction of the theories of rent and population led him to an attempt to determine the precise quantities of deductions;—an attempt which ended by irredeemably fogging the connection between wages and the productivity of labour, already made sufficiently obscure by the use of the wage fund in the *Wealth of Nations*. The result of his analysis of stationary equilibrium amounted to this: at the margin of cultivation rent is eliminated, and profits are at a known minimum rate, then either the number of labourers can be deduced given the standard of living, or, given the number of labourers, the standard of living. It is true, of course, that in order to determine the margin of cultivation the productivity of labour at that margin must be known, but the connection between the productivity and the wages of labour did not exactly leap to the eye because so many other considerations were involved. In explanation of this result it must be remembered that Ricardo's doubt as to the validity of the labour theory of value grew only as time went on, while the very completeness of this analysis made any further discussion of the connection between productivity and wages appear irrelevant. Until he was prepared to abandon it any direct approach by his followers to the determination of the value of labour other than the cost of the production of labour was impossible.

In the hands of James Mill and McCulloch the connection between wages and the productivity of labour was even more difficult to trace; while Torrens, and later J. S. Mill, though accepting Ricardo's last version of the cost of production theory of value, clearly saw no reason for striking out a new line.[1] Malthus protested vigorously, but spasmod-

---

[1] James Mill, *Elements of Political Economy*, third edition, 1826, chap. 2, p. 73. On McCulloch, see note 2 on p. 177 above. Torrens, *Essay on the External Corn Trade*, third edition, 1826, chap. 6, pp. 85–6, gave an uncompromising

ically, against the whole situation. In the first chapter of his *Principles* he asserted that the prices of factors of production depended on the same forces as the prices of commodities, that is on supply and demand, and only indirectly on cost of production.[1] But his limitation of wealth to material goods prevented him from using Say's theory of productive services which offered the easiest way of connecting the value of labour with the value of its product, and he failed to originate any serious theory of wages of his own.[2]

The only early English writer to consider the productivity of labour as the cause of the value of labour was Lauderdale, but he was too engrossed in his theory of public wealth to give much thought to the question.[3] In France, where Say and his followers had always derived value from utility, the English confusion did not exist. Say simply derived the values of all factors of production from the value of their products by demonstrating the parallelism between the service of factors and immaterial goods. Any cost of production theory of wages was therefore ruled out, and he treated wages like any other form of income. Say, however, was so much more interested in the general theory of mechanism of production than in distribution, that he offhandedly dismissed wage theory without any serious attempt to analyse the nature of the relation between capital and labour.[4] Similarly with other French economists; they accepted the general theory of productive services as

account of the cost of production or population theory, but in *Wages and Combinations*, 1834, chap. 1, introduced the cost of production of the labourer merely as a minimum, relying on a wage-fund theory for the actual determination of the rate of wages not limited merely to market price. J. S. Mill, *Principles*, Bk. II, chaps. 11–14, carried on Ricardo's theory and even in accepting Thornton's proof that it was impossible to define the wage fund as such (review of Thornton's *On Labour, its Wrongful Claims and Rightful Dues* in the *Fortnightly Review*, May 1869, reprinted in *Dissertations and Discussions*, Vol. IV) gave no hint as to the possible derivation of wages from the value of the product of labour.

[1] *Principles*, chap. 2, sect. 2, p. 65, first edition.

[2] See Part I, chap. 2, pp. 87–9 above.

[3] Lauderdale, *Public Wealth*, chap. 1, pp. 28–36, first edition.

[4] *Traité*, Bk. II, chap. 7, "Des Revenus Industriels," par. 4, "Des Profits de l'Ouvrier." For an account of Say's general theory of productive services see Part I, chap. 2, pp. 76–9 above.

applicable to labour and left it at that, without any attempt at precision. They at once were clearer than the Ricardians, and less interesting. They simply assumed that there was no difficulty.

In Germany, the generalization of the concept of rent to account for particular cases of wages and profits brought about a much closer approximation to modern analysis, since the complete form of the rent analysis is merely an application of the theory of marginal productivity. Though neither Hüfeland, Storch, nor Hermann improved upon Say's explanation of the determination of the value of a factor by its "relative productive importance," they all employed the rent idea to explain deviations of earnings from the average. Undoubtedly this prepared the way for von Thünen's evolution of the theory of marginal productivity from his study of the rent of the land, and for von Mangoldt's perfectly clear use of the theory in his *Grundriss* in 1863. It is highly improbable that the early users of the extended rent concept, such as Hüfeland, were fully aware of its implications. Nevertheless its application, in whatever form, to earnings of particular units and types of labour and capital is significant, for it began the breakdown of the traditional approach to distribution from the side of the total share of each generic factor of production. The application of the rent analysis involved asking the vital question of why a particular unit of a factor is valuable— a question that has been pushed into the background by the labour and cost of production theories of value.[1]

To explain Senior's views on the relation of the productivity of labour to wages is a matter of some difficulty. He utilized in his discussion of wages at one point or another

---

[1] Hüfeland, op. cit., Part B, sect. 2. Hermann's inclusion of land in capital on the ground that the income of capital was determined in the same way as that from land, seems to show that he understood the possibility of applying the marginal analysis to the former. It is possible that he really admitted its application to wages as well, but he paid comparatively little attention to wage theory, and it is possible only to guess that he had some grasp of the general ideas of the marginal analysis. *Staatswirtschaftliche Untersuchungen*, chap. 3. See Part I, chap. 3, pp. 133 et seq. above. Von Thünen, *Der Isolirte Staat*, Part II, pp. 162–93, 1849 edition. Von Mangoldt, *Grundriss der Volkswirtschaftslehre*, pp. 117 and 131, first edition, 1863.

practically all the ideas that had been canvassed by other writers, except the population theory: Say's theory of productive services, the produce-less-deductions theory characteristic of part of Adam Smith's and Ricardo's analyses, the wage fund, and the generalization of rent. It is only possible to fit them all together by taking the risk of selecting a probable explanation of the incorporation of each part, for Senior himself scattered his reflections on wages throughout almost every part of his *Political Economy* (except the section devoted to the theory of population). The alternative is merely to describe the isolated ideas and leave the confusion. The former course is obviously the most interesting, and I shall attempt to fit the pieces together in the light of his position in the development of the theory of value.

In the first place it is important to remember that Senior was very much influenced by Say's theory of value, and that he took special pains to explain why immaterial goods were to be included in wealth. Now immaterial goods are simply services, and Senior in illustrating their transferability took a wide range of illustrations of the sort of thing he meant, explaining that the skill of lawyers, the strength of a navvy, and the shelter afforded by a house are all immaterial goods, and must be considered in the elucidation of the general laws of value:

"Health, strength, and knowledge, and the other natural and acquired powers of the body and mind, appear to us to be articles of Wealth, precisely analogous to a residence having some qualities that are universally useful, and others peculiarly adapted to the tastes of its owner. They are limited in supply, and are causes of pleasure and preventives of pain far more effectual than the possession of Alnwick or Blenheim."[1]

In taking up the question of the distinction between services and commodities in the definition of production, he repeats this still more clearly:

"But, objecting as we do to a nomenclature which should consider producers as divided, by the nature of their products,

[1] *Political Economy*, p. 10.

into producers of services and producers of commodities, we are
ready to admit the convenience of the distinction between
services and commodities themselves, and to apply the term
service to the act of occasioning an alteration in the existing state
of things, the term *commodity* to the thing altered: the term
product including both commodities and services."[1]

This is, of course, on the lines of Say's theory of productive
services.

In the second place, Senior generalized the theory of rent
to account for the value of units of particular sorts of labour.
Now clearly, if part of a man's wages are derived according
to the theory of rent from the particular value of his product,
it is difficult to maintain that the whole of his wages are
not derived from the value of his product, unless we introduce
the idea of the cost of production. But since Senior ignored
the population theory of wages he did not do this. He was
in fact acutely aware of the difficulty of distinguishing rent
from wages and profits, maintaining that the ordinary
classification of incomes into these three categories was
highly unsatisfactory. In his discussions of nomenclature at
the beginning of the second part of the *Political Economy*
he pointed out that—

"The defectiveness of the established nomenclature is more
striking when we come to the third class. Wages and profits are
the creation of man. They are the recompense for the sacrifice
made, in the one case, of ease; in the other, of immediate
enjoyment. But a considerable part of the produce of every
country is the recompense for no sacrifice whatever; [it] is received
by those who neither labour nor put by, but merely hold out
their hands to accept the offerings of the rest of the community."[2]

and explained a little further on that this unearned income
is received by many people besides the owners of the land.
Any classification of incomes on a uniform principle he
concluded is impossible, and the classing of some incomes
as profits, or wages, or rent, is merely a matter of convenience:

"At a distance, these divisions appear clearly marked; but
when we look into the details, we find them so intermingled, that

[1] *Political Economy*, p. 53.   [2] Ibid., p. 89.

it is scarcely possible to subject them to a classification which shall not sometimes appear to be inconsistent, and still more frequently to be arbitrary. But it must be remembered that questions of classification relate rather to language than to facts; and that our object will have been effected if we can assist the memory by supplying a precise and consistent nomenclature.

"We will begin by recurring to a subject to which we have already alluded, the frequent difficulty of deciding whether a given revenue ought or ought not to be called Rent."[1]

A few paragraphs further on he discussed the problem with special reference to labour:

"Is, then, the extraordinary remuneration of the labourer, which is assisted by extraordinary talents, to be termed Rent or Wages? It originates in the bounty of nature; so far it seems to be rent. It is to be obtained only on the condition of undergoing labour; so far it seems to be wages. It might be termed, with equal correctness, rent, which can only be received by a labourer; or wages, which can be received only by the proprietor of a natural agent. But as it is clearly a surplus, the labour having been previously paid for by average wages, and that surplus the spontaneous gift of nature, we have thought it most convenient to term it rent."[2]

Since this treatment of wages is just the same as his treatment of profits, it is clearly legitimate to interpret it in the same way: that Senior considered the only distinction between rent and wages to be that rent has no minimum, while wages have a minimum determined by the necessity of rewarding the sacrifice of ease sufficiently to induce its continuation.

This interpretation seems entirely justified by the lecture *On the Cost of Obtaining Money*, which has not been generally taken into consideration in discussions of Senior's theory of wages. In this lecture Senior explained that England's competitive strength depends on the efficiency of English labour, and that high wages are a necessary consequence of that efficiency; that labourers, if artificially forced, e.g. by tariffs, etc., into comparatively unproductive employments, must be paid "according to the value of what

[1] *Political Economy*, p. 128.　　　　[2] Ibid., pp. 129–30.

they might produce if their labour were properly directed," and that to "complain of our high wages is to complain that our labour is productive."[1]

In fact the lecture taken as a whole is a statement of a productivity theory of wages, with some suggestion of the marginal analysis. The whole argument demonstrated that foreign trade is pushed to that point at which labour plus a given amount of capital ceases to be more profitably employed than in the home trade. This is the margin at which the money wages of labour are determined by their productivity, and by which wages in all other occupations are regulated. Or, as Senior put it in the elementary example in the lecture *On the Value of Money*, where gold is produced in an isolated community wages are determined by the amount of gold produced by a day's labour in the worst mine that, in all the given circumstances of tastes, etc., it is profitable to work. At least two of Senior's contemporaries believed that he held a productivity theory of some sort; Scrope paraphrased a passage from these same lectures about the Hindoo's and the Englishman's wages as Senior's theory of wages, and J. L. Mallet recounted in his *Diaries* a discussion at the Political Economy Club in which Senior maintained that the wages of labour are determined by the price of the products of labour.[2]

Finally there is an interesting passage in the 1847–52 Lectures in which Senior explained that he was not prepared to include labour in capital as well as land, because man is the controlling force in production.[3] Now if this is the only important distinction between labour and land it seems probable that Senior derived the wages of labour, like the rent of land, from the value of its product.

---

[1] *Three Lectures on the Cost of Obtaining Money, etc.*, London School of Economics reprint, Lecture 1, quotation from pp. 26–8. Cf. Part 1, chap. 6, p. 201 below.

[2] Scrope, *Quarterly Review*, January 1831, Vol. xlv, Art. I, pp. 31–3, repeated in his *Principles*, 1833, pp. 88–9. The passage in Senior's lectures referred to is on pp. 11–14 of the London School of Economics reprint of the *Lectures on the Cost of Obtaining Money. Proceedings of the Political Economy Club*, J. L. Mallet's *Diaries*, p. 226. Mallet said that Senior maintained that the real wages of labour always depended on the "value of the exchangeable produce of such labour."

[3] Lectures, 1847–52, Course II, lecture 3.

It seems fairly clear from all this that Senior started from the basic idea that wages were derived from the value of the product of labour, not vice versa. A further consideration in support of this interpretation is to be found in Senior's treatment of the relation of cost to value. He explicitly rejected the cost of production theory of value except in the one case of constant costs, in which he admitted that cost *regulates* value. Now, as Senior did not use the population theory of wages seriously at all, there is no reason for assuming that he had any idea that the value of labour was determined differently from the values of commodities; on the other hand, the presumption the other way is very strong. If this is correct, his peculiar theory of the wage fund based on a produce-less-deductions theory seems an unsuccessful attempt to determine ordinary wages residually, in a way which would explain the connection between wages and capital. It was this attempt which Senior himself considered as his theory of wages.

Before going on to the wage fund theory, Longfield's contributions to the productivity theory must be noted. Longfield, in his lectures at Dublin given a few years after Senior's first set at Oxford, expounded a definite marginal productivity theory of wages. It is one of the mysteries of the history of economic theory that Senior and Longfield, who evidently knew each other, and who held very similar theories of value, appeared to have no influence on each other whatever. Senior never mentioned Longfield's theory of wages even in the lectures of 1847, nor his theory of value.[1]

IV.

The wage-fund theory in itself contains nothing inconsistent with a productivity theory of wages. Its initial introduction by Adam Smith was, as we have seen, to explain the relation between capital and labour within the scope of the produce-

[1] *Lectures on Political Economy*, 1833, published 1834, lecture 10. Longfield's successor, Isaac Butt, attempted to take the analysis one step further by analysing the relation between the marginal productivities of labour, land and capital. See Part I, chap. 2, pp. 109–10 above.

less-deduction theory of wages. From this aspect it might be regarded as a part of capital theory at least as well as a part of wage theory. A long line of capital theories have, in fact, been generalized versions of the wage fund developed to explain the relationship between the value of present resources and the present values of their future products. This line started off from Ricardo, was taken up again by Jevons, and culminated with the Austrian theory; its relationship to the more recent Swedish developments is equally clear. In the restricted sphere of wage problems the same type of theory has turned up again in Taussig's discounted productivity theory of wages.

What appears surprising in the life history of the wage-fund theory is not that it was adopted, but that it became an object of ridicule—that J. S. Mill's recantation of it was hailed as a sign of emancipation from the thraldom of the classical tradition, and the essential preliminary to a reasonable theory of wages.[1] This situation has arisen, it seems, from the confusion between the wage fund as an explanation of the particular aspect of the wages question and the wage fund as a theory of wages, which originated in the *Wealth of Nations*. Instead of being part of the produce-less-deductions theory it gradually was substituted for it, partially perhaps as a short method of expressing the way in which wages are determined, and partially because the produce-less-deductions theory is insufficient alone to explain how the current payment of wages can be actually made.

It was apparently for both reasons that the wage fund was introduced by Ricardo and his followers as a short-period theory of wages. All Ricardo wanted to do to start with was to shelve the question of short-period wages. The obvious method was to adopt an explanation parallel to that of the short-period pricing of commodities. In contrast to the natural, the market price of commodities and of capital was thought to be determined by the accidents of supply and demand, and it was simple to say the same of the short-period price of labour. Adam Smith had said

[1] Review of Thornton's *On Labour, its Wrongful Claims and Rightful Dues*, reprinted in *Dissertations and Discussions*, Vol. IV.

that the demand for labour consists of the fund for the payment of wages, composed chiefly of circulating capital; this was accepted as an explanation ready to hand of the demand for labour, as well as an explanation of how the demand for labour is made effective.[1]

But this misleading, though initially harmless, application of the wage-fund theory led to the serious result that those economists who were dealing with short-period problems believed that they had a theory of wages. Thus we find cropping up again and again in discussions of short-period wages a complete divorce of the productivity of labour from the wages of labour, a cleavage far greater than in Ricardo's long-run analysis.

Senior's attempt to explain the average rate of wages by means of the wage fund is particularly interesting because he went back to the original idea that it was intimately connected with a produce-less-deductions theory. That he adopted it was not particularly surprising, as his theory of capital was based on the idea that capital arose from the abstinence from the consumption of resources in immediate enjoyment in order to secure future enjoyment. This is merely another way of saying that the function of capital is to advance funds for the support of labour while the produce is being produced. It is clear that the question of the relation between capital and wages must have cropped up anyhow, but, in the absence of any pretence of precision in the French theory of productive services, it was self-evident for Senior to attempt to achieve precision along these lines.

Senior started from the simple arithmetical statement that—

"The quantity and quality of commodities obtained by each labouring family during a year must depend on the quantity and quality of the commodities directly or indirectly appropriated to the use of the labouring population, compared with the number of labouring families (including under that term all those who depend on their own labour for subsistence); or, to

[1] Ricardo, *Principles*, chap. 5, pp. 71–5. Cf. Taussig, *Wages and Capital*, Part II, chap. 9.

speak more concisely, *on the Extent of the Fund for the maintenance of Labourers, compared with the Number of Labourers to be maintained.*"[1]

He then went on to an elaborate discussion, which is not of much interest, of seven opinions inconsistent with this obvious truism.[2] The next step Senior was aware was to find out the determinants of the fund, and it is in the search for these that his statement of the wage-fund theory is significantly different from others:

"On what, then, does the extent of the fund depend? In the *first* place, on the productiveness of labour in the direct or indirect production of the commodities used by the labourer, and, in the *second* place, on the number of persons directly or indirectly employed in the production of things for the use of labourers, compared with the whole number of labouring families."[3]

In this statement Senior had already created quite gratuitously a difficulty. Things produced for the use of labourers are sharply differentiated from things produced for other people. This idea had lurked in other statements of the doctrine in the assumption made that the wage fund is at any given time fixed in size by the supply of wage goods. J. S. Mill was the first person who explicitly got rid of this particular limitation, though it failed to help him as he clung to the idea that the size of the fund was irrevocably determined at the beginning of a definite production period.[4]

Senior first dealt at some length with the simple determinants of the productivity of labour under the following headings—

1. "the corporeal, intellectual, and moral qualities of the labourer. . . ."
2. "the natural agents by which it is assisted. . . ."

[1] *Political Economy*, p. 154. Senior's italics.
[2] Ibid., pp. 154–74. For an account of Senior's discussion of the seven opinions see note at the end of chapter.
[3] Ibid., p. 174.
[4] *Principles*, Bk. I, chap. 4, par. 1; Bk. II, chap. 11, par. 1; Bk. v, chap. 10, par. 5. Cf. Taussig, *Wages and Capital*, chap. 11.

3. "the degree to which it is assisted by abstinence, or, to use a more familiar expression, by the use of capital. . . ."

4. "the existence or the absence of Government interference. . . ."[1]

These are all perfectly straightforward, and include nothing peculiar either to Senior or to the wage fund.

The next step was to introduce the idea of produce-less-deductions. In the section devoted to the explanation of this second factor is headed "Causes which Divert Labour from the Production of Commodities for the use of Labouring Families. 1. Rent. 2. Taxation. 3. Profit," labour was described as diverted from production entirely for itself to produce things to be used by the respective owners of natural agents and capital, and by the Government.[2]

That Senior's chief object in embarking on the wage fund was connected with the problems of capital was shown by his remorseless elimination of first rent and then taxation from the picture. Rent he got rid of on the ground that it is a residual income dependent on the existence of natural agents of peculiar productivity. Thus it follows that—

"Such labourers may, in fact, be considered as existing only in consequence of the existence of natural agents of extraordinary productiveness. They draw their subsistence, not from the common fund, such as it would otherwise be, but from the addition made to that fund by that extraordinary productiveness."[3]

Senior seemed to have forgotten completely that he had here left out part of the problem; the number of labourers employed by rent, and therefore removed from the rest of the labour market, could only be decided if the total rent was divided by the average rate of wages, the very unknown that he had to find. Thus by eliminating rent he had only made the rest of the question indeterminate by making an unknown of the number of labourers to be supported.

---

[1] *Political Economy*, pp. 175–81. [2] Ibid., pp. 180–6.

[3] Ibid., p. 181. Senior added very lamely that these labourers can be regarded as extrinsic to the labour market proper, as rent is something extra (p. 185).

He went on, however, to invalidate his own argument quite hopelessly by admitting that where rent is due to an increase of population more rapid than the productivity of labour applied to land, it cannot be ignored in this way. He excused himself from explaining how it is to be treated in this case by the lame excuse that where there is no mis-government it is unlikely to occur, thus cheerfully asserting that diminishing returns in fact never exist in the main case relevant to his analysis.[1] Taxation was eliminated on the more reasonable ground that Government actions in general "are rather disturbing causes than necessary elements in the calculations of political economy."[2]

After all this Senior was free to get down to what he obviously considered the heart of the problem—the relation between profit and wages. The beginning is not very promising.

"The facts," he said, "which decide in what proportions the capitalist and labourer share the common fund appear to be two: first, *the general rate of profit in the country on the advance of capital for a given period:* and secondly, *the period which, in each particular case, has elapsed between the advance of the capital and the receipt of the profit.*"[3]

His explanation of the rate of profits is however curiously inadequate. He repeated that profits are the reward for the abstinence involved in advancing materials, instruments and subsistence to labour; in short, for the foregoing of immediate consumption on the part of the capitalist. The actual rate, he explained, is determined by the difference between the value of advance and the value of return, allowing for fixed capital.[4] This of course explained exactly nothing, and did not advance the question at all.

Senior next approached the general problem in a round-about way:

"It will be admitted that, in the absence of disturbing causes, the rate of profits in all employments of capital is equal. If we

---

[1] *Political Economy*, pp. 181–2.   [2] Ibid., p. 185.
[3] Ibid., p. 185–6. Senior's italics.   [4] Ibid., p. 186.

can ascertain, therefore, what are the causes which regulate the rate of profit in any one of the main employments of capital, we may infer that, in the absence of peculiar disturbance, either the same causes, or causes of equal force, occasion it to be the same in all others."[1]

He selected as an example the hypothetical case of a colony where land is free, where the number of capitalists and the amount of capital is known, and the number of labourers; where the period of production is of uniform length of one year and starts on the first day of the year for everybody, when wages (in goods) are advanced to be returned at the end of the year. Now this is a highly unrealistic example, but if Senior had worked out a solution with it he might have extended his analysis to deal with more complicated and realistic conditions. He doomed himself to failure, however, by his careful assumption that the wage fund is determined irrevocably at the beginning of the year, and that all production proceeds parallel through the period.

For since he had assumed to start with that wage goods are essentially different from other goods, he had assumed that the size of the wage fund is fixed for any given period, unless he had treated the periods of production of wage goods as variable. Only then could the size of the fund be varied during the year in response to higher wages offered on the basis of some anticipated change in the productivity of labour.[2]

The only conclusion he reached, after lengthy repetition, was that if the capitalists decide to increase their circulating capital by devoting more labourers than usual to produce wage goods for the succeeding year instead of income for themselves, in the next year they will have more capital, and this will drive up wages and lower the rate, but not the amount of profits.

[1] *Political Economy*, p. 188.
[2] That Senior should gradually forget that these were merely simplifying assumptions and so unrealistic as to invalidate the application of the conclusions drawn from the case based on them, is all the more surprising in view of a passage in which he criticized Adam Smith for giving a similar false impression. *Political Economy*, pp. 78–9. Cf. Part I, chap. 4, p. 147 above.

His final conclusion was merely that in this example the rate of profit appears to depend on

"the amount of labour which at a previous period was devoted to the production of wages, compared with the amount of labour which these wages when produced can command."[1]

and by analogy the rate of profits in all other employments is determined.

As to the second influence on proportionate shares, the average period of advance of capital, Senior stated rather in despair that it depends on the actual circumstances of the country and industry, and cannot be reduced to a general rule. Finally Senior came back to approximately where he began with the remark that the average rate of profits appears to depend on "the previous conduct of the capitalists and the labourers in a country."[2]

Without a shadow of doubt this was all a complete failure, but the attempt is nevertheless of importance. It was the first and practically the last attempt to explain what the wage fund really was, for after Senior the usual casualness of statement reappeared. When Longe again brought up the question it was not to explain the connection between wages and capital, but to point out that the examination of this connection was not in itself a theory of wages.[3] Thornton's attempt was on rather different lines; by showing that in some cases simple demand and supply curves for labour might intersect more than once, he thought he had got rid of the simplicity of the wage-fund idea.[4] So he had as far as it was merely a short-run theory of market wages. The criticism applied to the ordinary exposition, but not to Senior's, which was essentially meant to be an explanation of the continuous and changing relation between wages and capital, from which the average rate of wages might be deduced. Even Cairnes, in attempting

[1] *Political Economy*, pp. 188–94. Quotation from p. 194.   [2] Ibid., p. 199.
[3] F. D. Longe, *A Refutation of the Wage-fund Theory*, 1866. Longe's main criticisms were directed against the idea of fixity of the fund (pp. 17–56) and the divorce of wages from the productivity of labour (pp. 60–3).
[4] W. T. Thornton, *On Labour, etc.*, 1869, Bk. II, chap. I, "Of Supply and Demand, and of their influence on Price and Wages."

to reconstruct the whole wage-fund theory, considered it as chiefly significant as a theory of wages in the short period.[1]

In fact the situation was this: the ordinary post-Smithian treatment of the wage fund was simply as a crude statement of the determination of wages by supply and demand in the short period. Thornton's attack and Cairnes' reply were concerned solely with the question of whether it was adequate for this purpose. Longe's criticism was more fundamental in that it denied that the wage fund was a theory of wages at all, but it ignored the existence of the real problem altogether. The real interest of this controversy is that it illustrated the increased interest in short-period problems. Senior's contribution, on the other hand, was that of denying the relevance of the long-period analysis altogether, and insisting that a complete theory of wages must relate the productivity of labour to the theory of capital.

V.

It was not to be expected that the analysis of wages in different occupations would, in the general atmosphere of classical economics, develop much beyond Adam Smith's account. The bearing of the existence of different wage rates on the labour theory of value does not really concern us, as Senior had rejected the labour theory long before he came to wages, but as it played some part in Bailey's criticism of Ricardo it may have indirectly influenced him.[2] Ricardo and J. S. Mill simply assumed that differences in wage-rates are settled by higgling and bargaining, and can be treated analogously to differences in capital structures: Cairnes, though he admitted that the problem was of importance, and dignified it by discussing it under the head of non-competing groups, did not regard it as constituting a reason for overhauling the theory of value.[3]

[1] Cairnes, *Some Leading Principles of Political Economy*, Part II, chaps. 1 and 2.

[2] Bailey, *Dissertation on the Nature, Measures and Causes of Value, etc.*, chap. 11, pp. 207–15. Cf. Part I, chap. 2, p. 70, note 1 above.

[3] Cairnes, *Leading Principles of Political Economy*, Part I, chap. 3, pars. 5, 6, and 7.

Senior's concern with the problem was on a different basis, as a question of wage theory instead of as an exception to the general theory of value. His treatment of it was, however, surprisingly disappointing, and amounted to a reiteration of Adam Smith with a few modifications of details. He merely described in the usual way the causes of differences as agreeableness, facility of learning the business, constancy of employment, trustworthiness, probability of success.[1] The exposition might have been McCulloch's! In fact Malthus, in stating that high wages for responsible positions are due simply to the scarcity of persons suited to such positions, not to any inherent attribute of responsibility, threw far more light on the whole question.[2]

Why Senior did not apply or attempt to apply the rent analysis it is difficult to explain, unless he was simply bored with the whole business. In the final section on wages Senior, however, recovered himself to some extent in explaining the differences in wages caused by the immobility of labour:

"The inequalities in wages and profits which we have as yet considered arise from causes inherent in the employments themselves which have been the subjects of discussion, and would, generally speaking, exist even if one occupation could at will be exchanged for another. But great inequalities are found which cannot be accounted for by any circumstances leading men to prefer one employment to another, and which therefore continue only in consequence of the difficulties experienced by the labourers and capitalists in changing their employments."[3]

This opened up the way more promisingly, and he went on to explain the causes of immobility as the specialization of labour to few processes, and the general necessity of starting a trade young in order to acquire this specialized skill. As far as immobility between countries is concerned, Senior pointed out the moral, emotional and physical difficulties which prevent labour always moving so as to equalize wages in different parts either of one country or

---

[1] *Political Economy*, pp. 200–16.
[2] Malthus, *Principles*, chap. 2, sect. iii, p. 79, first edition.
[3] *Political Economy*, pp. 217–20. Quotation from p. 217.

of the world.[1] But he made no suggestion that any of this might have been stated in terms of rent analysis.

Senior's reviewer in the *Edinburgh Review* suggested that logically the rent analysis ought to be extended to explain the differences in wages both in different occupations and in different countries.[2] The former step Senior shrank from taking for no very obvious reason, for, if allowance is made for net advantages, it is perfectly logical, and may be enlightening. The latter step would have taken him outside the field to which he thought the extension of the rent analysis was useful, for he had introduced it to explain deviations from the current average rate of wages within one country due to natural or accidental advantages. The delimitation of the field in which it is useful to call particular incomes rent or wages respectively depends, as Senior pointed out, not on logic, but on convenience, and it is obviously not convenient to introduce the idea of rent when comparing wages in different countries. Senior was perfectly justified in not replying to his critic.[3]

VI.

The question remains of deciding how far these different elements in Senior's discussions on wages fit into anything

[1] *Political Economy*, pp. 220–5.

[2] *Edinburgh Review*, October 1837, pp. 73–102.

[3] Bibliographical Note.—Senior's lectures on wages, in which he expounded his theory of the wage fund, were given at Oxford in 1830 and published in the same year with the addition of a preface on "the causes and remedies of the present disturbances." The preface was clearly a diagnosis of the evils of the various systems of allowances in aid of wages given under the unreformed Poor Law, and was included in substance in his later writings on the Poor Laws. The actual lectures were reprinted without any important alterations in the *Political Economy*, pp. 142–3, and 147–74, with the exception of part of p. 150. There are no lectures on wages in the 1847–52 group except for a discussion of the variations of demand for labour in different employments and a diatribe against the violent attempts of Trade Unions to raise wages, in the sixth and only lecture remaining of the Fifth Course. The wage-fund theory was repeated very briefly in Senior's review of J. S. Mill's *Principles of Political Economy* and *Essays on Some Unsettled Questions* in the *Edinburgh Review*, 1848. For a bibliographical account of Senior's treatment of population and his extension of the rent concept, see Part I, chap. 3, note 1 on p. 118 and note 1 on p. 128 above.

like a coherent theory of wages. One thing emerges pretty clearly, that except in specifically dealing with wages in different employments he attached great importance to the influence of productivity on wages. In the earlier discussion of the general theory of value and generalization of rent, Senior derived the value of factors from the value of their product, which in turn depends on nothing physical but on marginal utility. He next showed the relevance of this analysis to the income of special factors of production by the extension of the rent analysis. This contained the characteristics of the modern analysis of the value per unit of factors of production. When, however, he came to the wage-fund theory this idea was lost. Productivity was still important, but it was physical productivity; instead of the analysis of the value of units of factors, the problem was considered in the usual way as that of the distribution of the total product in lumps between factors. The reconciliation of these divergences is, I think, impossible; whether it would have been if the result of Senior's wage-fund analysis had been more coherent is difficult to say. The question thus reduces to why the divergence crept in— Why Senior started with what promised to be a more complete version of Say's theory of productive services, and ended up with something like Adam Smith's produce-less-deductions?

A possible explanation, which is really a guess, is, I suggest, to be found in Senior's position between Say and Ricardo. Say's theory, on which Senior improved with the more precise analysis of the nature of rent, took him only up to a certain point. It explained neither the connection between capital and labour, nor the way in which the actual value of any particular factor is determined, except by a vague reference to "relative productive importance" without explaining how that is itself determined, except in general terms of the relative scarcity of different factors. In England, on the other hand, the relation of capital to labour had received more emphasis; it is obvious that Senior would naturally turn to the English analysis at this point. But further he had rejected Ricardo's long-run analysis of wages partly as irrelevant, since it is only applicable to a very hypothetical long run, and partly because it is based on a cost of production analysis. The wage fund which, between them, Adam Smith and Ricardo had elevated into a theory of wages, was open to neither of these objections, and there was good precedent in the *Wealth of Nations* for regarding it both as connected with productivity and applicable to more than mere market price. What could be more natural than that Senior should regard it as a solution to the question of how ordinary wages were determined?

Senior, if this interpretation is correct, thus appears as the reviver of the importance of the element of productivity in the theory of wages in England, an element which had never quite disappeared, but which had got badly mixed up with other considerations. And his theory of wages turns out as an illustration of the difficulty of reconciling the continental analysis with Ricardo's; a difficulty that has only been resolved with all the finesse of the application of mathematical analysis to the theory of marginal productivity, and the Austrian theory of capital.

In his attempt to grapple with this problem of wages and capital Senior was completely alone both in England and France, though in Germany an appreciation of the difficulties was displayed by von Thünen, whose results were little, if any, more satisfactory than Senior's. The work of Hermann and von Mangoldt, which had so much in common with Senior's in the field of value theory, resembled his on wage theory only in so far as it continued Say's tradition and generalized rent. Under the circumstances it is perhaps natural that Senior's theory of wages should have had no influence, for it was less a theory than inquiry, it posed a question without giving the answer.

NOTE ON THE SEVEN OPINIONS INCONSISTENT WITH SENIOR'S
STATEMENT OF THE WAGE-FUND THEORY

Senior summarized the seven opinions as follows:

1. "that the Rate of Wages depends solely on the proportion which the number of Labourers bears to the amount of Capital in the country,"

2. "that Wages depend on the proportion borne by the number of Labourers to the whole Revenue of the society of which they are members,"
3. "that the Non-residence of Unproductive Consumers can be detrimental to the Labouring inhabitants of a country which does *not* export Raw Produce,"
4. "that the general rate of Wages can, except in two cases, be diminished by the introduction of Machinery,"
5. "that the general rate of Wages can be reduced by the importation of Foreign Commodities,"
6. "that the Unproductive Consumption of Landlords and Capitalists is beneficial to the Labouring classes because it furnishes them with employment,"
7. "that it is more beneficial to the Labouring classes to be employed in the production of Services than in the production of Commodities."[1]

The first five opinions are uninteresting, and were regarded by Senior as such since they ignored the whole problem he was trying to investigate, the causes which determine the proportion of resources which will in some way or other be devoted to the production of wages.[2] The sixth Senior dismissed as irrelevant as concerned with employment independently of wages.[3] The seventh, however, is of some interest as it was advanced by Ricardo, and later elaborated by J. S. Mill,[4] and has cropped up in various forms recently. Senior argued that this theory must be wrong since—

"it is clear that the whole quantity of commodities provided for the use of labourers is not increased by the conversion of an artisan into a footman or a soldier."[5]

Ricardo's mistake, he thought, was due to double counting. No one, Senior argued, can spend their income more than once, and it can make no difference, *ceteris paribus*, if, instead of buying commodities from producers, those producers are employed as servants and paid wages in order that they

---

[1] *Political Economy*, p. vii.   [2] Ibid., pp. 154–69.
[3] Ibid., pp. 169–70.
[4] Ricardo, *Principles of Political Economy*, chap. 31, pp. 384–6. J. S. Mill, *Principles of Political Economy*, Bk. 1, chap. 5, par. 9.
[5] *Political Economy*, pp. 170–4. Quotation from p. 172.

may produce those goods within the master's house.[1] In short, it makes no difference whether cake is made at home instead of being bought from the baker, except to increase the demand for servants and decrease the demand for bakers as such.

This seems fairly obvious, and it has never been successfully refuted. It is clear that at any moment of time, in the absence of any hoarding or inflation, or a change of the velocity of expenditure of current income through time, nothing can increase the amount that can be spent, and it must either be spent in paying directly for services, or in enabling other people to do so.

The whole discussion as elaborated by J. S. Mill turned on the third condition. He argued that the demand for commodities is not a demand for labour, since this depends on advances of capital, the purchasing of commodities is not an advance of capital. It followed, he thought, that if income was spent on services it would increase employment of servants without decreasing employment in the production of commodities. To this must be objected that such a redistribution of expenditure prevents the release of capital already embodied in commodities, and therefore would theoretically cause unemployment corresponding to the increase in the employment of services. To this argument Mill replied that the newly employed servants would buy the commodities and release the otherwise frozen capital.[2] This is clearly illegitimate, as it assumes a sudden doubling of the velocity of circulation of money.

This confusion in both Ricardo and Mill is obviously related to their belief that the wages of servants, or unproductive labourers, were paid out of revenue, and those of productive labour out of capital. Their concentration on this distinction led them to ignore the stage in the circulating process at which circulating capital becomes free, and can either go back by devious ways into the process of production by being spent on services, or, more directly, by being spent on commodities, but cannot be spent in both ways

---

[1] *Political Economy*, p. 172.
[2] *Principles of Political Economy*, Bk. i, chap. 5, par. 9.

at the same moment. Now Senior treated all sorts of labour as productive, and all wages as being paid from the same wage fund, not some from capital and some from income, and thus he avoided this particular confusion. At any moment, he had declared, all income must, *ceteris paribus*, be spent either on goods or on services; it does not matter which.[1] The actual distribution is relevant only to future wages, and that only indirectly, since future wages depend on capital accumulation which may be influenced by the difference in willingness to save of artisans and servants respectively.[2]

[1] *Political Economy*, p. 170.
[2] Ibid., p. 173. Senior was not convinced by J. S. Mill's arguments any more than by Ricardo's. *Edinburgh Review*, October 1848, Vol. 88, p. 312. Review of Mill's *Essays* and *Principles*.

CHAPTER 6

MONEY AND INTERNATIONAL TRADE

RECENT discussions of the theory of international trade have brought out the fact that there are two ways of treating it, both theoretically valid. It is possible to analyse international trade as a problem distinct from ordinary value theory by investigating comparative physical costs, and then translating the analysis into money terms to show the relation between international trade and local price levels. On the other hand it is equally possible to treat the whole problem as part of ordinary value analysis where there are pronounced immobilities of factors of production.

The first method, developed by Ricardo when he realized that the labour theory of value was inapplicable to international trade owing to the immobilities of resources, is historically the older. Ricardo's theory of comparative costs, together with some supplementary analysis added by J. S. Mill, suffices to explain the conditions of trade between countries, and gives the basis for a comparison of local price levels. The theory has, however, very definite limitations in that, as it proceeds in terms of physical costs, it affords no means of comparing the costs of commodities produced with different capital structures, or different types of labour. In addition the analysis is singularly clumsy if applied to more than two countries, or more than two commodities. Various attempts have been made to get over these difficulties, notably by Taussig, Marshall, and more recently by Haberler. It may be fairly said, I think, that none of them have been really successful. Taussig's in particular seems to fail both from the points of view of clarity and precision, while Marshall in dealing with several commodities just evaded the issue by introducing the device of "bales." Haberler's is undoubtedly the best, largely because it demonstrates and admits, instead of trying to evade, the impossibility of attaining precision along these lines.[1] This unsatisfactory position is admirably illustrated by Edgeworth's remark that when several commodities and several countries are considered the analysis is best left to "the intelligence of the reader."[2]

Why in these circumstances has the Ricardian approach been retained? Ricardo himself in his analysis of the distribution of the precious metals demonstrated that it was quite possible to approach the whole question in terms of money values and value opportunity costs,[3] and J. S. Mill, in the famous chapter on International Values, set out to show that it was possible to consider the whole problem in terms of money values.[4] The possibility was recognized by Bastable, and by Edgeworth, who pointed out that the only difference between the analyses of domestic and international trade is that there are two more equations in the former than in the latter.[5] But with all this Ohlin is the only economist who has avowedly adopted this method, apparently believing that he has thereby made a revolution in international trade theory.[6]

The explanation of this rather curious situation is, I suggest, to be found in the sheer opportunism of exposition in a field where some means of appealing to the "man in the street" has always been regarded as peculiarly necessary. The comparative cost analysis is quite sufficient, and is indeed probably the best way, to show the general circumstances in which international trade takes place. Its application where there are more than two commodities and one scarce factor can be as it were extrapolated by general indications without losing clarity, whenever theoretical precision is not of great importance. As long, too, as a general picture of the relation of one country vis-à-vis the rest of the world is all that is wanted, the difficulties of

[1] Taussig, *International Trade*, Part I, chaps. 6–10. Marshall, *Money, Credit and Commerce*, Bk. III, chap. 6, pars. 4 and 5, and Appendix J. Haberler, *Der Internationale Handel*, 1933, chaps. 10–13.

[2] Edgeworth, *Papers relating to Political Economy*, Vol. II, p. 46.

[3] *Principles of Political Economy and Taxation*, chap. 7.

[4] *Principles of Political Economy*, Bk. III, chap. 18.

[5] Bastable, *Theory of International Trade*, chap. I, pp. 1–15. Edgeworth, *Papers relating to Political Economy*, Vol. II, p. 5.

[6] Ohlin, *Interregional and International Trade*, 1933.

applying the analysis to more than two countries can be evaded by considering the second country as the rest of the world. On the other hand the approach advocated by Ohlin, at least as at present expounded, is far from simple, and necessitates a knowledge of general value analysis.

As soon, however, as a more refined analysis is required to explain either the balance of payments, or the repercussions of changes in demand or supply which work indirectly by means of adjustments in several different countries, the comparative cost analysis will not do. Perhaps this is the reason why, in countries where the general doctrine of free trade has been accepted, there is still such complete public confusion as to the balance of payments and the effects of foreign competition in various markets. None of these things can be explained without the more complicated analysis in terms of income-levels throughout the world which was originally expounded by Ricardo in the second part of his chapter on international trade, and developed to deal with modern problems by Taussig. This distinction between the types of problems which the theory of international trade has to solve is of great assistance in considering the significance of Senior's work on international trade which developed Ricardo's suggestions as to the analysis of the latter type of problem.

Senior's lectures on money and international trade have unfortunately been published out of their context, and in this way their relation to his general theory of value has been overlooked, and the full unity of his analysis lost. As the lectures were originally delivered the first group published formed part of the course on the general theory of value, and were preceded by two lectures, "On the Nature of Exchange and Money," and "On the Nature of Money," respectively. These two lectures contained an explanation of the relation of international to domestic trade. The two sets of published lectures came at the end of the third course on the relation of costs of production to prices.[1] Altogether

---

[1] Lectures, 1826–30, Course 1, lecture 4, "On the Nature of Exchange and Money"; lecture 5, "On the Nature of Money"; lectures 6–8, *On the Transmission of the Precious Metals and the Mercantile Theory of Wealth*, published 1828,

the twelve lectures contained the whole of Senior's work on international trade as a coherent part of his theory of value. In view of the light shed on Senior's treatment of international trade by the hitherto unknown lectures, it is useful to give some account of the theory of all the lectures in the order in which they were delivered. It will be seen that Senior's theory of value and distribution described in the preceding chapters provided the necessary analytical basis for his lectures on money and international trade.

In the first lecture, "On the Nature of Exchange and Money," Senior explained the development of money in terms of attempts to facilitate barter in conditions of primitive credit by finding some generally acceptable form of credit. Money, according to Senior, is simply the commodity in which credit is crystallized, and hence it is simply a substitute for credit:

"My description of money as a mere substitute for credit may appear an unusual one. But when I give a legal opinion in exchange for a guinea it is not with a view to using the guinea myself. It would in 'fact be utterly useless to me. But I take it because my client has nothing else that I want, and because I trust that those who have what I want will readily give it in exchange for gold. The same reliance on the exchangeable quality of the guinea actuates every person to whom it is successively offered."[1]

This reversal of the ordinary treatment of the relation of money to credit indicates the starting-point of Senior's criticism of the quantity theory of money.[2] Since money was distinguished from credit in the first instance only by the fact that it was based on a commodity having value, any complete examination of the nature and value of money

Course III, lectures 5–11, *On the Value of Money* and *On the Cost of Obtaining Money and some effects of Private and Government Paper Money*. The greater part of lectures 5–8 were published under the former title in 1840, and part of lecture 8 and the whole of lectures 9–11 were published under the latter in 1829. The three sets have been reprinted as Nos. 3, 4, and 5 in the London School of Economics series of scarce tracts in Economics and Political Science. All page references refer to these reprints (see Appendix II).

[1] Lectures, 1826–30, Course I, lecture 4.

[2] This criticism was only completed in Course III, lectures 5–8. See p. 223, note 1 below, for J. S. Mill's reply to it.

must, Senior argued, include a consideration of the influences determining the value of the commodity of which it was made. The failure to appreciate this connection, owing to the apparent lack of a cost of production explanation of the value of a commodity which varies inversely with the quantity of the commodity, had led to the treatment of money by the quantity theory analysis as an exception to the general laws of value. Senior makes this point clear in a comparison of Aristotle's treatment of value with that of the Ricardians, very much to the latters' disadvantage.[1]

"But Aristotle's description of value as depending on demand approaches much more nearly perfect accuracy than Smith's, who, by adopting labour as a measure of value and talking of labour as never varying in its own value, has involved himself and his followers in inextricable confusion. . . . The only point in which Aristotle appears to me to have been mistaken is in supposing . . . that money may owe not only its currency, but also its value to convention.

"It might appear at first sight that a commodity which no person thinks of applying to his own gratification, which he takes only to part with as soon as possible, . . . need not possess any direct utility, but if limited in supply might circulate from hand to hand however useless each taker relying on his neighbour's willingness to receive it. But it is impossible to conceive how any useless commodity could have begun to circulate. Nothing but experience could shew its circulating power, and how could that experience have arisen? A banknote may be proposed as an instance of such a commodity. But a banknote is not money, it is a promise to pay money. The taker trusts not to the note but to the honesty and solvency of those who issue it."[2]

So much for the general nature of money as a commodity, which is a substitute for credit, which dominated Senior's approach to problems of international trade in which money had a place as a commodity.

The precious metals when used as money possessed a characteristic that Senior considered to be of fundamental

---

[1] Cf. Part I, chap. 2, above, for Senior's general criticism of the labour theory of value.

[2] Lectures, 1826–30, Course I, lecture 4.

importance as demonstrating the similarity between all inter-local trade, whether domestic or foreign: the uniformity of interspacial value which is characteristic of money, but not of anything else:

"I propose in the present lecture to consider a peculiar and important attribute of the precious metals when used as money. That their value is almost entirely independent of locality. The commercial ubiquity which I attribute to the precious metals may appear to some of my hearers questionable. It certainly is not the received doctrine. . . .

"Because 1,000 sovereigns will purchase 200 acres of land in Wales and not one in London, Mr. Mill considers money estimated in land of greater value in Wales than in London. But 1,000 sovereigns in London will purchase just as much Welsh land as 1,000 sovereigns in Wales. . . . The only inference from all these facts is, that 1,000 sovereigns in London, Wales, or Newcastle, though of precisely equal value themselves, exchange for different quantities of what are in fact different commodities."[1]

The explanation of this curious one-sided attribute of money Senior found in the way that debts are settled between different places by book transfers, or by bills of exchange. For it is only if, at current prices, the balance of indebtedness is not balanced that the exchange rate will deviate from par, and actual movements of money take place (if the variations of the exchange are greater than transport costs of money). These movements tend, of course, to bring about their own cure by altering the prices of goods in respective places in such a way that the place whose exchange is favoured buys more, and vice versa. It was by the absence of this possibility of using commodities, other than money, without transferring them through space, that Senior accounted for the difference in prices of commodities in different places by the amount of their transport

[1] Lectures, 1826–30, Course 1, lecture 5, "On the Nature of Money." Senior evidently attached considerable importance to this particular point, for he emphasized it in the third lecture of this course, "On the Nature of Value" (*Political Economy*, pp. 21–2), when explaining that in dealing with the value of commodities, commodities must always be defined in respect to locality. Cf. Mises, *Theorie des Geldes und Umlaufsmittel*, p. 153, second edition.

costs. In short, physically similar goods in different places are constituted different economic goods by the costs of transport, and may be expected to have different values in different places; since money, however, costs practically nothing to transport, it tends to have the same value in different places.

The same aspect of interspacial differences in values was treated at some length in Senior's discussion of distribution. After discussing the variations in incomes in different occupations, he went on to point out the differences of a more or less permanent nature which arise from the difficulty of transferring labour and capital from one occupation to another, and from one country to another. His analysis, it is interesting to notice, was closely similar to Cairnes' later development of the theory of non-competing groups, and applied to both domestic and international differences:

"The inequalities in wages and profits which we have as yet considered arise from causes inherent in the employments themselves which have been the subjects of discussion, and would, generally speaking, exist even if one occupation could at will be exchanged for another. But great inequalities are found which cannot be accounted for by any circumstances leading men to prefer one employment to another, and which therefore continue only in consequence of the difficulties experienced by the labourers and the capitalists in changing their employments."

and with respect to different countries—

"The obstacles which exist, even within the same neighbourhood and the same country, to the transfer of labour and capital from one employment to another, are of course aggravated, when not only the occupation, but the neighbourhood or the country is to be changed."[1]

Further light is shed on the importance of immobilities

---

[1] *Political Economy*, pp. 217–20, "Inequalities in Wages and Profits occasioned by the Difficulty of Transferring Capital and Labour from one Employment to Another"; and pp. 220–5, "Difficulty of Transferring Labour and Capital from one Country to Another." Quotations from pp. 217 and 220 respectively. The first passage has been requoted here for the sake of completeness. (See Part I, chap. 5, p. 194 above.)

on the organization of trade in connection with the division of labour—

"Nature seems to have intended that mutual dependence should unite all the inhabitants of the earth into one commercial family. For this purpose she has indefinitely diversified her own products in every climate and in almost every extensive district. For this purpose, also, she seems to have varied so extensively the wants and the productive powers of the different races of men. . . ."[1]

In conformity with Senior's analysis of value, all such immobilities prevent free competition and increase the influence of demand in the determination of prices. The whole of Senior's analysis of international trade was, therefore, based upon demand as well as cost of production, in just the same way as his analysis of domestic values. In this respect he differed from both J. S. Mill and Cairnes, to whom the necessity of introducing demand constituted a special case.[2]

This emphasis on the importance of immobilities was not of course original, but taken in relation to Senior's theory of value it constituted a new point of departure for the analysis of international trade. It is for this reason that I have devoted so much attention to it, for it shows that Senior was preoccupied not with the simple problems suited to the comparative cost analysis in its original and most satisfactory form, but with the more complicated and general problems of the relation between domestic and international price levels, to deal with which Ricardo had developed his theory of money in relation to the foreign exchanges.

To return to the main thread of Senior's argument, after analysing the local value of money within a country, he proceeded to explain how its local value is related to its international value:

[1] Lectures, 1826-30, Course III, lecture 9, *On the Cost of Obtaining Money*, p. 28; and also in *Political Economy*, p. 76.

[2] For J. S. Mill's criticism of Senior for neglecting the influence of demand in the lectures *On the Cost of Obtaining Money*, see below, note 1 on p. 223.

"I have hitherto considered only the local value of money in places using the same coin; or, as we usually call it in Great Britain, the inland exchange. The reciprocal value of the moneys of different countries using different coins, or, as it is usually termed, the foreign exchange, is governed by the same principles, although the application is more complex."[1]

These preliminary matters disposed of Senior's analysis of international trade was developed entirely in terms of money values, as, for instance, in the account of the way in which merchants estimate the profits of the export market—

"When a French jeweller sends his clocks to England he must first calculate in francs the expense of making and exporting them, then their price in sovereigns in London, then the silver bullion which those sovereigns will purchase in London, and lastly the francs which he can obtain for that bullion in Paris."[2]

Although the comparative cost analysis in its original form is quite capable of exhibiting the parallelism between domestic and foreign trade, it is necessarily limited by the labour theory of value on which it is based. Naturally an analysis of comparative money costs dependent on the general utility theory of value, which can be used without fundamental modification in both fields of analysis, displays the similarities more clearly. It is not surprising, therefore, to find that Senior constantly took examples from domestic trade to illustrate and explain foreign trade. He used, in fact, the closed community as the laboratory in which he worked out the principles governing all trade. For example, immediately after explaining the mechanism of the foreign exchanges, he added:

"If I have succeeded in explaining this very abstract subject, I have shown that the precious metals perform the same offices in international as in domestic commerce. But it may be objected that the trade between nations is a trade of barter. It is true that it is ultimately so, and so is that between the different towns and districts of the same country, but not primarily. The trade between London and Sheffield is ultimately a trade of barter in

[1] Lectures, 1826–30, Course I, lecture 5, "On the Nature of Money."
[2] Ibid.

which London receives hardware and returns the produce of
India and the Colonies. But the Sheffield cutler is not paid in
tea, nor does the Sheffield grocer make his payments in cutlery.
The cutler is entitled to be paid, and the grocer is bound to
pay in money. We have already seen that the passage of money
to and fro between London and Sheffield is avoided by means
of inland bills of exchange. . . . It is the same between different
countries. . . .

"The foreign exchange is the bartering the right to receive a
given amount of the money of one country for the right to
receive a given amount of the money of another country."[1]

The calculations necessary on the foreign exchanges are,
according to Senior, that of the gold value of the respective
coins, and the cost of transport of gold. The sole difference,
he concluded, between foreign trade and interlocal domestic
trade is caused by the necessity of equating the different
units of measurement. The ordinary manufacturer is
indifferent between the foreign and the home market,
provided they yield him equal profits; if the exchange
varies, his profit varies, and therefore his preference between
the two markets and the quantity he sells in each; this tends
to bring the exchange back to par.

It is evident that the complete avoidance of discussion of
comparative costs in Senior's approach to international
trade is due to the nature of the problems he was dealing
with. When he did more or less introduce the idea at a
much later point it was in terms of comparative value costs,
not comparative physical costs, to show the mutual relationships between productivity, price levels and the distribution
of trade.

The next lecture, *On the Transmission of the Precious Metals
and the Mercantile System of Wealth*, was devoted to further
elaboration of the working of the foreign exchanges. His
object was to prove, by explaining the balance of trade, that
specie movements caused by variations in the foreign
exchanges were of no harm to the country losing gold. Like
Ricardo himself and J. S. Mill, he realized that this was
essential to complete the case against mercantilism, and

---

[1] Lectures, 1826–30, Course i, lecture 5, "On the Nature of Money."

that this could not be done by the simple reiteration of the theory of comparative costs. Where, however, they were obliged to introduce the Equation of International Demand as an exceptional case of value, Senior was able to proceed without interruption from his theory of value.

He took as an example the sudden freeing of the trade between France and England, and analysed the effects on England of the consequent increased import of French goods, and outflow of gold. The loss of money, he pointed out, would be nothing but a benefit if nothing happened to prices, for we should have given away something quite useless, money, in return for goods which we wanted to consume:

"As money is not a source of gratification, but a mere instrument of commerce, if our prices were not affected by our parting with a portion of our money, we should be insensible of our loss; or rather we should have sustained no loss whatever, and have gained the five millions' worth of French commodities without any real sacrifice, while France would have parted with those commodities, and received no sensible equivalent."[1]

The process would involve a rise of prices in France and a fall in England, causing a decrease of imports to and increase of exports from England, and vice versa in France. The final result he explained in a way not accessible to the analysis based on comparative costs when it is, as usually, limited for the sake of simplicity to trade between two countries only:

"The commerce, which any country carries on with its neighbours, must depend on the prices of their respective exportable commodities. When commodities of the same quality, or which may be substitutes for one another, can be imported from different quarters, a slight variation of price will decide which will be preferred." [2]

France would therefore be at a disadvantage in all markets of the world:

[1] Lectures, 1826–30, Course I, lectures 6–8, *On the Transmission of the Precious Metals*, p. 6, in the London School of Economics series of reprints of scarce tracts in Economics and Political Science.

[2] Lectures, 1826–30, Course I, lectures 6–8, pp. 7–8.

"The same consequences, though to a less extent, would follow, even in the cases in which France had exclusive powers of production. Every commodity has among its purchasers some whose desire for it, or at least for that variable quantity of it which they consume, induces them to spend on it a given portion of their income, and no more. On the slightest rise of price they either discontinue, or diminish their consumption."[1]

The result would be, of course, a loss of gold for France, and the exact reverse process would take place in England, who would gain gold, until finally the whole of the original loss would be recovered. The significance of changes in price levels in international trade is finally summarized as follows:

"A universal balance against any country must soon so exhaust her stock of the precious metals, and consequently lower her prices, as to diminish and gradually destroy her motives for purchasing foreign commodities, while it increased the motives of all other countries to purchase hers. To suppose that it is possible to go on for ever buying without selling, or selling without buying, or even buying more than you sell, or selling more than you buy, are all equally irrational."[2]

The only result of such changes in the distribution of specie, he argued, is to change the actual channels of international trade. Instead of France taking goods directly from England, she would take them from other countries who would instead buy things from England as a result of the variations in price levels. An indirect trade takes the place of direct trade between France and England.

As a general rule, therefore, Senior believed outflows of specie set up tendencies which cause proportionate inflows except in two cases—mining countries, and countries which have undergone a change in their demand for money owing to changes in the volume of credit or notes. Senior apparently did not consider as important at this point the possibility that the increased demand for French goods, occasioned by the lowering of the tariff barriers, might necessitate a permanent slight fall in English prices—in

[1] Lectures, 1826–30, Course I, lectures 6–8, pp. 8–9.
[2] Ibid., pp. 17–18.

other words, a small deflation parallel to the recognized case of an inflation caused by the erection of tariffs.

The next two lectures *On the Mercantilist Theory of Wealth* were merely an elaboration of the theme of the first lecture, in order to show that opposition to free trade is based on a misconception not only of the nature of wealth, but of the part played by the mechanism of money values in its production and distribution. It is clear that Senior regarded these first five lectures simply as an explanation of the general problems of value caused by the existence of immobile factors and resources, and, where that immobility was across national boundaries, by the existence of different units of measurement of value. As such it is simply part of the general theory of value which formed the subject of his first course.

The more complex problems of the determination of the actual level of prices, or the value of money, in any country and its variations in different countries were taken up in the course devoted to the influence of cost of production on price, where they properly belonged.[1]

II

The first three lectures *On the Value of Money* were devoted to an elaborate criticism of the quantity theory of Money as expounded in particular by James Mill.[2] Senior's criticisms of the quantity theory were based on two objections closely connected with each other. First, that the quantity theory is the result of a failure to include monetary theory within the body of general economic analysis, and therefore it fails to examine the ultimate forces determining the value of money even within an isolated community; secondly, that the quantity theory of money is inapplicable to problems of international values and the price levels of different countries:

[1] Lectures, 1826–30, Course III, lectures 5–11, *On the Value of Money* and *On the Cost of Obtaining Money, etc.* See Appendix II, p. 342.
[2] *Elements of Political Economy*, chap. 3, sect. 7, pp. 131–4, third edition.

"Mr. Mill does not say in so many words that the value of money is decided by causes differing from those which decide the value of other commodities; but such is, in fact, the result of the statement which I have just read, if it be compared with his section on Exchangeable Value. . . . He does not mention rapidity of circulation; or, in other words, a frequent change of masters; or alteration of actual quantity, except for short periods, as among the actual elements of value. And if they are not the principles which regulate the value of other things, what reason is there for supposing that they regulate the value of money?"[1]

In short, the precious metals are produced in the same way as other commodities from sources of varying productivity; unless therefore it can be proved that their use as money fundamentally alters their character, the value of money must be determined by the same principles as the values of other commodities. The result of the vicious habit of regarding the amount of money as diffused by nature throughout a country was, Senior thought, the cause of certain economists considering the quantity theory to be the whole or most accurate statement of the value of money.[2]

Senior's first step was to eliminate from the problem the extraneous element of the rapidity of circulation by approaching the demand for money in terms of actual quantity to be held. The quantity of money held, he argued, depends on the money value of incomes and "the average proportion of the value of his income which each individual habitually keeps by him in money."[3] This latter, of course, depends on the exactness of coincidence of his receipts

[1] Lectures, 1826–30, Course III, lecture 5, *On the Value of Money*, p. 8. J. S. Mill defended the ordinary statement of the quantity theory of money by three arguments: (1) that the general principle of the law of value was that of supply and demand, which is "controlled, but not set aside" by the cost of production in the case of money as in most other cases; (2) that it is only in the case of money that a fall in the cost of production cannot cause a proportionate fall in value unless the quantity is increased in exact proportion to the fall in costs, since prices cannot rise except in proportion to an increase in the supply of money; (3) that the effect of changes in the cost of production influences its value only very gradually (this is with reference to a country possessing its own mines). Though Mill did not mention Senior as the critic of the quantity theory it is evident that he was in fact attempting to answer his arguments. *Principles of Political Economy*, Bk. III, chap. 9, par. 3.

[2] Lectures, 1826–30, Course III, lecture 5, pp. 8–10.   [3] Ibid., p. 11.

and payments, and will vary with the state of credit and confidence within the country at the present time.[1]

This was in fact a new method of approach[2] which followed directly from his earlier statement that money only arose because credit was imperfect. If credit was perfect there would, according to this argument, be no use for money as anything but a unit of account; neither the failure of receipts and expenditure to coincide, nor the numbers of persons with incomes, nor the money value of those incomes, would in any way affect the matter. Given the imperfections of credit, these three elements become the influences determining the demand for money, and the velocity of circulation is seen to be *not* an independent element affecting the value of money, but merely part of an algebraical identity describing the relation between the first factor and the other two.[3] Apart from the importance of this result in justification of Senior's refusal to consider the velocity of circulation as one of the determinants of the value for money, it has peculiar interest in connection with a recent version of the holding theory of money. The

---

[1] Lectures, 1826–30, Course III, lecture 5, pp. 11–17.

[2] J. S. Mill, for example, explained that the demand for money consists of the total volume of goods and services to be exchanged, explaining that this did not mean that it was necessary for the total quantity of money to equal the total volume of transactions because each piece of money might circulate several times. The demand for money therefore, according to him, equalled the quantity of money multiplied by the velocity of circulation; in fact, that the demand for money was fixed by demand in the ordinary sense of quantity demanded, and an effect of that demand, or more precisely an effect of the relations between the elements influencing that demand! And yet he maintained that the value of money was determined by supply and demand just like the value of other commodities! *Principles of Political Economy*, Bk. III, chap. 8, pars. 2 and 3.

[3] Looked at from this point of view the apparent inconsistency between the theory that in a community without risk the quantity of money can be infinitely small, the velocity of circulation infinitely great and prices infinitely high, and the fact that in a community in which risks are very great, e.g. with a large-scale inflation, the velocity of circulation and the quantity of money infinitely great and the value of money infinitely small, i.e. prices infinitely high, disappears. In the riskless community money as explained by Senior disappears, therefore there can be no velocity of circulation. In the community suffering from inflation, the demand for money nearly disappears because it fails completely to justify its *raison d'être*. No risk and infinite risk are simply the limiting cases.

modern version is based like Senior's on the conviction that the value of money is determined in just the same way as the value of other commodities. As a result the same conclusion is reached as by Senior, that the utility of money is due to the imperfections of credit, and that, therefore, the demand for money varies with the general state of credit and confidence; or, in other words, with liquidity preference.[1]

The demand for money disposed of, Senior turned to the heart of the problem, the analysis of the causes affecting the supply of money. For purposes of exposition he took the simplest possible case of a no-capital society with "an abundance of land" possessing alluvial deposits of gold which yielded gold at constant labour costs. Under these highly simplified conditions the gold price of labour would be determined by the labour cost of gold:

"the amount of labour which a certain quantity of it [gold] could purchase, would always correspond with its cost of production, except for short intervals, when any sudden increase or diminution of the demand for it should occasion the existing supply to be for a time relatively excessive or deficient. Under such circumstances the value of all other things would be estimated by comparing their cost of production with that of gold."[2]

The quantity actually produced would be determined, he added, by the demand for gold for plate and for money, which in stationary conditions would be limited to the replacement of annual wear and tear. Any increase in demand would merely lower all prices except that of gold, which would rise, bringing about a transference of labour to gold producing to take advantage of the higher earnings, until the price of gold again fell, and equilibrium was restored. In this way the gold prices of all commodities would be estimated in terms of the cost of production of gold. This analysis disposes of the claim of the mere quantity

[1] Cf. J. R. Hicks, *Economica*, February 1935, "A Suggestion for Simplifying the Theory of Money."

[2] Lectures, 1826–30, Course III, lectures 5–8, *On the Value of Money*, pp. 18 et seq. Quotation from p. 18.

of money in existence to determine its value, i.e. its price in other commodities, on the supply side:

"My principal object in this long discussion has been to show that the value of money, as far as it is decided by intrinsic causes, does not depend *permanently* on the quantity of it possessed by a given community, or on the rapidity of its circulation, or on the prevalence of exchanges, or on the use of barter or credit, or, in short, on any cause whatever, excepting the *cost of its production*. Other causes may operate for a time, but their influence wears away as the existing stock of the precious metals within the country accommodates itself to the wants of its inhabitants. . . ."[1]

This is the highly simplified constant-cost case of domestic money values, but the relation to the whole world is quite clear—

"In these respects my insulated community . . . is a miniature of the whole world. The whole world may be considered as one community, using gold and silver as money, and ascertaining the value of other commodities by comparing their cost of production with the cost of obtaining gold and silver. And though many causes may alter the quantity of the precious metals possessed by any single nation, nothing will permanently affect their value, so far as that value depends on intrinsic causes, unless it affect their cost of production."[2]

Up to this point the analysis of the cost of obtaining money is a simplified version of Ricardo's in so far as it only deals with an isolated non-capitalistic country. In the following lectures, however, Senior drops the unrealistic assumption of the constant costs of producing gold, and takes the further step of introducing capital without the assumption that all capital structures in the country are the same.

The hypothetical country is still isolated, but it is now a capitalistic one, in which the rate of profit is known, producing silver from mines of varying productivity. It is fairly evident that Senior also tacitly assumed that relative prices are given. The problem is to find the margin of

[1] Lectures, 1826–30, Course III, lectures 5–8, p. 30.   [2] Ibid., p. 31.

production of silver which will determine money wages, since the rate of profit is given. But Senior pointed out a special difficulty in doing this: that defining the margin in terms of the rate of wages which must be paid is merely reasoning in a circle—

"But this removes the difficulty only a little further, and the reasoning seems to move in a circle. What regulates the wages of labour? The cost of producing silver? On what does the cost of producing silver depend? On the amount of wages paid to the labourer. Which of these is the cause? which the effect?"[1]

This is yet another example of the impossibility of determining the margin of productivity on a pure cost of production basis, unless wages are given as well as profits. This obvious difficulty, Senior stated, can be solved only by the demand analysis, but since the utility of any amount of money is, *ceteris paribus*, exactly proportioned to its cost of production, it appears "that it is the cost of producing money which determines the demand for it, rather than the demand for it which decides to what extent the production shall be carried."[2]

As the examination of the demand for money gave no clue, Senior investigated the demand for the precious metals as plate, upon which ultimately the demand for the precious metals is based. His analysis can be summarized as follows: The total quantity of silver demanded in equilibrium in the stationary state is the amount necessary to replace the annual wear and tear of the precious metals as money and plate. Given all the assumptions explained above, and the further simplifying one that the capital structure of the mining industry is constant whatever the productivity of the mine, the solution is determinate. The position of the margin in silver mining is determined by the demand for the precious metals, which is, of course, assumed to be given. The average level of money wages will be fixed by the productivity of labour in the marginal mines after subtracting profits, and thus the standard for all monetary transactions will be set:

[1] Lectures, 1826–30, Course iii, lectures 5–8, p. 34.   [2] Ibid., p. 36.

"Under these circumstances 14⅖ ounces of silver must be the average annual wages of labour, and 16 ounces the price of every commodity produced under circumstances of equal competition by a year's labour; the labourer's wages having been advanced for one year; and the pivots on which all the money transactions of the country turn, are the existence of persons able and willing to give for 16 ounces of plate the commodities produced by the labour of one man for one year, his wages having been advanced for one year, and the power of the miner to raise, without payment of rent, 16 ounces of silver by a year's labour; in short, the amount of silver required, and the cost of producing that portion of it which is produced at the greatest expense."[1]

The treatment of capital and wages structures in this analysis are of interest in view of the continual criticism of the Ricardian analysis on the ground that it ignores differences between proportions of capital to labour, and differences in wage structures, in the international trade analysis. Senior's analysis of the cost of production of silver avoids this criticism, for it shows how, if the rate of profit and the relative price scale are given, some items of the relative price scale are equated to silver (i.e. money), and from these the silver values of all goods in the scale can be calculated in terms of simple proportion *whatever the capital or wage structure involved in their production*. It was just over this point that the Ricardian analysis came to pieces because, instead of starting from this device of a money cost of production analysis in order to find a common denominator of costs in both domestic and international trade, it was based on, and limited by, physical costs which afford no basis of comparison except under the assumption of equal capital structures, etc. In the field of international values, as in that of domestic values, the labour theory of value or the real cost theory can only explain a part, even though it may be the most significant part, of the phenomena.

The elaboration of the analysis of conditions of stationary equilibrium to deal with the four main cases in which changes in the data occur, presented no difficulties,[1] but

[1] Lectures, 1826–30, Course III, lectures 5–8, pp. 39–40.
[2] Ibid., pp. 40–55.

Senior's application of his conclusions to demonstrate his general theory of value is of some interest:

"It is a remarkable fact, particularly with reference to the opinion that the value of money depends on its quantity, that while the fertility of the mines is unaltered, every increase in the total amount of silver is preceded by an increase in its value, indeed, could not take place, unless so preceded; and that every diminution of the value of silver is followed by a diminution of the whole quantity. A striking illustration of the principle that, although value depends principally on limitation of supply, it is regulated not by the actual amount of the supply, but by the comparative force of the obstacles by which the supply is limited. And that, if those obstacles are increased, as must be the case whenever an increase of demand forces an increased cost of production to be incurred, the whole quantity produced, and the value of each portion of that quantity, will be increased together."[1]

The transition from the case of an isolated country to international trade proper merely involved the simple step of assuming that silver is produced in a different country. This change merely involves the application of analysis of domestic prices to international prices by considering the position of non-silver-producing countries *vis-à-vis* silver producers, in order to decide which mine will be the marginal one in the silver-producing country. The solution is clearly the same as in the former case expressed in slightly different terminology—

"The determining causes must have been that such was the desire, of the inhabitants of the rest of the world for silver, and such their powers of producing commodities desired by the Mexicans, and such the desire of the Mexicans for the commodities produced by the rest of the world, and such their power of producing silver, that the rest of the world annually offered to Mexico commodities sufficient to induce the Mexicans to produce annually for exportation 1,568,696 lbs. troy of silver, and the Mexicans offered annually to the rest of the world 1,568,696 lbs. troy of silver, in return for the commodities which were annually produced by it for the Mexican market.

[1] Lectures, 1826–30, Course iii, lectures 5–8, p. 55.

"And any alteration in one of these determining causes, unless neutralized by a compensating alteration in another, would produce a corresponding alteration in the value of silver."[1]

In these lectures *On the Value of Money* Senior was only concerned with the determination of the margin of production of the precious metals where they were produced, given all other conditions. The final completion of his theory necessitated an examination of all other causes which determine the cost of importing precious metals, and the amount imported by countries which do not produce them. In short, the last problem to be dealt with was the distribution of silver and/or gold throughout the world, and the determination of international relationships of domestic price levels.

III

This comparatively simple analysis of the lectures *On the Value of Money* led up to what is effectually a summary account of the theory of international trade in the lecture *On the Cost of Obtaining Money*. Senior stated the problem as that of "the difference in the cost of obtaining silver, or, in other words, in the wages of labour in silver, in different countries at the same period."[2]

These differences he pointed out have been attributed to almost everything but conditions of international trade; to differences in the real and the money cost of living, in taxation, in density of population, and in the rate of profit. None of these explanations are consistent with his theory of wages, and have not, he declared, even a plausible empirical foundation. His own explanation depends on the comparative productivities of capital and labour in various countries in obtaining money, or, in other words, in producing exportable commodities:

"The only mode by which I can account for the phenomena which I have been describing is, by supposing that the countries which have the precious metals to dispose of, either as producers,

---

[1] Lectures, 1826–30, Course III, lectures 5–8, pp. 61–2.
[2] Ibid., lectures 8–11, *On the Cost of Obtaining Money*, p. 1.

or as having a temporary superfluity at their own current rate of prices, are willing to give more than one-fourth more for the exportable commodities produced by the labour of one North American in a year, assisted by an advance of capital equal in value to his wages for a given period, than for the commodities produced by the labour of one Englishman, and more than ten times as much as for the commodities produced by the labour of one Hindoo, similarly circumstanced. Or in other words, that the diligence and skill with which English labour is applied enables the English labourer to produce in a year exportable commodities equal in value to those produced in a year by eight Hindoos; . . ."[1]

As when dealing with the value of money in an isolated community, Senior used the idea of a given proportion of labour to capital in the export industries merely as measuring-rod for all money prices within each country in dealing with international prices. He implied no fixity of proportions of capital to labour, and no reduction of all labour to terms of unskilled labour.[2] The law of one price in one market makes it possible, he pointed out, to express differences in these proportions in terms of the silver prices of labour and capital in the export industries. Thus he concluded his discussion by asking

". . . whether the price, or, in other words, the value in gold and silver of all those commodities which are not the subjects of a monopoly, does not depend, in a country not possessing mines, on the gold and silver which can be obtained by exporting the result of a given quantity of labour, the current rate of profit, and, in each individual case, the amount of wages which have been paid, and the time for which they have been advanced?"[3]

His preoccupation with the similarity between domestic and international trade is exhibited yet again in the following passage:

"In fact, the portableness of the precious metals and the universality of the demand for them render the whole commercial world one country, in which bullion is the money and the

---

[1] Lectures, 1826–30, Course III, lectures 8–11, p. 11.
[2] Ibid., pp. 14–16. See pp. 232–3 below.   [3] Ibid., p. 13.

inhabitants of each nation form a distinct class of labourers. We know that in the small market of every district the remuneration paid to the producer is in proportion to the value produced. And consequently that if one man can by superior diligence, or superior skill, or by the assistance of a larger capital, or by deferring for a longer time his remuneration, or by any advantage natural or acquired, occasion a more valuable product, he will receive a higher reward. It is thus that a lawyer is better paid than a watchmaker, a watchmaker than a weaver, a first-rate than an ordinary workman. And for the same reason in the general market of the world an Englishman is better paid than a Frenchman, a Frenchman than a Pole, and a Pole than a Hindoo."[1]

And again:

"The mine worked by England is the general market of the world: the miners are those who produce those commodities by the exportation of which the precious metals are obtained, and the amount of the precious metals, which by a given exertion of labour, and advance of capital, they can obtain, must afford the scale by which the remuneration of all other producers is calculated."[2]

It follows as a consequence that domestic money incomes move in sympathy with the value-productivity of labour and capital employed in the export industries; hence an increase in this productivity, by raising all money incomes, increases the command of all individuals over foreign commodities. Thus the landlord is enabled to travel "as a Milor Anglais, and drive the French and Italian aristocracy from the first floor to the garret, or the entresol.

---

[1] Lectures, 1826–30, Course III, lectures 8–11, p. 14. J. S. Mill's criticism that Senior had disregarded demand in his analysis is clearly invalidated by this passage. For Senior had explained that the willingness for example of Mexico to pay more for commodities exported from England than for those exported from Poland, accounted for the greater value of English labour, etc., in the international market and hence its greater value in silver. (*Principles of Political Economy*, Bk. III, chap. 18, par. 9; chap. 19, pars. 2 and 3.) Mill's failure to recognize this appears to have been due to the fact that he considered the efficiency of labour in physical terms, and therefore had to include the equation of international demand explicitly, while Senior regarded it in terms of its productivity of valuable commodities and thus included demand automatically. Cf. the account of Senior's theory of value in Part I, chap. 2, sect. iv, pp. 93 et seq. above.

[2] Lectures, 1826–30, Course III, lectures 8–11, pp. 15–16.

Little imagining that the greater part of the value of what he called his patrimony was, in fact, the creation of the chimneys and jennies of his neighbour, the manufacturer."[1]

In application to England this means, Senior explained, that her relatively high productivity enabled her to purchase goods from abroad at a less sacrifice of labour and capital than if they were produced at home, and even at a less sacrifice than they cost to produce in the countries from which they were imported. The contemporary fall in prices, or rise in the cost of precious metals, was due, he suggested, to a decrease in this relatively greater productivity and a consequent change in the terms of trade against England.

From this conclusion Senior deduced the important corollary that England is not necessarily benefited by an increased productivity of other countries, unless trade is assumed to be only between two countries. If the efficiency of the French in producing cottons increases, it will lower the cost in France of obtaining money, since her competitive position in general markets will be improved. England's, on the other hand, will be worsened to the same extent, with the opposite result. The value of all French labour will rise so that all French commodities will cost us more than before, except the cotton. In short, the loss of our relative advantage will decrease the demand for our goods abroad, while the cost of foreign goods in money will increase.[2]

For completeness, Senior should have added that the advantage or disadvantage in any particular case depends on the importance of the commodity to England with respect to which France increases her efficiency. His emphasis on the necessity of considering the position of any one country *vis-à-vis* each and every other country in analysing questions of the terms of trade, supports the suggestion put forward earlier that Senior's whole approach to inter-

---

[1] Lectures, 1826–30, Course III, lectures 8–11, p. 19. J. S. Mill must have overlooked this passage in criticizing Senior for not extending his analysis to all commodities. (*Principles of Political Economy*, Bk. III, chap. 18, par. 9.) Cf. note 1 on p. 223 above. It is clear that, according to Senior, high English money incomes were due to the low cost of importing gold, and imports bought with those incomes were really bought at this same low cost.

[2] Lectures, 1826–30, Course III, lectures 8–11, pp. 22–6.

national trade was determined by his interest in the interactions of trade in more than two commodities and between
more than two countries.

The famous controversy between Senior and Torrens
on the terms of trade, which was taken up again by J. S.
Mill, turned exactly on this question of the relevance of
an analysis confined to two commodities and two countries
to the real world. Torrens argued in two pamphlets that
one-sided free trade would diminish the free-trade country's
command of gold, and bring about a fall of prices and disas-
trous depression.[1] Senior criticized Torrens' argument on
two grounds. First, that Torrens overlooked the fact that
tariffs diminish the general efficiency of resources within
a country by limiting the division of labour and specialization, despite his own earlier teaching on international
trade.[2] Secondly, that since he had not considered sufficiently
the whole complex of international trade in many commodities between many countries, he had overlooked the fact
that the diminished efficiency of labour and capital in the
country imposing tariffs would increase the competitive
power of other countries both in the home and in the foreign
market. It followed, Senior said, that since the efficiency of
labour, etc., would be decreased, the cost of obtaining
money would be increased, and therefore the specie gained by
the imposition of tariffs in the first place would rapidly be
lost again. In the converse case of lowering tariffs exactly
the reverse process takes place, and apart from the temporary
inconvenience of altering the employment of resources the
country lowering its tariffs would gain.[3]

Senior did not deny, however, that retaliatory tariffs would
be useful if they achieved their object. But, like Adam

[1] *The Budget: A Series of Letters on Financial, Commercial and Colonial Policy*,
London, 1841. *A Letter to the Right Hon. Sir Robert Peel on the Condition of England
and on the Means of removing the Causes of Distress*, London, 1843.

[2] *Edinburgh Review*, July 1843, Art. 1, "Free Trade and Retaliation," pp. 12–16.

[3] Ibid., pp. 16–35. Pp. 18–20, 20–2, and 22–3 of the article are practically
word for word the same as pp. 11–18, 21–6, and 30–1, respectively, of the
lectures *On The Value of Money*. For Senior's treatment of gold movements
see above, pp. 209 et seq.

Smith, whom he quoted on this point, he was profoundly sceptical of such a policy being successful, and considered that the country attacked would not in the end lose as much trade as was generally supposed.[1]

There was more, however, of Torrens' argument against one-sided free trade. In a third pamphlet he maintained that it is possible to make the terms of trade more favourable by imposing tariffs, whether retaliatory or unprovoked. But he attempted to prove his argument by the case of trade in two commodities between two countries, each of which monopolizes one of them.[2] Senior admitted that Torrens would be right if these conditions were fulfilled, but he denied that his general deduction, that it was in fact possible to alter the terms of trade in this way, was valid.[3] In the first place, he pointed out that Torrens had excluded the use of money from consideration by limiting the analysis to two commodities.

"By that exclusion alone," he said, "he is able to represent international exchange as depending on demand and supply, instead of on cost of production. If France would receive in exchange for her silks nothing but yarn, she might force England to increase the proportionate supply of yarn, in order to obtain a greater or even the same supply of silk. But money the French Government has not the will, or even the power, to exclude or to subject to more than nominal duties. The French weaver has neither the will nor the power to refuse to sell his silks for money, at the cost of their production. The refusal, therefore, of France to receive yarn, would . . . affect the trade between England and France only by converting it from a direct into a roundabout trade—only by forcing us to alter the destination of the labour and capital now employed in producing yarn for the French market; and to send to France a larger portion than we now send of the bullion which is constantly passing through our ports, or under our control."[4]

[1] *Edinburgh Review*, loc. cit., pp. 43–4.
[2] *Postscript to a Letter to Sir Robert Peel*, London, 1843, pp. 5–15.
[3] *Edinburgh Review*, July 1843, pp. 35–6.
[4] Ibid., p. 42. For Senior's theory of the relation of cost of production to value under varying degrees of monopoly and competition, respectively, see Part I, chap. 2, sect. iv, above. For some discussion of the validity of Senior's argument about indirect trade see pp. 210–13 above.

In the second place, Senior argued, Torrens, in considering the possibility of altering the terms of trade by tariffs only in the case of two countries, had assumed that the second country could really be taken to represent the rest of the world; he had not realized that a uniform policy of monopolistic tariffs against one country by all other countries is completely out of the question. For although one country can exclude another country's products, it cannot shut them out of all other markets. Such a policy of exclusion, however, must damage its own competitive position, and thus help the goods it excludes to find a substitute market, and this must automatically check the change in the terms of trade in its own favour.[1, 2]

Most of the essential steps in Senior's refutation of Torrens were contained in his lectures *On the Value of Money*,[3] and both these and his article were well known to his contemporaries, among whom John Stuart Mill agreed with him

---

[1] *Edinburgh Review*, July 1843, p. 42.

[2] *A letter to N. W. Senior, Esq., in reply to the article "Free Trade and Retaliation"* in the *Edinburgh Review*, No. CLVII, 1843. This reply added nothing new to the controversy. Torrens refused to agree that the outflow of gold caused by the lowering of a tariff only involved temporary dislocation. It was for this reason that he continued to maintain that his analysis had a perfectly general application, since a loss of gold lowered prices in the losing country and raised them in the other, and therefore the free trade country sold its goods cheaper indefinitely. If Torrens had been prepared to limit the application of his analysis to special cases of inelastic demand or particularly rigid price structures, he would of course have been correct, but Senior's whole objection was that he neither did this, nor realized the further implications of the effect of tariffs on the general efficiency of resources. Thus in reply to Senior's assertion that tariffs, whether one-sided or not, diminished the efficiency of labour, Torrens tried to prove that the efficiency of labour could only be measured by the terms of trade, and that therefore to maintain favourable terms even at the expense of diminishing the volume of trade was to maintain the efficiency of labour. It is obvious, of course, that while Senior was considering the efficiency of labour in terms of the distribution of resources as a whole, Torrens was thinking of its efficiency in one particular direction, i.e. in the export trade. Nor did Senior deny that the terms of trade would be more favourable if all other countries lowered their tariffs as Torrens seemed to imply, but merely that this was not a reason for us not to lower ours. In justice to Torrens it must be remembered that he did not advocate tariffs on raw materials. He scored, too, a number of debating points on Senior's historical inaccuracies.

[3] See note 3 on p. 225 above. *The Three Lectures on the Value of Money* were printed privately on the advice of Senior's friends (advertisement to the book), probably the free trade members of the Whig Party.

as to the practical impossibility of Torrens' case being realized.[1] Practically all later writers on the terms of trade have admitted like Senior the theoretical validity of Torrens' argument in his particular case, and have used the same arguments as Senior to show the impossibility of generalizing it to the real world in which Torrens' assumptions are not likely to be realized. In so far as Senior's arguments have been generally known, either directly or through J. S. Mill's tacit acceptance of them, this particular treatment of tariffs must be considered as due in the first instance to Senior.[2]

The ultimate result of Senior's whole analysis was an explanation of the localization of different trades. The relatively great efficiency of English labour, he argued, caused wages to be higher in England than in other countries. Therefore it was advantageous for England to concentrate on the production of goods in which the advantage of her skill was greatest and vice versa. We could not compete with other countries in certain fields just because our labour was so productive in other directions that the high opportunity costs made money costs prohibitive--

[1] J. S. Mill, in his essay, "Of the Laws of Interchange Between Nations," argued, like Torrens, on the same assumptions as to the numbers of countries, that it was possible to increase (apparently permanently) the quantity of money and therefore the level of prices and incomes within a country by imposing a tariff on a particular commodity, and to decrease prices and incomes in the other country. It followed that the prices of imports other than the one on which the tariff was imposed would fall and the terms of trade alter in favour of the country with the tariffs. Mill recognized, however, that a change in the terms of trade might be brought about in this way at too great a cost by diminishing the volume of trade, for the diminution of the volume of trade by artificial means imposed sacrifices on consumers, *ceteris paribus*, as well as limiting the quantities of goods for which the more favourable terms would be effective. *Essays on Unsettled Questions*, Essay 1, par. 9. In the preface to the collection Mill explained that he disagreed with Torrens as to the practical application of the analysis.

[2] Cf., for example, Taussig, *International Trade*, Part 1, chap. 13. Edgeworth, *Papers Relating to Political Economy*, Vol. 11, pp. 6-13. Modern economists are more disposed to admit a remote possibility of the conditions of Torrens' case being fulfilled than Senior was. Taussig, in particular, agrees with Torrens' argument that the barter terms of trade would be permanently altered in favour of the country imposing tariffs.

"It is obvious that our power of competing with foreigners depends on the efficiency of our labour, and it has appeared that a high rate of wages is a necessary consequence of our efficiency. It is true, indeed, that if we choose to misemploy a portion of our labourers we must pay them, not according to the value of what they do produce, but according to the value of what they might produce if their labour were properly directed. If I call in a surgeon to cut my hair, I must pay him as a surgeon. So if I employ, in throwing silk, a man who could earn three ounces of silver a week by spinning cotton, I must pay him three ounces of silver a week though he cannot throw more silk than could be thrown in the same time by an Italian whose wages are only an ounce and an half. And it is true, also, that I can be supported in such a waste by nothing but an artificial monopoly, or, in other words, that I should be undersold by the Italian in every market from which I cannot exclude him by violence. . . . To complain of our high wages is to complain that our labour is productive—that our workpeople are diligent and skilful."[1]

This principle explains the distribution of industry throughout the world—

"The greater part of the advantage of rather importing than growing and manufacturing tea arises, without doubt, from the difference between the climates of China and England. But a great part also arises from the different values of labour in the two countries. Not only the cultivation of the tea plant, but the preparation of its leaves, requires great labour. The wages of labour are so low in China that these tedious processes add little to the cost of tea. In England the expense would be intolerable. When a nation in which the powers of production, and consequently the wages of labour, are high, employs its own members in performing duties which could be as effectually performed by the less valuable labour of less civilized nations, it is guilty of the same folly as a farmer who should plough with a racehorse."[2]

The last two lectures of this group, *On the Effects of Private and Government Paper Money*, added nothing new to Ricardo's

---

[1] Lectures, 1826–30, Course III, lectures 8–11. *Cost of Obtaining Money*, pp. 26–8.

[2] Ibid., pp. 29–30. The outstanding application of the analysis of this lecture was made by Cairnes in his famous articles on the Australian gold discoveries, reprinted in *Essays in Political Economy*, pp. 1–165, 1873.

treatment of sudden variations in the supply of money by means of issues of paper money.

IV

Two major questions arise immediately from a consideration of Senior's analysis—the precise nature of his premises, and the relation of his theory to the orthodox Ricardian theory.

The first of these questions throws considerable light on the second, but it may be simpler to dispose of a few minor points to start with. First, in conformity with Ricardian tradition, Senior did not treat land as a separate factor of production; since rent does not enter into costs it is irrelevant to the determination of price, and varying natural resources are reflected in the productivity of labour and capital. Secondly, Senior assumed complete immobility of factors of production between trading areas under consideration, and thus the analysis takes no account of capital movements between areas. But when regarding nations as units Senior does not necessarily imply that there is complete mobility of factors within national boundaries, for it is clear that since Senior's treatment of international trade was merely a development of that of domestic, he could assume the general solution of the problem of domestic immobilities which he had laid down earlier. Thirdly, how far did Senior deliberately exclude all consideration of transport costs? In view of his earlier definition of similar physical goods being only similar economic goods when in the same positions in space, it appears that transport costs are irrelevant to the general theory of international trade. For international trade can logically be based on the comparison of the values of goods at the place of import. China tea produced in England is compared with China tea produced in China and brought to England. The realism of this approach is indicated in a passage on the relative importance of domestic to foreign trade, in which Senior pointed out that under existing conditions of transport, Oporto and London are more nearly one market than Oxford and London.[1] Clearly,

[1] Lectures, 1826–30, Course III, lectures 8–11, pp. 31–2.

if separate consideration of transport costs can be left out of the general theory of interlocal domestic trade, it can be left out of international trade.

The more important points relating to the nature of Senior's assumptions can be summarized as follows: How did Senior's treatment gain on Ricardo's in the discussion of trade between more than one country? How far was Senior's treatment of capital more satisfactory than Ricardo's, and did he assume rigidly fixed domestic price relations?

Most of these questions are the subject of vigorous debate at the present time, and it is therefore not possible to compare Senior's analysis with any generally accepted modern standard. Nevertheless, it seems to me, that much of the belief in the emergence of revolutionary new ideas in the modern theory comes from a tendency to attribute far more rigidity to the classical analysis than is justifiable. Some discussion of the particular points in the light of recent criticism may at least indicate that a more modest attitude on the part of the revolutionaries would be appropriate.

Of the answer to the first question there can be no doubt. Taussig's chapter on two countries competing in a third[1] is sufficient evidence of the tediousness and unsatisfactoriness of the usual application of the theory of comparative costs to this problem. The ordinary mind simply refuses to contemplate the arithmetical complexities of applying this method to all countries in the world at once. Even the beautiful geometrical and algebraic constructions of Marshall and Edgeworth, though obviating the horrors of arithmetical examples, have to leave the final elaboration to the "intelligence of the reader." It is obvious from Senior's own remarks on the matter, that he thought that Ricardo's treatment of the theory of international trade was unsatisfactory in this respect, and that many of the most interesting and important practical questions could not be satisfactorily tackled without developing, or if we like reformulating, the accepted doctrines. His own work on international trade was directed to remedying this deficiency, and, either directly,

[1] *International Trade*, Part I, chap. 10.

or indirectly through John Stuart Mill, has become part of modern theory.

The second question is far more complex. Undoubtedly Senior's progress from the case of constant costs of production of gold to that of variable costs was a great improvement in increasing the flexibility and generality of the analysis, but he introduced two simplifying assumptions. Like all the early nineteenth-century economists he found the complexities of joint production peculiarly formidable, and to avoid some of these pitfalls, he assumed that capital structure in the production of gold was constant.[1] In itself this assumption merely amounts to selecting a particular cost function which is simple and easy to deal with, and though it naturally detracts from the generality of the analysis it does not alter it fundamentally. Senior himself appears to have regarded it in this light, for when he is discussing several countries in which the mines are the "general markets of the world," he takes the basis of comparison of one man plus capital equal to wages advanced for one year, merely as a convenient unit. His other simplifying assumption, that the rate of profits is given, is of much greater importance. It automatically excludes from the scope of his analysis all changes in trade which would alter the demand for capital relatively to labour, and therefore relative prices both of factors and commodities, unless the supply of capital is infinitely elastic. There is, however, no reason for thinking that Senior intended to imply the latter assumption. In consequence, Senior's analysis is applicable only to equilibrium conditions and not to changes in data, except such as affect relative commodity prices without affecting relative factor prices, or in those cases where all capital structures are alike and all costs constant (i.e. the single case to which the labour theory of value applies). To extend the analysis by dropping his assumptions of given relative prices and a given rate of profit, further equations are necessary to relate variations in the amount of capital

---

[1] It is important to remember that Senior only assumed a constant proportion of labour to capital in the export, or gold and silver mining, industries. Cf. pp. 218–21 above.

to variations in the rate of profits, as well as cost functions for each industry.

The principal differences between Senior and his contemporaries have already been pointed out in the account of his theory, but it may be a useful conclusion to this chapter to survey in a general way the origins of Senior's work.

Ricardo's theory of international trade fell into two distinct parts. In the first, he elaborated Adam Smith's exposition of international trade into the doctrine of comparative costs on the basis of the labour theory of value. Ricardo clearly assumed the influence of demand in bringing about an equality of exports and imports, so that the element of demand must be regarded as introduced before Senior, although it was not stated as a part of the theory of comparative costs before J. S. Mill. The second part consisted of the analysis of the distribution of the precious metals, and was contained both in the *Principles* and in the essays on monetary problems. This analysis used substantially all the main ideas worked up later by Senior. Not merely did Ricardo lay down the basic idea of the determination of the value of money by its cost of production, but he explained the differences in price levels in different countries in terms of the efficiency of labour and capital. But Ricardo's two sections were not joined together, except by the unsatisfactory paragraphs explaining that domestic and foreign trade were essentially barter trades, and that money made no permanent difference.

But any closer analysis of international trade in terms of monetary theory was blocked by his retention of the labour theory of value (even as modified by the comparative cost analysis) which forced him to treat opportunity costs in physical instead of value terms. To eliminate this dichotomy in the theory of international trade, it was necessary to start from a utility theory of value and show that the cost of imports depended, not on the physical efficiency of labour and capital in producing exports, but on their efficiency in producing commodities which had value in the world market. It was precisely this unification which Senior

achieved in his courses of lectures on money, which culminated in the lecture *On the Cost of Obtaining Money*.

Although John Stuart Mill retained Ricardo's division of
analysis into physical comparative cost theory and a
monetary theory of the foreign exchanges, he was obviously
greatly influenced by Senior in his treatment of the value
of money, particularly in his chapter on "International
Values." In the chapter on "The Value of Money, as dependent on the Cost of Production," he retained the ordinary
statement of the quantity theory of money, but admitted
that ultimately, even in a closed community, the value of
money depended on the cost of production. His analysis of
its value in a trading country was derived explicitly from
Senior's lecture *On the Cost of Obtaining Money*. It is even
reasonable to suggest that his introduction of the "equation
of international demand" was due, to what appeared to
him to be, Senior's neglect of the obvious fact that the cost
of obtaining gold depended not only on the actual cost of
the commodities exported, but also on the quantity which
had to be given to obtain any given quantity of gold.[1]

As we have endeavoured to explain, Senior's application
of his theory of value to money and international trade was
most fruitful in those fields where the interactions between
price and income changes in several countries are of fundamental importance. It is natural, therefore, that the value
of his work should be most generally recognized in discussions of the foreign exchange and price levels, rather than
in general treatments of comparative costs on which his
analysis has had influence, if at all, indirectly through
John Stuart Mill.

[1] See p. 223, note 1, and p. 224, note 1 above.

PART II
PROBLEMS OF SOCIAL POLICY

CHAPTER I

THE SCOPE OF GOVERNMENT AND SOCIAL POLICY

IF in the field of pure theory Senior has either been ignored or put a little on one side with a note of interrogation, in the sphere of the application of economic analysis to social questions he has received unenviable and quite unjustified recognition as the crude exponent of extreme *laissez-faire*. Abused by both contemporaries and historians as the dogmatic reformer and would-be destroyer of the Poor Laws, and ridiculed by Marx for his opposition to the Factory Act[1] any serious consideration of his real opinions on social questions has been considered superfluous. This attitude, it may be admitted at once, is to some extent excusable in so far as Senior published very little under his own name on problems of policy, and his best-known publication, the *Letters on the Factory Act*, is open to misinterpretation. The most important exposition of his ideas on the justification and possibility of Government intervention is only available in the second group of Oxford lectures, 1847–52, which, with the exception of those on method, are unpublished.

A study of these later lectures, together with his earlier contributions published and unpublished, leads to the conclusion that Senior started out without any very definite ideas on the theory and practice of Government intervention in economic affairs, but merely with a great interest in social problems. His final attitude seems to have been the

[1] Particularly strong criticisms of the Commission of Inquiry into the Poor Laws on the score of dogmatism have been made by the Sidney Webbs in the *History of English Local Government, English Poor Law History*, Part II, *The Last Hundred Years*, pp. 82 et seq., and by J. and B. L. Hammond in *The Village Labourer*, chap. 10. Evidence of the long survival of the belief that Senior was opposed to the Poor Laws root and branch all his life is to be found in *Annals of the British Peasantry*, p. 297, by Garnier. For references to contemporary criticisms of the reform of the Poor Law in 1834, see the next chapter. For Marx's criticisms of Senior's *Letters on the Factory Act* in *Das Kapital*, Part III, chap. 7, see below, note 1, p. 256.

result of a gradual process of evolution which was reflected in changes in his treatment of the nature and scope of economics.

In order to show this connection this chapter has been divided into three sections, each of which corresponds to a phase in his treatment of scope and method. The first phase covers his first appointment at Oxford in 1825 to his appointment on the Poor Law Commission in 1832; the second the period from 1832 to his second appointment at Oxford in 1847, or some unknown date in the 'forties, and includes the publication of the *Outline of Political Economy*; and the last from his second appointment at Oxford (or some date in the 'forties) until presumably the end of his life.

I

The exact avenue along which Senior entered the world of economists is unknown, but there is good evidence that the cause of his entry was his desire to reform the Poor Law. According to obituary notices, he grew up with a determination to reform the English Poor Law and re-establish English agriculture on a tolerable social basis.[1] His interest was not, however, confined to this one particular problem but included the main economic aspects of poverty as well as the more abstract questions of economic theory.

When Senior delivered his *Introductory Lecture* at Oxford in 1826, on taking up the Drummond Chair of Political Economy, he was far from clear as to what constituted the limits to the knowledge and authority of economists *qua* economists, and as a discourse on the scope of economics the lecture is chiefly remarkable for his obscurity on this matter. He did succeed, however, in making clear that he regarded the explanation and cure of the poverty of the bulk of the working classes as the main task and justification of the study of economics. This definitely normative idea which ran through the lecture was more or less concealed or eliminated in his later treatments of method,

---

[1] Obituary Notice in the *Cornhill Magazine*, 1864.

in which he attempted to disentangle economic science from political policy.

Senior explained in 1826 that the really important work confronting economists is to explain why some nations and some classes within nations are rich whilst others are poor, and to investigate those institutions most favourable to the production and diffusion of wealth. The science of economics he defined as explaining the nature of wealth and the laws of its production and distribution, and "the institutions and customs" which facilitate its production and regulate its distribution to give "the largest possible amount . . . to each individual."[1]

Further on slightly more light is thrown on the meaning which Senior attached to the criterion of the maximum wealth per head by the phrase "that diffusion of wealth which alone entitles a people to be called rich."[2] The normative element in this discussion was so obvious that Senior attempted to placate that section of opinion which regarded wealth as an unworthy object of human endeavour, by suggesting that a study of economics was necessary in order to prevent the accumulation of wealth, if for no other reason. But it is quite obvious that to him wealth was a highly desirable end in itself, owing to its intimate connection with both the happiness and moral welfare of the working classes:

"The pursuit of wealth . . . is, to the mass of mankind, the great source of moral improvement. When does a labourer become sober and industrious, attentive to his health and to his character?—as soon as he begins to save. No institution could be more beneficial to the morals of the lower orders, that is, to at least nine-tenths of the whole body of any people, than one which should increase their power and their wish to accumulate: none more mischievous than one which should diminish the motives and the means to save. If we have institutions eminently calculated to produce both the benefit and the mischief, how valuable must the science be that teaches us to discriminate between them, to extend the one and to remove, or diminish, or at least, not to extend, the other."[3]

[1] *Introductory Lecture on Political Economy*, 1826, published 1827, p. 7.
[2] Ibid., p. 13.   [3] Ibid., p. 12.

It may seem unnecessary to-day to labour the connection between wealth and happiness, but at the time of Senior's lectures there were considerable sections of opinion opposed to the importance attached by economists to wealth.[1] One section clung to the belief that riches were the source of evil; another, more cynical, argued that the poverty of the poor was a necessary condition of the supply of labour for the rich, and thus part of a divine order; and the most intellectually respectable section, inspired by Wesley, that the sufferings of poverty would be made up for in heaven. Against these varying shades of defeatism the economists proclaimed the necessity of at least examining the laws of the production and distribution of wealth, as an essential basis for judging as to the good or evil of wealth. There was therefore some reason for Senior emphasizing the close connection between tolerable security of existence and the maintenance of order and the development of culture:

"That state of society in which the productiveness of labour and the mode in which it is applied, secure to the labouring classes all the necessaries and some of the conveniences of life, seems to be not merely conducive but essential both to their morals and their happiness. . . . But, if proof be wanted, we have only to consider what are the effects on the human character of the opposite state of society, a state in which the mass of the people is habitually confined to a bare subsistence, and, consequently, exposed from time to time, from the accidents of trade or of the seasons, to absolute want. I will not dwell on the misery of those on whom actual want does fall; it is too painful to be steadfastly contemplated and forms only a small part of the

---

[1] Senior was by no means alone in regarding this type of opposition as important. Economists as divergent in outlook at Whately, Poulett Scrope and Samuel Read were equally preoccupied with it. Whately, for example, devoted most of his lectures as Drummond Professor in 1831 to explaining the compatibility of the study of economics with Christianity; Scrope explained at length that the science of economics was a necessary preliminary to that of happiness (Introduction, *Principles of Political Economy*, 1833); Samuel Read wrote *An Inquiry into the natural grounds of right to vendible property, or wealth* in 1829, to remedy the neglect of the moral aspects of economic laws by most economists, much as Bastiat wrote *Harmonies Economiques* in 1850. For a comparative account of the conflicting elements of public opinion in the first part of the nineteenth century see Halévy, *Histoire du Peuple Anglais au XIXe Siècle*, Vol. I, Bk. III.

evil. The great evil is the general feeling of insecurity; the fear which must beset almost every man, whose labour produces him only a subsistence, and who has no resource against contingencies, that at some period, how near he cannot tell, the want under which he has seen others sink may reach himself."[1]

As far as this goes it is a clear enough statement of the object of economics, but it leaves the limits of the practical branch of economics entirely undefined. Senior explained only that the conclusions of this branch must be based on a wide induction and understanding of the motives which permeate society, such as "dislike of labour, the desire for immediate enjoyment, and the love of accumulation," which he described as antagonistic forces producing "such opposite conduct, not only in different individuals but in whole masses of people," that it is extremely difficult to avoid mistakes in attributing motives to past conduct, or to predict the influence of a fresh motive.[2]

It appears indeed that Senior regarded the practical branch of economics as embracing all possible social and moral sciences, and thought that the economists' particular function was that of relating them to the criteria of the maximum production and diffusion of wealth. From the preliminary survey thus given in the *Introductory Lecture* it is impossible to deduce the justifiable extent of Government interferences. Was it limited *a priori* in Senior's opinion, as is generally believed, to a general policy of *laissez-faire*, of holding the ring? Or did he think the limits of Government policy could be determined by the hasty application of general economic theory to social problems? This latter conclusion is suggested by Senior's original expression of his hope of showing that economic science "is capable of all the certainty" of any recognized science not based on definitions, and that many of the most important conclusions of the practical branch are based so firmly on the conclusions of the science that they have the same "certainty and universality."[3] Nor can it be argued that Senior allowed more economic value to Government action at this time

---

[1] *Introductory Lecture*, pp. 13–14.
[2] Ibid., pp. 8–9.   [3] Ibid., pp. 10–11.

than did many of his contemporaries, merely because he deliberately defined wealth to include the services both of individuals and of Governments. The legitimate functions of government which he specifically described are confined simply to the traditional services of the protection of life and property.[1]

This strictly limited view of the legitimate scope of Government intervention was repeated in sundry writings throughout the period under consideration. For example, the following striking passage occurs in a memorandum which Senior prepared for Lord Melbourne on the state and efficiency of the law relating to combinations in 1830:

"We believe that it is the duty of the State to protect that property and that right, and that it may be guilty of a breach of duty by acts of commission or of omission. By acts of omission, if it does not protect the labourer from injury on the part of those who assume to dictate to him what he shall do and what he shall not do; by acts of commission, if it assume itself to dictate to him, and to force him to pursue or to abandon a given proceeding, not on the ground that he is interfering with the free will of another, but because his conduct may be detrimental to himself, or to his master, or to the general wealth of the society. We believe, in short, that in this, as in almost every other matter, the duty of the Government is simply to keep the peace, to protect all its subjects from the violence and fraud and malice of one another, and, having done so, to leave them to pursue what they believe to be their interests in the way which they deem advisable."[2]

The natural inference from all this, that Senior confined the scope of Government interference to narrow limits on traditional grounds philosophic and economic, is, however, completely upset by his *Letter to Lord Howick on a legal provision for the Irish Poor*, written and published in 1831.

[1] Lectures, 1826–30, Course I, lectures 2 and 9.

[2] Included in the *Report of the Commission on the Condition of the Hand-loom Weavers*, 1841, p. 98, and reprinted in his *Historical and Philosophical Essays*, 1865, Vol. II, pp. 121–2. It is curious that Senior did not omit this last sentence in the reprint as it directly contradicted the opinions expressed in the lectures of 1847–52, but it is impossible to attach any importance to this, as he frequently permitted reprints of earlier opinions which he had discarded. See note at end of this chapter for an account of Senior's opposition to trade unions.

Senior's attention had been drawn to Irish problems by Lord Howick who suggested that he should study the accumulation of reports and pamphlets on the state of the Irish poor. The results of his investigations were embodied in a letter to Lord Howick, of about a hundred pages, which was subsequently published as a pamphlet.[1]

The bulk of the letter deals with the state of the law in Ireland at the time, but there are important passages on the possibility of State intervention to alleviate Irish poverty, a problem which he evidently regarded as of more primary importance than the actual Poor Laws. He stated the problem as follows—

"it still must be admitted that the state of the lower classes in Ireland is inferior not merely to the situation which appears within the power of the labouring population of a country to attain, but even to the situation which in some countries— countries less favoured by nature than Ireland—has actually been attained by that class. And if this be admitted, it becomes our duty most anxiously to inquire how far the remedy for this evil lies within the province of Government."

He explained that economic theory shows that the size of the national income and the share obtained by the labourer depend principally on the providence and industry of the labourers, which determine the size of the wage fund and the numbers among whom it must be shared. But this explanation, he says, does not help those people who "by accident or error" fail to obtain a share adequate to subsistence. These unfortunates depend in a civilized society on charity. But private charity is nearly always inadequate and wastefully administered, so laws for the relief of the poor have been enacted "to make the supply of relief adequate to the demand for it, and, as far as the rich are concerned, to apportion equally the burthen of affording that relief, and by economizing and directing its distribution, to make that burthen as light as possible." To this account of the *raison d'être* of Poor Laws, Senior added his unequivocal approval—

[1] *Letter to Lord Howick on a legal provision for the Irish Poor*, p. 5.

"These are noble purposes, and as far as they can be effected without materially diminishing industry, forethought, and charity, it is the imperious duty of Government to effect them. We must remember, however, that the power of human laws directly to punish the want of these qualities is very slight; their power directly to create them, still slighter; their power to destroy them, almost irresistible."[1]

The proper sphere of Government action had thus suddenly grown from mere "police" to the alleviation and prevention of poverty, wherever this can be done without diminishing seriously the three sovereign qualities of industry, forethought and charity. These extensions embraced the whole field of public health as well as poor relief in the ordinary sense, for Senior argued that the treatment of infectious diseases was a matter of public concern, and that if the Government interfered it must also be prepared to pay the costs involved by its interference:

"In their treatment the public must interfere, and therefore must bear the expense. Nor is illness a contingency so present to the mind when in health as to warrant our depending on the providence of the uneducated to lay up a store against it. Without wishing to give to the poor, when in sickness, a right to assistance, I am anxious that public provision should be made for such assistance, as far at least as medical treatment is concerned."[2]

He went on to approve the suggestions of the Select Committee on the Irish Poor[3] for expenditure on the extension and improvement of the medical services. Similarly he wished to see ample provision made for the care of persons suffering from disabling diseases and accidents:

"Such are blindness, loss of limbs, and what is equivalent to loss of limbs, chronic infirmity, idiocy, and madness in any of its forms. No public fund for the relief of these calamities has any tendency to diminish industry or providence. They are evils too great to allow individuals to make any sufficient provision against them, and too rare to be, in fact, provided

---

[1] *Letter to Lord Howick on a legal provision for the Irish Poor*, pp. 6–7, 11, 11–12. Charity appears to be one of the customs which it is the duty of economists to study.   [2] Ibid., p. 13.

[3] *Report of the Select Committee on the state of the Poor in Ireland*, 1830.

against by them at all. Their permanency, too, is likely to weary out private sympathy. And the worst of them, madness, is perhaps the calamity with which we least adequately sympathize. Even to educated persons, the insane are too frequently objects almost of aversion. I wish therefore to see these evils met by an ample compulsory provision."[1]

It is indeed difficult to reconcile the author of such sentiments—sentiments which are more generous than those of many enthusiasts of health insurance to-day—with a diehard policy of *laissez-faire*, sink or swim.

On similar lines Senior complained of the provision for orphans, not that it was imprudent, but that it was inadequate and failed to give the children a fair start in life. Provision for deserted children and bastards was, however, he thought, a more complex problem. The poverty due to desertion, or the bearing of illegitimate children, was an evil which he pointed out was necessarily foreseeable, and public provision for it could only act as an encouragement to the absconding parent. Both English and Scottish experience appeared to bear this out, so that he decided against any increase of public charity for this purpose in Ireland, where the evil was comparatively rare.[2]

Consistently with this line of argument Senior came down rather reluctantly against a general public provision for old age, other than that provided incidentally by the medical services:

"Every man knows that in old age his personal wants will be greater than they are in youth and middle age, and his earnings less. Assure him that the difference will be made up by the public and you diminish in him the motives both of providence and of industry. You weaken still more the benevolent feelings of those around him."[3]

Similar difficulties were presented by the poverty of the able-bodied due to unemployment or crop failure.[4] It must not be thought that Senior was insensible to the misery of

[1] *Letter to Lord Howick on a legal provision for the Irish Poor*, p. 14.
[2] Ibid., pp. 17–18.   [3] Ibid., pp. 14–15.
[4] Ibid., pp. 19–26. For an account of Senior's opinion on relief in cases of crop failure, see Appendix 1.

unemployment, or unwilling that the State should help if a tolerably safe means could be found. The case for assistance he indeed stated in the most vivid terms:

"Indolence, and still more the want of self-denial, are so much more faults than crimes; the destitution by which they are followed so disproportioned to the offence, it falls on so many innocent persons who are dependent on the offender; the insensibility of the absentee landlord wringing his rents from misery, is so revolting; the hardship seems so manifest, of letting the whole burden of relieving distress fall, like a penalty, on the charitable, while selfish avarice affords an exemption."[1]

The only available method of relief appeared at that time to be something of the nature of the English Poor Law system.[2] An extension of the system to Ireland, with its continuous poverty due not only to unemployment but also to chronically low wages, was bound to result there in the rapid introduction of allowances in aid of wages and the attendant vicious circle which had wreaked havoc in the English countryside. In addition, it would have involved, or so Senior thought, the introduction of all the evils of Settlement Laws. But more important still, he believed it was fundamentally the wrong remedy: the English Poor Law was intended originally merely to assist the distress due to the contingencies and accidents of life, not to raise the general standard of living, but in Ireland the problem was to do this very thing, to cure the chronic poverty of the labouring population.[3] The introduction of the English right to relief would have left the main problem untouched

[1] *Letter to Lord Howick on a legal provision for the Irish Poor*, p. 26.

[2] See also the Preface to his *Journals, Conversations and Essays on Ireland*, Vol. I, pp. xiii–xiv, 1868 (the Preface was written in 1861). "In 1831, when I first wrote on Irish affairs, no Poor Law was known, except the unreformed Scotch Poor Law, and the unreformed English one. The first was illusory; the second was rapidly destroying the wealth of the richest, and the morality of the most civilized country in the world.

"A Poor Law affording, practically, only indoor relief had not then been tried, or even suggested. And I firmly believe, that if a Poor Law, on the English or Scotch system had been introduced into Ireland in 1832—and one of these models would certainly have been adopted—the ruin that I predicted would have followed."

[3] Senior stated this definitely in the *Letter to Lord Howick on a legal provision for the Irish Poor*, 1831, pp. 30–44 (particularly p. 33). He repeated the same

at the same time as it introduced a train of attendant evils of its own. Clearly the price of immediate alleviation was too high.

At this stage in the discussion Senior introduced proposals which should have made any serious believer in *laissez-faire* disown professional acquaintance with him. The cure of Irish poverty was not to be left to time and an enlightened policy of free trade. The Government, he suggested, should take measures both to increase the size of the wage fund and to decrease the number of claimants, or, in other words, to increase the productivity of Irish labour and decrease the population. The measures advocated were advances of capital by the Government to increase the productive capacity of Ireland by building roads, railways, harbours, docks and canals, and draining bogs and reclaiming waste; subsidies to increase emigration in order to relieve the pressure on the wage fund; and improved facilities for the clearing of estates and the consolidation of farms to pave the way for capitalistic farming. Summarizing his recommendations Senior declared:

"I am anxious that these provisions should be made as ample as possible: that public money should be advanced to facilitate emigration, and for the formation of roads, canals, and harbours; that the Irish should be relieved from one of the worst relics of feudal barbarism, the local taxation imposed on fairs and markets; that they should also be relieved from the absurd duties on timber, which are mischievous even in England, but, in a naked country such as Ireland, are powerful impediments to civilization; and above all I am anxious that they should be relieved from the expense of supporting the Catholic Church. I am anxious in short that every experiment should be tried for the relief of Ireland, except the adoption of that one measure which we are now discussing."[1]

In short, the Government was to assume the duty of directing the investment of capital instead of leaving it to private individuals to follow their own interests. It is

opinion in a *Letter to Lord John Russell on the 3rd Report from the Commissioners for inquiring into the condition of the Poor in Ireland*, April 14, 1836, published in 1837, *Parliamentary Papers*, Vol. LI (see Part II, chap. 2, note 1 on p. 295).

[1] *Letter to Lord Howick on a legal provision for the Irish Poor*, pp. 45–6.

important to appreciate that such Government-organized activities were not in any sense relief works. Their object was not to provide employment directly like the familiar parish works, but to increase the productive capacity of the country as a whole in order that in the future Irish labour should be more productive. The suggestion in itself is of considerable interest in a period when Government-organized works were frequently advocated both for England and Ireland as an obvious way of providing relief, but not, as far as I am aware, as a method of increasing productivity. It must be remembered that at the time Senior was writing private enterprise in providing first roads and canals, and then railways, was at the height of its glory. Against the old methods of would-be assistance to industry by various forms of monopoly, protective tariffs and subsidies, concealed or open, Adam Smith and his disciples had directed their most powerful criticisms which had been popularized in the theory that the Government was incapable of directing productive capacity better than, or even as well as, private individuals. Here, however, was one of the recognized economists of the day suggesting that in Ireland the Government could, and should, direct the investment of capital and undertake productive enterprises. Unfortunately Senior did not develop the theoretical implications of these suggestions anywhere, and his later discussions of intervention were limited to more strictly social questions.[1,2]

[1] The most interesting and important points of this letter have generally been overlooked by critics. Poulett Scrope for instance asserted that Senior wished to leave the relief of the poverty of the lower classes of Ireland to private charity, without referring at all to his suggestions for the development of Irish resources. As, however, Scrope believed that outdoor relief, limited only by a labour test, would cure the chronic unemployment he probably regarded Senior's suggestions as irrelevant. The question of relief to the non-able-bodied he considered of secondary importance. *Quarterly Review*, Vol. 46, January 1832, Art. iv, pp. 393–400. Similarly the Webbs refer to this letter in their *History of the English Poor Law* (op. cit., pp. 86–7, n. 1), but omit any mention of the careful analysis of the different causes of poverty and their respective remedies. After all the similarity between Senior's method of approach to the Irish problem in 1831 and their own treatment of the English problem in 1909 is much more remarkable than the difference.

[2] Similar suggestions were embodied in the *Third Report of the Commissioners* (of whom Whately was one) *for Inquiring into the condition of the Poor in Ireland,* 1836, together with a proposal for national rates to finance the health services

Senior's last major suggestion for solving the Irish question was connected with the Roman Catholic Church in Ireland. He attributed considerable responsibility for Irish poverty to the chronic political unrest of the country, and this to the dispossession of the Roman Catholic Church of its revenues by the Established Episcopalian Church. Not only did this constitute a permanent injustice of which agitators could make use, but it made the Roman Catholic priests into enemies of the Government and sympathizers, even if only passive, with rebellion. In addition the financial support of their Church was a heavy tax on the slender resources of the peasants, the majority of whom were Roman Catholics. As a simple remedy, but one which profoundly shocked a great number of people, he proposed the confiscation and transfer to the Catholics of the property of eighteen out of the twenty-two bishoprics and the benefices of a number of the ordinary clergy of the Episcopalian Church as soon as they became vacant. During the interval he suggested that the Imperial Parliament should make an annual grant for the support of the Roman Catholic priests, and the provision of adequate churches for them.[1]

and the care of children, the aged and lunatics, in order to relieve the poorer districts. Senior expressed his approbation of the whole report, including the latter proposal. *Letter to Lord John Russell*, see note 3 on p. 246 above, also Appendix I below.

[1] *Letter to Lord Howick on a legal provision for the Irish Poor*, 1831, pp. 54 et seq. The same ideas were elaborated in a *Letter to Lord Howick on Commutation of Tithes and a Provision for the Roman Catholic Clergy in Ireland*, cf. p. 22, note 3 above. They were fiercely attacked in the *Quarterly Review*, Vol. 46, January 1832, Art. v. It is said that Senior lost his professorship at King's College, London, on account of the opinions he expressed on this subject. (*Proceedings of Political Economy Club*, Vol. vi, pp. 236, 261. J. L. Mallet's *Diaries*.) The subsequent history of these suggestions is of some interest. Among Senior's papers there is an account of a conference held at Lord Melbourne's house on May 31, 1835, to discuss Senior's proposals for reform of the Irish Church, etc. These proposals were apparently embodied in a preface intended for the fourth edition of Senior's pamphlet *On National Property and on the Prospects of the present Administration*. (All four editions appeared in 1835, cf. Appendix II, p. 345 below.) It was finally decided not to publish the preface as the members of the conference were afraid that it might damage the prospects of the Bill which the Government was intending to introduce to deal with the problem.

In this pamphlet Senior explained the principles according to which a Government ought to treat individual and corporate property, particularly

Senior was under no delusion that these measures would produce a rapid cure of Irish poverty, but any immediate improvement in the standard of living in an overpopulated country was, he considered, out of the question. The best that could be done was to break the vicious circle of poverty and unrest by opening up the resources of the country, and thus giving the disease of a redundant population the chance to cure itself. It must be remembered that Senior had no belief in the extreme form of Malthusian doctrine and believed that continuous progress was possible.[1]

It is not at all easy to summarize Senior's attitude to Government interference during this period of the first Oxford lectures. According to his statement on method, the economist was to decide what institutions were conducive to the production and diffusion of wealth, and these decisions were to be based largely on the conclusions of his theoretical analysis. One of these conclusions was that, under conditions of competition, resources would be distributed among the most profitable occupations and that the production of wealth would thus be maximized. The Government's function seemed to be limited to keeping the ring. On the other hand, Senior could scarcely have been more eloquent in describing cases where individuals failed to look after

with regard to reversions and expectations. "We affirm," he wrote, "not that every lawful interest which is capable of valuation is inviolable, but that no interest can be held inviolable as against the public, unless it be capable of valuation" (pp. 10–11, second edition). He considered that corporate property was legitimately only a life interest, for "our ancestors have had their full swing of posthumous power" (pp. 20–1), and that it was the duty of the Government to use all corporate property in the best interests of the community, irrespective of the wishes of the original owners, but with regard to the legitimate claims of current life interests. It followed that the Government had a right and a duty to decrease the endowments of the Episcopalian Church in Ireland, reform the municipal corporations, and open the Universities to Dissenters, since in all these cases the control by present owners of these properties was against the public interests (pp. 26–48). The rest of the pamphlet was devoted to political and constitutional questions, reform of the criminal code, and a discussion of the best method of endowing the Irish Roman Catholic Church.

(Leon Levy apparently saw the preface, cf. Senior's *Industrial Efficiency*, Appendix I, p. 379, Vol. II, but I have not been able to trace it, and have only seen the notes of the conference at Lord Melbourne's, which do not state what pamphlet the preface was intended for.)

[1] Cf. Part I, chap. 3, sect. i, above.

their own elementary economic interests, and where it was the duty of the Government to look after them. (Senior does not seem to have regarded such failures merely as the results of *imperfect* competition in the sense in which the term is ordinarily used.) This duty, moreover, involved not merely making laws, but also taking active steps to bring about a redistribution of income in favour of the poorer classes. Perhaps this position might be accounted for by the assumption that economic theory justified *laissez-faire* in the sphere of production but not in the diffusion of wealth. Then it followed that Government action was to aim at bringing about some ideal of distributive justice and welfare as far as possible without destroying the three vital sources of further progress—industry, providence and charity.

At any rate if we are to take the *Letter* on Irish Poor Law problems into account we cannot deny Senior's admission that the maximization of wealth might easily conflict with that of welfare. Nor did Senior hesitate to draw conclusions from this as to policy, for it would be the merest sophistry to try to argue that the proposals in this letter were aimed primarily at the maximization of wealth. The letter on the Irish Poor Law question was in fact an exposition of the economics of welfare in which the conflict between private expediency and social ideal was stated in the clearest terms.

The characteristic of Senior's attitude did not consist in his dislike of poverty and his desire to diminish it. In varying degrees such feelings were common to all the classical economists. The difference between him and many of his contemporaries[1] was that he thought it was desirable and possible for the State to influence the distribution of income and capital between different classes and districts, not because it would increase *total* wealth by doing so, but because it would help those districts and classes in the greatest distress. State interference to make the supply of relief adequate to the demand and to apportion the cost of that relief is, he declared, "a noble purpose."

[1] E.g. Malthus, James Mill, McCulloch. For some account of their attitude to Government intervention, see sect. iv below.

It is possible to argue that Senior's original definition of the scope of economics deliberately included problems of welfare, and, therefore, that his excursions into these fields under the title of economist were not inconsistent. Nevertheless, it seems to me improbable that he had started out with any prevision of the position he actually reached. The confidence with which he originally asserted the close connection between economic theory and the art of economics, the latter defined in generous terms, indicates that he started out from the prevalent individualistic premise that private and social interests tend to coincide.

It seems a reasonable explanation that when he went up to Oxford in 1826 to lecture he had not worked out any distinctive economic or political philosophy of his own, and only evolved it during the following five or six years. In that case it was natural for his *Introductory Lecture* to start from some received definition of scope. (The definition of the *Lecture* was in fact the same as McCulloch's.) That he should find after some years that it was unsuitable is surely not surprising. If this interpretation is correct, Senior's opinions as to the legitimate functions of Government in Ireland must be regarded as the first published expression of the attitude he took up with increasing determination as time went on—that questions of policy cannot be resolved by a simple appeal to the general principles of economic science. The *Letter*, in short, may be said to mark his emancipation from the confusion between Bentham's philosophy of individual liberty and the economic analysis of perfect competition. His complete restatement of the method and scope of economic science in the *Outline of Political Economy* of 1836, together with his increasing emphasis on the difference between economics, political philosophy and ethics, gives a good deal of plausibility to this explanation.

II

From 1832 to 1834 Senior's attention was confined to the work of the Commission on the English Poor Laws. The detailed discussion of the analysis and recommendations of the Commission will be taken up in the next chapter, but some explanation of the difference between Senior's proposals for dealing with the Irish problem in 1831 and with the English one in 1834 must be included here, in order to appreciate his attitude towards Government intervention. In the former case his main preoccupation was with the problem of the chronic poverty of the labouring classes in Ireland, and the question of Poor Laws, i.e. particularly relief to the able-bodied, was only the excuse for this general discussion. In England, on the other hand, he was concerned primarily with the social and legal status of the agricultural labourer in relation to the Poor Laws. In this latter case the problem confronting him was to find a way of guaranteeing to the agricultural labourer a position in which he could reach the standard of living theoretically possible if the degrading influence of the unreformed Poor Laws was abolished. It is in this difference that the explanation of the contrast between Senior's views on Irish and on English Poor Laws is to be found.

The English inquiry turned on the evil effects of indiscriminate relief to the able-bodied in reducing the agricultural labourer to a semi-servile status, rather than on the evil of a low standard of living. In consequence the functions of government appeared to be more limited in England than in Ireland. In the former, beyond the provision for the "true poor," the principal object of policy was to give to each individual freedom to make the most of his economic surroundings—the radical policy of holding the ring; in the latter it was hoped to change those economic surroundings by Government intervention. The efforts of the English Commission were, therefore, devoted to evolving a means of providing against destitution of the able-bodied without infringing the real freedom of the individual, or impairing the stimulus to make use of that freedom. The new element in the solution, besides the more efficient organization of State help to the "true poor," was of course the principle of "less elegibility" by means of the workhouse system.[1] It was hoped that its introduction would make it

[1] It is questionable how far the celebrated workhouse test was the adaptation of an old institution for a new purpose, or the revival of an old principle. Cf. C. R. Fay, *Life and Labour in the Nineteenth Century*, Part I, chap. 9.

possible for the first time since the end of the eighteenth century to provide for both the aged and the unemployed without diminishing the incentives to providence, industry and charity. Senior's continuous opposition during these years to the introduction of the right to relief into Ireland, even safeguarded by the workhouse test, was due to his conviction that the nature of the problem was different in the two countries. Any system of relief could, he saw clearly enough, have little constructive effect where the primary difficulties were lack of capital and over-population.[1]

Senior's treatment of the English Poor Law made it really impossible for him to preserve his original vague formulation of the scope of economics in relation to policy. It is difficult to include his discussions of Irish welfare in 1831 in the field he had reserved to economists, but it was impossible to maintain that his insistence in 1834 on the independence of the agricultural labourer, based largely on the philosophical ideal of individual freedom and responsibility, had anything to do with economics. It was necessary for Senior to decide how far he was justified in claiming the authority of an economist when considering these general problems of policy.[2]

It would be rash to claim that the important changes introduced into the discussion of the scope of economics in the *Outline of Political Economy* in 1836 were due entirely to Senior's appreciation of the obscure position he had got into, but it is at least reasonable as a partial explanation.[3] The new definition of the scope of economics in 1836 was diametrically opposed to the original one of 1826. Any inquiry into customs and institutions favourable to the production and diffusion of wealth was rigorously excluded, so also was any normative attitude as to the desirability of

[1] See Appendix I.

[2] Senior was recommended for appointment to the Poor Law Commission by Hyde Villiers as a "practical Political Economist." Letter from Hyde Villiers to Lord Howick, 1832, see below, chap. 2, pp. 285–6.

[3] The only part of the *Outline of Political Economy* which differed significantly from the lectures of 1826–30, besides the section on population which included an account of the dispute with Malthus, was the preliminary discourse on scope and method (as far as can be judged from the MS. remains of the lectures). See Appendix II, pp. 340–3, below.

wealth. Economics was defined as the "science which treats of the nature, the production, and the distribution of wealth." This limitation Senior justified by explaining that it was easier to reach clear and definite ideas in a small field than by straying into a consideration of the fascinating problems connected with the best method of distributing wealth in different stages of society. These problems, he declared, do not belong to economic science, at least in his sense of the term, any more "than Navigation forms part of the science of Astronomy"; they belong to the science of legislation which, though it must have some foundation on economic principles, deals with welfare instead of wealth, and therefore differs from economic science "in its subject, its premises, and its conclusions."

The function even of giving advice, he declared, is out of the sphere of economists, their job is merely "to state general principles, which it is fatal to neglect, but neither advisable, nor perhaps practicable, to use as the sole, or even the principal, guides in the actual conduct of affairs." The actual decision how far to rely on economic principles in this way is part of the art of government.[1]

Thus by 1836 Senior had proceeded a negative stage towards defining the scope of government. It could in no way be limited by the conclusions of economic analysis. If the mere economist advocated *laissez-faire* as most conducive to the production of wealth, this did not justify him in criticizing encroachments on this principle by the Government, unless it was aiming at some specifically economic object, as for example trying to increase national wealth by a mercantilist policy.

The best-known example of Senior's attempt to confine himself as an economist to the field laid down in the *Outline* is his opposition to the Factory Act in 1837.[2] He opposed it bitterly not as an infringement of individual liberty, but

---

[1] *Outline of Political Economy*, pp. 1–3.

[2] *Letters on the Factory Act as it Affects the Cotton Manufacture, addressed to the Right Honourable the President of the Board of Trade (to which are appended a letter to Mr. Senior from L. Horner, and minutes of a conversation between Mr. E. Ashworth, Mr. Thompson, and Mr. Senior)*, 1837, second edition, 1844. For differences between the two editions see Appendix II, pp. 345–6 below.

for an entirely economic reason: that it would be ruinous to English commercial supremacy, and thus indirectly to the workmen it was intended to assist, who, he thought, would end by being still worse off.

This criticism was based on Senior's once famous calculation that the whole of a manufacturer's profits were derived from the last two hours' work of the day. The logic of the calculation was sound enough, that the value of the product is only sufficient to yield profits if there is a balance after all current costs of production have been covered. But the values of the variables of the equations of costs and output were taken from a completely inadequate survey of capital structure, costs and rates of profits made during a brief visit to Lancashire to show Lord Shelborne the cotton manufacturing districts. This was pointed out with some vigour by various members of the Political Economy Club, as well as in the general Press; no one, however, thought of suggesting that the assumption of unchanged productivity per man-hour, whether the length of the working day was ten hours or more, used in the calculation might not be valid.[1]

Senior also raised an objection of a less economic character. This was based on an equally partial survey of the conditions of the cotton factories, principally those belonging

---

[1] *Proceedings of the Political Economy Club*, Vol. VI, pp. 46 and 273–5. According to J. L. Mallet's *Diaries*, Senior's letters were discussed at a meeting of the Club in May 1837, at which Horner, the factory inspector for Lancashire and Yorkshire, was present. Horner showed the inadequacy of Senior's data and apparently convinced everyone present except Senior and S. J. Loyd (Lord Overstone). Afterwards Senior asked Horner to write out his criticisms in the form of a letter, which he published with his own letters in 1837. The calculation was also criticized in *The Times*, March 26 and 29, 1844, because (1) it seemed to imply that a manufacturer expected his capital to be returned in one year, (2) it made no allowance for reductions in raw materials, etc., if output was reduced. It was suggested in an article in the *Spectator*, March 23, 1844, that manufacturers might be content with smaller profits; that if not, and prices were forced up, the increase of price and diminution of output would be a small price to pay for the reform. Senior's replies to these criticisms were included in the second edition of the letters, 1844. Cf. Hutchins and Harrison, *History of Factory Legislation*, pp. 88–9. Marx's criticism amounted to a more extreme form of that in *The Times*, and a most complicated calculation based on the Labour Theory of Value supposed to show that the product of all but $5\frac{3}{4}$ hours' labour was net profit. *Das Kapital*, Part III, chap. 7, sect. iii.

to enlightened manufacturers. The damaging effects of factory work on the health of the operatives, Senior argued from this survey, had been exaggerated,[1] and the main reason for the ill health of the operatives overlooked. The real explanation was to be found in the frightful housing conditions of the industrial towns, which were sufficient to undermine the health, however good otherwise, of their inhabitants. Instead of the Ten Hours Bill he suggested legislation to deal with housing, in order to make proper provision for drainage and ventilation incumbent on the landlords and to lay down regulations to prevent the worst evils of jerry-building.

Throughout the *Letters* Senior made no suggestion whatever that the principle of factory legislation was wrong, unless his rather excessive sympathy with the complaints of the manufacturers of tiresome and clumsy restrictions is interpreted in that way.[2] As far as State regulation of the employment and education of children were concerned, neither Senior nor any other economist had anything but approval for the scheme. Up to 1847, as far as there is any

[1] For an interesting but not entirely convincing defence of this opinion see Hutt, "The Factory System of the early Nineteenth Century," *Economica*, March 1926.

[2] It is obvious that the *Letters* were directed primarily against the legal ten-hour day for adults and not against Factory Acts as such. Those historians who have quoted the remark in the actual *Letters* that the factories were airy and the children's work was so light as to be negligible, ought in justice to have quoted also the opinion that Senior expressed in the preface to the first edition of the *Letters*, p. 9. "No facts have been proved to me, and I do not believe that any exist, which show that it is proper to keep a child of eleven years old, for twelve hours a day, in attendance on the employment, however light, of a factory." He wanted to see, he went on, the enforcement of the eight-hour limitation for children worked by the relay system. In a letter, written apparently in 1841, he was willing to go further, for he warmly approved of an education scheme of Sir James Graham's which involved (1) cutting the hours of children's work from eight to six, (2) raising the upper age limit of children coming under the limitation from thirteen to fourteen years. (Letter written from Bowood from Senior to Whately, undated.) Cf. Hutchins and Harrison, op. cit., chap. 4, pp. 64–70. It is interesting to notice that in 1861 Senior was urging the extension of the Factory Act safety regulations and control of the conditions of labour of children and young people to all trades and industries, and had no patience with the cotton printers who said it would ruin them. He also referred to the pioneers of factory legislation as the "wise and courageous men" who carried through the legislation in the face of great opposition. (*Suggestions on Popular Education*, 1861, pp. 186–228.)

evidence, Senior's opposition to Factory Acts to regulate the conditions of work of adults was apparently on grounds of expediency, not on *a priori*. theoretical grounds of the economics of individual self-interest.

Senior's other excursion into the field of social policy between 1831 and 1847 was in connection with the Commission on the Distress of the Hand-loom Weavers of which he was a member. It seems probable that Senior was himself responsible for the writing of the Report, and it bears all the marks of his style and methods of arrangement.[1] That he attached importance to the analysis and conclusions of the Report, and to his own work on it, is shown in a letter from him to de Tocqueville:

"I take advantage of the privilege of General Hamilton to send you a copy of a Report on Hand-loom Weavers, which I printed a few days ago, after having given to it the leisure of nearly two years. If you can find time to look through it, you will find that it treats at some length many important questions."[2]

After a comprehensive and sympathetic account of the condition of the hand-loom weavers, the Report goes on to the analysis of the causes of those conditions by an application of wage theory. Since wages depend on the supply and demand for labour, it is argued, unduly low wages in any occupation must be due either to an excessive supply of labour, or to a diminution of demand.[3] On the side of supply in hand-loom weaving there were continuous

[1] This is suggested also by an unpublished letter to Whately (Senior MSS.) dated February 1, 1841. "I send you a little pamphlet which together with the Hand-loom Weavers Report has occupied all my leisure since November. I have inserted in the Hand-loom Weavers Report besides this, two considerable articles on Embezzlement and the Irish Linen Board, [and] an elaborate paper on combinations among workmen. It is a frightful picture and has cost the perusal, painful in every sense, of many folios. I have nothing more on [that] report now than Emigration, which I shall dismiss rather summarily, for the weavers are not good emigrants, and education—on which I shall have Kay's assistance."

[2] Letter to de Tocqueville, February 27, 1841, *Correspondence and Conversations of Alexis de Tocqueville with N. W. Senior*, published 1872, Vol. 1, pp. 21–2.

[3] *Report of the Commission on the Condition of the Hand-loom Weavers*, 1841, pp. 22–3.

tendencies to excessive supply, due to the agreeableness and freedom of independent working, to the ease of learning to weave and of hiring looms, and to the fact that it was an occupation in which it was possible for every member of a family to contribute to income, since children could be employed on the subsidiary occupations. As a result, according to the Report, weavers in many ways suffered from all the disadvantages of a casual supply of labour, and had a tendency to increase in numbers despite the appallingly low level of earnings.[1]

On the side of demand the competition of power looms and the instability of trade diminished both the volume and the regularity of the demand for their labour. The bulk of the fluctuations in the demand for weavers fell on the hand-loom weavers, who as a class had been reduced to the reserve of the industry for times of active trade.[2] The problem was summarized in the following way:

"The general result of our inquiries as to the condition of the hand-loom weavers and its causes may be thus summed up. We have shown that though there are many differences in the respective conditions of different branches of hand-loom weavers, yet as a body they are in a state of distress; and that the great cause of this distress is a disproportion between the supply of hand-loom labour and the demand for it: the demand being in many cases deficient, in some cases decreasing, and in still more irregular, while the supply is in many branches excessive, in almost all has a tendency to increase, and does not appear in any to have a tendency to adapt itself to the irregularities of the demand.

"If we are right in believing that the low rate of the wages of the hand-loom weavers arises principally from a disproportion between the supply of their labour and the demand for it, it must follow that no measures can effectually raise their wages except by getting rid of that disproportion, or even improve them except by diminishing it; still, however, while this low rate

[1] The Hand-loom Weavers inquiry led Senior to raise as an additional objection to the allowance system of outdoor poor relief, that it acted as a subsidy to a decaying branch of industry encouraging the formation of pools of underpaid labour subsisting partly on the rates. *Remarks on the Opposition to the Poor Law Amendment Bill by a Guardian*, 1841, pp. 78–83.

[2] *Report on the Hand-loom Weavers*, p. 23.

of wages continues the condition of the weaver would be improved by any cause which should render the demand for his labour more steady, or should diminish the price or improve the quality of the commodities on which his wages are expended."[1]

The problem confronting the Commission was similar in many ways to that of the modern depressed areas—that of a declining industry dependent to some extent on a foreign market in a period of considerable trade fluctuations. It was no more possible to produce a remedy like a rabbit out of a hat then than now, and the Commission was reduced to making general recommendations with the objects of steadying the demand for the labour of the hand-loom weavers, lowering the cost of living, and increasing the mobility of the weavers themselves. In this connection a discussion of the mischievous effects of the Corn Laws in causing sudden and unforeseeable changes in the state of trade came into the Report. Apart from the hampering effects of these Laws on the expansion of trade, the variations in the price of corn and in the quantities imported caused, according to the Report, sudden fluctuations in the home demand for manufactured goods, and dislocated credit and markets by necessitating sudden movements of specie. These variations were bad for all industries, but *a fortiori* for the marginal producers of a depressed industry, since a bad harvest not merely raised the price of food, but increased the supply of labour among those who, like the hand-loom weavers, had the opportunity to work harder to make up their wages, just at the times when the demand for their labour had fallen off. The inevitable results were a fall in money wages and a rise in the cost of living at the same time. The Commission attempted to bring home the distress caused by these disturbances:

"Very few even of our best-paid workmen have the economy and providence which enable the high wages of one period to meet the low wages or inactivity of another. With almost all of them low wages produce immediate distress, and want of

[1] *Report on the Hand-loom Weavers*, p. 48.

employment immediate destitution. We do not believe that anyone who has not mixed with the working classes, we do not believe that we ourselves, can adequately estimate how much mental and bodily suffering, how much anxiety and pain, how much despondency and disease are implied in the vague terms 'a fall of wages' or a 'slack demand for labour.' "[1]

Although the Commission was convinced of the harmful effects of the protective system and of the Corn Laws in particular, it pointed out that their removal could not produce any fundamental change in the conditions of the hand-loom weavers, since the principal cause of their distress was the competition of power looms. It made, however, a general recommendation in order to help the weavers by improving the quality of some of the goods they bought, particularly house room. The duty of the Government was intervention in this matter:

"Of the modes in which the labourer can expend his income, the legislature ought to encourage those which contribute to the general welfare of his family; and of these the principal is the improvement and adornment of his habitation. Where that is miserable, nothing else that is for the common benefit is likely to be attended to."

On the following page of the Report the way in which this might be done is explained:

"With all our reverence for the principle of non-interference, we cannot doubt that in this matter it has been pushed too far. We believe that both the ground landlord and the speculating builder ought to be compelled by law, though it should cost them a percentage on their rent and profit, to take measures which shall prevent the towns which they create from being the centre of disease. . . . If like the higher classes the labourers were aware of the danger and refused to encounter it, better habitations would be provided for them. But where tenants are to be found for every hovel and cellar where family after family occupy rooms which are vacant by the disease or death of the previous tenants, the builder has no pecuniary motive to provide

---

[1] *Report on the Hand-loom Weavers*, p. 67. According to the Report the hand-loom weavers attached great importance to the reform of the Corn Laws.

better accommodation than his customers require. We repeat, therefore, our belief that this is not one of the matters which can be safely abandoned to the parties immediately concerned."

The Commission was in fact prepared to support the recommendations of the public health enthusiasts as to regulation and examination of plans for new buildings, compulsory drainage, inspection and disinfection of old, and the condemning of those past repair. The Commission made the further suggestion that in order to prevent these restrictions raising the cost of houses to the labourers the duty on Baltic timber should be abolished.[1]

Of those remedies which might apply specifically to hand-loom weavers by increasing their mobility and willingness to enter other industries, education occupied the chief position, and the Commission had no hesitation in recommending compulsory education provided gratis by the State.[2] Emigration was turned down as unsuited to the physique and inclinations of the weavers themselves.[3] Finally, Senior himself regarded legislation to prevent trade unions limiting entry into certain trades, as one of the easiest and most effective remedies.[4]

From the tone of the Report it is obvious that if Senior and his colleagues had known a remedy for the distress of the hand-loom weavers, they would not have turned it down for the sake of the principle of non-interference. But inevitably the only real solution lay in the hands of the weavers themselves—the abandonment of the branches of hand-loom weaving which were economically dead, and the decrease or limitation of the supply of labour in those which were not. Thus the Report concludes:

"But we must add, and we make the statement with great sympathy for the persons on whose situation we are commenting, that there are branches of hand-loom weaving which no conduct on the part of those engaged in them is likely to make adequate sources of comfortable support for a family."[5]

[1] *Report on the Hand-loom Weavers*, pp. 71–3 et seq.
[2] Ibid., pp. 121–4. See pp. 267–8 below for an account of Seniors' views on education.
[3] Ibid., pp. 118–20.   [4] Ibid., p. 118.   [5] Ibid., p. 120.

But neither this Report, nor anything else Senior wrote during this period, contains any general statement as to the proper scope of Government interference. We can only glean that Senior thought that the principle of non-interference could be carried too far. In 1847, however, Senior at last came into the open with a definite theory of the function of the Government and a modified one of that of the economist in relation to it.

III

It is evident that though a considerable part of the analysis contained in the *Hand-loom Weavers Report* was purely economic, a large part fell outside the field of economists as Senior had defined in 1836, just as part of his *Letters on the Factory Act* had. The Report naturally contained, too, recommendations on both economic and only indirectly economic matters. How did all this fit in with Senior's precept of 1836, that economists were not to give "a syllable of advice"? Obviously he had found it just as impossible as other economists to refrain from giving advice, particularly when asked for it, but he had never explained the status of such advice, whether it had all the weight of economics behind it or not. In 1847, however, when he went up to Oxford as Drummond Professor for the second time, he formulated his mature views on the relation of economic analysis to policy, devoting the greater part of the first course of lectures to a further elucidation of the scope and method of political economy and the theory of Government intervention.[1]

According to his new point of view economics is divided into three sections, the pure and exact science of theoretical economics, and two arts of political economy, the one embracing the study of customs and institutions, the other the relation of wealth to happiness or welfare. Now according

---

[1] A summary of Senior's new position was published in his review of J. S. Mill's *Principles* and *Essays* in the *Edinburgh Review*, October 1848. The actual lectures on the scope and method of economics were published in 1852, the lectures on Government intervention were not published.

to Senior's judgment of the progress of economics, insufficient agreement on fundamental principles had been reached to enable anyone to treat the art in either sense without explaining his opinions on the science first.[1] This meant that the art of economics, though methodologically respectable, had not yet any certain foundations.

Accordingly, Senior explained, he could only speak as an economist when he was analysing the abstract principles of economic theory; in the treatment of practical problems he could only express his personal opinions based on his own interpretation of theory. Naturally even if economic science were sufficiently advanced for the precepts of the arts of economics to be worked out, the final decision as to the weight to be attached to those precepts must be taken by statesmen, not by economists.

This is certainly a modest enough opinion for any economist to hold as to the validity of his own judgments outside the field of pure theory. By emphasizing this attitude Senior made clearer than in 1836 that, though the legitimate functions and policies of Government intervention in economic and social problems were not matters on which, as an economist, he could claim any particular authority, he was prepared as "a statesman or moralist" to discuss them.[2]

In two later lectures in the same course, entitled "The Power of Government to alter the degree in which Wealth is Desirable,"[3] Senior explained his view of the legitimate scope of Government in general terms. After describing the means at the disposal of a Government, he discussed the question of whether, if it can affect the advantages of the possession of wealth, it is justified in doing so:

"This is an attempt so liable to fail, so liable to produce results precisely the reverse of those intended by the legislator,

---

[1] Lectures, 1847–52, Course I, lecture 3, *Reasons for treating Political Economy as a Science*, pp. 51–3.

[2] Ibid., particularly pp. 52 and 55. For a more detailed discussion and references see Part I, chap. I, pp. 54–5 above.

[3] Lectures, 1847–52, Course I, lectures 6–7, "The Power of Government to alter the degree in which Wealth is Desirable."

so liable to aggravate the evils which he proposes to remedy, and to introduce others which could not have arisen without his intervention, that many political writers have affirmed that it ought never to be made. They have declared that the business of government is simply to afford protection, to repel or to punish internal or external violence or fraud, and that to do more is usurpation. This proposition I cannot admit. The only rational foundation of government, the only foundation of a right to govern and of a correlative duty to obey, is expediency—the general benefit of the community. It is the duty of a Government to do whatever is conducive to the welfare of the governed. The only limit to this duty is its power. And as the supreme Government of an independent State is necessarily absolute, the only limit to its power is its moral or physical inability. And whatever it is its duty to do it must necessarily have a right to do.

"The opinion which I am controverting appears to have been produced by the fact that the expediency of the exercise of some of the powers of government is more obvious than that of the exercise of some others. It is obviously expedient that a Government should protect the persons and the property of its subjects. . . . But if it can also be shown to be expedient that the Government should perform any other functions, it must also be its duty and its right to perform them. The expediency may be more difficult of proof, and until that proof has been given, the duty and the right do not arise. But as soon as the proof has been given they are perfect. It is true that in such matters the Government may make mistakes. It may believe its interference to be useful where it is really mischievous. There is no Government that does not make such mistakes, and the more it interferes the more liable it must be to make them. On the other hand, its refusal or neglect to interfere may also be founded on error. It may be passively wrong as well as actively wrong. The advance of political knowledge must diminish both these errors, but it appears to me that the most fatal of all errors would be the general admission of a proposition that a Government has no right to interfere for any purpose except for the purpose of affording protection, for such an admission would prevent our profiting by experience, or even acquiring it."[1]

[1] Lectures, 1847–52, Course 1, lecture 6. Cf. J. S. Mill, *Principles of Political Economy*, particularly Bk. v, chap. 11. Senior's and J. S. Mill's views on government coincided in many respects, for although the latter laid down the general principles of *laissez-faire*, his discussions of all possible and probable exceptions reduced it from a principle to the shadow of a maxim.

In short, the Government has a roving commission and duty to do anything that it can do. The sacred and respected principle of non-interference was thrown overboard as a principle: it was on the same footing as interference—whether it was expedient or not. On this basis Senior could satisfactorily explain his general outlook on the function of government in social and economic problems. To this he devoted the rest of these two lectures under the headings, "The Power of Government to decrease the Desirability of Wealth," and "The Power of Government to mitigate the Hardships of Poverty." Under the first he included the ordinary examples of misgovernment, insecurity of life and property, arbitrary taxation, and failure to open up social and economic opportunities to each individual. These merely correspond to the usual classical exposition of the police functions of government, the preservation of economic and legal freedom, and Adam Smith's criteria of taxation. Under his second heading, however, Senior included all the various measures of social reform in which he had from time to time been interested, e.g. housing, education, destitution, and regulation of conditions of labour.[1]

As before he pointed out that the Government can prevent some of the worst evils of bad housing:

"It cannot of course enact that every family shall have five well-built, well-ventilated rooms, any more than it can enact that every family shall live on roast beef, but it can prohibit the erection of houses without drainage, or in courts, or back to back. It can require the streets to be paved, it can regulate their width and the thickness of the walls. In short, it can provide prospectively against the creation of new seats of disease and vice. To deal with those which already exist is more difficult. No one denies the right in the State to interfere to prevent a man from injuring others. It exercises this right when it forbids him to build a row of undrained cottages. But the right of the State to interfere to prevent a man from injuring himself supposes that the legislator knows better how to manage the affairs

---

[1] Lectures, 1847–52, Course 1, lecture 6. Senior further distinguished measures designed to prevent poverty, such as restrictions on early marriages, inheritance laws, etc., but he did not discuss them.

of an individual than the man himself does. In the present case this supposition is true."[1]

It followed that a policy of inspection, disinfection, enforcement of repairs and condemnation of dwellings was the duty of the State. This much, which Senior had favoured for a long time, had already, at least theoretically, been realized in Liverpool,[2] but the supreme difficulty of providing for the rehousing of the inhabitants at rents they could afford (a difficulty pointed out in the *Hand-loom Weavers Report*) was still unsolved, and to a large extent is unsolved at the present day. Senior had no remedy to propose, he could only state the difficulty:

"But admitting that in this instance the formidable objection to the interference of Government to prevent men from acting unwisely, does not exist, a still more serious one is the physical difficulty of providing residences for those whose habitations it condemns. It is remarkable that this class of difficulties is one which those who attempt to legislate on what they call the principles of humanity generally refuse to take into account."[3]

As regards education, he realized that the ideal of a complete education for everyone was outside the bounds of contemporary possibility, but he maintained the Government could at least do something by providing good elementary schools:

"Another of the evils of poverty which a Government can palliate is defective education. Here again it can only palliate. A really good education implies leisure. It implies that the acquisition of knowledge shall be the principal business of childhood, and even of adolescence. But this is incompatible with the condition of the labouring classes, that is to say, with the condition of the bulk of a people. They cannot afford to lose

[1] Lectures, 1847–52, Course 1, lecture 6. Senior had favoured some such policy in 1837, see above, p. 257.

[2] An Act for the Promotion of the Health of the Inhabitants of Liverpool, June 18, 1842 (5 & 6 Vic., Cap. XLIV).

[3] Lectures, 1847–52, Course 1, lecture 6. Senior illustrated this difficulty from the evidence given before the House of Commons Committee on the Administration of the Act, 1846.

all the wages which their children and young persons can earn.
. . . But it is obvious that a further, or rather previous step is
to secure the existence of good schools. And this is in the power
of every civilized Government. No country is so poor as to be
unable to bear the expense of good elementary schools. Strictly
speaking, it is not an expense. The money so employed is much
more than repaid by the superiority in diligence, in skill, in
economy, and in health. . . . The defect of the Factory Act is that
it does not provide such schools."[1]

On destitution Senior had very little to add to what he
had already said from time to time in connection with the
Poor Law, but he gave it a slightly different emphasis. He
now placed the desirability of removing all fear of destitution in the foreground, while the dangers of bad administration are only referred to at the end of the discussion.

---

[1] Lectures, 1847–52, Course i, lecture 6. Senior had always been in favour of
provision for education of the working classes, and his matured ideas on it are
contained in his *Suggestions on Popular Education*, 1861, which was, as he explained,
of the nature of a minority report to the Royal Commission on Popular Education, 1857–61. He stated that he differed from the majority in thinking that the
expense of ensuring universal elementary education would not be overwhelming,
that centralized control, inspection and grants ought to be retained and
extended, that school hours were too long to be educationally useful and should
be shortened, and that measures should be taken, i.e. by extending the Factory
Acts, to make possible the education of children in unregulated occupations.
(Preface.) He started from the principle that it was as much the duty of the
State to educate children as to feed them when their parents could not afford to.
His actual plan was that the Privy Council education inspectors should be made
responsible for finding out those places where the existing provision of education
was inadequate, and empowered to levy an education rate to pay for bringing
and maintaining the provision up to standard, while the Privy Council should
continue its system of grants. The great difficulties he foresaw were those of
inducing parents to send their children to school because they were either
apathetic or unable to do without their earnings. To get over the first obstacle,
he suggested that the employment of children except at home should be made
conditional on the possession of an education certificate, as he felt the time
was not ripe for the open compulsion of parents. To get over the second
difficulty, he advocated the extension of the half-time system. As regards
pauper children he urged (1) the foundation of district schools where the
children could be brought up outside the workhouses, and (2) in cases of
outdoor relief the introduction of attendance at approved schools as a condition
of relief, if necessary making up the loss of the children's earnings by increasing
the relief given to the parents. More general recommendations as to the general
type of education included the introduction of drill, and an increased emphasis
on education as an intellectual training instead of the customary system of
fact cramming. Cf. next chapter, pp. 330–1.

The comparative success of the new Poor Law in depauperizing the agricultural labourer without removing all provision for contingencies had in fact finally proved, Senior
thought, that it was within the power of the Government
(and therefore was its duty) to eliminate the worst of this
particular disadvantage of poverty.[1] A well-arranged Poor
Law, like other social legislation, could be regarded in
1847 as a safe and valuable part of the social code.

On factory legislation Senior clearly felt uncertain. Its
object, he stated, is to prevent that particular evil of poverty,
overwork. This in itself constitutes a change from his earlier
statement in the *Letters on the Factory Act* that the evils of
factory conditions were exaggerated. Nor did he reopen
the question of the possible effect of such legislation on the
industrial prosperity of the country, he confined himself to
discussing the validity of the assumption that the Government knew better than individuals what was best for them
in regard to hours of work. With regard to children and
young persons under sixteen there was and never had been
any doubt.[2] But the burning question of the period was the
regulation of women's work, and on this he adopted John
Stuart Mill's opinion that there was no sound reason for
believing that women were less capable than men of looking
after their own interest:

"I believe them," he said, "to have as clear a perception of
their interest, and as much determination and as much power
to follow it as belong to their brothers or to their fathers. I utterly
disapprove therefore of the principle of the Act of 1844 and of
the present Bill so far as they place adult women on the footing
of children. And I am inclined to agree in the doctrine that,
so far as respects persons, whether male or female, above the
age of sixteen the interference of the legislator to force them to
manage their own affairs in the way they do not think most
conducive to their welfare, is an interference so likely to be
mischievous that it is better to forbear it altogether. It must be

---

[1] Lectures, 1847–52, Course 1, lecture 7. See next chapter. On Senior's
Letters on the Factory Act see above, pp. 255 et seq

[2] The age at which children ceased to be counted as members of their
parents' family for the purposes of the Poor Law Amendment Act.

recollected that as the supreme authority is necessarily unrestrained, as there is no arbiter between it and its subjects, there is no medium between its interference with their conduct as affecting themselves whenever it thinks fit, and its abstaining from such interference altogether. The Government itself must be the judge as to the truth of the premises which it assumes, and as to the correctness of the conclusions which it draws from them. There is no authority to which they can appeal against its errors as to facts or as to interferences."[1]

Senior's doubt about the radical doctrine was perfectly genuine; in all matters of health and housing, in matters relating to provision for contingencies and calamities and the regulation of female labour in the mines, he admitted the failure of the radical theory to fit the facts. He was prepared even to object to J. S. Mill's use of the term "optional"[2] with regard to any functions whatever of the State; if their expediency was proved, they must according to Senior's view be performed. The question of general legislative regulation of the labour market was, however, one of great difficulty; its answer depended on the answers given to two preliminary questions: does the workman know his best interests? if so, is he able to act up to them? On neither point does Senior appear to have been altogether decided. He was convinced that as far as rapid adjustments to changes in the conditions of demand were concerned, ignorance, which could only be cured by better education, prevented a full use of opportunities.[3] In matters of wages, he believed that neither employers nor workmen had ultimate power; strikes and lock-outs were therefore clearly to be depreciated as dangerous and wasteful, but he was not prepared for legal prohibition.[4] On the whole, he thought that the labourer was the best judge of how long and how hard he was willing to work at any given rate of wages.

---

[1] Lectures, 1847–52, Course I, lecture 7.

[2] Op. cit., *Edinburgh Review*, October 1848, p. 331. "We agree with him [J. S. Mill] that there is absolutely no limit, no exception, to the doctrine of expediency. And we are even inclined to disapprove of his use of the word 'optional' as applied to any of the functions of Government."

[3] See p. 262 above on the *Report on the Hand-loom Weavers.*

[4] See note on Senior's opinions on trade unions, pp. 277–81, below.

Further, he was impressed by the serious hardship caused by sudden attempts at legal regulation of such matters. These had been made sufficiently clear in 1844, by the reports of the inspectors appointed to enforce Shaftesbury's Coalmining Act of the plight of the women who had suddenly been deprived of their sole means of earning a living.[1] What neither Senior nor many of his contemporaries appreciated was the difficulty or impossibility of the ordinary individual factory operative enforcing his own desires with regard to his own conditions of work.[2] The most obvious means at his disposal besides legal enforcement of some agreed minimum was a trade union, but the only recognized way by which a trade union could hope to be effective was by some policy of exclusion; this, however, Senior naturally condemned as causing great hardship to persons not admitted to the union.[3]

Senior's hesitancy on the question of whether the ordinary adult was either the best judge of his own interests, or able to follow them, is not in the least surprising, nor his consequent doubt as to the expediency of factory legislation for adults. He realized that it was still experimental, and likely to be pushed further, for he remarked in concluding the discussion that this "sort of legislation is at present in its infancy."[4] But he refrained from expressing a final opinion on it, explaining that he had

"given this brief outline of the factory question merely as a specimen of the attempts made by Governments to palliate that

[1] Lectures, 1847–52, Course I, lecture 7. Senior felt that not merely a hardship was involved but also a gross injustice, and he more or less implied that displaced workers should, in common justice, be compensated. "If any of the higher classes, any of those who can force the public to hear their case, had been thus sacrificed to the public good, they would have demanded compensation and would have received it. I ought perhaps to include among the evils of poverty, the carelessness with which the individual interests of the poor are dealt with by the legislature, and particularly, as I have before remarked, by those who profess peculiar humanity."

[2] In contrast to Senior, J. S. Mill, Thornton and Cairnes appreciated this difficulty and therefore sympathized with the whole trade union movement. Cf. Mill, Principles, Bk. v, chap. 10, par. 5. Thornton, On Labour, Bk. II, chap. 4, and Bk. III. Cairnes, Some Leading Principles of Political Economy, Part II, chaps. 3 and 4.

[3] See pp. 277–81 below.   [4] Lectures, 1847–52, Course I, lecture 7.

portion of the evils of poverty which arise from overwork, and the dangers incident to such attempts."[1]

On the positive side of improving the amenities of the lives of the poor, Senior suggested that the Government might take steps to secure opportunities for entertainment and recreation by providing parks, open spaces, museums, and picture galleries. In this respect, as in that of education, England, he declared, was far behind continental countries.[2] Senior summed up his conclusions, saying:

"On the whole this sketch of the influence of Government in bringing nearer to a level the happiness of the rich and of the poor is an illustration of the general rule in human affairs that it is much easier to do harm than good. It is not in the power of the best Government so to remove or palliate the evils of poverty as to make it nearly as desirable as wealth. It is as difficult to elevate the poor as it is easy to depress the rich."

Further on he added:

"Much without doubt remains to be done, and perhaps something to be undone, and the greater part of what has been done is mere seed in the ground, to be reaped by the next or by a still more distant generation. But even already the interval as respects happiness which twenty years ago separated in England the rich from the poor has been narrowed. And all who believe in the improvement of mankind must believe that it will be still further narrowed. Not I trust by pushing back the former, but by advancing the latter. That it should ever be altogether removed is not to be expected or to be wished."[3]

IV

In considering the quarter-century 1825–52, during which Senior took his most active interest in economics, the rough

---

[1] Lectures, 1847–52, Course 1, lecture 7. Senior had no doubt as to the desirability of the Act of 1842 preventing female labour in coalmines. He considered that in this case that it had been proved that the Government knew better than the individual workers what was right.

[2] Lectures, 1847–52, Course 1, lecture 7. [3] Ibid.

parallelism between the evolution of his views and those of the general public on reform emerges most strikingly. Up to 1832 the ordinary progressive person interested in public affairs was chiefly interested in questions of political reform and the realization of free competition at home. After 1832, when the Liberals had become potentially victorious with increased representation both of the radicals and the industrial interests in the House of Commons, reforming energy flowed into social channels, and during the next twenty years the main lines of the social code of the rest of the century were sketched out. As far, however, as the general public were aware the economists dug their heels in in 1832 and refused to consider the new trend of activity. But in fact, far from being in the rear of the reformers, clinging despite everything to the shibboleths of *laissez-faire*, Senior was, as we have seen, in the van of the movement, and with him in varying degrees the rest of the economists.

It is perhaps simple to account for the popular opinion that, with the shining exception of J. S. Mill, who has been given a niche as the apologist for, and humanizer of, classical economics, the classical economists were rigid supporters of *laissez-faire*. Popularly economics in England were associated with Bentham, who it was believed provided the philosophical content of the analysis of Adam Smith and his disciples. The first generation of economists, Ricardo, Malthus, James Mill and McCulloch, were known as his disciples, and it appeared to follow that they therefore refused to consider any possibilities of economic and social policy beyond those included in the popular misinterpretations of his philosophy.[1] Add to this the circumstance that these economists attracted attention largely by their teaching of the theory of population and by their advocacy of free trade in general, and abundant ground is available for the

[1] Ashley's paper on "The Present Position of Political Economy" (*Economic Journal*, 1907) may be cited as an example of the common misconception and the sort of criticisms it has always inspired. The inadequacy of the data on which these are usually based is illustrated by the ease with which Ashley was answered in the Introduction to the *Proceedings of the Political Economy Club*, Vol. VI, pp. xi et seq.

growth of the popular tradition.[1] The bulk of the argument is of course all wrong and has been demonstrated as such time and again, but in order to dispel the surviving legend of Senior as the arch-apostle of *laissez-faire*[2] it is essential to emphasize a few of the salient points. It is unnecessary to point out that Benthamism is not an intrinsic part of classical economics, but it is perhaps important to point out that the adherence to Bentham of Ricardo's generation did not involve them logically in opposition to Poor Laws, health regulations, Factory Acts, or education.[3] The early nineteenth-century education movement owed much both to Bentham personally and to his disciples, and in common with Robert Owen he attached the greatest importance to the effect of environment and education on personality. He himself sketched a plan for the reform and centralization of poor relief, while Chadwick, the greatest leader of the public health movement, was his trusted personal friend and disciple. Among Ricardo's generation of economists there is practically no concrete evidence of *a priori* opposition to any of these particular movements. Ricardo himself was largely immersed in banking and monetary problems which were the burning questions of the last decade of his life, and published nothing on social reform. James Mill and Malthus were keen supporters of the education movement, while their attitude to the Poor Law was determined by their general belief in the theory of population, but Mill at any rate approved of the Poor Law

[1] For admirable sketches of the way in which the tradition has grown see Nicholson, "The Use and Abuse of Authority in Economics," *Economic Journal*, 1903, and J. M. Keynes, *The End of Laissez-Faire*, 1926. The classical economists themselves were aware of the misinterpretation to which they were exposed; Senior, for example, in his controversy with Malthus, urged him to state his theory of population in a way less likely to give apparent support to opposers of social reform (Letters from Senior to Malthus, March 26 and April 9, 1829, published with Senior's *Two Lectures on Population* in 1829, cf. Part i, chap. 3, sect. i, above); while Cairnes devoted an introductory lecture at University College, London (1870), to explaining that economic science had nothing to do with *laissez-faire*. ("Political Economy and Laissez-Faire," published in *Essays in Political Economy*.)

[2] Cf. R. Opie's review of *Senior's Industrial Efficiency*, etc., edited by S. Leon Levy, *Quarterly Journal of Economics*, 1929, pp. 373 and 374.

[3] See Leslie Stephen, *English Utilitarians*, Vol. i, chap. 6.

Amendment.[1] McCulloch, the only one to survive as an active economist into the era of factory and public health agitation, was a warm supporter of both.[2]

All this must be admitted by anyone who takes the trouble to inquire as to what these economists actually wrote or said on social problems, but as with most long-lived misconceptions there is some real justification for this one. The only thing is the critics have proved too much. A great deal of Bentham's energy was directed to criticizing restrictive customs and interference by Government, and to justifying individual freedom. According to his philosophy there was an *a priori* argument in favour of *laissez-faire* to which exceptions existed in the difference between enlightened and unenlightened self-interest (the exact definition of enlightened self-interest was never satisfactorily formulated).[3] The reforming energies of his immediate followers found, however, plenty of scope in the fields in which it was obvious that self-interest was unenlightened—among the uneducated and the young, etc.—while regarding State intervention in general as mistaken. Hence it is perfectly correct to regard them as supporters of the basic

[1] Letter to Robert Harrison, December 12, 1864, in the *Letters of J. S. Mill*, edited Hugh Elliot, Vol. II, p. 14, and *James Mill*, by Alexander Bain, p. 372. Though James Mill was a close disciple of Bentham he was active on behalf of numerous philanthropic causes, accepting the distinction between enlightened and unenlightened self-interest and applying it to certain fields. For an account of Malthus' opinions see Bonar, *Malthus and his Work*, Bk. II, chap. 4, and Bk. III. Malthus approved of Government intervention to provide education, restrict children's labour, provide medical relief, help families with more than six children, assist emigration, and to protect home industries in certain cases. He probably approved of the principle of the Poor Law Amendment Act, 1834.

[2] McCulloch, *Principles of Political Economy*, Part I, chap. 10, and Part III, chaps. 3 and 4, fourth edition, 1849. The field outlined by McCulloch for Government intervention was extremely wide, including factory legislation, housing and health regulations, education, poor relief, employers' liability, and on some occasions the building of canals, railways, etc. Nevertheless, he laid down *laissez-faire* as the dominant principle, and objected to the Government undertaking any intervention by way of experiment. Cf. next chapter, note 1 on p. 284.

[3] Bentham admitted his own difficulty as to the exact significance of enlightened self-interest with great candour in the famous remark: "I am a selfish man, as selfish as any man can be. But in me, somehow or other, so it happens, selfishness has taken the shape of benevolence." *Works*, Vol. XI, p. 95.

principle of *laissez-faire, but* it is grossly unfair to maintain that they were blind or indifferent to the social problems of the time.

It is evident that the attitude of Senior and John Stuart Mill marked an important breach with the preceding generation. It is one thing to maintain, as a principle, that the duty of Government is to keep out except in special cases, however liberally that phrase is interpreted. It is quite another to assert the right, duty ànd possibility of intervention for the common good, and that the only limit to the duty of Government is its power, without any first principle limiting that power. This is what Senior and effectually J. S. Mill were asserting in 1847.[1] Senior's own evolution and application of this principle of government is sufficient evidence of his divergence from the original Benthamite principle of non-intervention. The same may be said of John Stuart Mill. Nor is it difficult to explain why this has not been realized in the former case, while it has in that of the latter. Most of the writings in which Senior's evolution is displayed are either embodied in Government reports, or are in the form of memoranda written for various members of the inner circle of the Whig party to which he acted as general adviser on social and economic questions, or else are contained in his unpublished lectures. Of the few non-theoretical writings published, the most important, the *Letter* on the Irish Poor Laws, naturally had a circulation limited to people interested in the Irish question; the *Letters on the Factory Act* were certainly open to *laissez-faire* interpretation in view of the common habit of reading a general condemnation of a wide movement into criticism of a particular part of it; while the only article directly connected with English social problems, viz., "The English Poor Laws," was published anonymously in the *Edinburgh Review*.[2] It was thus not to be expected that any outside the circle in which he moved should know anything

[1] Cf. Leslie Stephen, *English Utilitarians*, Vol. III, chaps. 3 and 4. J. S. Mill, *Autobiography*, chap. 7.

[2] This article was reprinted in 1865 in *Historical and Philosophical Essays*, Vol. II.

about those of his opinions which might modify the popular idea that economists had got left behind.

Sufficient has been said to show that Senior, no less than John Stuart Mill, thought that the function of government was not limited to intervention in special cases outside the general category of police, and that *laissez-faire* was not necessarily the normal rule. Surely if the two most distinguished members of the second generation of classical economists had reached this position, it is unreasonable to suggest that the teachings of the classical economists have been a dead weight on later generations. Indeed there is little doubt that much of the actual work of reform has been carried out by people who have been educated and influenced by either classical economics or utilitarian philosophy, or both; it is impossible to deny the debt of such reformers and administrators as Chadwick, Sir James Stephens, the Cornewall Lewises, Lansdowne and Sir Robert Peel, and Lord Howick, to mention only some of Senior's contemporaries, to both Bentham and the classical economists.

SENIOR ON TRADE UNIONS

In 1830 Senior was asked by Lord Melbourne to consider the position of the law of trade combinations, and to make recommendations for reform. Lord Melbourne and his colleagues in the Cabinet considered that the existing position of the law gave far too much encouragement to strike organizations. In this Senior agreed with them, and he believed that a drastic strengthening of the law was necessary.

Assisted by another lawyer, Tomlinson, he made inquiries, and finally recommended the most intolerant measures which, if they had been enforced, and provided they had not provoked a revolution, would have effectively hampered the Trade Union Movement. This group of proposals may be summarized as follows:

1. A law making clear the common law prohibitions of all conspiracy and restraint of trade.

2. All solicitations, peaceful or otherwise, to form unions,

all threats to blacklegs or to masters were to be forbidden and severely punished. Picketing, however peaceful, was to be prohibited and ruthlessly punished.

3. Employers, or their assistants, were to be authorized to arrest men soliciting or picketing without warrant, and take them before any Justice of the Peace.

4. Masters who encouraged combinations and strikes were also to be severely punished.[1]

If these measures were not found to be adequate, Senior recommended that funds subscribed for the purposes of combinations and deposited in savings banks or elsewhere should be confiscated.

After deliberation, Lord Melbourne and his colleagues decided that that these astounding recommendations were politically impossible, and in any case probably undesirable, and the Report was relegated to the files of the Home Office. The Report, however, contained a good deal of other interesting material, and numerous recommendations which Senior incorporated in the *Report on the Hand-loom Weavers* in 1841, and published in his *Historical and Philosophical Essays*. Whether in 1841 he still really thought that the recommendations of his original Report were satisfactory it is impossible to say, but it is evident that in 1830–1 he was sufficiently alarmed to make recommendations which in practise would have undone the work of the Philosophical Radicals in achieving the repeal of the Combination Laws in 1824–5.

In 1841 he explained his objections to trade unions as due to the effect that their restrictive policy had on the mobility and freedom of labour:

"As the object of the combinations among workmen is the increase of their wages and the general improvement of their condition, and as they have adhered to them for many years, at the expense of great and widely spread occasional suffering, at a sacrifice of individual liberty, such as no political despotism has ever been able to enforce, and with a disregard of justice

[1] The original report is not available. This account is taken from the Webbs' *History of Trade Unionism*, chap. 3. The Webbs had access to the original.

and of humanity, which only the strongest motives could instigate, it may be supposed that combinations have been found to produce the benefits for which such enormous evils have been voluntarily incurred. We believe, however, that, with a few exceptions, the tendency of combinations has been precisely the reverse of their object, and that, as hitherto directed, they have led to the positive deterioration of the wages and of the condition of those who have engaged in them, and of the far more numerous body who are excluded from them."[1]

It must be remembered that at the time of Senior's early Report, and even when he wrote again in 1841, that the active unions were practically confined to skilled trades. Naturally, therefore, strikes were called without much regard for the large body of workpeople who would, for the time being, lose their wages quite involuntarily. Although Senior seriously failed to appreciate the significance of the Labour Movement in its early nineteenth-century phases, its contemporary appearance was in fact not such as to encourage anyone who was a sincere believer in individual liberty, though his original recommendations cannot be justified on any grounds whatever. Even the most ardent opponents of the old Combination Laws, such as Francis Place, hoped that their abolition would bring about the natural death of active trade unionism.

The duty of the State in this matter was, Senior believed, to protect the right of the labourer to dispose of his labour as he liked. The Government, he said, would be guilty of "acts of omission if it does not protect the labourer from injury on the part of those who assume to dictate to him what he shall do and what he shall not do." It would fail on the other hand by acts of commission if it should oblige labourers to do and not to do things because such actions might damage their own interests or those of their employers, and the wealth of the community. In short, Senior declared that, apart from keeping the peace and protecting individuals from each other, the duty of the Government is

---

[1] *Historical and Philosophical Essays*, 1865, Vol. II, p. 117. Reprinted from p. 31 of the *Report on the Hand-loom Weavers*, 1841.

to leave everyone to follow what they believe to be their own interests.[1]

It is evident that Senior felt the difficulty that most Liberals have always felt with regard to the position of trade unions with respect to individual freedom. Whether or not we agree with his particular opinion of the real influence of trade unions at the time he was writing (and in this connection the Webbs' extremely sympathetic account of the early nineteenth-century Labour Movement gives very considerable support to it[2]) it must be admitted that Senior had laid his finger on one of the most important of the economic and social aspects of trade unionism in emphasizing the lack of solidarity of interests between different sections of the working classes.

Despite his fierce recommendations, it appears that he had not any real desire to return to the pre-1824 state of the Combination Laws, for he stigmatized the old laws as oppressive and demoralizing, since, he explained, they confounded "men's ideas of right and wrong" by laying down that—

"each man's separate attempt to raise his own wages was blameless, but that any concerted effort was a crime; that a mere agreement to make such an effort was a crime, and that an assault or a riot exposed its actors to far severer punishment when used as evidence of a combination to raise wages, than when regarded as merely endangering the persons and property of their fellow-subjects."[3]

He admitted, too, that the administration of the old law had been "partial and oppressive."

His suggestions were, he said, tentative, as he felt that he did not know the complete facts. In the first place, he recommended that the common law against conspiracies should be modified, as it still made practically every act of a workman, as a member of a combination, illegal. Secondly, that the law should be strengthened against

---

[1] *Historical and Philosophical Essays*, 1865, Vol. ii, p. 122. These opinions and those discussed below were reprinted from pp. 98–118 of the *Report on the Hand-loom Weavers*, 1841. Cf. p. 242 above.

[2] *History of Trade Unionism*, chaps. 2 and 3.

[3] *Historical and Philosophical Essays*, Vol. ii, pp. 124–5.

combinations to force discharges of individual labourers, or to force the use or prohibition of certain sorts of machinery. Thirdly, that the encouragement of strikes and combinations by masters should be severely punished by fines. Fourthly, that picketing should be made a criminal offence. Fifthly, that injury to witnesses or to people who stood out against combinations should be compensated from public funds. Finally, he added in a true philosophical-radical spirit:

"We have to add . . . only an earnest wish that no preamble in the spirit of that of the 6 George IV denouncing combinations as 'injurious to trade and commerce, and especially prejudicial to the interests of all concerned in them' [should be included]. We firmly believe in the truth of this preamble. We believe that the general evils and general dangers of combinations cannot easily be exaggerated. We believe that if the manufacturer is to employ his capital, and the mechanist and chemist his ingenuity only under the dictation of his shortsighted and rapacious workmen, or of his equally ignorant and rapacious rivals; if a few agitators can command and enforce a strike which first paralyses the industry of the peculiar class of workpeople over whom they tyrannize, and then extends itself in an increasing circle. . . . we believe, we say, that if this state of things is to continue we shall not retain the industry, the skill, or the capital, on which our manufacturing superiority, and, with that superiority, our power, and almost our existence as a nation, depends. But though we believe in the truth of these premises, they are not the grounds on which we wish now to proceed. Our immediate object is to give freedom to the labourer; and we firmly believe that as soon as he is made master of his own conduct he will use his liberty in the way most useful not only to himself, but to the rest of the community."[1]

Altogether Senior's attitude to trade unions was a peculiar combination of panic fear of turbulent workpeople, a genuine belief in the damage and injustice done by them to the excluded groups such as the unskilled, the hand-loom weavers, etc., and to industry as a whole, and too great a willingness to think of the instigators and organizers of unions as unscrupulous ruffians imposing on the ignorance of their fellows.

[1] *Historical and Philosophical Essays*, Vol. II, pp. 171–2.

CHAPTER 2

THE POOR LAW PROBLEM

BY 1830 the necessity of reforming the administration of the Poor Laws, if not the actual content of the Laws themselves, had been brought home in no uncertain way by the outburst of terrorism and rebellion in the agricultural districts of the south and west. The Government could not afford to continue to ignore the confusion which had gradually developed in the organization of relief since the ill-fated decision of the magistrates at the Pelican Inn, Speenhamland, in 1795. It was, however, a remarkably tough problem to handle, and the only immediate step taken after the riots of 1830 by the unreformed Parliament was to set up a House of Lords Inquiry, which took evidence in 1831. The newly reformed Parliament in 1832 found itself faced with the uncomfortable position of having the power to do something, but not knowing what to do. There were two parts to the question: the reform of the administrative abuses which were at least as rampant as in any other public service of the period, and the theoretically more difficult task of checking the continually increasing burden of the poor rates, due to the growth and scope of the relief to the able-bodied agricultural labourer.

Two points must be noticed here: first, the problem was primarily one of agriculture as distinct from manufacturing industry; secondly, before the 1832 Commission got to work it was envisaged more as a question of saving the rates than of depauperizing the agricultural labourer as an end in itself.

This is shown, I think, sufficiently by the numerous Acts which had been passed in the preceding ten years or so, gradually removing the stigma from the receipt of poor relief and facilitating its grant. Most of these Acts contained some administrative reform, but their promoters failed to envisage the problem of depauperization as either possible or desirable. The riddle they aimed at solving was not how to make the agricultural labourer independent and self-supporting, but how to maintain him out of the rates at a less cost to the ratepayers, or to some special section of them. Even the more far-thinking members of the Whig Cabinet undoubtedly shared this view until Senior had explained the problem as redrawn in the Report of the Commission.[1]

Senior's main contribution to the poor law problem lay just in this transformation of the conception of the reform from one of, if we like, class-reform dictated by political necessity, to one of a large-scale social reform based on a philosophy of a free society. To Senior the essence and the interest of the problem lay in the rescue of the labourer from the degraded status of a pauper, at least as much as, probably more than, in the salvation of the agricultural interests. This does not mean, of course, that he was alone in thinking the question one of far-reaching social importance; his point of view was essentially that of the Liberal and Radical economists of the day. The desire of Ricardo, James Mill and Malthus, for the abolition of the Poor Laws, was not necessarily based on a crude dislike of State interference of any sort, but was rather part of the ideal of self-determination derived from the radical philosophy of the revolutionary era. In so far as they were Malthusians, they naturally believed that the existence of relief (at least as then administered) encouraged population, and hastened the approach of a stationary state at a low level of subsist-

---

[1] There is no doubt that the idea of a necessary dependence of the poor on the rich was still widespread at the time of the Amendment. A section of opinion headed by Dr. Chalmers were led by it to wish to abolish the Poor Laws altogether, and there is no doubt that the same belief influenced many nineteenth-century reformers. Senior himself was not entirely free of it. On the other hand, authorities like Poulett Scrope (*Quarterly Review*, Vol. 46, January 1832, Art. IV), W. F. Lloyd, Whately's successor at Oxford (*Four Lectures on the Poor Laws*, delivered in 1834, published 1835, and *Two Lectures on the Justice of the Poor Laws*, delivered in 1836, published 1837, etc.), Samuel Read (see note 3 on p. 303 below), and Longfield (*Four Lectures on the Poor Laws*, 1834), asserted that the poor had a natural right to relief. For a general account of contemporary opinions on the Poor Laws, cf. Mackay, *History of the English Poor Law*, Part I, chaps. 11–12, and Webb, *English Poor Law History*, Part II, *The Last Hundred Years*, Vol. I, pp. 1–14.

ence.[1] On this ground alone they were bound to condemn poor laws.[2] To such a group of thinkers the problem of poor law reform was more than a merely administrative and financial one. It was the problem of the moral and social degradation and the threat to the standard of life of the agricultural labourer by pauperization.

The Commission of 1832 was set up in conditions unfavourable to this wider view. To the Government it was a dire political necessity fraught with the certainty of offending by reform some section or other that benefited from the abuses, or thought it did. The main classes wanting reform wanted immediate relief from rates, while the labourers,

[1] Actually it appears that some English economists approved of relief to the able-bodied even before it had been shown that it could be administered without the devastating consequences of the unreformed Poor Law. In 1833 McCulloch was supporting the principle of relief to the able-bodied at the Political Economy Club (*Proceedings of the Political Economy Club*, Vol. VI, p. 252), and in 1834 pointed out that some sort of provision must be made for the urban proletariat if trade was slack. (Ibid., p. 259.) Torrens, in 1834, suggested that some scheme of national insurance was essential to deal with workers displaced by inventions (*On Wages and Combinations*, 1834, p. 44), and supported the proposals of the Poor Law Commission at the Club (*Proceedings, etc.*, p. 259). James Mill was converted to the Amended Poor Law (see Part II, chap. I, pp. 274–5, above). Even Malthus wanted medical relief and assistance to special families, and although he disapproved of granting a right to relief as such, it seems probable that he approved of the main principle of the Poor Law Amendment of 1834. (Bonar, *Malthus and his Work*, Bk. III). Cf. also Part II, chap. I, note I on p. 275 above.

J. S. Mill, in a letter to Cherbuliez, November 6, 1863, explained that as a result of the Inquiry and Amendment of 1834, most English economists had become favourable to relief to the able-bodied. *Collected Letters of J. S. Mill*, edited Hugh Elliot, Vol. I, p. 306. It is not beyond the pale of possibility that Ricardo would have conformed in the same way if he had lived to 1834, though his opposition to the Poor Laws was not based entirely on population theories. (See Cannan, "Ricardo in Parliament," *Economic Journal*, 1894, and Ricardo's *Principles*, chap. 18.)

[2] The Webbs appear to attribute too much importance to the influence of the wage-fund theory in the Poor Law controversies (op. cit., pp. 7, 22). Similarly Halévy (*Histoire du Peuple Anglais au XIXe Siècle*, Vol. III, 1830–41, pp. 112–13) falls into the usual confusion as to the wage-fund theory. It has been shown conclusively by Prof. Taussig (*Wages and Capital*, Part II, chaps. 9–12) that the economists had little idea as to the fixity of the wage fund. Senior himself explained that if production decreased there would be less to distribute and therefore, *ceteris paribus*, lower wages per head; that if population increased, *ceteris paribus* this would also be the result. But he certainly did not regard the fund as fixed. (Letter to Lord Chancellor, September 14, 1832, see sect. ii, pp. 298–9, below, and cf. Part I, chap. 5, above.)

about whom Senior was chiefly anxious, were bound to resent any threat to their parish money. There was little prospect, therefore, that any Government would be willing to carry through a plan of long-period social reform on first principles.

These difficulties are admirably summarized by Hyde Villiers in a letter to Lord Howick on January 19, 1832, in which he urged the importance of immediate action by the Government—

"The difficulties which would be in a degree peculiar to this task appear to me to be these. Almost all the principles to be observed are of an unpopular character. The Clergy and the Magistracy have, for the most part, no idea of the mischief they have done, and are therefore not likely to assist in tying up their own hands. . . . See also the change which would be desirable with a view to introducing and fostering a spirit of prudence in the people—all of an unpopular character. Those who think it is religiously charitable, at all rates, to promote marriages and build cottages—those who think it profitable to the parish, that the law of bastardy should remain as it is, and to themselves, that wages should be paid out of the rates of the parish, will be against the reform. The looseness and the uncertainty of the law have given rise to a great variety of practice, much of which must be interfered with by any useful Bill proceeding upon general principles. . . . Thus in short it is, that the reform, however salutary—the reformer, however benevolent—both the piece and the actor—would stand an excellent chance of being hissed off the stage."[1]

In addition, of course, Villiers pointed out the usual complications of party politics embittered by the recent struggle over the Reform Bill. A way round these dangers could, he maintained, be found by setting up a Commission of Inquiry with instructions to draw up its own Bill upon which, after it had been circularized and discussed, the Government could proceed with authority as on a technical question. The Commission, to be useful and to start in good favour, must begin by making contact with the clergy, the country magistrates and gentry, the Radicals and the

[1] A letter from Hyde Villiers of the India Board to Lord Howick, January 19, 1832. (A copy of this letter is among the Senior MSS.)

economists, who he evidently expected to produce the solution. He mentioned James Mill as a suitable contact with the Radicals, and Senior as "a practical Political Economist, who has written well on the subject."

It was largely in accordance with these suggestions that the Poor Law Commission was set up in 1832, consisting of Senior, the Bishops of Chester and London, Sturges Bourne, the Rev. Henry Bishop, Walter Coulson and Henry Garler. They were instructed to appoint assistant commissioners to carry out the actual inquiry, and they themselves were to digest the information collected and make recommendations. Edwin Chadwick and Henry Traill were added to the actual Commission in 1833.

Senior appears to have been the chief analytical force on the Commission, and he carried it beyond the field of a mere Government inquiry into administration into the sphere of social economics. Throughout the period of the inquiry frequent discussions on the desirability and methods of giving relief were held at the Political Economy Club, to which several members of the Cabinet belonged, as well as Walter Coulson, Senior, and Cowell (an assistant commissioner). Chadwick attended as a visitor.[1]

[1] December 6, 1832. Senior proposed the following three questions for discussion: "(1) Would it be advisable to vest in Government Officers the collection and distribution of the fund for the relief of the Poor, leaving the assessment of that fund to the parochial authorities? (2) Would it be advisable to vest also the assessment of that fund in Government Officers, leaving it still a parochial charge? (3) Would it be advisable to make that fund a country, district, or national charge?" (*Proceedings of the Political Economy Club*, Vol. VI, p. 39.) These questions were discussed at two meetings, December 6, 1832, and January 10, 1833. Chadwick and Blencowe, another Assistant Commissioner, came to the first discussion. The general feeling was that the Government would never accept the scheme for a national poor rate. According to J. L. Mallet, Senior stated the scheme and made the estimate of the expense involved, but did not actually venture to recommend its acceptance. (Mallet's *Diaries, Proceedings of the Political Economy Club*, Vol. VI, pp. 242–5.) There were further discussions on Settlement, February 6, 1834 (see note 1 on p. 304 below), and on the proper principle of regulating relief to the able-bodied, April 10, 1834. Sturges Bourne, Senior, and Coulson attended the first of these meetings and Chadwick the second. (*Proceedings*, loc. cit., pp. 254–7.) At the time of the Amendment Bill the following Cabinet Ministers were members of the Club: Lord Althorp, Spring Rice (Lord Monteagle), George Villiers (Earl of Clarendon), and within the next few years Lords Lansdowne and Howick joined. (List of Members. *Proceedings*, loc. cit., pp. 358–60.)

But Senior's activities did not end here, he wrote the bulk of the Report and organized the inquiry into foreign methods of relief.[1] He acted as chief interpreter and co-adjutor to the Government, writing lengthy letters to the Lord Chancellor explaining the point of view of himself and/or that of the Commission as well, long before the actual Report was ready. After the Report was finished and the Commission's Bill drawn up, Sturges Bourne and Senior were requested to explain it to the Cabinet. It immediately became clear that Senior was the important member of the partnership. Not merely did he defend the Bill at the Cabinet meetings, but he carried the fire into the enemies' camp in frequent private discussions with Lords Lansdowne and Althorp. In fact it appears from Senior's History of the passing of the Act that he and Lord Althorp spent much of the time between formal meetings competing as to who should produce the most amendments to the amendments introduced by the Cabinet and the Houses of Parliament. During the whole period of the passage of the Bill he was called upon for advice on amendments, no member of the Cabinet feeling sufficiently confident to decide anything on his own responsibility. The passing of the final Act in a form so closely similar to the original draft was largely due to Senior's passionate interest in the matter.[2]

[1] See Mackay, *History of the English Poor Law*, Part I, chap. 3. In a private letter to Senior's daughter (afterwards Mrs. Simpson), December 12, 1864, Nicholls implies that Senior was the most important member of the Commission. Similarly Meadows White, solicitor to the Commission, in a letter to Senior, March 5, 1835 (published at the beginning of a pamphlet, *Parochial Settlements, an Obstruction to Poor Law Reform*), stated that not only did Senior write or revise the bulk of the *Extracts of Evidence* in 1833 and the Report itself in 1834, but that "all the instructions of the Government were received through [him], and after its preparation by Counsel and during its passage through both Houses of Parliament every clause and line, and I may almost say every word, with the exception of the bastardy clauses, and a few other additions by individual members of the legislature, were considered and revised" by him. This is still further borne out by J. L. Mallet's *Diaries* (op. cit., pp. 242, 244), where Senior is referred to as "the head of the Commission" and "the most active Commissioner." For discussion of Chadwick's influence see pp. 328–9 below.

[2] For an account of the contemporary criticism of the membership of the Commission see Webbs (op. cit., pp. 82–90). A writer in the *Quarterly Review*,

His influence on the Poor Law did not stop with the passage of the Act, as the appointments to the Administrative Commission were made largely on his recommendation. In a letter to Lord Melbourne he recommended that the selection should be made from Chadwick (who became secretary), James Stephens, Frankland Lewis, Captain Nicholls and Thomas Whately. He himself refused a seat on the Board.[1]

We are not, however, concerned with the historical facts of the passing of the Poor Law Amendment Act, but Senior's own outlook and views on the nature of the problems and the efficacy of the proposed reforms. The first sections of the chapter are devoted to an attempt to describe the former, and the last two to the latter, and particularly to estimating the importance that Senior attached to the workhouse system.

I

It is necessary to point out that although Senior was not a diehard supporter of the policy of *laissez-faire*, he was on general grounds to begin with opposed to the principle of the Poor Laws, and in particular to that of relief to the able-bodied. So far the historians are correct, but they have not, with the exception of Mackay, made any attempt to discover the extent of, and reasons for, this disapproval

(Vol. 50, January 1834, pp. 349–51) took particular exception to Senior's appointment, declaring that he was from the beginning well known as an opponent of the English Poor Laws. The writer did not bother to explain how the Report took its final shape if Senior was as diehard as he seemed to think. McCulloch, it is well known, objected to the centralization by the Amendment (*Principles*, Part III, chap. 3, third edition, and *Literature of Political Economy*, 1845, p. 291) and declared that the evidence was selected in a most biassed fashion. On the other hand, J. S. Mill regarded the Report itself as a great achievement. (*Collected Letters*, Vol. I, pp. 50–1.) There is no doubt that much of the criticism that the Report was deliberately arranged so as to carry conviction, and that most emphasis was laid on the evidence from places where the administration was bad, was justified. But there seems little basis for the assertions sometimes made that the evidence was tampered with.

[1] Letter to Lord Melbourne, June 30, 1834. (Senior MSS.) The main source of information as to Senior's influence on the Cabinet is the unpublished History of the passing of the Act written by him for Lord Lansdowne in 1834.

in the light of either the Poor Law Report or the Amendment Act itself.[1] It would be possible to some extent to reconstruct Senior's philosophy of the Poor Law, as we may call it, from these sources together with the Preface to the *Foreign Communications on the Poor Law*. But there is, fortunately, a perfectly clear statement in an article by him in the *Edinburgh Review* of 1841,[2] which, together with the published and unpublished letters and papers of the period of the inquiry itself, give us ample material. The objection that the article of 1841 contains wisdom after the event is not valid, as the earlier papers give adequate though scattered support to the same view. It was at a somewhat later date towards the end of the 'forties that Senior's opinion underwent some modification.[3] There is a real difficulty, however, in using the earlier papers in that some purport to be the expression of the views of the whole Commission, though as Senior was without doubt the most active member of it, it is obvious that he at least agreed with the ideas expressed. As to whether they were original or not, it is unimportant. On a subject which had occupied public attention, and that of economists in particular, for as long as the Poor Laws had, it would be invidious to attempt to decide.

Senior himself was under the influence of the prevailing ideas of individual freedom and self-determination, and it was from this angle that he considered the place of the Poor Laws in the social fabric. His opinions can be summarized as follows from the 1841 article. He saw the progress of society as the gradual evolution of individual freedom. The first major step in the process had been taken with the abolition of serfdom, which gave the individual labourer

---

[1] The Webbs (op. cit., p. 86, n. 1) appear to be surprised that Senior changed from opposing relief to the able-bodied to supporting it. If they had not been so convinced that all the economists, including Senior, were dogmatic and prejudiced they would have appreciated the reason for his original opposition better. (See Part II, chap. 1, pp. 246–7 above, and pp. 294–5 below for Senior's own explanation.)

[2] "English Poor Laws," *Edinburgh Review*, October 1841; reprinted in *Historical and Philosophical Essays*, 1865, Vol. II.

[3] Lectures, 1847–52, Course I, lecture 7. See Part II, chap. 1, pp. 268–9 above, and pp. 296–7 below.

legal personal freedom. Legal freedom of occupation had, however, only evolved gradually with the decay of the guild and apprenticeship system, while actual freedom had been hampered by the existence of the Poor Laws and the Laws of Settlement which were an integral part of their administration. The effect of the Settlement Laws on the effectual mobility, and therefore freedom, of labour was obvious, but the connection of the actual Poor Laws with it needed some explanation. Senior's view of personal freedom was that of the recognition of personal responsibility for self-support, and the support of a family, in ordinary contingencies of life, such as old age and sickness, as well as for the other actions for which responsibility was recognized by the civil and criminal law. The fundamental principle of the Poor Laws was inconsistent with this concept, for they were based on the idea that the labouring classes were peculiarly unfitted to look after themselves in a way tolerable with common ideas of humanity or compatible with the safety and welfare of the State. The abolition of the Poor Laws was therefore an essential step in the recognition of the freedom and responsibility of the labouring classes. The Poor Laws were a badge of their fundamental inferiority. It followed that if poor laws were considered necessary they must be framed so as to hinder the process of emancipation as little as possible.

This point of view is illustrated frequently throughout the Commission papers, in which both current practice and proposed remedies were examined from this aspect. Thus in a letter to Lord Althorp about the labour-rate, he says, after examining its numerous disadvantages:

"The great fault of a Labour-rate is that it destroys the distinction between pauperism and independence. The inquiries of the Commissioners have convinced them that it is only by keeping these things separated, and separated by as broad and as distinct a demarcation as possible, and by making relief in all cases less agreeable than wages, that any thing deserving the name of improvement can be hoped for. But under the Labour-rate system, relief and wages are utterly confounded. All the wages partake of relief, and all the relief partakes of wages. The labourer is employed not because he is a good workman, but because he is a parishioner. He receives a certain sum not because that sum is the value of his services, but because it is what the vestry has ordered to be paid.—Good conduct, diligence, skill, all become valueless. Can it be supposed that they will be preserved? We deplore the misconception of the poor in thinking that wages are not a matter of contract but of right; that any diminution of their comforts occasioned by an increase of their numbers without an equal increase of the fund for their subsistence is an evil to be remedied not by themselves, but by the magistrate—not an error, or even a misfortune, but an injustice."[1]

Further on in the same letter he adds:

"When what now remains of repugnance to relief or of degradation in accepting it has been destroyed by its being merged in wages, when all the labourers have been converted into a semi-servile populace, without fear but without hope, where can we look for the materials of improvement?"

Similarly in an earlier letter in 1832 he expresses his fundamental criticism of the Settlement and Poor Laws:

"To suppose that a man can support his family by his wages; that he is to exercise any providence or economy; that anything is to be hoped from voluntary charity; that the poor can manage their own affairs without the interference of the rich; that a man's wages ought to depend on his services, not his wants; seem to be views which those who have long resided in pauperized districts reject as too absurd for refutation. . . .

"The present system gives the labourer low wages, but at the same time easy work. It gives him also, strange as it may appear, what he values more, a sort of independence. He need not study to please his master, he need not bestir himself to seek work, he need not put any restraint on his temper, he need not ask relief as a favour, he need not fear that his idleness, or drunken-

---

[1] Letter to Lord Althorp, March 1833, explaining the views of the Commission on the Labour-rate with reference to a proposed Bill for the better employment of Agricultural Labourers, by facilitating the introduction of a Labour-rate. *Appendix D to the first Report from the Commissioners on the Poor Laws,* p. 2. *Parliamentary Papers,* 1833, Vol. XXXII. The Bill was passed in March 1833 as a temporary measure, was twice amended, and finally expired in 1834. See Appendix II.

ness, will injure his family; he has, in short, all a slave's security for subsistence without his liabilities to punishment."[1]

It is difficult to decide just how far at this period Senior regarded a poor law offering relief to the able-bodied as advantageous in the backward state of development of England. It seems to me probable that, while wishing to leave open the way to future development by breaking down the traditional right to relief, he considered some provision for relief to be desirable, if some safe method of administering it could be devised. In a letter in 1832 on a proposed Agricultural Labourers' Employment Bill which aimed at facilitating the introduction of the labour-rate, on which his opinion had been asked by Lord Melbourne, he inveighed against the provision of additional "eleemosynary funds" on account of the discouragement they offer to foresight and thrift:

"I have gone through the Agricultural Labourers' Employment Bill, and I must say that next to the 43rd Elizabeth, the usury laws, the apprentice laws, and a few other choice specimens, it appears to me as mischievous an attempt at legislation as ever was made.

"It aims at providing a new fund for eleemosynary assistance. Now we know that it is the nature of any such fund to create its own demand, to raise up a fresh body of claimants; after which the distress is greater than before the fund was created. It is the old story of the children who made a wall across the valley to keep the cuckoo in. They raised the wall just over the level of the bird's usual flight, and when they found that it just skimmed over the top they thought that if they had laid only another row of stones it would have been kept in. So it is with every definite provision for the poor. Fresh and fresh applicants appear encouraged to depend on such support, and to relax their own industry and frugality; fresh funds must be raised, and in turn fall short of the distress. The cuckoo still skims over the wall."

---

[1] Letter from Senior to the Lord Chancellor, September 14, 1832 (Senior MSS.), written to explain Senior's general opinions. At this date he explained that the Commission were agreed as to the nature and sources of the evil of the Poor Laws, but had not discussed remedies. Almost exactly similar passages occur in Senior's Preface to his *Lectures on Wages*, published 1830.

Finally, his last criticism of the Bill is that it admits "the most dangerous of all principles, the principle that the poor are in fact the owners of the land, and that to the extent of their wants."[1]

In the later papers frequent passages occur in which he objects to the recognition of a right to relief both on the grounds given above, and because he sees no logical limit to the principle between admitting relief from some people's incomes and confiscation of the whole of rent and profits. There is, for instance, a passage in his History of the Passing of the Poor Law Amendment Act, in an account of the discussion of the labourer's right of appeal against the Guardians, etc., as follows:

"If therefore the guardians or vestry expressly commanded the overseer to refuse relief to A B, and A B should consequently perish, it did not appear that any body could be punished. Now though this is the law in the greater part of Europe, and is a much safer system than our own, yet it seemed to me a change which Parliament would not knowingly sanction, and which ought not to be introduced surreptitiously."[2]

He was unable, nevertheless, to resist the temptation to slip in an amendment while the Bill was in the Lords, which enabled all relief to be treated as a loan, of which he says that it was:

"a most important change in principle, as in fact, by enabling all relief to be treated as a loan, it amounts to a denial of the right to gratuitous relief: a right which has existed from the 43rd Eliz. until the present time."[3]

[1] Letter to Lord Melbourne, March 10, 1832. (Senior MSS.) This Bill appears to be the same as the one about which Lord Althorp made inquiries, see note 1 on p. 291 above.

[2] Senior's History of the Poor Law, pp. 81-2 of the MS. (There are several copies of the manuscript, including one in the Goldsmiths' Company's Library of Economic Literature (University of London) and one deposited in the Library of the London School of Economics. The paging varies in the different copies, and all page references given here are to the latter copy.)

[3] Ibid., p. 228. It is interesting to notice that in 1848 he had changed his opinion and thought that a right to relief must be admitted where relief was administered by officials. Course 1, lecture 7. The statement that a right to gratuitous relief was admitted in 43 Eliz. is not strictly accurate. According

He also expressed his approval of the general anti-Poor Law sentiment of the speech in which Brougham introduced the Bill into the Lords, for though he admitted it to be untimely he remarked:

"Indeed as these views, though perhaps unguardedly expressed, are in a great measure, indeed almost to the whole length, founded on truth, I am not sure that this powerful exposition of them by suggesting to many persons doubts as to the justice and expediency of the whole system, did not induce them to concur more readily in its restriction and modification.[1]

The inference from these passages seems obviously that Senior submitted to relief to the able-bodied merely as a concession to public opinion in England. On the other hand, in a letter to Lord John Russell in 1836, on the Third Report of the Commission of Inquiry into the Condition of the Poor in Ireland, he said that he had changed his mind on this matter, as far as England was concerned, since writing the *Letter to Lord Howick on a legal provision for the Irish Poor* in 1831. He explained that his chief objection in the past had been due to the difficulty of administering relief to the able-bodied:

"In that letter [i.e. to Lord Howick in 1831] I protested against any compulsory provision for the able-bodied or their families. The only change that subsequent experience has produced in my opinion is that I now believe that in England, or in any country in which the standard of subsistence is high, a provision for the able-bodied in strictly managed workhouses, in which their condition shall be inferior to that of the independent labourer, may be safely and even advantageously made. But as this is not the state of Ireland, as the standard of subsistence in that country is so low that any provision which the State could offer must be superior, as far as physical comfort

to the law, relief to the able-bodied was to be given only in the form of employment and thus was only in return for work. This, of course, Senior knew, but the failure to make the employment effective had in his opinion resulted in gratuitous relief and he generally spoke of it as such.

[1] Senior's History of the Poor Law, pp. 203-4. Senior had sent Lord Brougham a summary of the Bill preparatory to the latter introducing it in the House of Lords. Brougham's speech consisted of a violent and most untimely denunciation of the principle of poor laws.

is concerned, to that obtained by the independent labourer, this change of opinion does not apply to Ireland, and I am forced, therefore, so far as Ireland is concerned, to adhere to that letter."

Though it is impossible to give any exact date to this change of view, it would, I think, be fair to put it at the beginning of the period between writing the letter to the Lord Chancellor in September 1832, and the writing of the Introduction to *Statement of the Provision for the Poor in Parts of America and Europe* in the first few months of 1835. In any case the letter to Lord John Russell seems to prove fairly conclusively that, considering the stage of development and the traditions of England, Senior did not ever really believe that abolition of all relief to the able-bodied was desirable if its abuse could be prevented.[1] It will appear more clearly in later sections describing the possible remedies that he recognized the necessary slowness of a process of depauperization, only expressing a pious hope that some time the ideal state would be realized in which the necessity for provision would be so small that the Settlement Laws would be altogether abolished.

It must be remembered that neither Senior himself, nor the Commission, ever suggested at any time the desirability of abolishing relief for old age, sickness, sudden emergency or catastrophe, but on the contrary were anxious to make it more effective.[2] From among the numerous references to

---

[1] "Letter to Lord John Russell, etc.," April 14, 1836, published in *Parliamentary Papers*, Vol. LI, 1837.

In the *Statement of the Provision for the Poor in Parts of America and Europe*, 1835 (see Appendix II, p. 349, below), he remarked that in those countries such as Switzerland where a right to relief had been admitted, the system had worked well where the principle of "less eligibility" had been enforced. pp. 84–8. The Advertisement to the *Statement* is dated June 10, 1835.

It has sometimes been thought that Senior's conversion to the idea of relief to the able-bodied was only forced upon him by circumstances, since he had stated in the *Introductory Lecture*, 1826, and the Preface to the *Lectures on Wages*, 1830, that relief would inevitably produce over-population. This is not correct. All he said was that the abuse of the Poor Law had produced local over-population in some districts, and that emigration would enormously facilitate the carrying through of a reform—an opinion that he still held in 1834.

[2] Cf. account of the *Letter to Lord Howick on a legal provision for the Irish Poor*, 1831. Part II, chap. I, pp. 242 et seq. above.

this we may perhaps select the following from a letter to Lord Lansdowne in 1834 explaining the main objects of the Commission's Bill. Referring to their recommendation of the workhouse test, Senior wrote:

"In the first place our recommendation applies only to the able-bodied and their families. The aged and impotent, the true poor as they are called in the 18th Eliz., are excluded. It is true, that even for the aged and impotent, the workhouse will in many, perhaps even in most cases, be the least objectionable mode of bestowing compulsory charity, and we trust that by a proper classification of workhouses, and assigning distinct and comparatively comfortable abodes to the impotent, they will be far more effectually relieved than at present. But we have carefully avoided making such a measure obligatory."[1]

Senior's general standpoint, which seems to have remained unchanged between 1832 and 1841, was that under the unreformed system relief of all types tended to create its own demand by destroying the incentive to energy and providence; that reform must by definition remove this discouragement by making the position of the independent able-bodied labourer more eligible than that of the able-bodied pauper; that it must also differentiate as far as possible between those who attempted to provide for old age, sickness, etc., and those who did not.[2] It is obviously consistent with this eminently reasonable attitude that machinery should exist to deal with any distress that eventually arose. To this end the Poor Law must distinguish between poverty and pauperism; between a low standard of living and inability and/or unwillingness to reach even that low standard. If this vital distinction was lost sight of the Poor Law would always be a machine for increasing pauperism, and would finally ruin the hope of an ultimately higher standard of living

[1] Letter to Lord Lansdowne, March 2, 1834, explaining the main objects of the Commission's Bill. (Senior MSS.)

[2] It is interesting to notice in this connection that, while the Bill was in the House of Lords, Senior and Sturges Bourne suggested that overseers should be enabled, under certain regulations, to make contributions from the rates towards the establishment of benefit and saving societies, and help with the subscriptions of members. Senior's History of the passing of the Poor Law Amendment Act.

by the destruction of the means of achieving it—the efficiency of labour.[1]

Substantially Senior held this opinion when he went to lecture at Oxford for the second time in 1847, but he had modified his emphasis, showing more appreciation of the difficulties of providence on a very small income. He pointed out that the Government can mitigate the hardships of poverty by providing that no one shall perish by destitution, and regarded this as desirable, something worth while achieving for itself, not merely as a provision necessitated by the imperfect development of the country. On the intrinsic dangers of such provision and its liability to abuse his opinion was unchanged, but it is clear that he had been impressed by the success of the reformed Poor Law both in depauperizing the agricultural labourer and in proving the possibility of administrative efficiency.[2] The soundness of the general principles of the 1834 Act had shown that it was possible to make provision of this sort without increasing the need which it was supposed to relieve.

II

The inquiries of the Commissioners brought to light the existence of widespread corruption in the administration of the Poor Laws. They showed up the wholesale pauperization in various districts caused by the working of the systems of allowances and labour-rates, the arbitrary hardships and the impediments to the mobility of labour

[1] This opinion was restated in the pamphlet published during the controversy as to the continuance of the centralized administration in 1841. (*Remarks on the Opposition to the Poor Law Amendment Bill by a Guardian.*) In this pamphlet he maintains that the allowance system has been put down; the industry, etc., of the labourer have again become of value to him; the comfort of the aged and infirm secured; the education of pauper children commenced; and early marriages decreased; also that wages had risen, employment had become steadier, and corruption been repressed (p. 54). This optimistic account, not by any means altogether unjustified, was written, it must be remembered, before the problems of the general mixed workhouse had come to the fore.

[2] Course 1, lecture 7. Senior's letter on the Irish Poor Law is sufficient evidence that he distinguished not only between destitution and poverty but also between the different causes of destitution. See sect. vii below.

due to Settlement Laws, the encouragement of bastardy in some places by disproportionate relief given to the mothers of illegitimate children, and finally the enormous waste of money on futile litigation under the laws of settlement and bastardy.

The Laws of Settlement[1] and the pauperization of the labourer were the subjects upon which Senior had the clearest ideas and convictions and were the problems most closely connected with the general principles of the Poor Laws. Although he had expected to find the situation serious, it is clear that the revelations of the Assistant Commissioners' reports were unexpectedly alarming. Thus in 1832 he wrote:

"I was prepared also to find the system most injurious to the diligence and skill of the labourers, the profits of the farmers, and the rental of the landowners; but on these points, too, the results of the inquiry are worse than I had anticipated. Where the system does not prevail the general answer to our question, as to the character of the labourers, has been 'much the same,' 'never were better'. . . . But in the pauperized parishes the reply has generally been 'diligence destroyed,' 'skill much diminished,' —'none of the young men good workmen or care to be so,'— 'piecework refused.' 'Young men won't engage in any business that requires care or exertion.' Until we come to a place like Royston, in which all the work is done by out-parishioners, and the settled population is maintained from the rates in idleness. At the same time the land is imperfectly cultivated, the labour, however lowly paid, being very dear even at that low money price."

Not merely was the labourer demoralized and inefficient under the system, but the position, Senior thought, was bound to get worse with the decrease of the fund for the payment of wages and the amount of land kept in cultivation at all. The fund consisted of

"commodities which must be periodically reproduced by the industry and skill of the labourer assisted by the farmer's capital."

[1] See sect. iii below, pp. 301–5.

Both these ingredients were being decreased, the efficiency of the labourer by pauperization, the investment of capital from fear of the threats of the terrorists. Even the land itself was falling out of cultivation wherever the rates equalled or exceeded rents.[1] The situation with regard to rents he went on to describe as follows:

"The agricultural variations of the last forty years have very much diminished the number of leases, and as to those which still exist, the bargain seems in general to be considered binding on the landlord, not on the tenant. Every increase in poor rates is considered, by the farmer, as a ground for requiring a diminution of rent, which he enforces if a tenant from year to year or at will, and generally obtains even if tenant for a term. He is indifferent, therefore, to the increase of pauperism, if he thinks he can obtain any immediate advantage; and he generally thinks that he does gain by it, by being enabled to beat down the wages of unmarried men, and to throw on other persons part of the wages of his married men. Farmers maintain that 'they do not see the justice of forcing the farmer to pay the unmarried wages equal to those of the married.' "

The interests that would be opposed to reform were revealed as so widespread that Senior was almost prepared to give up the attempt, declaring in the same letter, "on the whole the obstacles to reform are so formidable that if I thought the evils of the present system stationary, I almost think that I had rather submit than grapple with the difficulties and dangers and real suffering that are incident to any alteration." For though the evils of the present system were so great, most parties concerned were unwilling to attempt reform:

"It might have been hoped that under such circumstances a general feeling would have arisen that the evils of the system are intolerable, and must be put an end to at any risk or any sacrifice. Half of this is true. Everyone that replies to our questions describes the evil as intolerable, but they oppose any plan of Amendment if they think that it must be, or may be, accompanied by any immediate inconvenience. They seem to expect

[1] Letter to the Lord Chancellor, September 14, 1832, op. cit.

us to cure an inveterate disease without exposing the patient to any suffering or even discomfort."[1]

Not only the administrative abuses, the vested interests and the apparent benefactors from the allowance system or one of its variants had to be dealt with by reform, but a change in ·the Settlement Laws was, at least in Senior's opinion, an essential part of any far-reaching improvement. The problem of settlement will be taken up in a separate section,[2] but its importance and difficulty, as seen by Senior, can be summarized under the headings of immobility of the labour market, corruption and litigation. As long as relief was dependent on the possession of a settlement in a particular parish, there was strong discouragement to any labourer venturing beyond his own parish in hope of acquiring a new settlement in new employment, as he would live under the threat of being turned out of his house and employment in order to prevent him acquiring a right to relief in that new parish. At the same time employers were unwilling to take on anyone who might become a burden on the parish. This would have been a deterrent in any case, but where either the allowance system or the labour-rate was in force, no farmer would, unless desperate, employ out-parishioners, as he in any case had to support his own parishioners. In the train of the complicated laws and the conflicting interests of different parishes a rich harvest of litigation was reaped, which did no good to anyone except the lawyers, and caused great hardship to the labourers with doubtful settlements.

The laws of bastardy were similarly fruitful of dispute, and allowances in some cases were so graded as to make the bearing of bastards financially attractive.[3]

Even the whole rating system on which the edifice was raised worked in favour of the perpetuation of the abuses.

[1] Letter to the Lord Chancellor, September 14, 1832, op. cit.

[2] See sect. iii below, pp. 301–5. Sturges Bourne thought Senior exaggerated the evils of the Settlement Laws. Comments on Senior's Letter to the Lord Chancellor of September 14, 1832, by Sturges Bourne (October 1832). (Senior MSS.)

[3] Senior's Letter to the Lord Chancellor, September 14, 1832, op. cit.

The employers of labour could shift part of their wages bill on to the non-employers, landlords, tradesmen, tithe-owners, etc., who were almost always in positions from which they could exercise little influence even when they realized that it was in their interest to do so. The landlords, if resident occupiers (the only case in which they could vote), were generally magistrates and unwilling to lose popularity and lay themselves open to revenge by protesting against, or refusing, allowances; the shopkeepers believed that they were more likely to have their bills paid when the labourers were firmly supported by the parish, and frequently had an interest in contracts with the overseers; the tithe-owners were in a hopeless minority.[1]

A few months later Senior wrote another letter to the Lord Chancellor, in which he declared that the policy of making the Poor Law a local business in order to secure that he who paid the piper called the tune had been a complete failure.[2] It had become obvious that the Commission were confronted with the task of breaking with the whole tradition of local government based on parish control in order to make any start on the problem at all.

The problems before the Commissioners were thus: first, to reform the administration of the Poor Laws; second, to reform the actual Poor Law itself, and all the subsidiary laws relating to settlement and bastardy, etc.; and finally third, to persuade an unwilling Government and Parliament to pass an unpopular measure.

The proposals for dealing with these difficulties will be discussed later, but Senior's interest in and contribution to the solution of the second group were so important that it is necessary to explain his views on these points in some detail first.

III

The Settlement Laws

Enough has already been said to indicate Senior's general views on settlement, but the question of his detailed opinion

---

[1] Senior's Letter to the Lord Chancellor, September 14, 1832, op. cit.
[2] Ibid., January 7, 1833. (Senior MSS.)

is of some interest as he attached more importance to it than did other members of the Commission. In his letter to the Lord Chancellor in 1832 he pointed out that particular forms of settlement, such as settlement by hiring and service, were specially harmful:

"Hiring and Service, besides producing fraud and injustice, is described as narrowing the market for labour, preventing the continuance of labourers in the same service, and contributing largely to the alienation of labourers from their employers. I should without the slightest hesitation abolish them all. Nothing would then remain but birth, marriage, and parentage."[1]

Six months later Senior was willing to go even further and considered the abolition of all Settlement Laws as the greatest point in favour of making the whole burden of the Poor Law relief a national charge. The whole of the discussion is so interesting that, though it more properly belongs to the section on general remedies, it seems appropriate to insert it here. He had been discussing the failure of the system of local rates to induce competent administration of the Poor Law, and he continued:

"If therefore the principal advantages of making the charge parochial are unattainable, I certainly think the propriety of making it national a debatable question.

"The advantages would be great and immediate:—

"It would put an end to settlements. With settlements would go passes, removals, labour rates, and all the other restrictions and prohibitions by which each agricultural parish is endeavouring to prevent free trade in labour and to insulate itself by a conventional cordon as impassable to the unsettled workman as Bishop Berkeley's wall of brass. There would no longer be any motive for preferring in employment the men with large families to those with small, the married to the unmarried, the destitute to those who have saved, the careless and improvident to the industrious and enterprising. We should no longer have these local congestions of a surplus, and therefore half employed and dissolute population of serfs *adscripti glebae*, some driven not by the hope of reward, but by the fear of punish-

---

[1] Letter to the Lord Chancellor, September 14, 1832.

ment to some useless occupation, and others fed on condition of being idle. Character would again be of some value to the poor man."[1]

From this passage it is evident that Senior regarded the Settlement Laws as one of the worst of the abuses of the Poor Law system,[2] without which the whole tangle of allowances and labour-rates would not exist. On the other hand, it is equally obvious that, if the latter had not been so prevalent, the evils of the Settlement Laws would have been to a large extent dormant. As Senior rejected the idea of making relief national for other reasons, he had to turn back to the less harmful heads of settlement.[3] Of these he selected settlement by birth as the least damaging, pointing out that—

[1] Letter to the Lord Chancellor, January 7, 1833. That part of the letter dealing with poor relief as a national charge was published almost word for word in the *First Report of the Commissioners for Inquiring into the administration and operation of the Poor Laws*, more familiarly known as the Poor Law Report of 1834 (p. 148 of the 1894 reprint).

[2] The Webbs state that the Commission was so absorbed in destroying the allowance system that among other things they neglected the evils of the Settlement Laws (op. cit., p. 89). This contention is scarcely supported by the published, not to mention the unpublished, discussions of it.

The Laws of Settlement were really modifications of the early confinement of serfs to the parishes where they were born. The chief modifications gradually introduced made it possible to acquire settlement in places other than that of birth, and formed the Laws of Settlement. The chief methods of acquiring a new settlement, i.e. right to relief from a parish, were by serving an office, by being hired or in service for a year, by serving apprenticeship, by renting or purchasing land, or renting a tenement for a certain length of time, by marriage (in the case of a woman), or parentage in the case of a legitimate child. Apart from the simplifications introduced by the Poor Law Amendment Act of 1834, changes were made in 1846 introducing 'irremoveability' after five years' residence (by 1865 the period had been reduced to one year), and in 1865 the system of union instead of parish chargeability was established. For a detailed account see Mackay, *History of the English Poor Law*, Part II, chap. 16.

[3] Letter to the Lord Chancellor, January 7, 1833, op. cit. The idea of nationalization of the Poor Rates was by no means new. It had been advocated in particular by Samuel Read, an acute but neglected writer, in 1829. (*The Natural Grounds of right to vendible Property or Wealth*, Bk. II, chap. 9, sect. i.) The Commissioners considered the suggestion so important and hopeful that they dealt with it in their Report (pp. 147–9) in detail. Senior himself had raised the question at the Political Economy Club, December 6, 1832, see note 1, p. 286. Cf. Part II, chap I, note 2 on p. 248, for Senior's opinion with regard to a national rate in Ireland.

"it could not occasion the removal of the unmarried, though it might deter from marriage, their employers threatening dismissal if they created burdens to the parish, and . . . as to the married few persons could turn away a good servant in the fear of a possible burden sixteen years hence."[1]

This proposal of radical simplification caused great perturbation throughout the country; it was immediately suggested that married men would be dismissed, and that the independent labourers would be alarmed by the suggestion. Senior's reaction to this was characteristic of his dislike of the whole Settlement Laws—

"I felt a strong objection to leaving the question untouched, being convinced that the present Settlement Laws greatly aggravate the existing evils, and add materially to the difficulties of improvement. But I was much tempted by the proposal of substituting nothing for the abolished heads of settlement. It was quite clear that the immediate effects would be admirable. Every man's settlement being unchangeable, he would be able to carry his services wherever they were wanted, without even the possibility of rejection lest he should be a burden on the parish. Thirty or forty years hence without doubt the evil of a pedigree settlement would be intolerable. But might not the remedy then be found either by substitution of a district or country settlement, or if the new system should work as well as we hope, by the abolition of all settlement? In the meantime, the dangerous crisis, the period in which any increase to the inherent difficulties of the change of system might render them overwhelming, would be got over."[2]

[1] Senior's History. Reply to the Duke of Richmond at a meeting of the Cabinet Council on Sunday, March 30, 1834. The whole question of settlements was brought up at the Political Economy Club on February 6, 1834. Senior, Sturges Bourne (who appears to have come into line with the rest of the Commission on this point) and Coulson "drew a melancholy and I fear a hopeless picture of the effects of these laws. It seemed to be agreed on all hands that there ought to be but one claim to settlement, namely, birth, all other means of gaining settlement leading to perjuries, deceit, and misdoings of every kind, both on the part of the labourer and the capitalist." (J. L. Mallet's *Diaries, Proceedings of the Political Economy Club*, Vol. vi, pp. 254–5.)

[2] Senior's History, pp. 105–7. The proposal to introduce birth Settlements had been communicated to various parts of the country and produced a considerable outcry.

As a result of this conviction Senior persuaded Althorp to omit birth as a head of settlement, although it had been in the Commission's original Bill.[1] He summarized the effect of the changes in the Laws of Settlements in the Bill as it finally left the House of Commons:

"The 64th, 65th, and 66th clauses abolish the most mischievous heads of settlement, hiring and service, and apprenticeship, and impose an additional restriction on settlement by renting a tenement. Their effect will be to throw open the labour markets. I am inclined to wish that settlement by serving an office, and by estate, were also abolished."[2]

By the time the Bill was through the Lords other changes had been made by which settlement by apprenticeship (except sea apprenticeship) was restored, but settlement by office omitted, and further restrictions made on settlement by estate which Senior professed not to understand.[3] His hope of radically simplifying the Settlement Laws was thus only partially fulfilled.

Allowances

The system of allowances in aid of wages was of course one of the oldest of the abuses of the Poor Law, and by far the commonest. Senior's main objections to the unreformed Poor Law largely applied to allowances to able-bodied labourers, and as they have already been given in some detail it is not necessary to repeat them here in full. It may, however, be useful just to summarize them. Senior considered that:

I. (a) Allowances destroy the connection between work and wages and the responsibility of the labourer for his own family, differentiating against the independent labourer and the unmarried in favour of the pauperized and married.

(b) Their existence brought into operation all the hindrances to mobility of labour involved in the Laws of Settlements.

[1] Senior's History. Before the Bill was introduced into the Lords, pp. 107–8.
[2] Ibid. Summary of the Bill sent to Lord Brougham, pp. 189–90.
[3] Ibid. Final Summary of Amendments, pp. 269–70. Senior did not approve of the re-inclusion of settlement by apprenticeship.

II. Allowances enabled the employer of labour, particularly the farmer, to shift part of his wages bill on to the general body of ratepayers, of whom, in general, the farmer was not a member as he shifted his rates on to the landowner.

These were the inevitable consequences of a system of allowances to the able-bodied, but there were others which were in fact a part of the system, though not necessarily so. For instance, the scale of relief was so arranged that it was profitable to have a large family. Senior's attitude to this point was shown in the discussion in the House of Lords which arose from Lord Ellenborough's amendment to the Bill, which attempted to facilitate outdoor relief to the aged infirm, and to children under three years old, by giving discretionary power to magistrates to deal with these classes. Senior described the proposal of this amendment in the following way:

"The next committee was on Friday, 25th, a memorable day, as it produced results which, if they had not been got rid of, would have left the poor laws worse than they found them, and produced a striking confirmation of the remark in the Report, that pauper legislation has in general been worse than unsuccessful, has created whatever it was intended to prevent, and fostered whatever it was intended to discourage."

Against its acceptance he urged the following considerations:

"I said that I thought it would be ruinous; that as to children it would legalize head money, the worst form of allowance, and that as to the old it would destroy benefit societies, and subject a large portion of the population to magisterial interference, to an extent even beyond that which now exists. The part respecting children was resisted and abandoned, but the proviso in favour of the aged was so specious, and so favourably received by the House, that the Government acceded to it, and it was passed, without a division."[1]

In 1841 Senior came to the conclusion, probably as a result of the knowledge gained on the Commission on the Distress among Hand-loom Weavers, that if the allowance

[1] Senior's History, pp. 207-8, 209-10.

system once got started in industry its results were likely to be even worse than in agriculture. The Settlement Laws, he thought, had the one useful effect under the unreformed system that the pauperism of one country parish did not necessarily spread to another. (This is the only remark of Senior's in favour of settlement in the whole of his papers on Poor Laws that I have found.) Senior explained that this was because the amount a farmer produced was limited by his farm, not by the wages he paid, and therefore he had no motive to try and undersell his neighbours if the wages were low in his particular parish. This argument is a curious example of the influence of the scarcity of land in England on early nineteenth-century economists. The other part of the comparison has a more modern flavour. Since the most important element in manufacturing costs is wages, Senior argued that a reduction of wages at the expense of the rates in one parish enabled manufacturers in that parish to undersell their competitors and expand their output. This forced similar reductions in wages in the other parishes, and hence subsidies out of the rates. The introduction of the allowance system in one parish thus forced its introduction in all others in which there were competing manufacturers.[1]

The Labour-Rate

At the time of the Commission the labour-rate scheme was one of the most popular panaceas for the difficulties of the rural areas. Under it all ratepayers were assessed for quotas of certain numbers of labourers on some basis of their supposed ability or duty to employ labour. Anyone who failed to employ his quota at the current rate of wages (fixed by the parish) had to pay over to the parish the resultant deficiency in his theoretical wages bill, and the proceeds were then used in direct relief, or as a subsidy to those who employed more than their quota.

The apparent advantages of this system over the ordinary variants of the allowance system were considerable. Rates

[1] *Remarks on the Opposition to the Poor Law Amendment Bill by a Guardian*, pp. 78–9.

actually collected in money were diminished, for all those who employed their quota or more were relieved of most of the Poor Rate, and at the same time it afforded a direct encouragement to employ labourers, for obviously, *ceteris paribus*, if up to a certain limit it cost as little to employ labour as not, some sort of work would be found for the extra labour. Thus, it was argued, rates would fall, employment would increase, and the erstwhile pauper would help to produce some of his subsistence, if not all, and land would cease to go out of cultivation. After the disturbances of 1830, the prospect which it appeared to offer both of relieving rates, and of getting rid of the menace to law and order of the paupers either completely idle, or nominally engaged on the demoralizing parish relief works, was clearly extremely attractive.

The pertinacity with which it was urged on the Commissioners was of course a consequence of the prevalent idea that poor law reform was to consist primarily in finding a way of lowering rates and diminishing the danger to property. The argument that agricultural wages ought to be a *quid pro quo* for services and kept distinct from relief was entirely unappreciated by its supporters, for the labour-rate was based on the assumption that the parish, or in some instances the county, was responsible for the employment of all who happened to be settled in it, irrespective of whether the labour was worth its wages or not. This is of course exactly the same idea as that at the back of the argument that many forms of uneconomic public works are cheaper than maintenance on the dole. This is obviously true now, and was true then, but Senior and the other members of the Commission regarded the matter from a different angle. The universal application of the labour-rate in rural areas, as a permanent remedy, would be an admission that a considerable number of labourers were superfluous economically, and had a claim to perpetual support whatever their habits, numbers, or their efficiency. In short, that some form of agricultural pauperism was a natural part of the social fabric, was incurable, and not even particularly undesirable.

Of course if each ratepayer had been assessed to the labour-rate in exact proportion to his demand for labour, the scheme would have had no influence except in so far as adjustments would have been cumbrously inelastic. But this was necessarily not the idea, even where the existence of a surplus of labour was not important. Respectable support of the scheme was based on the belief that the maintenance of the labourers was a duty incumbent on all ratepayers equally, irrespective of the different needs for labour of different individuals; in other words the possibility that labour was employed for the advantage of the employer *not* as a social duty was completely ignored. Frequently of course influential groups tried to introduce it merely in the hope of lining their own pockets. *A priori*, then, the rate must not be adapted strictly to demand for labour, but rather to income ability to employ labour. Its effect in practice was therefore similar to allowances: those who had a large demand for labour had their wage bills subsidized by those with a small demand, i.e. the shopkeepers, tithe-owners, and farmers (or ultimately their landlords) who had farms requiring little labour, as, for instance, pasture. As far as the landlords were concerned, the system merely differentiated to the disadvantage of those who happened to own an unusually large amount of pasture land, except in so far as the actual burden of the labourers was decreased by increased production.

Senior's opinions on the labour-rate are to be found in a memorandum he wrote on behalf of the Commission answering a question of Lord Althorp's.[1] Their reply to the common suggestion that the labour-rate increased the extent and intensity of cultivation was merely that if profitable cultivation was not undertaken it was due either to lack of capital or to sheer perversity. In the former case the labour-rate could not help, in the latter it ought not to help. If, however, the labour-rate was intended to make the

---

[1] Letter to Lord Althorp, March 1833 (see note 1 on p. 291 above). Cf. also Senior's letter to Lord Melbourne in 1832 (see note 1 on p. 293 above), and his reply to Mr. Hillyard (see below), whose scheme was published in the *Poor Law Report*, 1834, pp. 174–6 of the 1894 reprint.

surplus labour contribute to its own support by earning some part of its subsistence, it might be successful. On the other hand, the disadvantages of the labour-rate were so important that they objected to its use even for this apparently reasonable purpose. The Commission pointed out that it was intrinsically unjust, as it benefited the farmer with a large demand for labour at the expense of everyone else, and that its ultimate consequences were bound to be fatal to the mobility of the agricultural labourers:

"Another consequence of a labour-rate, and a still more mischievous one, since it affects many more persons, is its interference with the distribution of labour. In ascertaining how far each ratepayer employs his quota of labourers, those labourers only are reckoned who have *Settlements in the Parish*. Those who have Settlements elsewhere are consequently discharged: long connection, fidelity, excellence, all the qualities that ought to bind the employer to his servant, must be disregarded."

Finally, and most important of all, the labour-rate was no improvement upon the allowance system in that it equally blurred the distinction between wages and relief. Thus it led to the familiar circle of demoralization, inefficiency, and unrest, since the labourer was just as much guaranteed his subsistence under the labour-rate as under the allowance system.

The general views of the Commission on the whole question were summarized as follows:

"On these grounds, the Commissioners believe that the Labour-rate system purchases, at the expense of enormous and permanent mischief and injustice, whatever immediate advantages it may appear to afford, and as all the proposed enactments are intended to facilitate and extend that mischief and injustice, the Commissioners disapprove of them *in toto*."

In this letter Senior was merely expressing the opinions of the whole Commission, but that he agreed with them is not open to question. His individual disapproval of the labour-rate is summarized very briefly in a letter to a Mr.

Hillyard, March 23, 1834, which is among the Senior papers. He repeats the objections set out above, and adds:

"On the whole, therefore, it appears to me that your scheme, like every that I have seen, is a scheme of general pauperization, is a scheme for confining all the labourers to the accidental boundaries of their parishes, without reference to the demand for their services, to be employed by a scale of allowances fixed by the vestry, without reference to their ability or their conduct."

IV

It was suggested at the beginning of this chapter that Malthus' theory of population was regarded by some people as an *a priori* argument against the existence of poor laws at all. This was not Senior's opinion. Senior, as we have pointed out before, was unorthodox in his views of population in general. He did not think that, other things being equal, population tends to increase faster than subsistence.[1] Nevertheless, he thought that institutions which definitely encouraged population might well destroy the balance, and, *a fortiori*, any which at the same time weakened ambition and self-respect. The whole of the Poor Laws in so far as they discouraged providence and ambition were dangerous, but in particular such customs as "head money" were obviously so when graded so as to encourage early marriages and large families. Thus far he agreed with the Malthusians, and he went still further in agreeing that any system which should make the unmarried labourers' position less eligible than the married, as, for instance, allowances which reduced the unmarried man's wages below those of the married, highly undesirable.[2] But in agreeing that if institutions had any influence on population it would be better that they should discourage it rather than the reverse, he was

---

[1] Senior's attitude to the population problem was not realized by all his contemporaries, e.g. *Quarterly Review*, Vol. 45, April 1831, Art. III, pp. 104–5; no doubt because in the correspondence with Malthus he ended up by saying that they agreed. (See Part I, chap. 3, sect. i above.)

[2] Letter to the Lord Chancellor, 1832, September 14, op. cit., see above, pp. 298 et seq.

far from thinking that the incentive they offered to increases of population was the main, or in any way the most, important danger involved in the unreformed Poor Laws.

The principal object of reform in his opinion, as we have emphasized already, was to depauperize the rural population as an end in itself, and to increase its independence and ambition; that reform would at the same time do away with the stimulus to irresponsible breeding of a degraded class was an additional advantage. This is clear enough from the significant omissions in his writings. In criticizing the reintroduction of children's allowances, for instance, he did not mention population problems at all, but referred only to this affording a back door to the whole reintroduction of pauperization through indiscriminate relief.[1] Similarly, in alluding to the objects of reform, it is always the evil of pauperism as such that he harped upon. In one of the letters already referred to, he pointed out as among the advantages of an abolition of settlements the dispersion of the local pools of surplus labour which had resulted from the immobility of labour; he did not believe that there was any large surplus due to over-population.[2] Sturges Bourne, on the other hand, maintained that the Settlement Laws were not as important as the actual right to relief in immobilizing labour, and suggested that the real problem was one of over-population.[3] Pauperism, in short, according to Senior, was essentially a result of the wrong administration of the Poor Laws, and could only be cured by the reform of the Poor Laws.

It is really on his theory of the wage fund that Senior's antipathy to any increase in the agricultural population was based. Briefly the wage-fund theory amounted to saying that the average level of wages depended on the size of the fund divided by the number of labourers. He thought that the effect of pauperization was to decrease the size of the fund by decreasing the efficiency of labour, driving away

[1] See sect. iii above.

[2] Senior's Letter to the Lord Chancellor, September 14, 1832 (see next page).

[3] Sturges Bourne's comments on this letter in October 1832, op. cit.

capital, and putting land out of cultivation, at the same time that it tended to increase the population by lifting all responsibility for children off the shoulders of the parents.[1] This is merely one way of stating the obvious: that if the efficiency of a factor diminishes at the same time as its supply increases, its reward per unit must inevitably fall. Over-population might well result according to Senior from the mere dwindling of the wage fund quite apart from the increase of population; *a fortiori* if population increased at the same time wages must fall until they were below subsistence level.[2] The necessity of immediate reform lay just in the fact that this process of decline in the theoretical level of wages had already begun, but had not proceeded so far as to make over-population in the crude sense a reality. This all seems so clearly implied in the passages already quoted, that it is unnecessary to repeat them or search out new ones. Senior was, however, all his life an ardent advocate of emigration, and there is little doubt that the clauses in the Bill enabling Poor Law Unions to borrow money to encourage emigration met with his approval; but this was more as a palliative to help the transfer of the local congestions of labour than as a necessary part of reform. Thus, in the letter of 1832 to the Chancellor, he said, in recommending emigration:

"In order to prevent the labourers from having a real cause of complaint, I think the Government ought to afford to the labourers in those parishes having a real surplus population . . . the means of emigration, and to supply a fund for that purpose, as to half by adding a percentage to the whole of the rates of England and Wales to be paid by the occupiers, but allowed by the landlords, and as to the other half by a rate imposed on the parish. . . .

"If any other persons are to share it [the expense], it should be the owners of land and houses, who have been the principal creators of pauperism and surplus population, and who will be more benefited by their diminution than the owners of any

---

[1] Letter to the Lord Chancellor, September 14, 1832. Cf. sect. iii above, especially pp. 305–7.

[2] Letter to the Lord Chancellor, September 14, 1832.

other property. But in fact I do not believe that much emigration would take place. The real surplus population is not great, though the poor law system accumulates it in a most inconvenient degree in particular places.''

This passage is the nearest to an admission of over-population that I have found, but even here he did not admit that the Poor Law had done more than accumulate it in particular places. From his other writings on population of the same period approximately and his later lectures, it appears, indeed, that he did not think England was over-populated in the crude sense. But it must be remembered that he always admitted that if population increased more slowly wealth per head would probably increase more rapidly, and that the labourer would derive a benefit from a decrease in supply of labour in the form of increased wages. Emigration was therefore always of advantage to labour.

Senior's attitude to wages generally has been made abundantly clear in an earlier chapter, and it is only neces-sary to summarize it here for the sake of completeness. He was entirely untainted by the idea that wages were deter-mined by subsistence. They might be above or below subsistence, but there was no magic attraction about any particular level. Wages, *qua* wages, were the payment for valuable services, not payment for subsistence. They had no necessary connection with needs, but depended largely on productivity. It followed that the mere size of a family was no measure of its claim on the produce of the community. Only in so far as labourers produced what they needed had they first claim on the produce. It followed that, if a right to maintenance for unlimited numbers was admitted, the persons who would pay that maintenance over and above wages ought to have some means of preventing the unlimited and indiscriminate increase of population. This was the basis of his somewhat sanctimonious attitude towards landlords as preordained to limit the population trying to live on any given piece of land through the rights of property. This aspect of the functions of landlords is not apparent in the English Poor Law papers, but it turns up

again and again in the Irish *Journals* and in his criticism of
the application of even the reformed English Poor Law to
Ireland.[1] As far as England was concerned, he believed that
the modifications of the Settlement Laws to free the labour
market, and the increased efficiency of labour, as soon as
reasonably depauperized, would provide amply for the
subsistence of the population, and agricultural wages would
rise to a sufficiently high level, if not higher than the old
wages plus allowances.

V

The analysis of the abuses and nature of the Poor Laws was
to some extent a straightforward application of first principles to a particular problem, but evolving a workable
scheme for reform was far more complex. Not merely had
general policy to be translated into the major provisions of
a Bill, but a large number of detailed questions springing
from the complexity of the old administration of the Poor
Law had to be dealt with. It was not simply a general code
of conditions of relief that was needed, but the drawing of
that code in such a way that it would work almost automatically under a system of administration that was bound,
ex hypothesi, to be subject to local variations. In order to
make any reform effective some form of central control
was obviously required; at the same time the nature of the
problem was such that a rigid system laid down by Act of
Parliament was foredoomed to failure. Further, any reform
of the code of relief had to be of such a nature as to admit
of gradual introduction. These difficulties were fully appreciated by Senior in 1832, and he appears to have evolved
a scheme of central administration independently of the
rest of the Commission by the time he wrote to the Lord
Chancellor in September of that year.[2] In view of this later

---

[1] Senior, *Journals, Conversations, and Essays on Ireland*, 2 vols. The advocates
of the right to relief on the ground of the legal protection given to property
in land overlooked his fundamental objection that this implied a right to
increase the population indefinitely with the possible result of diminishing
everyone's share; e.g. pp. 153–5. See Appendix 1 below.

[2] It is not certain whether he knew Chadwick at this time, but it is probable
that he had seen some of his writings on administration. According to J. S.

development it is interesting to examine an early draft scheme among Senior's papers which appears to have been drawn up by Senior in 1831.[1] The first provision of this draft abolished all allowances on an appointed day on the ground that:

"Whereas the practice of giving parochial relief in aid of wages to persons earning wages from their employers has much tended to lower wages and diminish industry, be it enacted," etc.

The second clause contained an attack on improvident marriages, and was apparently suggested by Sir E. Sugden.[2] It proposed that no relief should be given to persons who married under thirty for seven years, or to persons who married over thirty for four years, it being explained—

"whereas much of the distress among the poor arises from improvident marriages contracted in the expectation of Parish relief. . . ."

These enactments, however, are specifically prevented from applying to the following cases:

"Provided always and be it enacted that nothing in this Act contained shall be construed to make it unlawful to afford necessary parochial relief or allowances in cases of illness of any such labourer or other person or of his or her family or to afford parochial relief or allowance to any widow or wife deserted by her husband left with a family which she is unable by her and their labour wholly to support or to afford parochial relief or allowance to those who through old age or any infirmity shall be unable by their labour wholly to maintain themselves and their families or to afford temporary parochial assistance to those who by fire flood or such calamity shall be in urgent distress."

Mill some papers by Chadwick on administrative problems first attracted Senior's attention to him. (Letter from J. S. Mill to James Henderson of Glasgow, August 22, 1868, *Collected Letters of J. S. Mill*, Vol. II, p. 119.) Letter to the Lord Chancellor, September 14, 1832.

[1] There is no indication of the purpose for which this scheme was drawn up.

[2] There is a set of notes among Senior's papers on previous changes in the Poor Laws in which this plan is attributed to Sugden. See Appendix II, g. i, p. 348 below.

His suggestion for the reform of the Settlement Laws was the abolition of all heads except those of birth, marriage, or parentage, and three years' residence. All persons under sixteen years were to follow their parents' settlements, and were not to be regarded as separate entities from the point of view of the Poor Law.

It was obviously a roughly thought-out scheme but it contains some suggestions to which Senior attached importance later on. The abolition of allowances was rejected by Senior slightly later as being too sudden and too crude. It is obvious that in 1831 he had not discovered any harmless way of affording relief to the able-bodied, and hence thought abolition of allowances to be the only cure. Actually there is no indication in this draft that he thought that relief to the able-bodied in return for parish labour ought to be abolished. He continued, of course, to think the simplification of the Settlement Laws was very important, and in his later attempts aimed at still more drastic reforms. The choice of the age of sixteen as the age of independence was a point he continued to attach importance to, as closing the door to allowances to able-bodied labourers by means of their children.[1]

By 1832 Senior's ideas had developed much further, as well as his appreciation of the complexities of the problem. It is noticeable that the early draft contains no project for reform of the administration, but in the following year he proposed a system of inspection and the removal of power from the magistrates, as well as the introduction of the workhouse test. This again may have been suggested by Chadwick, but it is equally likely to have been suggested by the evidence of the Assistant Commissioners. In his letter to the Lord Chancellor in the September of this year, he made the following suggestions for general reform which he had apparently not discussed with the other members of the Commission:

I. *Administrative Reform.*—(a) Reform of accounts and

---

[1] This age was selected in the Commissioners' draft Bill, but lowered to twelve in subsequent discussions, and finally raised again in the House of Lords. Senior's History.

audit to make possible the attachment of responsibility to
the actual administrators of relief. (*b*) Transfer of all power
of ordering relief from the country magistrates to the overseers, making the latter entirely responsible for taking
proper steps for the provision of relief instead of the existing
system in which the magistrates were the ultimate authority.
(*c*) Appointment of special poor law magistrates, who should
move on circuit, as the ultimate seat for appeal, with
powers and duties of general inspection; these magistrates
were to be appointed by the Government for this special
purpose.

II. *Relief.*—(*a*) Introduction of workhouses which were
ultimately to become the sole means of relief to the able-
bodied. He explained that:

> "It appears from the evidence before us, that a well-regulated
> workhouse is one of the most effectual means by which a pauper-
> ized parish can be reclaimed. The dissolute poor hate its cleanli-
> ness, its regularity, its confinement, its classification, its labour,
> and its absence of stimulants; qualities which to the only proper
> inmates of the workhouse, the infirm, are either indifferent or
> agreeable. On the other hand, an ill-regulated workhouse
> which resembles in everything their own cottage, except that
> it is larger and affords more society, is a place of misery to the
> decent and the infirm, and of sluggish sensual ease to the idle
> and profligate. By far the greater number of workhouses appear,
> from the information before us, to be either ill-regulated, or
> subject to no real regulation whatever . . . they are subject to
> no superintendence except sometimes the periodical visits of
> Guardians or Visitors, whose principal object is to see that
> 'the poor are well taken care of'; that is, that they are much
> better fed, clothed, and lodged, in idleness than they could be
> by honest labour."

(*b*) Workhouses to be subject to the general inspection of
his proposed poor-law magistrates.

He hoped that by this means the specific prohibition of
allowances to the able-bodied could be avoided by giving
instructions that they were to be repressed as soon as possible
except in extreme cases.

III. *Settlement.*—Senior was now in favour of the abolition of settlement by residence, as well as all other heads, except those of parentage and birth.

The other suggestions in the letter are of little importance except that for subsidized emigration, which has been mentioned already in the preceding section.

Sturges Bourne in his comments on Senior's letter[1] considered that the suggestions on settlement were not of much value, and largely impracticable; he also attached less importance to the reform of the system of control, and exhibited no enthusiasm for the idea of independent inspection by poor-law magistrates or anyone else. The suggestions as to workhouses he approved, and also those for emigration, though he thought the proposed plan difficult.

Henry Garler, the only other member whose comments are available in the unpublished papers, expressed far more agreement with Senior, and urged that the overseers should be full-time paid officials[2]—a suggestion that Senior adopted in the following months.

By January 1833 Senior had worked out his scheme of administration still further, though he added nothing to the suggestions for the workhouse. In his letter of this month to the Lord Chancellor, he says that he suggested in his last letter[3] a definite central committee consisting of a chief and two assistants, who should control a body of inspectors, one to each seventy parishes. He now added a number of administrative details—the most important of which was the adoption of Garler's suggestion for paid overseers—and took the important new step of advocating the compulsory union of parishes by the inspectors. (This was almost certainly suggested by Chadwick.) But the real interest of this letter is the discussion of the failure of the local system and possibility of the whole matter of relief being made a function of the central Government:

[1] Comments on Senior's letter to the Lord Chancellor of September 14, 1832, by Sturges Bourne in October 1832.

[2] Comments on the same letter by Henry Garler in November 1832.

[3] This letter is missing.

"I foresee that the whole of this scheme will be objected to on the ground of the patronage which it will give to the Government.—So far as that objection is founded on a supposition that the general influence of Government, or, to speak more properly, the influence of Government in general would be mischievously increased, I should treat it with great contempt; believing the influence of Government to be, and to be likely to be, far too small. . . . A year ago, or even six months ago, I should have laughed at the proposal of making it any other than a parochial charge.

"I had supposed that the only possible mode of keeping it within endurable limits was to make the distributors the payers so that every vestryman and overseer should be urged by his own interest to diminish the common burden. And I still think that if that course had from the first been pursued in this country, as in fact it has been in Scotland, we should have been not certainly in a healthy state, but in one not much worse than that of the assessed Scotch districts. But this has not been the system either of the law or of the practice. The law gives the power to the overseers, who are only required to be householders in the Parish, and to the Justices who need not have, and indeed seldom have, any connection with it.—The practice vests it either in the Justices or in the vestry, who, even when they do not profit, or think that they profit, by the abuse as shopkeepers, cottage landlords, farmers, or manufacturers, are in general indemnified against loss by a proportional reduction of rent. The real payer, the landlord, has not as landlord the slightest control over the expenditure, or even the power of objecting to the most illegal and most glaring malversation, and though the objection might be diminished by giving the landlord the vote, still if paid superintendence is to be adopted, and in the existing state of our population it seems to me impossible to dispense with it, he can have nothing to do with the actual distribution."

Senior then went on to explain the advantages to be derived from a national responsibility for relief as the abolishment of settlement, the economy of administration, and the disappearance of causes for litigation, and finally its general popularity among the existing ratepayers. Nevertheless he turned this idea down in favour of the detailed proposals he had already enumerated, on the general grounds that it would be a highly objectionàble and desperate expedient "to make the Government the general insurer against misfortunes, idleness, improvidence, and vice."[1] He also, and this was his deciding reason, believed that efficiency and strictness under a national administration would only last a short time, explaining that he feared—

"that in time the vigilance and economy, unstimulated by any private interest, would be relaxed. That the workhouses would be allowed to breed a hereditary workhouse population; and would cease to be an object of terror. That the inability of receiving in them all the applicants would occasion a recurrence to relief at home; that candidates for political power would bid for popularity by promising to be good to the Poor, and we should run through the same cycle as was experienced in the last century, which began by Laws prohibiting relief without the sanction of the magistrates, commanding those relieved to wear badges, and denying relief out of the workhouse; and when, by these restrictions the immediate pressure on the rates had been relieved turned round and by Statutes with preambles reciting the oppressiveness of the former enactments, not only undid all the good that had been done, but opened the floodgates of the calamities we are now experiencing."[2]

In consequence he concentrated his attention on an administrative scheme which would combine central inspection with local financial responsibility.

The final scheme of administration adopted was undoubtedly due to Chadwick, but it is interesting to notice that Senior had already reached the similar general conclusions in 1832 without, as far as can be seen, any assistance from him. It is legitimate to leave the details of the actual scheme adopted in the Act of 1834 on one side as not being

[1] Senior's letter to the Lord Chancellor, January 7, 1833. For the connection of these suggestions with the reform of the Settlement Laws, see sect. iii, pp. 301–5 above.

The voting system was changed by the Amendment Act of 1834, in order to give the landlords some sort of control.

[2] Letter to the Lord Chancellor, January 7, 1833. Clapham (*Economic History of England*, Vol. II, p. 350) points out that this objection is equally applicable to a parish rate, remarking that the Commission were really trying to make the right to relief a low-grade sort of right, which could only be admitted by low-grade authorities.

specifically connected with Senior, and to concentrate on his efforts to insure the introduction of the workhouse system, to which he attached so much importance.

VI

The emphasis laid by Senior, and more gradually by other members of the Commission,[1] on the double function of the Amendment Act has not always been sufficiently recognized. The principal objects of reform as they saw them were to depauperize the agricultural labourer and to create a system which might be expected to prevent such pauperism either spreading to the towns or recurring generally in the country.[2] The realization of the first aim necessitated an administrative machine which would be able to proceed gradually and piecemeal to the destruction of pauperism. This was the reason for the enormous powers given the Central Administrative Commission to legislate separately for each parish according to its individual circumstances, and for the lack of the wholesale enforcement of the workhouse system in the towns, or even in the northern country districts, immediately the Bill was passed. The stress the Commission put on this policy of gradualism is illustrated in the following passage from Senior's explanation of the Bill to Brougham:

"If it be admitted, (1) That the administration of the Poor Laws requires extensive amendment; (2) That an amendment by the express and strict provisions of an Act of Parliament is a remedy which the constitution of the patient cannot endure, it must follow that the proposed mode of amendment, namely, by means of a new authority empowered to introduce its changes step by step, to feel all its way, to act according to the different states of different parts of the country, according to the state of public feeling, according even to the accidents of the seasons, and according to the success of its previous measures, is not

[1] As far as the information goes Sturges Bourne had little hope to begin with of the possibility of this, and Henry Garler had no opinion either way. (Comments on Senior's letter to the Lord Chancellor of September 14, 1832.)

[2] The fulfilment of these schemes implied, of course, considerable relief to agriculture in general.

only the only safe, but the only practicable mode of amendment."[1]

The most concise and lucid statement of the objects of the Bill is to be found in the same summary, as follows:

"The objects of the Poor Law Amendment Bill are two: (1) To raise the labouring classes, that is to say, the bulk of the community, from the idleness, improvidence, and degradation into which the maladministration of the laws for their relief has thrust them. (2) To immediately arrest the progress, and ultimately to diminish the amount of the pressure on the owners of lands and houses."

The order in which Senior arranged these two aims is characteristic of his belief that the main object of the reform was the social one of rescuing the agricultural labourer, and that the need for rescue was due to the maladministration of the law, not to any inherent tendency for the labouring population to be unable to look after itself.

He went on to explain the dependence of the realization of the second object on the first.

"It is to be observed that these two objects are intimately connected. Even if the whole amount of the poor rates were raised without expense to the proprietors, if it were a tribute, for instance, from a foreign country, yet if its effect were to destroy the diligence, skill, and morality of the labouring classes, the proprietors would be as effectually ruined as if they themselves contributed it, since lands and houses are valueless without the aid of a laborious and skilful body of workpeople. And on the other hand, if the expenditure on the poor had no immediate effect on their moral character, yet if it were to go on at the rate at which it has increased for the last fifty years, it would ultimately throw the whole land out of cultivation, and destroy by famine or pestilence all who had not the means of emigration."[2]

It was by the enforcement of the workhouse test that Senior believed these aims could be realized. It offered a

[1] Senior's History, pp. 196–7. It is of some interest to notice the difference between Senior's proposals for reform in 1831 and this later attitude. Cf. sect. v above.   [2] Senior's History, pp. 159–61.

solution of the fundamental problem of relief to the able-bodied, for it provided a simple method of distinguishing between idleness and real need. At the same time, by making the position of the pauper less eligible than that of the independent labourer, it differentiated between those who attempted to maintain their independence and those who did not. Senior's opinion both of its efficiency and importance is shown in a letter in 1834 explaining the Commission's Bill to Lord Lansdowne[1]:

"There remain therefore only the able-bodied and their families, and all the evidence shows that there are very few cases in which they need enter, or in fact will enter, a well-regulated workhouse. . . . Supposing the whole number of able-bodied paupers, including their families, now to amount to a million, which I believe to be above the mark, there is no reason to suppose that one-tenth, or one-twentieth, or even one one-hundredth part of them, would continue inmates of workhouses, even under their average regulation. Still less if they were properly governed.

"So much for the economical part of the question.

"To those who object to the scheme from motives of compassion, it must be urged that the proper objects of compassion are the independent labourers, whom the present system defrauds of the wages and the respect to which they are entitled, and still more the actual paupers and their families on whom it inflicts the worst evils that misgovernment can inflict, degradation and vice.

"To say that our scheme will make poverty punishable is the grossest misrepresentation, if by poverty is meant the situation of the man who has to earn his bread. It is the present system which, by confounding poverty with pauperism, and tainting wages by the admixture of relief, punishes poverty with a severity which I should be sorry to see applied to crime. Our scheme will reward independent poverty. It will punish, if affording subsistence to those who voluntarily implore it is a punishment, not poverty, but pauperism; and if some cases occur in which the subsistence we offer would be felt as un-merited punishment, those seem to be the cases for voluntary charity."

[1] Letter to Lord Lansd owne, March 1834. (Senior MSS.)

THE POOR LAW PROBLEM

That the workhouse system was infinitely superior to any other he had no doubt. He had nothing but scorn for the ignorance of the past displayed by those who suggested that general administrative reform and pious hopes would be sufficient. The possibility of giving relief in return for labour he objected to as difficult to carry out,[1] and in the same letter he wrote:

". . . I think that there are other means by which our object, that of making the situation of the pauper less eligible than that of the independent labourer, the only result which we should call a real improvement, might be effected. We have stated in the report (p. 147) that all that is necessary is that those who receive relief should work for the parish exclusively as hard and for less wages than those of the independent labourer. But we have also stated (p. 21) that this would require strict superintendence; a superintendence, indeed, much more strict than that usually exercised by those who are superintending their own workmen. It would be vain to expect this superintendence from the existing parochial officers.

" If instead of the simple, and almost self-acting plan of the workhouse, the more troublesome, and more easily evaded one of parish employment is adopted, it appears to me that it will be necessary to arm the central board . . . with extensive and almost arbitrary powers of appointing and removing the paid officers, and of employing the paupers in work not merely within the parish or the incorporated district, but wherever it can be obtained."

He concluded:

"I think the process would be less certain of ultimate success and probably be slower in operation."

The importance that Senior attached to the workhouse system is further illustrated in his account of the passage of the Bill. Early in the discussion with the Cabinet the workhouse clause was struck out, largely owing to the influence of the Duke of Richmond. In its original form the clause

[1] Lord Althorp had suggested parish labour as a test instead of the workhouse at the Cabinet Meeting, Monday, March 17, 1834, at which Senior and Sturges Bourne had been present. (Senior's History, pp. 2–3.)

prohibited outdoor relief to the able-bodied in such places as the Administrative Commissioners should think ready for the step (that is, principally, where they thought the workhouse would provide sufficient accommodation for those who really needed relief and were willing to enter rather than seek independent means of support). But by the next clause the Commissioners were empowered to permit outdoor relief in special cases despite their general order. This clause the Cabinet also insisted on modifying to give the overseers and vestries powers to proceed contrary to the Commissioners' rules in special circumstances, subject to the final disallowance by the Commissioners. This change lost, of course, most of its point by the omission of the workhouse clause.[1]

As a counterblast Senior almost immediately proposed a clause which was accepted, forbidding allowances after an appointed date. But he himself introduced a modifying clause "enabling Commissioners to permit allowance in such places and to such persons . . . as they should think fit." He was never happy, however, about the allowance clauses, and explained that—

"the Clause forbidding allowances . . . . was the only clause in the Bill as to the working of which I felt any apprehension, that it was not in pursuance of any recommendation in the Report, but had been introduced as a substitute for the workhouse system."

The objections that he felt to it were that it introduced too sudden a change, and that paupers who would have refused the workhouse would take to parish employment in large numbers if allowances were refused; that the provision probably would not be enforced; that, if it were it would inflict great hardship on individuals "by the abrupt and total cessation of a long-established practice."

The Government was finally convinced by these arguments, although the clause had been popular in the House of Commons, and agreed to the insertion instead of a proviso in the form of a preamble:

[1] The whole of this account is from Senior's History, pp. 27 et seq.

"reciting the prevalence of the *illegal* practice of allowance and the difficulty of applying a universal remedy, and therefore leaving it to the Commissioners to suppress it gradually."[1]

In this incomplete state the plans for the introduction of the workhouse system were left, despite the recommendations of the Report and Senior's efforts in persuasion. Its institution depended hereafter entirely on the energy of the Commissioners who were given specific power to compel the erection of workhouses out of rates in addition to general powers for determining the method of relief.

Even this obviously necessary financial power was not won without a struggle. According to the original draft of the Bill the Commissioners were to be able to order the necessary expenditure, which was to be financed from the rates. This was whittled down by the Cabinet Committee first to a year's rates, and then made dependent on the consent of the majority of the ratepayers or owners.[2] According to Senior this would have meant the complete failure of the scheme for depauperization. The Commissioners, besides not being instructed explicitly to introduce the workhouse system, were to be robbed of the power to introduce it at all. He therefore went to Lord Lansdowne to suggest that the Commissioners should have full power to force expenditure up to one-tenth of the year's rates. He explained that the omission of this power was "so fundamental an injury to the Bill" that without this power the Bill might be "entitled an Act to amend the laws for the relief of the poor in such parishes which shall consent thereto."[3]   So far he got his way, but when he tried to raise the limit from one-tenth to one-fifth on the Bill having a favourable reception in the House of Commons, Lord Althorp, though agreeing in principle, thought it too risky a change to make.[4]

[1] Senior's History, pp. 64, 69, 214–15. The discussion on this matter took place with Lord Althorp on Sunday, April 27th, shortly before the Bill went to the Lords.

[2] At meetings on Sunday, March 23rd, and Friday, April 4th. Senior's History, pp. 23–4, 49–50.

[3] Senior's History, pp. 51–2.   [4] Ibid., pp. 55–6.

With this partial acceptance of the Commission's original proposals for the establishment of the workhouse system Senior had to be content. On the whole he was satisfied that despite numerous detailed amendments, some good, some bad, and a few major amendments of a damaging kind, sufficient of the original provisions for reform had been preserved during the passage of the Bill through the Cabinet and Parliament to assure a considerable measure of improvement in the organization and administration of poor relief.[1]

VII

It remains only to attempt to estimate Senior's influence on the amendment of the Poor Laws. It is clear that the realization of so many of the Commission's original recommendations in the actual Act was due to Senior's untiring persistence, and in this sense his own statement that for good or evil the main responsibility for the inception of the system of 1834 rested on him is undoubtedly correct.[2] But it is impossible to disentangle the respective parts played by him and Chadwick in making the particular suggestions. Senior was certainly responsible for most of the suggestions for the reform of the Settlement Laws, though Chadwick agreed with him.[3] It seems probable that they decided independently on the merits of the workhouse test.[4] On the administrative side Chadwick is known to have been the dominating influence, but Senior appears to have decided on the necessity of some sort of centralization independently. In any case it is evident that they had much in common in their views, and we know that Senior's attention was drawn to Chadwick by some of his papers on administration.[5] That he finally got him into the main Commission of Inquiry and recommended with great warmth his appointment as one of the Central Administra-

---

[1] Senior's History. Final summary of changes made in the Bill.
[2] *Correspondence and Conversations of Alexis de Tocqueville with N. W. Senior*, 1872. Letter from Senior to de Tocqueville, March 18, 1835, pp. 12–13.
[3] See pp. 300–305 above.
[4] See pp. 317 et seq. above.   [5] See note 2 on p. 315 above.

tive Commissioners shows that he relied considerably on his judgment.[1]

Whether Senior or Chadwick was originally responsible for any particular suggestion is really, however, unimportant, for practically every suggestion included in the Report had been recommended at some time or other by people not connected with the Commission of Inquiry. But it is clear that the introduction of the workhouse system and the sweeping simplification of the Settlement Laws were the two objects that Senior had most at heart; in both cases he met with only partial success. By the time the Bill was passed the former had been left entirely dependent on the Commissioners, and its enforcement would depend on their personal views. This, of course, was what happened; the first Administrative Commissioners, appointed largely on Senior's recommendation, introduced the workhouse test into the majority of pauperized rural areas, but as the memory of the old abuses faded, the restrictions on outdoor relief to the able-bodied slackened, and another burst of liberality appeared in the 'fifties.[2] As to settlement, Senior was really more successful; he managed to dispose of at least a number of heads and leave it simplified to marriage, parentage, apprenticeship with some limitations, a qualified form of residence, and a qualified form of settlement by estate.

This success, partial though it was, at least sufficed to get rid of the worst pauperization of the agricultural labourer, an achievement largely due to Senior's insistence that this was the essence of the problem. His further hope of gradually eradicating all pauperism has only partially

---

[1] In a letter to Lord Melbourne on Appointments. June 30, 1834, (Senior MSS.) He wrote of Chadwick as "the only individual among the Candidates, perhaps I might say in the country, who could enter into the office of Commissioner with complete prearranged plans of action. He was the principal framer of the remedial measures in the Report and the sole author of one of the most important and difficult portions, the union of parishes," and as having "communicated more information than any other of our Assistant Commissioners, indeed, almost as much as the rest of them put together," when he had been an Assistant Commissioner.

[2] For an account of the administration of Poor Relief after 1834 see Mackay, op. cit., and Webb, op. cit.

been realized, and by modern methods of insurance rather than by the workhouse system; but even to the most enthusiastic supporters of the principle of "less eligibility" realization of this ultimate aim was always something of an Utopian aspiration. The failure of the workhouse scheme to take the form recommended in the Report of 1834 was a much greater disappointment, and in 1862 Senior regarded the cherished workhouse system from which he had hoped so much with something like horror. He had never anticipated the evolution of the general mixed workhouse with every sort and grade of pauper jumbled up together, nor the complete failure of the Poor Law Commissioners to make adequate provision for the education of pauper children. Thus in his evidence before the Select Committee on Poor Relief in 1862, in answer to a question about the intentions of the original Commission as to classification, he said:

"Yes, we recommended that in every union there should be a separate school. We said that the children who went to the workhouse were hardened if they were already vicious, and became contaminated if they were innocent, and we recommended that in every union there should be a building for the children, and one for the able-bodied males, and another for the able-bodied females, and another for the old; we supposed the use of four buildings in every union."

and added in reply to a supplementary question:

"We never contemplated having the children under the same roof as the adults."[1]

On education he was equally critical of the administration and vigorous in his defence of education for pauper children. In reply to the suggestion that it was unfair to the independent labourer to educate pauper children at the expense of the rates, he said:

"I feel that if a guardian refused to allow a child to be educated because some money could be saved to the parish by so refusing, it would be an act of wickedness and cruelty."

[1] Third Report of the Select Committee on Poor Relief, 1862, *Parliamentary Papers*, 1862, Vol. x, Senior's evidence, questions 6905 and 6906.

and again:

"I think that parents who send their children to work instead of allowing them to be educated, are guilty of cruelty and wickedness to their children, and I do not think the guardians ought to require any parent to be guilty of such conduct."

He went on to maintain that children had a right to education, in replying to a question as to whether a parent had the right to claim education for his children at the public expense:

"Certainly at the public expense, if he cannot do it at his own. I take it that the duty to educate children is as much a duty as the duty to feed them."

Finally, he emphasized his old theory that ignorance and pauperism have a great deal to do with each other:

"I believe that there is nothing which creates paupers so much as ignorance, and that to require a child to work, perhaps that he may earn sixpence a day by scaring birds, instead of going to school would be not only very wrong, but very short-sighted."[1]

It is perfectly clear that this was not mere wisdom after the event. The Report of 1834 had recommended the education of pauper children; the Report on the Hand-loom Weavers had recommended free education without specific limitation to any particular class; he had pointed it out as one of the most useful fields for Government intervention in his lectures in 1847.[2] No one, however, is disposed to

[1] Third Report of the Select Committee on Poor Relief, 1862, *Parliamentary Papers*, 1862, Vol. x, Senior's evidence, questions 6686, 6687, 6690, 6694. The Committee suggested that, in his enthusiasm for education, Senior had under-rated both the achievements of the Poor Law authorities in educating indoor pauper children, and the objections and difficulties to their undertaking the education of outdoor paupers' children.

[2] *Poor Law Report*, 1834, pp. 253, 255–8, 301 (1894 reprint). *Report on the Hand-loom Weavers*, see Part II, chap. I, p. 262 above. Lectures, 1847–52, Course I, lecture 6; see Part II, chap. I, pp. 267–8 above. In the pamphlet *Remarks on the Opposition to the Poor Law Amendment Bill by a Guardian* (p. 54; cf. p. 297, note I above) Senior cited as one of the achievements of the Act of 1834 that the education of pauper children had been started.

deny the educational enthusiasm of the Utilitarians or of the classical economists, and it is unnecessary to enlarge upon it, but it has been less generally realized that the workhouse system visualized in the *Poor Law Report* of 1834 and that evolved by the Administrative Commissioners were two very different things.

In its Report in 1834,[1] the Commission of Inquiry recommended a strict classification of the inhabitants of workhouses just in order that different types of destitution should be treated differently: that the aged and infirm should be looked after in reasonable quiet and comfort; the children educated, and kept away from the depressing influence of the adults, so that they at least might start with a fair chance of independence; the sick of all sorts given proper medical attention in infirmaries; the able-bodied separated from the rest and the two sexes from each other, in order to make possible a more rigorous treatment.

Senior summarized the recommendations in a letter on the Forest of Dean[2]:

"I should recommend four Workhouses to be built: one for ible-bodied men, one for able-bodied women, one for the old and sick, and one for the children. The two for the able-bodied should be at a distance from one another, and need be very small; for if tolerably managed (that is, cleanliness and regularity enforced, stimulants prohibited, and work required) they would scarcely ever have half-a-dozen inmates. That for children would of course contain a school. That for the aged and sick would be an Almshouse and Hospital."

It is strange to find the word "almshouse" used in connection with any part of the workhouse system, but it undoubtedly conveyed the idea of the Commission of Inquiry with regard to the aged.[3]

Why, with all these good intentions, did the plans for distinctive treatment of the main categories of poverty miscarry so completely between 1834 and 1839 that the first

[1] *Poor Law Report*, 1834, pp. 252–9.
[2] Letter to Robert Gordon, Esq., India Board, April 4, 1834, on the Relation of the Forest of Dean to the new Poor Law. (Senior MSS.)
[3] See pp. 295–6 above.

three or four decades of reforming effort in the twentieth century have been devoted to destroying the workhouse system that resulted?[1] In the first place, no doubt, part of the trouble was due to the failure of the Commission of Inquiry of 1834 to think out all the administrative difficulties involved in their plan. Not only did the urgency and complexity of the problem prevent the laying down by law of the details of the new system, but the unpopularity of the proposed reforms forced the Commission to acquiesce in leaving out specific references to the organization and administration of the workhouses from the final Bill.[2] It is fairly evident, however, that considerable responsibility for the miscarriage of the original plans rests with Sir G. Nicholls, perhaps the most energetic and the least subtle of the Administrative Commission.[3]

Despite these admitted failures of the Amendment, there is much to be said in favour of Senior's attempts to deal with the problem of destitution. His attitude may, I think, be fairly summarized as follows: He believed that over-population in the crude sense did not exist in England, that every able-bodied adult could earn enough to live on if unhindered in his attempts. The various forms of allowances not only dragged wages down so as to make this impossible, but assisted the survival of irregular and decaying trades by a concealed form of subsidy. The result was a serious obstacle to the most productive distribution of labour. Apart from philosophical considerations these arguments were and still are the main justification of the principle of "less eligibility." Unemployment as a recurrent phenomena Senior was not prepared to deal with except on this principle, for, while he admitted the difficulty of providence on a small income, to make no distinction between those who did and those who did not save was, he believed, unjustifiable. Apart from this problem of unemployment, however, he favoured the provision of relief in what may be

---

[1] See Webbs, op. cit., pp. 122–48.   [2] See pp. 325–8 above.

[3] Nicholls appears to have been mainly responsible for the introduction of mixed workhouses both in England and Ireland. Cf. Webbs, op. cit., pp. 122–33; and Nicholls' own *History of the English Poor Law*, Vol. II, chaps. 16–18.

called cases of personal misfortune.[1] The criticism that the workhouse test failed to distinguish between unemployment due to personal and impersonal causes is legitimate, and is the most serious that can be made against the Amendment. But it must be remembered that though everyone has been aware of this for a long time, the remedies, such as they are, have only been found after prolonged and stormy experience.

To us, in the complacency of the twentieth century, it appears that, in common with others of his generation, Senior under-estimated the difficulties of saving on a small income and over-estimated the flexibility of the economic system. That neither he, nor his contemporaries, were blind to the human difficulties of adaptability is, however, certain; and his greatest failure, the analysis of and provision of relief for urban destitution due to unemployment, lay in just that field in which modern failure is so painfully evident. Senior, too, it should be remembered, recognized several classes of destitution due to infirmity, childhood, and old age, and was clear that each of these should be treated differently, in infirmaries, schools, and almshouses. Even for these classes he avoided recommending rigidly uniform treatment, and the Commission carefully refrained from recommending the application of the workhouse test to them.[2] At least the fundamental principle that a poor law is not and cannot be a general cure for poverty was enunciated once and for all in the Report of 1834.

Thus although the classification and the administrative machine recommended by the Commission are out of date to-day, and were open to criticism even in their own day, it is difficult to see any really significant difference between its outlook and the outlook of the modern reformers of the Poor Law on these problems.

---

[1] Cf. also the discussion of Senior's *Letter to Lord Howick on a legal provision for the Irish Poor*, Part II, chap. I, pp. 242 et seq. above.

[2] See pp. 295–6 above.

SENIOR ON IRELAND

SENIOR's interest in Ireland dated more or less from 1830 when Lord Howick suggested to him that it offered an important field for study. From then on, no doubt partly because Whately was made Archbishop of Dublin in 1831, Senior spent a great deal of time in Ireland, and wrote at length on Irish problems. Most of his writings, though possibly of general historical interest, were more political than economic, and do not concern us. In any case it would need a competent student of Irish history to pronounce on the value of his discussions of the causes of the Irish *malaise*. All that will be attempted here, therefore, is a summary account of his opinions on various points which seem of interest in connection with his general opinions on Poor Laws and State intervention, and which it was difficult to include in Part II.

There is a point raised by the *Letter to Lord Howick on a legal provision for the Irish Poor* which is of some interest: Senior's objections to State assistance to Irish farmers and peasants in the event of crop failure. He admitted that—

"Such a provision, if confined to extreme cases, can scarcely be said to have any tendency to diminish industry or providence. The failure of a crop is not a contingency against which a labouring man can be expected to make a provision. When such a failure is general throughout a district it is not in the power of neighbours or friends to give adequate assistance; public relief therefore could not be said to come in lieu of ordinary charity, and the principal objections to it seem at an end."[1]

Rather surprisingly, however, he rejected compulsory assistance on the grounds that it would be impossible to decide what really constituted crop failure, and that assistance would naturally become a "resource to be drawn upon in all unfavourable seasons." It would further, he thought, diminish private charity and frugality, and would provide the farmers and peasants with free insurance at the public expense, while the fear it would give rise to of indefinitely high rates would check the investment of capital in improvements.[2]

---

[1] *Letter to Lord Howick on a legal provision for the Irish Poor*, 1831, p. 21.
[2] Ibid., pp. 19–24.

These general objections Senior held throughout his life, but rather curiously he altered his early opinions as to the possibility of effective Government action to alleviate Irish poverty by reclamation of waste and general development schemes. In 1837 he approved apparently without serious reserve the proposals of the Whately Commission on all these matters, and condemned the proposal to introduce the workhouse system.[1] He also changed his mind on another matter. We learn from Nicholls that Senior disapproved of his suggestion to introduce the English Poor Law into Ireland in 1836, either in a modified form entirely confined to indoor relief, or as giving a right to relief.[2] Writing to Senior's daughter in 1864 Nicholls explained in an account of a discussion with her father in 1836 that the latter—

"viewed the case of Ireland as so essentially different from that of England, that the same principle did not apply to both countries.— I thought it did, and so after discussing the matter, we each retained our own opinion."

In 1861, however, Senior wrote that he considered the Irish Poor Law, which was then a modified version of the English, as having worked well, and to be "the best which any country has ever adopted."[3] Some explanation of this change is to be found in the course of events in Ireland after 1837, discussed in his three articles on Ireland written in the 'forties.[4] By 1843 he was mainly concerned with the iniquities of the Tory Government in failing to deal with the Irish Church and education questions, and with the violence of the Trade Unions. At that date these

[1] Letter to Lord John Russell in the third Report of the Commissioners for Inquiring into the Condition of the Poor in Ireland, 1836, published 1837. See Part II, chap. 1, p. 248, note 2 above.

[2] Letter from Sir George Nicholls to Senior's daughter (Mrs. M. C. M. Simpson), December 12, 1864. See also Nicholls' *History of the Irish Poor Law*, pp. 129 et seq.

[3] Preface to *Journals, Conversations, and Essays on Ireland*, published 1868, Vol. 1, pp. ix and x. Senior admitted in this Preface that some of the plans for Ireland (apparently including the Irish Poor Law), which he had opposed, had worked well.

[4] "Ireland in 1843," "Proposals for extending the Irish Poor Law (1846)," "Relief of Irish Distress in 1847 and 1848," published in the *Edinburgh Review*, January 1844, October 1846, and October 1849, respectively, and reprinted in *Journals, etc., on Ireland*, 1868, Vol. 1, with a preface written by Senior in 1861. These articles caused considerable excitement to the Whig leaders, and there are a number of lengthy letters among the Senior papers about them from various people who saw them in draft.

matters seemed more important to him than the Poor Laws. These running sores, as he thought them, were the real cause of Ireland's poverty and lack of capital, and fundamental improvements could not be expected until these were relieved.[1] The two later articles were concerned, however, with the problems arising out of the famine. The first was an attack on the proposal advocated, particularly by Poulett Scrope, to extend the Irish Poor Law so as to give a right of relief in return for labour on public works.[2] This mere suggestion was, of course, bound to incite Senior to eloquent opposition, since it was merely the old enemy, the labour-test.[3] But this was by no means the sum total of his objections. The burden on the rates would be sufficient, he declared, to drive much of the land out of cultivation.[4] State-aided improvements, he considered, in contrast to his opinions of 1837, were wrong in principle as giving unfair assistance to private individuals, and would probably be, he thought, inefficient. The recommendations of the Whately report of 1837 for subsidized emigration and public works in general came in for sceptical disapproval, though he conceded that the reclamation of waste might still be of some slight use. In the same article, however, he lamented the rise of the general mixed workhouse and the absence of a right to assistance for the aged or infirm or for children.[5]

But these objections to Scrope's suggestions were as nothing compared with Senior's dislike of his doctrine that the poor had a natural right to be maintained by the landlords in Ireland:

"He [Scrope] complains," he said, "that his scheme is called a *confiscation*. We really know of no word that, as far as the landlords of Ireland are concerned, more adequately expresses the case. But that word does not adequately, or nearly adequately, represent the whole mischief of the proposal. Confiscation signifies merely a forced ademption of property, literally an ademption by the State. Such an ademption, of course, is a severe evil to the possessor. It probably destroys his whole happiness; but there the injury ceases . . . but if the rental

---

[1] "Ireland in 1843." (See previous footnote.)

[2] *Letters to the Rt. Hon. Lord John Russell on the Expediency of Enlarging the Irish Poor Law, to the full extent of the Poor Law of England*, by G. Poulett Scrope, 1846.

[3] "Proposals for extending the Irish Poor Law (1846)," pp. 171–83. (All page references to the Irish articles are to the reprints in *Journals, etc., on Ireland*, Vol. 1.

[4] Ibid., pp. 150–3.   [5] Ibid., pp. 167 et seq.

of Ireland, instead of being transferred, were exhausted—if the ownership of land ceased to be worth having—if estates were abandoned to
avoid payment of rates—the consequence would be, not the ruin only
of the proprietor, but of the whole island."[1]

The reason for this insistence on the importance of maintaining
the existence of rents paid to someone or other is to be found
in Senior's gloomy conviction that the uneducated Irish, lacking
either ambition or prudence, would always over-populate the
land if they had the chance—in short, that they were not suited
to peasant proprietorship. As to its social desirability, he agreed
with Thornton and John Stuart Mill, but he considered that in
recommending it in Ireland they had ignored the half-savage
state of the West of Ireland peasant. The impossibility of this
remedy being effective necessitated, he thought, the maintenance and protection of the receipt of rents by primarily non-
cultivating landlords.[2] He explained that—

"The existence of rent, that is to say of individual property in land,
is the only means by which the population of a country is proportioned
to the demand for labour. In this, as in many other cases, nature has
provided that the interests of the landlord and of the public shall
coincide. It is the interest of the landlord that his estate shall be occupied by precisely the number of persons which will produce the largest
surplus above their own consumption; or, in other words, by the
number of persons whose labour can be beneficially employed. The
proportion, of course, varies according to the habits of the people. A
labouring population eating meat must be more thinly scattered than
one eating corn; . . . A population thus proportioned to the demand for
labour never can be in want of employment. If it is frugal it cannot,
except from unforeseen misfortune, want public assistance . . . if the
great duty of the landlord be so to manage his estate, as to render it the
seat of prosperous tenants, and moral, industrious, and well-paid
labourers—the first step in the performance of this duty is to prevent
it from being occupied by an excessive population."[3]

All Senior's argument amounted to was the obvious: that
there is some optimum density of agricultural population, which

---

[1] "Proposals for extending the Irish Poor Law (1846)," pp. 152–3. It is
not clear how far Senior's objection to Scrope's proposals for public works
was because they were suggestions for relief works financed from the rates,
instead of general works undertaken not so much in order to give relief as to
increase the productivity of Ireland. Cf. Part II, chap. I, pp. 246–7, above.
[2] "Proposals for extending the Irish Poor Law (1846)," pp. 153–63, and
"Relief of Irish Distress in 1847 and 1848," pp. 270 et seq.
[3] "Proposals for extending the Irish Poor Law (1846)," pp. 153–4.

can only be realized if the owners of land have the will and the power to keep the population down. This he admitted to be possible under a variety of forms of tenure in theory, but in Ireland only by giving the landlords effective power to prevent the sub-division of their estates and the indiscriminate increase of houses. Obviously the allowance of sub-division as well as a right to outdoor relief would be doubly fatal. The argument, as far as I can see, has no theoretical significance to the theory of rent, though it is perhaps not altogether clear whether Senior thought it had.

Senior's third article on Ireland[1] was mainly a description of the inevitable results of the extension of the poor law under the pressure of famine in 1847, the discouragement of cultivation by the small farmers and peasants, and the partial ruin of the landlords. As a historical account it is probably of considerable interest, though I am not historian enough to judge, but it adds nothing new to our knowledge of Senior's views on the Poor Laws.

[1] "Relief of Irish Distress in 1847 and 1848."

BIBLIOGRAPHY OF SENIOR'S WRITINGS, ETC. PUBLISHED AND UNPUBLISHED [1]

I

Published Works on Economics (excluding articles, pamphlets, and Lectures published separately)

1. Ambiguous Terms in Political Economy. Appendix to R. Whately's Elements of Logic. First Edition. London, 1826.
2. An Outline of the Science of Political Economy. First edition published as the article on Political Economy in the Encyclopaedia Metropolitana, 1836 (a few copies were struck off for private circulation).

   Five more editions were published separately between 1850 and 1872 without alteration, except for the insertion of more paragraph headings than in the first edition.
3. Principes fondamenteaux de l'Économie politique, tirés de leçons édites et inédites de N. W. Senior par le Cte. J. Arrivabene. Paris, 1836.

   This volume was arranged by Arrivabene quite separately from the English Outline, etc., with Senior's approval (cf. its Preface). It contained the substance of some of the original lectures, altered only by the insertion or omission of various paragraphs and observations, and in order of arrangement, for the sake of clarity to French readers, but without alteration of the sense. The following are the lectures included:

Lectures 1826–30. Course I, Lecture 1 (French edition, pp. 35–71).

Lectures 2–4 (French edition, pp. 72–125).

Lectures 5–9 (French edition, pp. 125–219).

Course II, Lecture 9 (French edition, pp. 220–9). [2]

Lectures 7–8 (French edition, pp. 230–83).

Lectures 1–5 (French edition, pp. 284–400).

[1] This bibliography is, I believe, complete as to Senior's identified writings on economic subjects; it does not, however, include his non-economic articles except in so far as they were reprinted in volumes containing economic articles.

[2] See sect. IIA below. As I have not seen these lectures, the references are merely based on a comparison of the lecture headings with the French edition.

The substance of all these lectures, except Course I, Lecture I, is in the Political Economy, pp. 6–86, 88–9, and 118–23 (sixth edition).

4. Principii di economia politica. [Bibliotheca dell'Economista, first series: Trattati Complessivi. Vol. v, Turin, 1854.] This was an Italian translation of the Principes Fondamenteaux.

5. Presidential Address to Section F of the British Association for the Advancement of Science, 1860. Report of the British Association, etc., 1860.

II

Lectures delivered at Oxford. A. 1826–30. B. 1847–52. (Unless otherwise stated the original MSS. or copies of the originals are still in existence in the possession of Mrs. St. Leo Strachey.)

(a). LECTURES 1826–30.

Course I, 1826–7

1. Introductory Lecture on Political Economy. Delivered December 6, 1826. Published 1827, also in the Pamphleteer, Vol. 29, No. 57, 1828.
2. On the Nature of Wealth. Published in the Political Economy, pp. 6–11.
3. On the Nature of Value. Published in the Political Economy, pp. 11–22 (except for one example).
4. On the Nature of Exchange and Money.
5. On the Nature of Money.
6, 7, and 8. Three Lectures on the Transmission of the Precious Metals from Country to Country, and The Mercantile Theory of Wealth. Delivered June 1827. Published 1828. London. Reprinted as No. 3 in the London School of Economics Series of Reprints of Scarce Tracts in Economics and Political Science, 1931. (MS. missing.)
9. On the Various Scientific Definitions of Wealth. Part of the Lecture published in the Political Economy, pp. 53–6.

Course II, 1827–8

The MSS. of this Course are missing, and only the two lectures on population were published separately. The following list of headings is taken from Appendix I, p. 377, of Senior's Industrial Efficiency, edited by S. Leon Levy, 1929, who apparently saw the MSS.

1. On Production and Consumption.
2. On Abstinence.
3. On Capital and Machinery.
4. On Division of Labour.
5. On Application of Capital to Land.
6. On the Corn Laws and the Poor Laws.

7 and 8. On Population. Delivered Easter Term 1828; published together with A Correspondence between the Author and the Rev. T. R. Malthus. London, 1829. The substance of these lectures, with a short account of the correspondence, was republished in the Political Economy, pp. 29–50.

9. On the General Desire for Wealth.

Course III, 1828–9

1. On the Cost of Production. Published in the Political Economy, pp. 95–102.
2. On Price where Competition is Unequal. Published in the Political Economy, pp. 102–10.
3. General Laws of Price (continued). Published in the Political Economy, pp. 111–18 (with one example omitted).
4. Some Effects of Corn Laws.
5, 6, 7, and 8. On the Value of Money. Delivered 1829. The greater part of the four lectures were printed for private circulation under the title Three Lectures on the Value of Money. London, 1840. Reprinted as No. 4 in the London School of Economics Series of Reprints of Scarce Tracts in Economic and Political Science, 1931. The last section of Lecture 8 was published at the beginning of the Lecture 9. (See below.)
9, 10, and 11. On the Cost of Obtaining Money, and on Some Effects of Private and Government Paper Money. Delivered Trinity Term, 1829; published 1830, together with the last section of Lecture 8. Reprinted as No. 5 in the London School of Economic Series of Reprints and Scarce Tracts, etc., 1931.

Course IV

The MSS. of this course are missing, and only three of the lectures on Wages were published separately. The following list of headings is taken from Appendix I, pp. 377–8, of Senior's Industrial Efficiency, edited by S. Leon Levy, 1929.

1 and 2. Rent, Profit, and Wages.
3. Variations in Wages and Profits in Various Employments.
4. Effects of Uncertainty on Profits.
5. Meaning of High and Low Wages and High and Low Price of Labour.
6 and 7. Popular Errors Respecting the Causes which Influence the Rate of Wages.

Lectures 5, 6, and 7 were delivered in the Easter Term 1830, and published with a preface On the Causes and Remedies of the Late Disturbances. London, 1830.

8. Causes which Influence the Rate of Wages. (a) Productiveness of

Labour. (*b*) Proportion of Labourers not Employed for the Benefit of Labourers.

9. Effect on Wages of Rate of Profit.

[Lectures 5, 6, and 7 were reprinted in the Political Economy, pp. 140–4 and 147–53 (some of p. 150 is not in the lectures), pp. 154–62, and pp. 162–74 respectively.]

(*b*). LECTURES, 1847–52

Course I, 1847–8

1. Causes that have Retarded the Progress of Political Economy.
2. Political Economy a Mental Study.
3. Reasons for Treating Political Economy as a Science.
4. Political Economy a Positive not an Hypothetical Science— Definition of Wealth.

These four Lectures were published together as Four Introductory Lectures on Political Economy, London, 1852. The MSS. are missing.

5. Universal Desire of Wealth.
6 and 7. Power of Government to alter the Degree in which Wealth is Desirable.
8. Production of Wealth. Published 1849. The MS. is missing.
9. Direct and Indirect Production. MS. dated by Senior July 26, 1847. Much of it is the same as Course I, Lecture 9, 1826–7.

Course II, 1848–9

1. Classification, Nomenclature, and Definition. MS. dated February 14, 1848.
2. Classification of the Instruments of Production. MS. dated 1848.
3 and 4. Definitions of Capital.
5 and 6. National Capital. MS. of Lecture 6 dated April 20, 1848.
7. Capital—Division of Labour.
8. Capital—Instruments—Abstinence. MS. dated August 28, 1848.
9. Abstinence.

Course III, 1849–50

1, 2, and 3. Efficiency of Capital applied to Agriculture. MS. of Lecture 3, dated March 25, 1849.
4. Population: Preventive checks.
5. [Missing.]
6. Population: Preventive checks concluded. [Effects of Inattention of Landlords.]
7 and 8. Population: Destructive checks.
9. Population: Remedial checks. MS. dated December 8, 1849.

Course IV, 1850–1

1. Population: Remedial checks concluded.
2. Colonization.
3 and 4. Recapitulation: Production.
5. Recapitulation concluded. Efficiency of Capital applied to Agriculture.
6. Exchange—Value—Cost of Production.
7. Monopolies.

Course V, 1851–2

6. Cost of Gold.
[All the other Lectures of this Course are missing.]

Lecture on the Retardation of Capital by Unwise Legislation. [This is only a fragment in Senior's handwriting, and is undated. Levy dates it 1849 or 1850. (Senior's Industrial Efficiency, p. 380.) It deals with the expense of war and the folly of commercial legislation.]

III

ECONOMIC ARTICLES

I. *Quarterly Review*

Corn Laws, July 1821[1]

II. *Edinburgh Review*[2, 3]

1. Grounds and Objects of the Budget, July 1841.
2. English Poor Laws. October 1841. (Reprinted in Historical and Philosophical Essays, Vol. II, 1865.)
3. The Budget of 1842. April 1842.
4. Free Trade and Retaliation. July 1843.
5. Ireland in 1843. January 1844. (Reprinted in Journals, Conversations, and Essays relating to Ireland, Vol. I, 1868.)

---

[1] Attributed to Senior in *Dictionary of National Biography*. S. Leon Levy apparently saw the original MS. (Senior's *Industrial Efficiency*, Vol. II, p. 378.)

[2] The rest of Senior's articles in the *Edinburgh Review* (eighteen in number) were of a non-economic character and, with the exception of one on The Revolution of 1848 (January 1850), were reprinted either in his *Historical and Philosophical Essays* or in his *Biographical Sketches*. (See sect. viii below.)

[3] The first and third articles were identified by Levy from the *Selections from Correspondence of Macvey Napier*, 1879 edition, pp. 352, 355, and 387. The fourth article was criticized by Torrens, who knew it to be written by Senior, in his *Letter to N. W. Senior, Esq., in reply to the article on Free Trade and Retaliation in the "Edinburgh Review," July 1843*, published 1843. The seventh article was identified for Levy by Messrs. Longmans, Green & Co., the publishers of the *Edinburgh Review*.

6. Proposals for extending the Irish Poor Law. October 1846. (Reprinted in Journals, etc., relating to Ireland, Vol. 1, 1868.)
7. J. S. Mill's Principles of Political Economy and Essays on Unsettled Questions. October 1848.
8. Relief of Irish Distress in 1847 and 1848. October 1849. (Reprinted in Journals, etc., relating to Ireland, Vol. 1, 1868.)

IV

ECONOMIC PAMPHLETS AND MSS.

(Except those on the Poor Laws)

1. Memorandum on the present state of the Law relating to Trade Combinations. 1831.

   The Memorandum was prepared at Lord Melbourne's request in 1830 and completed in 1831, but was not published. A considerable portion of it was incorporated in the Report on the Condition of the Unemployed Hand-loom Weavers in 1841 and this portion was reprinted in Historical and Philosophical Essays, Vol. II. See Introductory Note to the Reprint. The original Memorandum was in the Home Office Library, but cannot be found at present.

2. Letter to Lord Howick on a Commutation of Tithes and a Provision for the Roman Catholic Clergy of Ireland. Second edition. London, 1831.

3. (a) On National Property and on the prospects of the present Administration and of Their Successors. January 1835. Four editions.

   The pamphlet was written at the request of Lord Lansdowne during Sir Robert Peel's Government in January 1835. Senior wrote a preface to the fourth edition, recommending a congregational instead of a territorial system of Irish Church endowments. This preface was not published for political reasons. (See note by Mrs. Simpson to the reprint of part of this pamphlet in Journals, etc., relating to Ireland, Vol. 1, 1868.) The preface is referred to in S. Leon Levy, op. cit., Appendix 1, p. 379, but it is now apparently lost.

   (b) Minutes of a Conference held at Lord Melbourne's House to consider this Preface, May 31, 1835 (unpublished).

   (c) Outline of a pamphlet on the Consideration due to individual interests and on the measures which the present crisis demands of Government must be undertaken by the present administration and by their successors. This is missing, but from its title seems to have been a draft of the pamphlet on National Property. It is stated by S. Leon Levy to have been annotated by prominent Whigs, op. cit., Appendix 1, p. 379.

4. (a) Letters on the Factory Act as it affects the cotton manufacture, addressed to the Right Honourable the President of the Board of Trade, by N. W. Senior. To which are appended a letter to Mr.

Senior from L. Horner, and minutes of a conversation between Mr. E. Ashworth, Mr. Thomson, and Mr. Senior. London, 1837.

Horner's letter was written at Senior's request as a result of the former's criticism of the letters at a meeting of the Political Economy Club, May 15, 1837. Proceedings of the Political Economy Club, Vol. VI, J. L. Mallet's Diaries, pp. 273–5.

(b) Second edition, 1844, containing the criticisms in the Spectator, March 23, 1844, a reply to them in the Morning Chronicle, March 25, 1844, the criticisms from The Times of March 26 and 29, 1844, and a reply to them.

V

BOOKS, PAMPHLETS, AND PAPERS (PUBLISHED AND UNPUBLISHED)
ON THE POOR LAWS

(a). *Early Documents relating to the Poor Law.*
Bound in One Volume, MSS.

1. Draft of an Amendment Bill, signed by Senior.
2. List of principal subjects of investigation. Undated.
3. Reply to Lord Althorp's question on the Labour Rate by the Commissioners.

   Neither signed nor dated, but evidently by Senior from the style of writing. It was published practically without alteration as the reply to Lord Althorp's letter (February 23, 1833) on a Bill for the Better Employment of Agricultural Labourers by the Commissioners (March 1833), signed by all the Commissioners but Sturges Bourne. Ordered to be printed, August, 5, 1833. Parliamentary Papers, 1833, Vol. XXXII.
4. Letter from Senior to the Lord Chancellor on the Poor Laws, September 14, 1832.
5. Comments on Senior's Letter to the Lord Chancellor by Sturges Bourne, October 1832.
6. Ditto by Henry Garler, November 1832.
7. Letter from Senior to the Lord Chancellor on the Poor Laws, January 7, 1833.

   (There seems to have been an intermediate letter, which is missing.)
8. Miscellaneous notes, undated and unsigned, and not in Senior's writing.

(b). *Poor Law Amendment Bill while before the Cabinet.*
3 Vols. Printed Papers.

Volume I

1. Measures submitted by the Poor Law Commissioners to His Majesty's Government: notes of the heads of a Bill, etc., as amended in consultation with witnesses.

2. Remedial Measures; Evidence.
3. Letter from Senior to Lansdowne explaining the proposals, March 2, 1834. (See F below.)
4. Abstract of clauses for the Bill. (Marked by Senior 1st Edition).
5. Ditto (Marked by Senior 2nd Edition, and annotated by him).
6. Ditto (Marked by Senior 1st Edition, and annotated by him).

Volume II

1. Third edition of Abstract of Clauses, 1834 (annotated by Senior).
2. A Bill for the Amendment of the Poor Laws, etc., 1834. (Annotated by Senior.)

Volume III

1. A Bill, etc. (Marked J. Stephens, Esq., by Senior. Annotated.)
2. Ditto (Marked Senior's copy, and annotated by Senior).
3. A Bill to alter and 'amend the Laws of Settlement, 1834. (Annotated by Senior.)
4. A Bill to Alter and Amend the Laws of Bastardy, 1834. (Annotated by Senior.)

(c). *Poor Law Amendment Bill while in the House of Commons.*
1 *Volume printed*

1. A Bill to Amend the Poor Laws. (Annotated by Senior and others.) April 18, 1834.
2. Ditto.
3. Ditto.
4. A Bill, etc., June 21, 1834. As amended on recommitment.
5. A Bill, etc., as passed by the House of Commons, July 2, 1834.

(d). *Poor Law Amendment Bill.* 1 *Volume printed*

1. A Bill to amend the Poor Laws. July 2, 1834. (Annotated by Senior and others.)
2. A Bill, etc., as amended by Committee, August 4, 1834 (Annotated by Senior and others), and clauses to be added on Report.
3. A Bill, etc., as Amended by Committee, August 4, 1834. (Marked White's copy, annotated.)

(e). *Poor Law Amendment Bill and Act.* 1 *Volume printed*

1. A Bill for the Better Administration of the Laws relating to the Poor, etc., as amended on recommitment. April 18, 1834.
2. Ditto, as amended on recommitment, June 21, 1834.
3. A Bill, etc., Intituled an Act for the better Administration, etc., as passed by the House of Commons. July 2, 1834.

4. A Bill, etc., with the amendments made by Committee, July 31, 1834.
5. A Bill, etc., with the amendments made by the Lords, August 9, 1834.
6. An Act for the better Administration of the Laws relating to the Poor, etc., August 14, 1834.
7. A Letter from J. Meadows White to Senior on lawyers' fees. August 4, 1834.

(f). *Senior's History of the Passing of the Poor Law Amendment Act*, 1834, *written for Lord Lansdowne*. 1 *Volume, MS.*

It also contains Senior's letter to Lord Lansdowne explaining the objects of the Commissioners' recommendations. March 2, 1834.

(There are several copies of the History, one of which belonging to Sir George Nicholls is in the Goldsmiths' Company's Library of Economic Literature at the University of London.)

(g). *Miscellaneous Papers on the Poor Law* (*Unpublished*)

1. Notes on Poor Law Bills, 1819–29 (undated and unsigned).
2. Letter from Hyde Villiers to Lord Howick. January 19, 1832 (copy).
3. Letter from Senior to Lord Melbourne on an Agricultural Labourers Employment Bill. March 10, 1832 (copy).
4. Letter from J. Audley, of Gore Court, on The Instructions to Assistant Commissioners and the Extracts of Evidence of 1833. August 3, 1833.
5. Correspondence between J. W. Cowell and George Nicholls. March 1834 (copy).
6. Correspondence between Senior and Lo. Hillyard, of Thorpelands, near Birmingham, on the Labour Rate. March 1834. (Hillyard's opinions on the Labour Rate are mentioned in the Poor Law Report, 1834, pp. 174–6, 1894. Reprint.)
7. Letter from Senior to Robert Gordon, of the India Board, on the relation of the Forest of Dean to the New Poor Law. April 4, 1834 (copy and original draft).
8. Letter from Senior to Lord ——, describing the making of amendments to the Poor Law Bill, May 3, 1834 (original draft).
9. Letter from the Marquis of Salisbury to Senior on the minutes of a conversation between them on the Poor Law Bill preceding its introduction into the House of Lords (copy undated).
10. Letter to Lord Melbourne, June 30, 1834 (marked Mr. S. on Comm.).
    On appointments of the three Commissioners and their secretary under the Poor Law Amendment Act.
11. Draft of instructions to and election of Assistant Commissioners (probably 1834).

12. Letter from John Meadows White to Senior on corrections in the History of the passing of the Poor Law Amendment Act (probably written in 1834).
13. Part of a letter (presumably from Senior) to Lord Howick on a paper by the latter on the Irish Poor Law, 1837.
14. Letter from Senior to —— on appointments to the Irish Poor Law administration, and Senior's brother's in particular (undated copy).
15. Letter to Lord —— on Chadwick on the distribution of relief. April 4, 1841. (Probably copy of a letter from Senior to Howick.)
16. Memorandum on the centralized administration of the Poor Law by Senior, marked 1846 (original).
17. Letter from Sir George Nicholls to Miss Senior, December 12, 1864.

(h). *Publications on the Poor Laws*

1. A Letter to Lord Howick, on a legal provision for the Irish Poor, commutation of tithes, and a provision for the Irish Roman Catholic Clergy. London, 1831. Third edition, 1832, with a preface on measures to be taken in the present crisis, MS. now missing. Stated by S. Leon Levy, op. cit., Appendix I, p. 378, to have been annotated by Malthus and others.
2. Statement of the Provision for the Poor and of the condition of the labouring classes, in a considerable portion of America and Europe. . . . Being the preface to the foreign communications contained in the appendix to the Poor Law Report. London, 1835.
3. Letter to Lord John Russell (Home Secretary) on the third Report of the Commissioners for inquiring into the Condition of the Poor in Ireland. April 14, 1836. Published together with a letter agreeing to publication, May 12, 1837, Parliamentary Papers, Vol. LI, 1837.
4. Remarks on the Opposition to the Poor Law Amendment Bill by a Guardian. Published anonymously 1841. Generally attributed to Senior from internal evidence, and because the copies are said by the publisher, John Murray, to have been evenly distributed between Senior and Sir George C. Lewis. See Mackay (Nicholls') History of the English Poor Laws, Vol. II, p. 25 note.
5. Horton and Senior. Inquiry into the Causes and Remedies of Pauperism. Fourth series. Explanation of Wilmot Horton's Bill in a letter and queries addressed to N. W. Senior with his replies. London, 1830.

VI

Published Writings on Education

1. Resolutions and Heads of a Report on Popular Education proposed by Mr. Senior to the Royal Commission on Popular Education. London, H.M. Stationery Office, February 1, 1860.

2. Suggestions on Popular Education. London, 1861. Reprint of Resolutions and Heads, etc., practically unaltered, plus some additional proposals.

3. Address on Education delivered to the National Association for the Promotion of Social Science at its seventh annual meeting, October 1863. London, 1863. Senior was President of the Department of Education of the Association for 1863.

VII

Reports wholly or partly written by Senior, and Evidence before various Commissions

1. Extracts of Evidence received by the Poor Law Commission, 1832–3, published 1833.

2. Poor Law Report, 1834. (First Report of the Commission for Inquiring into the administration and operation of the Poor Laws in 1834.)

3. Report on the Condition of the Unemployed Hand-loom Weavers. Parliamentary Papers, Vol. x, 1841.

4. Section on Pauper Education in the Report of the Royal Commission on Popular Education, 1861. (Senior admitted to this in his evidence before the Select Committee on Poor Relief in June 1862.)

5. Evidence before the Select Committee on Poor Relief, June 1862. 3rd Report. Parliamentary Papers, 1862, Vol. x.

VIII

Miscellaneous Books

1. Biographical Sketches. London, 1863. (Principally reprints of articles from the Edinburgh Review.)

2. Essays on Fiction. London, 1864. (Reprints of reviews of Sir Walter Scott, Thackeray and Bulwer Lytton, from the Quarterly, Edinburgh, and North British Reviews, 1821–57.)

3. Historical and Philosophical Essays. 2 vols, Edited by Mrs. M. C. M. Simpson. London, 1865. (Reprints of Articles, etc.)

4. Correspondence and Conversations of Alexis de Tocqueville with N. W. Senior, 1834–59. 2 vols. Edited by Mrs. M. C. M. Simpson. London, 1872.

   (Part of the correspondence was reprinted in French in "Alexis de Tocqueville et la démocratie libérale." by Eugene d'Eichthal, Paris, 1897.)

5. Conversation with M. Thiers, M. Guizot, and other distinguished persons, 1852–60. 2 vols. Edited by Mrs. M. C. M. Simpson. London, 1878.

6. Conversations with distinguished persons during the Second Empire, 1860–3. 2 vols. Edited by Mrs. M. C. M. Simpson. London, 1880.

IX

Senior's Journals

1. A Journal kept in Turkey and Greece in 1857 and 1858. London, 1859.
2. Journals, Conversations, and Essays relating to Ireland, with a preface written by Senior in 1861. 2 vols. Edited by Mrs. M. C. M. Simpson. London, 1868.
3. Journals kept in France and Italy from 1848 to 1852. With a sketch of the Revolution of 1848. 2 vols. Edited by Mrs. M. C. M. Simpson. London, 1871.
4. Conversations and Journals in Egypt and Malta, 1855–6. 2 vols. Edited by Mrs. M. C. M. Simpson. London, 1882.

QUESTIONS PROPOSED BY N. W. SENIOR FOR DISCUSSION AT THE POLITICAL ECONOMY CLUB[1]

1. June 2, 1823. "Can there be an increase of Riches without an increase of Value?"
2. January 9, 1826. "Would it be convenient to define capital to be 'All that portion of the produce of industry and frugality which is *not* actually in the hands of those by whom it will be *unproductively* consumed,' or 'All that portion of the produce of industry and frugality which is consumed *reproductively*,' or is there any other more convenient definition?"
3. February 6, 1826. "What decides what shall be the least productive mine of Gold or Silver that shall be worked?"
4. April 3, 1826. "To what extent would the Rent of Land in money and in commodities be affected by a Free Trade in Corn, and for how long?"
5. January 8, 1827. [Question of February 6, 1826, repeated.]
6. December 7, 1829. "Can the value of Money in any two countries differ more than is expressed by the Exchange?"
7. May 5, 1831. "Would a Remission of Taxation occasion an immediate fall of wages?"
8. June 2, 1831. "Would it be practicable and advantageous to form a Society on an extended scale for the improvement and diffusion of Political Economy; and how should it be set about?"
9. January 19, 1832. "If an alteration is to be made in the existing Corn Laws, would it be advisable to impose any Duty on Corn? And if any, should that duty be imposed for the purpose of obtaining Revenue, or for that of countervailing the specific burdens on Agriculture?"
10. December 6, 1832. "(a) Would it be advisable to vest in Government officers the collection and distribution of the fund for the relief of the Poor, leaving the assessment of that fund to the parochial authorities? (b) Would it be advisable to vest also the assessment of that fund in Government officers, leaving it still a parochial charge? (c) Would it be advisable to make that fund a country, district, or national charge?"
11. March 7, 1833. "Suppose two countries similar in extent, fertility, climate, government, and civilization, but one to have been from time immemorial subject to Tithes, the other Tithe free: would these countries differ as to rent of land, the density of population, the price of raw produce, or the price of manufactures?—first, supposing them not to have a free intercourse with other countries;

[1] *Proceedings of the Political Economy Club*, Centenary Volume (Vol. VI), 1921.

second, supposing them to have such an intercourse. And what would be the effects in them respectively as to these points: first, to the imposition; and second, of the removal of tithes?"

12. April 10, 1834. "Is a compulsory provision for the Able-bodied Poor a beneficial provision; and if so, by what principles ought it to be regulated?"

13. February 5, 1835. "What would be the effect on the wealth of Great Britain if all the principal Landholders and principal Stockholders were to devote all their revenues, beyond their own subsistence, to Productive purposes?"

14. February 4, 1836. "Under what circumstances is the Absenteeism of Landed Proprietors detrimental to the wealth of a country?"

15. February 2, 1837. "Ought the new Poor Law Bill to authorize any, and what, outdoor relief? and ought it to give any, and what, legal claim to the applicant?"

16. May 4, 1837. "What have been the effects of the Factory Regulation Act; and should any, and what, alterations be made in it?"

17. December 7, 1837. "What is the most convenient definition of Rent?"

18. December 7, 1837. "On what does the increase in the value of certain articles which accrues during the Lapse of Time, and is independent of the application of either Capital or Labour, or of any monopolized appropriation of natural Agents, depend?"

19. May 5, 1838. "Is it expedient to adopt an exclusive Silver currency, or a double currency of Silver and Gold, each being a legal tender to any amount?"

20. December 6, 1838. "What is the natural limit to the Accumulation of Capital?"

21. July 4, 1839. "In what mode is it most advantageous that the expenses of a Church Establishment and public Education should be defrayed in New Colonies—for example, by Grants from the general revenue of the Settlement, by reserved lands, or by Corn rents?"

22. July 4, 1839. "What have been the effects on the production and distribution of wealth, of the Observance of a Seventh day?"

23. March 5, 1840. "What is the connection between the price of Provisions and the price of Labour?"

24. May 6, 1841. "Does the value of Gold and Silver depend in any, and, if in any, on what principle, different from those which govern the value of the other metals?"

25. May 5, 1842. "Which is best? A tax upon Property, upon Income, or upon Expenditure?"

26. May 4, 1843. "What determines the extent to which a duty imposed upon an article of Raw produce, partly produced at home, and partly imported, raises prices?"

27. March 6, 1845. "Does Taxation on the Commodities consumed by the labourer, raise Wages under any, and what, circumstances?"

28. June 5, 1845. "Are expenditure upon Wages, and expenditure upon Commodities, equivalent, or different, in their effect on the remuneration of the labourer?"

29. July 6, 1848. "Is it expedient that the rights of Tenants occupying land in Ireland should be enlarged, so as to render their tenure virtually perpetual at the existing rents, as actually paid?"

30. July 6, 1854. "Is it desirable, and if so, under what circumstances, that a Government should endeavour to oblige its subjects to Accumulate?"

31. March 25, 1858. "What have been the effects on the production and distribution of Wealth, of the observance, as a period of rest, of one day in seven?"

32. July 7, 1859. "What is the connection between the Price of Provisions and the Price of Labour?"

33. July 4, 1861. "What is the most convenient definition of Political Economy?"

INDEX OF NAMES

(References to footnotes shown by page numbers in italics)